MI *matic*
rd.

GROUPS:
INTERACTION
AND
PERFORMANCE

GROUPS: INTERACTION AND PERFORMANCE

Joseph E. McGrath
University of Illinois, Urbana

Prentice-Hall, Inc., Englewood Cliffs, N.J. 07632

Library of Congress Cataloging in Publication Data

McGrath, Joseph Edward
   Groups, interaction and performance.

   Bibliography: p.
   Includes index.
   1. Social groups.   2. Social interaction.
3. Performance.   I. Title.
HM131.M377 1983   302.3   82-24016
ISBN 0-13-365700-0

Editorial/production supervision: Dee Amir Josephson
Cover design: 20/20 Services, Inc.
Manufacturing buyer: Ron Chapman

Printed in the United States of America

10 9 8 7 6 5 4 3 2 1

ISBN 0-13-365700-0

Prentice-Hall International, Inc., *London*
Prentice-Hall of Australia Pty. Limited, *Sydney*
Editora Prentice-Hall do Brasil, Ltda., *Rio de Janeiro*
Prentice-Hall Canada Inc., *Toronto*
Prentice-Hall of India Private Limited, *New Delhi*
Prentice-Hall of Japan, Inc., *Tokyo*
Prentice-Hall of Southeast Asia Pte. Ltd., *Singapore*
Whitehall Books Limited, *Wellington, New Zealand*

CONTENTS

EXAMPLES OF RESEARCH TECHNOLOGY (EXRT)

PREFACE

This is a book about the study of groups. Over the past hundred years, we have gathered much evidence about groups through application of scientific methods of study. These include the empirical methods that involve laboratory experimentation, field studies, surveys and the like, and the theoretical methods that involve hypotheses, prediction, interpretation and so on. In my view, we have done the former much better than the latter. We have become much better at gathering evidence about groups than at building good theory to help us understand it. That is both the central difficulty of the field, and the central challenge for anyone trying to write a textbook for that field.

To deal with that challenge, a textbook writer must find some way to present the voluminous evidence so as to give it shape and meaning. That requires more than just to present the empirical findings, without interpretation, however comprehensively. It requires some kind of overarching schema through which the writer tries to integrate, and make sense of, the whole body of information. I have tried to provide such an integrative conceptual framework for the body of research information we have gathered about groups.

One interesting feature of the group research area is that it contains three large and relatively separate bodies of work—each reflecting interests in a different subset of outcome or dependent variables about groups, and each associated with a different subset of group researchers. One of these bodies of group research studies concentrates on the consequences of group activity for the group's members and for the group itself. This work is associated with social psychologists such as Lewin, Festinger, Thibaut, Kelley, Schachter, Back, J.R.P. French, Zander, Cartwright and many others. Conceptually, this part of group research deals with *groups as vehicles for delivering social influence.*

A second body of group research has emphasized the process by which groups carry on their interactions with one another, or, in the language of this book, an emphasis on the group interaction process itself. Such an emphasis is distinctly associated with the work of R.F. Bales, and many of his colleagues such as Couch, Borgatta, Slater, Strodtbeck, Hare, Mann, and many others. Conceptually, this part of group research deals with *groups as structures for patterning social interaction.*

A third body of group research has emphasized group productivity and other aspects of group task performance. That work is associated with social psychologists such as Steiner, Fiedler, Davis, Hackman, Kerr, Komorita, Laughlin, Shifflet, Stassar, and many others. Conceptually this part of group research deals with *groups as task performance systems.*

A colleague has suggested that I dub these three bodies of work the Michigan school, the Harvard school, and the Illinois school, respectively, because so many of the most notable practitioners of each of them have some connection, past or present, with those three universities. Although labeling by schools would provide a very useful device for communicating about them, I hesitate to attach such labels because I certainly do not want to imply thereby that good work on groups gets done only at those institutions or only by people who are or were associated with them. Much good work in group research has been done by scholars whose work does not fit such neat institutional affiliation categories—Altman, Argyle, Dabbs, Deutsch, Gottman, Helmreich, Levinger, Myers, Morley, Rubin, Rutter, Shaw, Sherif, Stephenson, Taylor, Thomas, to name but a few. So I will simply call these three bodies of work, respectively, the social influence school, the interaction process school, and the task performance school of group research.

It is not remarkable that there are distinctive subsets of work within a field and that different researchers pursue them. Such is probably the case for most fields. What seems to me remarkable is the degree to which those separate bodies of work within the small group field do not seem to touch each other, to take each other into account, to reckon with the findings or even the questions posed by the other two schools. Even textbooks, and other writings that aspire to full coverage of the group research area, seem usually to do full justice only to one of these three points of view, seldom to all three. Yet from my perspective, all three are a part of the same overall set of phenomena—how people behave in groups and what consequences ensue therefrom—and need somehow to be integrated. In the early 1970s, Steiner talked about the fractionation of group research, and used the analogy of a number of little islands of work, separated from one another by relatively uncharted seas. Here I am suggesting that there are three relatively compact groups of little islands, within each of which there is considerable commerce but between which there is a surprising lack of cross-cultural contact.

I have tried to construct a textbook that does reasonably full justice to all three of these points of view, or bodies of work, and does so in a way that shows some of the connections between them. The work on groups as social-influence systems is reflected especially in chapters 17 and 18, but also in chapters 14, 15, and 16. The work on groups as interaction process systems is reflected especially in chapters 12 and 13, but also in chapters 14, 15, and 16. The work on groups as task performance systems is reflected in chapters 5–11. A relatively thorough treatment of all three bodies of work, in a way that ties them to one another, is an important goal for this book and could be one of its major contributions.

Many people helped me in many ways in the writing of this book. I owe them all my thanks. Irwin Altman and Richard Hackman challenged me to rethink portions of the material, and thereby to make major improvements in portions of the book. Janice Kelly helped me develop the Examples of Research Technology (EXRT) boxes that appear in the book, and to cross check their accuracy. Careful reviews and extensive comments on drafts of the manuscript were provided by the following reviewers: Vernon L. Allen, University of Wisconsin; Alonzo Anderson, University of California, San Diego; Michael L. Berbaum, Brandeis University; Robert Bray, Research Triangle Institute in North Carolina; Norbert L. Kerr, Michigan State University; Rosina C. Lao, East Carolina University; H. Andrew Michener, University of Wisconsin; Garold Stasser, Miami University; Dalmas A. Taylor, University of Maryland. I also had the advantage of review and comment on various parts of the material from a number of other colleagues, including David Brinberg, James Davis, Sam Komorita, David Kravitz, Patrick Laughlin, and Philip Runkel. Kimberly Carter and Kathleen Karr gave invaluable help in preparation of the manuscript. I owe all of them, and other colleagues and students, my gratitude for their help.

I had the good fortune to be a Resident Summer Fellow at the Baldwin Institute for Research and Scholarship, Baldwin, Michigan, for several summers during the preparation of the book. I am grateful for that opportunity and for the physical, intellectual, and spiritual support I got from the experience. Finally, I want to thank Marion McGrath. Throughout the project, her interest and support sustained me, and her wisdom and humor helped me keep this project in its proper perspective in the cosmic scheme of things.

Joseph E. McGrath
University of Illinois
Urbana, Illinois

PART ONE
AN INTRODUCTION TO THE STUDY OF GROUPS

This is a book about *human groups.* It deals with how groups behave, as groups, and how individuals behave when they are in group settings. The main focus is on what goes on when people interact with one another. *Group Interaction Process* is the term used here to refer to that dynamic interplay of individual and collective behavior of group members, acting in a complex environment. The book explores the nature of that group interaction process; its causes or antecedents; and its consequences for members, for the group itself, and for the environment in which that interaction takes place. These three basic questions—the nature, the causes, and the consequences of group interaction process—when they are considered in detail, become a large and complex set of questions indeed. That detailed set of questions provides the stuff of which group research is made. What we have learned about those questions is the main substance of this book.

This is also a book about the *study of human groups.* It assumes that to understand groups, in general and in any particular case, requires that we study them in some systematic and objective way. The book further assumes that we can use the methods of behavioral and social science to carry out such systematic and objective study. Thus, the second focus of the book is on how group behavior has been studied; on the substantial strengths but also the major limitations of those methods of study; and on how those methods themselves affect how we can interpret the evidence from those studies on groups.

The book, then, is concerned with what we have learned and what we could learn about groups and group behavior by applying the tools of the behavioral and social sciences. It adopts the point of view that what we can and do learn, at any given time, from any given study, is crucially affected by (a) what we *already* know, from earlier studies and from current interpretations of them; (b) what we *expect* to learn, because of our guiding theories and hypotheses—our preconceived ideas and biases, if you will; and (c) what we *can* learn, because of the constraints imposed by the methods we use to do that study. This book will, therefore, continually view each piece of evidence from three perspectives: (a) from an *historical perspective,* for interpretations of problems and solutions; (b) from a *theoretical perspective,* for considering the "meaning" of specific research findings; and (c) from a *methodological perspective,* for understanding the limitations of such findings and the constraints within which they must be interpreted.

History is important to understanding. Henry Ford, the industrialist, is alleged to have said: "History is bunk." But Santayana wrote that if we fail to remember history we are doomed to repeat the mistakes of the past. And Abraham Lincoln said that we need to know where we are and from whence we have come if we are to be able to predict "whither we are tending." In the present case, we can profit in at least two ways from a look at the history (approximately 100 years of it) of group research. First, a look at the past can show how topics, methods and concepts have waxed and waned in popularity, and perhaps give perspective about the variability to be expected in the future. Second, it can highlight what the persistent, and thus perhaps fundamental, problems of the field have been.

Theory is important too. There is no such thing as research with no theory. What there can be, of course, is research guided by unrecognized, implicit theoretical premises. In order to observe anything, we have to have some concepts to guide our observations; we have to know what to look at, and what to look for, and the answers to those questions necessarily draw upon some theoretical foundations. After we have made those observations (theory-guided, willy-nilly) we then draw further on theoretical concepts when we interpret those observations—when we give them meaning. It is important that such underlying theory be recognized and made explicit. If not, we are liable to base our studies on theories that have untenable and/or mutually inconsistent premises without knowing we have done so. Furthermore, we need theory to guide subsequent research, and to relate results of one study to those of other studies. Theory is both compass and rudder for research.

Just as history is important to give us perspective about current and recent work, and theory is important to guide our search for evidence and to give meaning to such evidence, so too is research methodology important. All methods have limits; and those limits set limits on what we can learn and with what degree of confidence we can learn it. Research on groups has drawn on the methodology of social and behavioral science, in general, and social psychology in particular. It is assumed that the reader is familiar with that methodology, at least in a general way: questionnaires, observation procedures, experimental design, statistical analysis, and so on. But some findings of group research, and some of its key problems, arise in conjunction with the use of some very specialized data collection and analysis methods (e.g., interaction process analysis systems, complex analysis of variance designs, and the like). Some of these matters need discussion, so that their implications for the meaning and limitations of evidence can be appreciated. A short chapter on method is offered in the first part of this book.

Part I of the book has four chapters. The first introduces the topic of groups, discusses some definitions and boundary conditions, and offers a conceptual framework that will provide a guide for the organization of the rest of the book. The second chapter provides a brief outline of past research on groups, notes some trends in that work, and discusses the role of theory in the past. Chapter 3 is about methods, how they both offer opportunities to gain information and limit the information thus obtained. The final chapter of Part I discusses the variety of kinds of social entities that have been called groups, and that have been used in research intended to apply to groups; provides a classification schema or typology of such groups; and describes certain other features of the technology of group research.

CHAPTER ONE
GROUPS
AND
HUMAN BEHAVIOR

Groups are everywhere. We live in families. We work in teams, crews, and committees. We eat, exercise, and play with others, in organized teams, or in informal groups, or in friendship or romantic pairs. Much of the world's business, and a lot of its pleasure, take place in groups—that is, with two or more people, who have some prior relationship with one another and an expectation of some future relations, doing something together.

Groups also are important. Groups are the instruments through which much work gets done. They are also the contexts that pattern and shape many other kinds of activities. Moreover, groups are instruments for influencing, shaping, changing the individuals who are their members. So, interest in learning about groups is a natural consequence of how widespread and important they are.

Of course, much human behavior does not take place in groups, but rather occurs alone or in other kinds of aggregates (crowds, audiences, and so on; see discussion to follow). Furthermore, it is possible to talk about all these behaviors without ever bringing up the concept of a group. One can describe human behavior solely as individual behavior—treating the other people involved as stimuli, as part of the environment, that is, as objects, rather than as co-interactors. While such a thoroughgoing individualistic perspective is often taken by experimental psychologists, and even by some social psychologists, and while it is doubtless useful for some purposes, such is not the perspective to be taken here. Rather, this book will take a group perspective, and will regard much of human behavior as relevant to that group focus. I am not arguing that one or the other perspective is right, the other wrong. On the contrary. Both are right, or neither is. But they are useful for different purposes.

WHAT IS A GROUP?
DEFINITIONS
AND BOUNDARIES

What is a group? There are many definitions (e.g., see Shaw, 1976). Most of those definitions stress the ideas of interaction, interdependence, mutual awareness, a past, and an anticipated future. Groups are not just any aggregation of two or more people. Indeed, there are many kinds of social aggregates; some of them are groups, some are not. It may be worth noting some of them, and pointing out why they do or do not qualify as groups for present purposes. (See discussion of Social Groups in *Encyclopedia Britannica,* third edition, 1974, p. 960.)

Types of Social Aggregations

Artificial aggregations:

A statistical group, or social category: Members have some property in common (age, sex, social class, etc.) but otherwise are not necessarily in any relation to one another, nor aware of one another.

Unorganized aggregates:

An Audience: This is a collection of individuals whose members are all attending to the same set of stimuli (e.g., the same mass-media presentation; or an eclipse), but otherwise are not necessarily in any relation to one another nor aware of one another's common activity.

A crowd: This is a collection of individuals who are attending to a common set of stimuli and are in physical proximity, hence are interrelated at least in terms of mutual sensory stimulation.

A public: This is a set of individuals who are attending to a common set of issues; have some form of indirect interaction regarding these issues; and are aware of their common interest, though they are not necessarily in direct physical proximity or interaction.

Units with patterned relationships:

A culture: In this, all of the members share a common and patterned set of value orientations and common language, dress, and customs, although with patterned variations. Members are interdependent with respect to those and other aspects of the culture, though they are not necessarily aware of all those relations.

A subculture: Members share a set of value orientations, language, and so on, common to members of that subculture and in contrast to—often a variant of—the patterns common to members of the surrounding culture; but subculture members likely also share many aspects of the surrounding culture.

A kinship group: All members are related by birth and/or marriage; the network defined as kin is extensive in some cultures, more limited in others; cultures also vary in terms of what other aspects of social relations are kinship structured.

Structured social units:

A society: A large social aggregate, usually within a single culture, in a defined geographical region and with an integrated political system, whose members have structured relations, formal and informal, that are characterized by high degrees of interdependence.

A community: A location based subdivision of a society whose members live close together, are highly interdependent, interact frequently in many relationships and for an extended time, and are aware of their mutual interaction and interdependence.

A family (also, the kinship group, above): A kin based and/or residence based basic unit of social structure, whose members are highly and pervasively interdependent and are aware of it.

Deliberately designed social units:

An organization: A large aggregation of people and other resources deliberately designed to pursue certain (limited) aims; members are recruited for specific roles, and are formally related to one another via demands of such roles.

A suborganization: A portion of a large organization, within which a particular individual is located and fulfills his or her interdependent roles.

A crew (or work team): A relatively small set of persons within an organization who are the role incumbents with whom a given individual interacts, and who are highly interdependent in terms of those organizational roles.

Less deliberately designed social units:

An association (or voluntary organization, or interest group): An aggregate of individuals who share and are aware of common interests in certain issues and deliberately seek interactions on those issues. When interpersonal relationships remain limited, these resemble publics; when interpersonal interactions and interdependence become substantial, these resemble organizations.

A friendship group: A relatively small aggregation of individuals, all or subsets of whom interact voluntarily, frequently, and on a broad band of activities, with positive interpersonal feelings, and with rewarding interpersonal interaction the main goal of those interactions.

These social aggregations, of course, are not mutually exclusive: a friend can be kin, a coworker in an organization, a fellow audience member. They differ along two major axes. They differ in the degree to which there are structured interrelations among the members, the bases of those structured relations, and the degree of deliberateness of development of these structures. Second, they differ in size or scale—from cultures and societies down to work crews, friendship groups and families. These two axes are precisely the key bases on which we will distinguish groups from other aggregates.

Groups are those social aggregates that involve mutual awareness and potential mutual interaction. Hence, they are the social aggregates that are relatively small and relatively structured or organized. On these bases, the term group will be used in this book to include families (kin groups and other residential groups); work crews and other organized task performance teams; and friendship (or social) groups. We will not count as groups those social aggregates that fit the definitions of audiences, crowds, publics, associations or interest groups, because generally they do not involve potential mutual interaction. Of course, subsets of persons in any of those aggregations can become involved in mutual interaction, and thereby become a group (a task group, or a social group, conceivably a residence based group), while remaining part of some other kind of aggregate. We will also not count as groups those social aggregates identified as cultures, subcultures or extended kinship networks; societies or communities; organizations or suborganizations. All those terms refer to aggregates too large to consider that all members are mutually aware of and potentially interacting with one another. But each such aggregate is teeming with potential teams, crews and groups. Finally, we will not consider statistical groups as groups because they do not involve interactive relations among members. (In chapter 6, though, we will discuss a kind of aggregate very much akin to this one: a "statisticized" group. Such groups are created for research purposes, with members usually assigned at random, and do not necessarily even have a property in common. They, too, are not regarded as groups, but serve as a "nongroup" baseline for comparison.)

A Definition of Groups as "Fuzzy Sets"

There is a relatively new subbranch of mathematics that deals with "fuzzy sets." Groups, as I will use the term in this book, are appropriately called "fuzzy sets"—both in this technical-mathematical sense, and in a looser, more metaphorical sense.

The discussion thus far has more or less specified the key features of the definition of group that I will try to use in this book. For an aggregation to be a group, it must include two or more people, but it must remain relatively small so that all members can be mutually aware of and potentially in interaction with one another. Such mutual awareness and potential interaction provide at least a minimum degree of interdependence; that is, members' choices and behaviors take one another into account. Interdependence, in turn, implies some degree of continuity over time: these relationships have, or quickly acquire, some history, and some anticipated future. *A time based, mutual interdependence can reasonably be termed "dynamic."* In other words a group is an aggregation of two or more people who are to some degree in dynamic interrelation with one another. In terms of the list of aggregations given previously, this definition of group would normally include families (at least the residential unit core), work crews, and many social or friendship groups, but would normally not include units that fit all of the other kinds of aggregations in that list (cultures, communities, organizations, etc.).

But that definition leaves a lot of questions still unanswered about what kind of "bunches" are and are not to be regarded as groups. Groups fitting that definition can still vary a lot in number of members, from at least two up to as many as twenty or thirty, perhaps even more under circumstances favorable to mutual awareness and interaction. They can vary a lot in the range of behaviors and situations over which members are interdependent, and the degree of interdependence—from families or romantic dyads whose members exercise broad-band and all-encompassing influences on each other, to recurrent but occasional work pairs who do one specific task together once in a while. Groups within that definition can also vary widely in the temporal patterns of their relationship, from groups where members have interacted for years (such as families in which the adult pair were childhood sweethearts) and expect to continue for years, to groups that have in common only the "history" leading up to the specific current interaction, and who anticipate limited or no interaction beyond some near time-boundary (such as the ad hoc groups of college students that are the subjects of so many group research studies, but also such as the jury that hears any one specific case). All three of these features—size, interdependence, temporal pattern—really reflect degrees of "groupness." An aggregate that is a group by my definition becomes less of a group as (a) the number of its members increases, and/or there are barriers to mutual awareness and interaction; (b) the range of content of the members' interaction decreases, and/or there are barriers to free interaction; and (c) the members' "history" decreases, and their anticipated "future" shrinks toward the time-bounds of the current interaction, unless this is somehow offset by an emotionally intense focus for that interaction (such as would be the case for hostages in a bank robbery, the set of people trapped in a disabled elevator, or the participants in a marathon encounter group).

This is a "fuzzy" definition. I am not trying to set some arbitrary and categorical boundaries, inside of which are "real" groups and outside of which are "nongroups." Rather, I am trying to specify certain features that make one collection of people more like a group than some other collections, while recognizing that some groups have some but not all of those features, and/or have some of those features to a greater degree than others. So, I am proffering not so much a "fuzzy" definition of a group, but a definition of a group that establishes a "fuzzy" boundary between groups and nongroups. But there are important differences *among* the aggregations that are to be classed as groups. As we examine the theoretical ideas and empirical findings of group research, it will be important to keep track of features such as size, broad- or narrow-band scope of interaction and interdependence, barriers to or constraints on interaction, and the temporal pattern of relations of these groups. A classification of groups, making use of these and other distinctions, is laid out in chapter 4, as a typology of social units that have been used in research on groups.

A Fuzzy Definition of Membership

Groups have members. And individuals are members of groups. But no group "has" certain individuals as its members in the total and exclusive sense that a certain table *has* a certain four legs as its parts, or that a certain building *has* a certain set of rooms. Individuals, as members, *do not belong to groups in the sense of logical proper parts.* Rather, they are members in the logical or mathematical sense of "members of a set." In such a formulation, a given element (individual) can be, and remain, a member of set (group) A, while at the same time being a member of another set (group) B; and this can be so under any of a variety of relations (including independence) between the two sets, A and B. Individuals belong to, participate in, partake of many groups, but they are not the exclusive property of any one group. Individuals, thus, have temporally overlapping relations to multiple groups.

There are further complications to the matter of membership. Persons continue (in their own and others' eyes) to be members of certain groups even when they have not interacted with others in that group for a long time. You continue to be a member of your family of orientation even after you leave home—and even if you never phone, write, or visit. You remain a member of your sixth-grade class even if you never attend a reunion. At some point, though, these memberships become pretty tenuous. Again, the boundary is a "fuzzy" one.

Thus, there is a certain indeterminacy, a certain "fuzziness," about just exactly who is a member of a given group, at a given time. How long can it be since member M last interacted with the others for M to still be a member of group G? For that matter, what is M's status if M is *present* during, but does not participate in, group interaction? What if M participates only a little, or in only one modality, or on only a very narrow band of content? Is the star player, who is on the disabled list for the season, still a member of the team? What about the player recently traded away? What about the player recently traded *to* the team but who is not yet physically present? And what about the father who is away from the family at war, in prison, separated or divorced? Under what conditions, and in what sense, and to what degree, are they still members of the group? Intuitively, it seems as if we can answer such questions definitively in every specific instance. But it is much more difficult to develop answers that we could comfortably apply to the general case.

Groups as Real and Not Real

In the first quarter of the century, there was a long and bitter argument—most often between sociology-trained and psychology-trained social psychologists—about whether or not groups were "real." Much of the logic and the rhetoric of that argument seems nowadays quite inappropriate. Sometimes the issue was argued on the basis of some notion of tangibility: groups are not real, it was once argued, because you can't bump into a group (Allport, 1924). At other times it was argued in terms that seemed to mirror present day concerns about the logical, mathematical form of the model by which members were combined: groups were asserted to be either "merely," or "greater than," the sum of their parts. Perhaps the most cogent basis of argument was Lewin's (1948) assertion that groups are real because they have real effects.

More modern epistemological positions in social science would not accept as cogent most of the grounds on which those arguments were based; indeed, they would not accept as appropriate the question as it was posed (i.e., are groups "real"). Such views would, instead, take the position that the existential "reality" of concepts in science is not to the point; what matters, rather, is the *usefulness* of those concepts in making sense of observations and other evidence, and the *fit* of those concepts within networks of theoretical and empirical relations (i.e., within nomological networks). My position in this book is in accord with those later views, and with Lewin's assertion about the effects of groups. In my view, "groups" and related concepts are very useful, and occupy a rather central location in our theoretical and empirical networks. Both in terms of available research evidence (as will be examined in this book), and in terms of our everyday lives (as the reader knows from direct experience), *groups have pervasive, persistent and powerful effects* on human behavior.

Groups—the family, but also friendship and task groups—are the vehicles through which culture is transmitted from one generation to the next. They are the media through which the individual develops his or her "self"; learns a language, and with that develops cognitive processes and contents; and develops repertoires of emotions, motive patterns and behaviors. Groups are the arbiters of what is proper, permissible and taboo. In large part, they define the *right* ways to think about many things—"right" in both the logical and the moral meanings of that word. The bulk of this book deals with such effects of groups, and with how those effects are brought about via social interaction.

This point of view bypasses the question of whether groups are real, at least as that question was argued in the past. It takes the position that the phenomena we are dealing with under the rubrics of "group," "group interaction process", and related concepts, are very important ones in human affairs, and that we can gain a lot of conceptual leverage, so to speak, by viewing them from a group perspective rather than from some other perspective, such as a "purely" individualistic one. In this view, it is neither appropriate nor useful to ask whether groups are real; but it is both appropriate and crucial to ask whether certain aggregations of individuals constitute "real groups." This question has already been discussed here—leading to a fuzzy definition of groups, and of memberships in them; and to the fuzzy position that *some groups are more "groupy"* (that is, they exemplify the category more fully) *than others.* The question will be raised and discussed again, in chapter 4, in the context of examining and comparing the many different kinds of social units that have been used in studies of groups.

A Static/Dynamic Difference

Several remarks earlier in this chapter hinted at the idea of a distinction between *membership* and *interaction*. A person can be a *member* of many groups at one and the same time, but is likely to be *interacting* in only one of those groups—if any—at any one time. Often, when we talk about groups we really refer to the former: the groups of which a given individual is a member, or characteristics of the persons who are members of a given group. But when we consider group interaction process—and that will be the central focus of this book—we are really talking about the latter meaning of group. This is a sufficiently important distinction that I think it merits the use of two different labels. In this book, I will refer to the first of those meanings—*the continuing patterned relations among individuals who are members*—as a *Standing Group*. I will label the second of these—*patterned relations among the behaviors of the individuals*—as an *Acting Group:* The *standing group* is the "location" for those patterned relations we will talk about as *group structure*. The *acting group* is the "location" for those patterned relations we will talk about as *group interaction process*. These distinctions will be presented, defined and used in the next section of this chapter, which presents a conceptual framework for the study of groups.

A CONCEPTUAL FRAMEWORK
FOR THE STUDY OF GROUPS

There are many different perspectives from which one can view a group, and many ambiguities already noted in defining groups and their membership. For such a complex and ambiguous set of concepts, it is often useful to adopt a frame of reference, a map, that models or lays out systematically the various parts of the topic as a research problem. This section offers such a conceptual model for the study of groups (see Figure 1-1).

The point of such a model is to lay out the underlying logic of the problem in a way that can serve as a guiding framework for exploring the problem in its various aspects. For a complex problem, you cannot study everything at once, you cannot think about everything at the same time. This kind of model lets us take the total problem apart, so we can think about and examine evidence about a manageable chunk of it, and then be able to fit the parts back together again. Furthermore, such a framework tells us what batches of things to look at—what sets of variables are likely to be important—and at the same time offers a logic for deciding what sets of relations among these variables are likely to be important to consider.

Note that this is intended to be a model of the problem (i.e., studying groups systematically), rather than a theory or model of groups. Such models are sometimes called "metatheories." They reflect a way of looking at the problem that encompasses a whole family of possible substantive theories. But they do not specify any one particular theory. Here, we are talking about *classes* of properties or variables, and the logical relations between those classes. But there is no specification of specific sets of relations between specific sets of variables—as there would be in a substantive theory.

Main Classes of Variables

The central feature, the "essence," of a group lies in the interaction of its members—the *behaving together*, in some recognized relation to one another, of two or more people who also have some past and/or future relation to each other. So *group interaction process* is the centerpiece of the model.

Certain things go into that group process. For one thing, there are participants, or group members. They come to a group interaction with all their "properties" (traits, characteristics, beliefs, habits, etc.). A member may be strong, or extroverted, or wise, or old, or female, or bellicose, or clumsy, or many other things. *Some* of these properties of members may affect group interaction. So, if one wants to understand and perhaps predict aspects of group interaction process, one must take these group member properties into account.

These participants make up the group being considered, and one can think about the pattern of relations among group members, *prior to* any group interaction process, as another batch of potentially important properties or

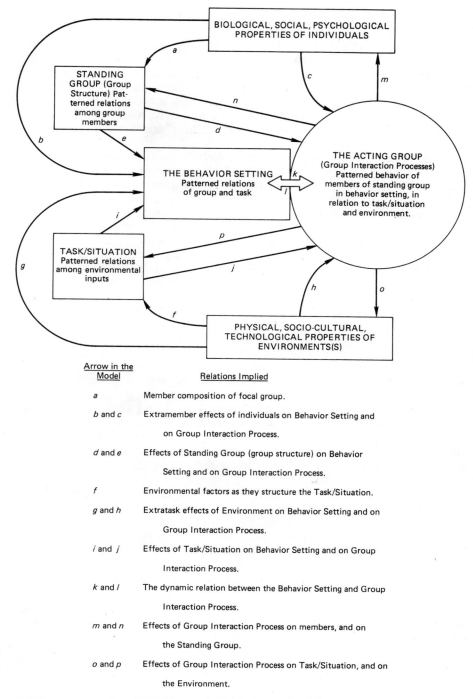

Arrow in the Model	Relations Implied
a	Member composition of focal group.
b and c	Extramember effects of individuals on Behavior Setting and on Group Interaction Process.
d and e	Effects of Standing Group (group structure) on Behavior Setting and on Group Interaction Process.
f	Environmental factors as they structure the Task/Situation.
g and h	Extratask effects of Environment on Behavior Setting and on Group Interaction Process.
i and j	Effects of Task/Situation on Behavior Setting and on Group Interaction Process.
k and l	The dynamic relation between the Behavior Setting and Group Interaction Process.
m and n	Effects of Group Interaction Process on members, and on the Standing Group.
o and p	Effects of Group Interaction Process on Task/Situation, and on the Environment.

FIGURE 1-1   A Conceptual Framework for the Study of Groups

variables. Do group members like each other? Do they have differential influence on each other (for example, does one person exercise more leadership or dominance than the others)? How many members are there and how long have they belonged to this group? Group members are related to each other in many ways; a lot of those relations affect how they behave in relation to one another when they interact. These patterns of relations among members—aspects of *group structure*—also must be taken into account if one wants to understand and predict group interaction process.

Group interaction takes place somewhere, in some *environment*. It may involve a group of workers doing their jobs in an assembly plant; a set of executives holding a conference in a company meeting room; a County Planning Board having its monthly meeting; a family eating dinner on a Wednesday evening in April; a football team getting a dressing room talk between halves of a game; a group of kids playing with some old tires in a dump; two couples at a night-club; an airplane crew flying from Texas to Toronto; a Broadway company rehearsing in a theater. In all of these cases, the group interaction is taking place in an environment that includes both physical and social aspects. Many of these can make a difference in how members behave, hence can alter group interaction process.

Group interaction not only takes place somewhere, it involves the group *doing something*. One very important aspect of all of those settings just enumerated is the "task." Any group interaction (actually, any intact portion of such an interaction) can be characterized in terms of the task(s) that the group (or its members) is trying to carry out: giving (and receiving) a lecture or a sermon or a play; processing steel; assembling an auto; choosing a new vice president; deciding on a zoning variance; preparing a budget justification; arbitrating a grievance; enjoying dinner; having a good time at the nightclub, on the backpacking trip, or in the dump. The task, as you can see from those examples, involves informally assumed goals (e.g., having a good time) as well as assigned jobs (e.g., assembling an auto). What the group is doing, or trying to do, as well as where this is taking place, affects group interaction process in many ways. So, the task situation represents another class of "factors" one must take into account if one wishes to understand and predict group interaction process.

These major classes of inputs—properties of group members; properties of the standing group (group structure); properties of the task/situation; and properties of the surrounding environment—set the conditions under which group interaction takes place. Furthermore, the effects of these four sets of properties, singly and in combination, are forces that shape the group interaction process.

The group interaction process itself is both the result of these shaping forces and the source of some additional forces. While group interaction is greatly affected by those sets of input variables—properties of members, of the group, of the task, and of the environment—it is also patterned, in part, by forces internal to (or indigenous to) the interaction process itself. The latter part of this chapter delves further into the internal forces of group interaction process.

Furthermore, the interaction process and its results represent sources (forces) that potentially lead to changes in those very input conditions: changes in the members themselves; changes in the group structure, or the patterns of relations among members; and changes in the relation of the group to its tasks and to its environment. So, these sets of outputs (or outcomes, or consequences) of group interaction process are parallel to the input classes and, in fact, represent changes in those input variables.

These classes of factors, or "panels" of potentially important variables, are related to one another in relatively complex ways. These panels, and the relations among them, are diagrammed in Figure 1-1. The parts of that model are discussed next.

A Model of Effects by and on Groups

The conceptual framework for study of groups starts with two givens: individual people, who are the members of the group in question (what will be referred to, at times, as the focal group, for clarity of reference); and the environment in which those people are embedded. So we begin with two panels of potentially relevant properties: properties of the group members as individuals; and properties of the physical, socio-cultural and technological environment(s). The former panel includes biographical and demographic characteristics (age, gender, etc.); personality dispositions; beliefs, attitudes and values; moods, feelings, states of mind; and drives, needs, motives, goals and expectations. The latter, environmental, panel includes conditions of the general physical environment (noise, heat, lighting, etc.) and of the social environment (inter-group conflict, loyalty, alienation, etc.).

Both of these panels of variables are huge, perhaps even infinite. So it is necessary to be very selective in terms of what properties are to be included in a study. Such selectivity is one of the functions of theory, as noted earlier. That is, theory functions as a guide to the investigator in selecting variables for study that are thought to be germane to the problem.

When people become interrelated, as when they are members of a group, they develop patterned relationships among themselves—patterned in terms of status, of power, of affection, and of many other aspects. These patterned relationships among group members constitute a group structure. There are many such patterns, such group structures—as many as there are variables or properties on which members can be connected to one another. These include, *at least:* structures defined in terms of composition of members; structure defined in terms of division of labor on tasks; communication structures; power structures and interpersonal relations structures. In the model, the *collection* of all these structures is called the *standing group* (to distinguish it from the *acting group*).

Environmental properties, too, are patterned; and one particular portion is of special importance in the present discussion. That important part is the set of environmental demands/constraints/opportunities that combine to form a particular task and situation. Environmental properties "play into" more than one task/situation, of course, and even more than one at the same time, just as group members "belong to" more than one group, and even more than one at the same time. So, for clarity, we probably should designate our referent as the focal task/situation, recognizing that the environment abounds with "tasks."

We can consider the juxtaposition of the standing group and the task as the Behavior Setting. The term, behavior setting, is borrowed from the work of Roger Barker and his colleagues (Barker, 1965; Barker & Wright, 1955). But the reader should be warned that I am changing the use of that term in one important respect. When Barker talks of the behavior setting, he is dealing with individuals behaving in environments, or individuals behaving in task/situations; but Barker does not use concepts of group, group structure, or group process at all. Barker sees individuals, and their behavior, as related to one another primarily through the demands of the situation.

In the model, the behavior setting represents a pattern—a fit—between the group as a structured entity (the standing group) and the task/situation as a structured set of requirements/demands/opportunities/possibilities/constraints. Notice, too, that the framework has both properties of individuals and properties of the environment "playing into" the behavior setting directly, as well as indirectly through the group and the task. This is equivalent to saying that, while a particular concert (behavior setting and group interaction process) is to be viewed as *mainly* a juxtaposition of a particular orchestra (standing group) with a particular set of musical compositions (task/situation), properties of the orchestra members (M) and of the concert hall, the city, and perhaps the time of year (E), can also have effects on the results.

All of these form the "inputs" for what I am calling group interaction process (GIP), or the *acting group*. GIP refers to the *processes* that take place when group members actually interact, in behavior settings that carry task structures and environmental effects. Such activity can be described in terms of many processes, including (at least) general structural properties such as level and rate of interaction, distribution of participation, extent of member involvement, and so forth, all of which might be labeled *morphological properties;* the flow of work; the flow of information or communications; the flow of influence; and the flow of interpersonal affect. The *acting group* is the term used in this book for the collection of all of these interactive processes. In a sense, the behavior setting refers to the time-place-thing-person complex that serves as the site for the behavior of the acting group. The acting group and the behavior setting are the "action" and "state" sides of the same coin. In Barker's terms, the behavior setting is "circumjacent to" the group interaction process. This is represented in Figure 1-1 by showing the behavior-setting-to-group-interaction-process relation, and the reciprocal relation, as a double arrow, K and L.

The group interaction process feeds back into, and has effects on, all the panels of input variables out of which it has sprung. Individuals are often changed (for example, their attitudes are influenced) as a result of being members of an acting group. Group interaction can change the structure of the standing group; for example, it can change the pattern of attraction among members. Group interaction sometimes results in effects on the environment;

and it quite often results in a shift in the relation of the focal group to its task/situation. Such changes are usually dealt with in terms of task performance effectiveness or task productivity.

All of these effects (the eleven input arrows, *a* to *k,* and the five feedback arrows, *l* to *p,* in Figure 1-1) are important in principle, and are worthy of study. But many of them have been more thoroughly studied than others, and some of them are of more theoretical or practical significance than others. So the organization of later parts of this book will reflect selective treatment of some of these classes of relations more thoroughly than others. One basis for the selection of particular sets of relations for special attention is my particular conception of the interaction process and what it entails. That conceptualization will be presented next.

A MICRO-VIEW OF THE INTERACTION PROCESS

When two or more people interact—that is, when they do something together— a rather complex set of processes take place. That interaction can be viewed in terms of three stages or modes. First a behavior by one member (A), verbal or otherwise, can be regarded as a *communication* from A to others (B, C, and so on). A series of such behaviors, by a set of interacting persons, can be regarded as the *communication process.* The *form* or structure of such a series of interactive behaviors or communications entails such factors as the communication channels and modalities used, the distribution of acts among persons and over time. That form or structure can be regarded as a *communication pattern.*

Each such behavior also can be considered with respect to its *content.* In principle, every interactive behavior can be regarded as having both a *task component* and an *interpersonal component.* The task oriented aspects of the participants' activities can be viewed as the *task or action process,* which results in a *task performance pattern.* The interpersonal oriented aspects of those activities can be viewed as the *attraction or acquaintance process,* which results in an *interpersonal relationship pattern.*

The third stage of the interaction process has to do with its *impact.* The three patterns resulting from the interaction (the communication pattern, the task performance pattern and the interpersonal relationship pattern) in turn have effects on one another and on the participants. Such effects constitute the *influence process,* which involves the outcomes or consequences of the interaction for the participants, for their relationships to one another, for their task performance and for their subsequent communications. These relations are shown in Figure 1-2 and listed in Table 1-1.

This trimodal perspective, along with the overall conceptual framework presented earlier, provides the basis for the organization of much of the rest of the book. Part II, (chapters 5 through 11) is devoted to the *task content* of group interaction; that is, the task performance process. In terms of the overall

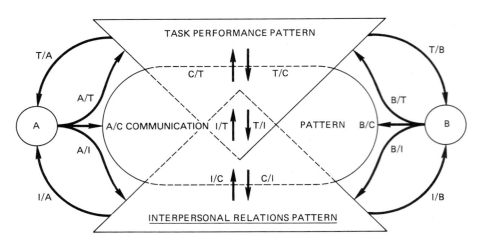

A, B	Group members	Outcome	
		T/A, T/B	Effect of task performance on members
Form			
A/C, B/C	Communication process	I/A, I/B	Effect of interpersonal relations on members
Content		C/T, T/C	Effect of communication pattern and task
A/T, B/T	Task Activity		performance on one another
	(Action Process)		
		C/I, I/C	Effect of communication pattern and interpersonal
A/I, B/I	Interpersonal Activity		relations on one another.
	(Attraction Process)		
		T/I, I/T	Effect of task performance and interpersonal
			relations on one another

FIGURE 1-2   Interaction as a Three-Stage Process

conceptual framework, those chapters deal with "arrows" i, j, and p. (See Figure 1-1). By treating the task performance material earlier in sequence than the logic of the models would imply, I want to give that material special prominence. Much of the continued interest in groups over the years has focussed on groups as potential vehicles for improving task performance. Following those chapters on task performance, Part III deals with groups as systems for structuring interaction. Chapters 12 and 13 deal with the form or pattern of interaction and with the communication process. Chapters 14, 15 and 16 deal with the interpersonal content of interaction; that is, with the *acquaintance or attraction* process. Chapters 17 and 18 deal with outcomes or consequences of interaction; that is, with the *influence process.*

Before these presentations, though, the remaining chapters of Part I (chapters 2, 3, and 4) provide some background needed to make the detailed analyses of later parts of the book understandable. First, in chapter 2, there is a brief outline of past research on groups, of trends in that research, and of the role that theory (and its absence) has played in past group research. Chapter 3 presents a discussion of some general features of research methods in the social

TABLE 1-1   Interaction as a Three-Stage Process

PROCESS	*Communication Process*	*Action Process*	*Attraction Process*	*Influence Process*
ASPECTS OF INTERACTION	*Form of Interaction* Modalities Participation patterns Temporal patterns	*Content of Interaction* Task component: Generate Choose Negotiate Execute	Interpersonal component: Affect Control	*Consequences of Interaction* Impact of communication, task and interpersonal patterns on participants A & B and on each other
RESULT	*Communication Pattern*	*Task Performance Pattern*	*Interpersonal Relations Pattern*	*Pattern of Change in:* Participants; Communication; Task; Interpersonal relationships

and behavioral sciences and how those features both enable and constrain research on groups. Chapter 4 takes the concern with method one step further, providing a discussion of the various kinds of social units that have been used in the study of groups and classifies them in terms of their relations to the definition of groups given earlier in this chapter.

CHAPTER TWO
BACKGROUND
FOR THE STUDY
OF GROUPS

In any field of science, and especially in the social sciences (hence in the group research field), what we know about any given problem at any given time is very much constrained by at least three features of the context within which that problem is studied. One constraining feature is the history of past study of the problem: what we have already learned in the past about that problem, and how those results have been interpreted. A second constraining feature is theory: how we conceptualize the problem; what pattern of relations we assume/imagine/hypothesize to be involved; which aspects of the problem are inferred to be crucial causes, and which to be consequences. The third constraining feature is method: what "rules of evidence" do we use to assemble, integrate and interpret that evidence; what means do we use to assess the biasing effects of the methods themselves.

Fields of science are dynamic. History, theory and method change over time, and with such change there often is a change in the "meaning" of any given piece of evidence. As time goes on, we learn more about a problem, and also learn more about related problems. Our theoretical conceptions change, sometimes sharply redefining the problem. New methods are developed that make it possible to gain more detailed or more accurate information about the problem, or even to study some aspects of the problem that heretofore could not be studied. In all these ways, any given problem and any given piece of evidence about a problem can shift in meaning over time.

This chapter offers some background on the first two of these three constraining features of the context of group research. The first section offers a very brief overview of the development of group research over the past century;

the second section notes certain themes, dilemmas and issues that have marked that history. The third section provides a brief discussion of the role of theory in the development of an empirical science, and of how a lack of attention to theory has handicapped the group research field.

AN OUTLINE OF PAST RESEARCH ON GROUPS

The study of groups, within modern social science, grew out of work of sociologists and social psychologists of the late nineteenth and early twentieth centuries, although the roots of some of the issues in that field go back much further. The French sociologists Tarde (1903) and LeBon (1896) were concerned with mobs and crowds—"pathological" groups. Simmel in Germany (1950) and Cooley (1902), Mead (1934), and Ross (1908) in the United States, focussed on social interaction, on the family as a basic unit of society, and on the complexities of relationships in very small, two- and three-person groups. (Useful reviews of this and later periods can be found in G. W. Allport, 1954; McGrath & Altman, 1966; McGrath, 1978; Cartwright & Zander, 1953, 1960, 1968.)

These early efforts mainly dealt with broad theoretical issues: What are the basic human instincts, and how important are they in human behavior? How do experience, learning, habit, affect human social behavior? Are groups "real"; and, if so, is it reasonable to talk about "group consciousness" or "group mind"? What are the fundamental principles of human behavior (e.g., imitation, suggestion, sympathy)? These efforts were theoretical, in the sense that they built from speculative thought, based on personal experience and reading. They were not empirical, based on systematic observations, and they certainly were not *experimental* in the sense that we use that word in modern times.

This theory-oriented period ended in the 1920s and the field of social psychology (and group research) came under the sway of logical positivism (Compte, 1853), with its emphasis on the collection and interpretation of empirical data, based on experiment and direct observation. The social psychologists (and group researchers) of that day borrowed the paradigms and methodology of the physical sciences; they tried to bring their problems into the laboratory. F. H. Allport (1920) for example, tried to use controlled laboratory conditions to study what he termed "social facilitation": effects on individual task performance that arise from the presence of other people (see discussion of social facilitation in chapter 17) (F. Allport, 1924).

By the 1930s social psychology and group research, still strongly empirical, had broadened their base beyond the laboratory and had begun to grapple with problems in real life settings: mass movements, lynchings, prejudice, gangs and delinquency, and the like.

In the 1930s, also, the group dynamics movement began, under the leadership of Kurt Lewin. That movement, in large part, shaped the field of group research for years to come. (See Lewin, 1948, 1951, 1953; Lewin, Lippett and White, 1939). In its early years, under Lewin's genius, the group dynamics movement was a balanced blend. There was a strong concern with theory.

There was a central focus on application of science to socially significant problems: frustration, leadership styles, attitude change, and so on. At the same time, there was strong effort to harness the power of experimental, laboratory methodology in the service of these problems. This effective marriage of theoretically based ideas, socially significant problems and experimental methodology had not occurred before in group research—and, sad to say, it has for the most part not occurred since.

The war pressures of the 1940s engulfed group research, along with most other enterprises. The new problems opened up by the group dynamics movement, and the "boom" aspects of the wartime situation, yielded much research. That research paid off for the field in two ways: by providing much new evidence on certain substantive problem areas—such as leadership, communications, attitude change in groups; and by producing much in the way of new and refined methods for study—such as techniques for measuring interpersonal feelings, methods for constructing experimental groups of desired composition, and the like. The strong theoretical orientation of Lewin's early work, however, did not survive the war. But social psychology, and with it the group research field, became established as a legitimate field of science.

During the 1950s, the lack of concern with theory continued, and the strong and near-exclusive attachment to laboratory methods returned. There was an unprecedented research boom in the United States throughout the 1950s and well into the 1960s, fueled by the cold war and the Korean conflict and later by the manned space-flight programs. Since social psychology and group research were now established as fields of science, they also participated in this expansion of research. The number of studies increased enormously, perhaps ten-fold in a decade. Most of the research was done in the laboratory; the vast majority of it failed to reflect the earlier concerns either with real world problems or with theoretical development.

By the late 1950s and early 1960s there had begun to be signs of concern among scholars about the lack of integration of knowledge in the group research field. (See, for example, Roseborough, 1953; Kelley & Thibaut, 1954; Reicken & Homans, 1954; Cartwright & Zander, 1953; Hare, Borgatta & Bales, 1955, 1965.) That concern grew stronger by the middle 1960s. There were many efforts to catalogue, synthesize, or otherwise integrate the vast quantities of empirical facts that seemed to be piling up in all those atheoretical laboratory studies. (See, for example: Argyle, 1957; Thibaut & Kelley 1959; Hare, 1962; Collins & Guetzkow, 1964; McGrath & Altman, 1966.) Among these, only the Thibaut and Kelley (1959) effort offers a theory. But the occurrence of all of these attempts to integrate the evidence points to certain serious limitations of group research at that time, namely; techniques for generating empirical evidence, especially in laboratory settings, had been developed and used with a vengeance; support for such work had flowed fairly freely; but there had been little support for—indeed, nearly a disdain for—theoretical development. As a consequence the group research field was in danger of drowning in an ocean of fragmented evidence.

The group research field changed sharply in the late 1960s and early 1970s in two related ways. First, the rate of production of studies that would readily be identified as "group research" dropped sharply. Many scholars who had focussed on the group as a unit of inquiry turned their efforts to problems at the individual level (e.g., Festinger, 1957), or at the level of larger aggregates such as organizations (e.g., Bass, 1960; Fiedler, 1967). At the same time, many of the conceptual issues raised by the voluminous research of the 1940s and 1950s were still being investigated; but for the most part, those issues were being studied as basic individual behavior processes *abstracted from their occurrence in concrete groups.*

SOME MAJOR TRENDS IN GROUP RESEARCH

Experiential Groups

One offshoot of the early, Lewin-led group dynamics movement was the development and application of "group methods" as means for improving practices in a wide range of endeavors—psychotherapy, schools, business management. These began with the early "T-groups," or training groups. Since then, there have been many variations, under labels such as sensitivity groups, encounter groups, integrity groups, and a host of others. These efforts grew out of, but soon became isolated from, the more basic-science-oriented efforts of group researchers in the group dynamics movement and elsewhere. They have had enormously widespread use, and have many ardent advocates, although there is a very noticeable lack of research evaluating their effectiveness in achieving their claimed gains. (For good reviews, see Back, 1972; Campbell & Dunnette, 1968; Hartman, 1979; Lieberman, 1976; Smith, 1975.) It is notable that, in the early work, the emphasis was on group processes as such. Later, the emphasis shifted to using groups as a basis for *changing individuals.* That shift, from concentration at the group level to near exclusive concentration at the individual level, occurred at about the same time as a similar shift in the basic research stream from a focus on groups to a focus on individual level concepts. It is not unreasonable to suppose that some forces outside of the group research area, and outside of social science entirely, might have had influences on both the basic and the "engineering" side of the group movement. Such forces, which in the late 1960s and early 1970s led to a social milieu that has been dubbed the "me-decade", might also have produced a parallel shift in both the applied and basic "wings" of the group area, from group to individual level concerns. (For other interpretations of these shifts see: Back, 1972; Steiner, 1974.)

Some Polarities

These tracings of history point up several polarities, or perhaps dilemmas, that underlie that history. One such polarity is a nature/nurture dichotomy. Since the demise of the early instinct theorists (for example, McDougall, 1908; see discussion later in this chapter) the "nurture" end of that polarity has been in clear ascendency. That is, there has been a broadly shared consensus among social scientists (and, indeed, in the lay culture) that *experience,* rather than innate characteristics, is of central importance in shaping social behavior. But a flat rejection of the "nature" pole has been repeatedly challenged, although often implicitly. It is challenged, for example, by some proponents of Freudian views that stress the importance of innate unconscious motives. It is also challenged, implicitly, by proponents of theories that propose that group behavior reflects mainly built-in personality patterns of members. The recent boom in sociobiology is another example showing that the nature/nurture issue is not closed. Nonetheless, the experience or nurture pole has remained dominant for the past sixty years.

Another polarity of long standing in group research hinges on the relative emphasis that should be given to theory and to empirical evidence. Since the early speculative theorists gave way before the onslaught of the positivist philosophy (see further discussion later in this chapter), except for Lewin's early group dynamics work, group research has been totally dominated by the empirical end of that polarity. Indeed, the very success of that emphasis, the development of a highly efficient and sophisticated data generating technology, brought with it, as the other side of the same coin, the virtual absence of emphasis on development of broad-, or even middle-range, theoretical structures. The group research field is in urgent need of good theory. There is some basis for hope that efforts toward such theory building are increasing.

Yet a third polarity is the relative concern with basic and with applied problems. Group research has shown a cycle of emphasis in regard to this polarity. The field itself initially grew out of concerns with and attempts to grapple with the very pressing problems of how people come to behave so differently in crowds and mobs than they do in other situations. But in the 1920s there was a turning toward a concern with method, and a parallel concern with problems growing out of the conceptual and methodological issues of the field, rather than out of social concerns of the world outside the laboratory. In the 1930s and 1940s there was a resurgence of concern with problems in the "real world"—perhaps fueled by the depression and the war. In the 1950s and well into the 1960s, the emphasis once again returned to basic research on problems originating from within the discipline, with relatively little emphasis on problems arising from surrounding social conditions.

There is another polarity, between laboratory and field research, that is frequently but not inherently related to the polarity between basic and applied problems. There has been a similar cycling of emphasis, on laboratory then field then lab again, that parallels the cycles of emphasis on basic, applied, then basic research. There seems to have been at least some resurgence of emphasis on applied problems and on field methods—along with, rather than in place of, basic problems and laboratory methods—in the latter part of the 1970s.

Shifts in Topical Emphasis

The substantive topics dominating group research also have shifted from period to period, reflecting both the state of the research field and the state of social forces quite outside research and social science. In the 1920s, the central problem on which research focussed was the effect of the presence and behavior of others on the individual's performance. In the 1930s one main thrust was on ethnic prejudice and attitude change. In the wartime 1940s, group research seemed to focus on leadership and communication. In the 1950s, conformity and its consequences had center stage. In the 1960s the leading theme was conflict and its resolution. The focal problem of the 1970s is hard to state because we are still close to that time. It is reflected in such topics as altruism and aggression; personal space, territoriality and crowding; attribution of causality; stress from stimulus and information overload. The key problem common to those topics can reasonably be stated as the question: How can individuals effectively relate to one another amidst the complex physical and social forces of this highly technical and inter-dependent world? That problem remains unanswered in the 1980s—just as do the problems of prejudice, leadership, conformity, and conflict resolution inherited from earlier decades. But all of those problems are at a different—more advanced—stage now than they were in previous times. And what we know about each of them has been affected by being filtered through that history. Now it is time to consider further how such knowledge is affected by similar advances (or lack of them) in theory and in methods for research.

THE ROLE OF THEORY, AND THE CONSEQUENCES OF ITS ABSENCE

The early social psychological work out of which the group research field was developed relied largely on broad, speculative, "armchair" thinking, bolstered by anecdotal evidence drawn from personal experience and reading. It had very little concern for *systematic* collection, analysis and interpretation of empirical evidence (i.e., direct or indirect observation of behavior). Furthermore, much of that early work tried to identify and argue for one single sovereign theoretical principle that would "account for" all human behavior. (See G. W. Allport's review, 1954.) One such single factor, for example, was *imitation;* another was *sympathy;* still another was *suggestion.* Those early principles can be seen as the ancestors of many ideas still current in the field (e.g., modeling, empathy, and conformity, respectively), and also as the progeny of much earlier concepts (such as the knowing, feeling and striving threesome—the cognitive, affective and conative trio—that goes back at least to Plato). But theories in which one of them was taken as the *single* principle to account for all the complexities of human behavior were simply too simple to remain viable.

Another early thrust—also based on speculation, not systematic observation—was a kind of multiple attribute approach. McDougall (1908), for example, posited a set of "instincts," and suggested that different people had more or less of each of them. This approach had an advantage over single factor approaches in that it apparently could account for a much wider range of individual differences. But others offered their own lists of instincts to add to the McDougall list. Since these were not based on observational evidence, the sole test of whether any proposed instinct should stay in the list was the strength of verbal argument that its proponents could make for it. Hence, the lists grew, and eventually the approach collapsed under the weight of the ever-expanding list. (This approach—and its waxing and waning—have been mirrored within a number of other areas of psychology and social psychology, including the cataloguing of basic mental abilities or aptitudes and the proliferation of personality traits.)

Both the various single factor theories, and the theories that consisted of lists of traits or instincts, were inadequate on several grounds. First, they were not derived from any set of systematic evidence. Mostly, they were based on the particular experiences, idiosyncratic preferences, interests and ideas of their promulgators. They often drew on the writings of earlier scholars, but did so with much selectivity; and, in any case, those writings were also the product of the unsystematic speculations of those earlier scholars. Second, the basic formulations of the early theories provided no criterion or standard in terms of which one could *assess* the validity of the assertions and assumptions of the theory. Logical argument and, often, rhetorical virtuosity were the sole bases for choosing between competing ideas. Third, those particular theories consisted mainly of concepts (single ones or lists) that purported to "explain," but that in fact simply relabelled, the behaviors to which they were applied. We are not much enlightened, for example, if we "explain" why person B does what person A has just done by asserting that people "imitate." Nor are we enlightened to learn that the reason some people interact in a friendly fashion is because they have a high amount of the "gregarious" instinct. These "theories," in effect, simply described some aspect of behavior, and then asserted that descriptive label as an "explanation." (This is by no means a problem only of the past. Such labelling-as-explanation frequently creeps into current theories, and the group research scholar must continually guard against it.) If the main theoretical terms are merely descriptions of what is observed, eventually there will be as many theoretical concepts as there are observables to be accounted for by that theory. Such a state of affairs does not provide any conceptual leverage, which is one of the key functions of theory.

These early theoretical efforts—both the sweeping single factor theories and the cumbersome lists of instincts or traits—were thus quite inadequate on several grounds. Their inadequacies were becoming quite troublesome to their proponents, and quite apparent to their critics, at about the time that another very fundamental set of changes was about to take place in the social sciences. The philosophy of logical positivism was being applied to the social sciences (e.g., Compte, 1853), and a parallel viewpoint, behaviorism (partly derived from positivism), soon gained ascendency in psychology. Positivism and behaviorism both put a strong emphasis on "objective" evidence, on the collection of systematic observations of behavior. They rejected both introspection and speculation as bases for "knowing." Not only did this view overwhelm the already toppling single-factor and instinct theories—a useful outcome, because of the serious inadequacies of these approaches already noted—but it also gave *all* theoretical endeavor a bad name for many years to come. The upshot was a field (social psychology and, within it, group research) with heavy emphasis on the collection and analysis of empirical data, but with a moratorium—a virtual taboo—on the development of theoretical/conceptual ideas to guide that empirical effort. It is as one-legged as its predecessor—though there was a switch from one leg to the other, from data-less theory to theory-less data—and is equally, though differently, inadequate.

Theory is important in science, not as a substitute for data but as a framework to guide the collection and interpretation of data. Similarly, data are important in a science, not as a substitute for theory but as the substance with which theoretical ideas can be induced, tested and revised. The key limitation of the earlier speculative period was the lack of data, not the presence of theory, or even its speculative form. And the key limitation of the more recent empirical era has been the lack of theory, not the presence of data or even its fragmented form. After all, without theory, data could only be fragmented; and without data theory could only be speculative. Both theory and data are necessary, each to strengthen the other. Theory strengthens a data-based science in several ways: (a) as a means for identifying problems worthy of study; (b) as a means for connecting one problem or one piece of evidence with another, even when they have been given different labels; (c) as a means for estimating (hypothesizing/predicting) the pattern of data likely to be found in a yet-unstudied area; (d) as a means for anticipating what aspects of a problem are most likely to be important, hence worth focus in research, and what aspects might be of less central importance for research. In short, theory serves as a means for *understanding* the problem to be studied and the evidence thus gained.

If an entire field develops vast bodies of data, with little or no underlying theory—as has largely been the case in group research for nearly fifty years—it is inevitable that the work in that field will have certain undesired features. First, its results will be highly fragmented, because there is no basis for connecting one set of data with another. The group research field is highly fragmented, and is marked by having many labels that appear to refer to the same phenomena (for comment on this, see McGrath & Altman, 1966; Zander, 1979). Second, it will be very much shaped by considerations of efficiency and cost of available tools. Without theory, these provide a very compelling basis for deciding how to do a study. This effect has led to an extreme emphasis within group research on relatively narrow laboratory experiments. Third, work in the field is likely to be very much shaped by currents of popularity. Without theory, these provide a normatively compelling basis for deciding what to study. This tendency has left the group research field pockmarked with the residue of fifty years of fads and passing fancies. This is not to say that group research has no theory at all. The rest of this book contains mention or description of a number of useful theoretical efforts, many fairly recent. But it also contains much evidence of the undesired effects that have arisen because, broadly speaking, there has been a half-century of neglect of, and retreat from, theory in the small group research area.

CHAPTER THREE
METHODS
FOR THE STUDY
OF GROUPS

Science is the systematic use of theoretical and empirical methods to try to increase understanding of some set of phenomena or events. In the social and behavioral sciences, those events involve states and actions of human beings, and the by-products of such actions. In the study of groups, the relevant phenomena involve states and actions of groups and their members, and the by-products of those actions. This chapter is about some features of the methods by which researchers in the small group area go about "doing science" in that area.

Methods are the tools—the instruments, techniques and procedures—by which a science gains and interprets information. (For readers familiar with computer jargon, methods include both the hardware and the software; and, as with computers, things often go awry if there is too little emphasis on the latter.) Like tools in other domains, different methods can do different things. Each method should be regarded as offering *potential opportunities not available by other means;* but also as having *inherent limitations.* You can't pound a nail if you don't have a hammer or some functional equivalent. But if you do have a hammer, that hammer won't help you much if what you need to do is to cut a board in half. So it is with the tools or methods of science, of social science, and of the social science area dealt with here: the study of groups.

Many students find the subject of methodology boring. It is nevertheless true that the *meaning* of scientific evidence (in any area of science) is inherently tied to the means or methods by which that evidence was obtained. Hence, an understanding of that evidence, its meaning, and its limitations, requires an understanding of those methods. Becoming highly knowledgeable and skilled in all the methods of any one area of study, such as the group area, takes a lot of work and a lot of time. It would not be possible to embed a full treatment of research methodology within a chapter of a textbook such as this. Nevertheless, the reader needs some grounding in research methodology in order to understand the reasons why researchers working in the group area have proceeded as they have done; why they asked some questions and not others; why they have interpreted some results and not others; and what degree of confidence ought to be placed in their interpretations. Furthermore, since the *meaning* of evidence depends on how it was obtained, there will be references throughout the book to various data gathering and analysis methods, as various findings are talked about. These references to methods will necessarily be brief. They will often use acronyms or jargon labels (e.g., PDG; or the Asch technique; or mock jury studies; or Bales's IPA). So the reader needs to be able to find out what those labels mean. What is needed is a kind of catalogue of the "technology" of the small group trade.

I will attempt to deal with the need for information about the methods of group research in three ways within this book. First, this chapter discusses some general features of research methods in the social and behavioral sciences, and raises some issues that underlie all work in those areas. Those issues arise at strategic, design and operational levels. Second, chapter 4 presents a discussion of the kinds of social units that have been used in the study of groups, and provides a classification of those in terms of how they relate to the working definition of groups presented in chapter 1. Third, a large number of examples of the more widely used techniques for research on groups, or items of group research technology, or "study paradigms", are presented in brief, digest form, in boxed inserts, throughout the chapters of Parts II and III of the book. These boxes will identify the techniques by the names or acronyms that are used to talk about them in other places in the book, and will cite at least one reference from which the reader can learn more about that study paradigm or item of group research technology.

OVERVIEW: METHODS AS OPPORTUNITIES AND LIMITATIONS

When we learn something in science, that knowledge is based on use of some combination of empirical and theoretical methods. The meaning of that knowledge and the confidence we can have in it are both contingent on the methods by which it was obtained. All methods used to gather and analyze evidence offer both opportunities not available with other methods and limitations inherent in the use of those particular methods.

In the group research area, the use of questionnaires or other forms of self-report provides a good example of this dual nature of methods. On the one hand, self-report measures (questionnaires, interviews, rating scales, and the like) are a direct way, and sometimes the only apparent way, to get evidence about certain kinds of variables that are worthy of study: attitudes, feelings, retrospective recall of experiences early in life, and the like. On the other hand, such self-report measures have some serious flaws. For example, respondents may try to appear competent, to be consistent, to answer in socially desirable ways, to please the researcher. These flaws limit and potentially distort the information gained from such measures. Alternative data collection approaches, such as observation of overt behavior, may avoid some of these particular weaknesses but will suffer other ones. In any case they may be difficult or impossible to adapt to measure particular kinds of variables. For example, how do you observe a feeling?

Such is the dilemma of empirical science: *all methods have inherent flaws—though each has certain advantages.* These flaws cannot be avoided. But what the researcher can do is to bring more than one approach, more than one method, to bear on each aspect of a problem. If only one method is used, there is no way to separate out the part that is the "true" measure of the concept in question from the part that reflects mainly the method itself. Multiple methods, carefully picked so that they each have different weaknesses, can add strength to one another by offsetting each other's weaknesses, and can add strength to the resulting evidence if they show consistent outcomes across divergent methods.

The same problems, and the same prescription for dealing with them, apply at the level of research strategy as well as at the level of methods of data collection. Laboratory experiments, for example, have some great strengths. They can permit precise measurement of effects, deliberate manipulation of presumed causes, and strong inferences about cause-effect relations. But they also have some serious flaws. They often greatly narrow the scope of the problem; they study it in artificial settings; and researchers using laboratory experiments are likely to make the matter worse by using obtrusive and artificial procedures and measures. There are several alternatives to laboratory experiments, including field studies and sample surveys. (There are at least five other strategies; see the next section of this chapter). Each of these other strategies offers different strengths, some of them offsetting the weaknesses of the laboratory; but each also has different inherent weaknesses, some of these being the very strengths of the laboratory method. *No one strategy, used alone, is very useful;* each of them is far too flawed. But again, the researcher needs to take advantage of multiple approaches—not so much within a single study, which usually must use a single strategy as a practical matter, but over several studies of the same problem. The approaches need to be chosen so that the weaknesses of each can be offset by the strengths of another strategy. If we obtain *consistent outcomes across studies using different strategies,* we can be more confident that those outcomes have to do with the phenomena we are studying, not just with our methods.

Incidentally, one can view the kind of interplay between theory and data suggested in chapter 2 as a specific form of use of multiple strategies. Some of the possible alternative strategies are theoretical, not empirical. (See next section of this chapter.) When we yoke a formal theory with a laboratory experiment, or with a sample survey, we are applying two alternative strategies with different strengths and weaknesses, and the *consistency* between them is the core of the resulting evidence.

The central notions in all this discussion, concerning methods at both the strategy and measure levels, are (a) that *methods enable but also limit evidence;*

(b) that *all methods are flawed, but all are valuable;* (c) that the *different flaws of various methods can be offset by* (simultaneous or successive) *use of multiple methods;* and (d) that such *multiple methods should be* chosen to *have patterned diversity,* so that *strengths of some offset weaknesses of others.* Given these principles, it follows that one ought not ask whether any given study is flawless and therefore to be believed ("is it valid?"). Rather, one should ask whether the evidence from that study is *consistent with* other evidence on the same problem, from other strategies, done by other methods. If two sets of evidence based on different methods *are consistent,* both of those studies gain in credibility. If the two sets are *not consistent,* that raises doubts about the credibility of *both* sets—equal or unequal doubts, depending on what else is known about the problem from still other studies, what methods are involved and what is known about their usefulness and limitations, and so forth. Conversely, if all of the studies of a given problem are based on the *same methods,* then the body of information thus gained is very much contingent on and limited by the flaws of those methods; and that information must be regarded with some degree of skepticism until it can be shown to hold for a broader array of methods. The fundamental principle is that *empirical knowledge,* in group research as elsewhere in science, *requires consistency or convergence of evidence across studies or sets of data that are based on different strategies and methods for acquiring that evidence.* These issues are discussed further, and a more detailed listing and description of strategies and methods is given, in the following parts of this chapter.

STRATEGIC LEVEL ISSUES: CHOOSING A SETTING FOR A STUDY

Research evidence, in social and behavioral sciences, always involves *somebody doing something, in some situation.* When we get such evidence, we can, therefore, "reference" it on three aspects or facets: Whose behavior is it about (which Actors)? What behaviors is it about (which Behaviors)? What situations is it about (which Contexts)?

When you gather a batch of research evidence, you are always trying to maximize three things:

1. The *generalizability* of the evidence *over populations* of actors (A).
2. The *precision* of measurement of the *behaviors* (and precision of control over extraneous facets or variables that are not being studied) (B).
3. The *realism* of the situation or *context* (in relation to the contexts to which you want your evidence to refer) (C).

While you always want to maximize A, B, and C simultaneously, *you cannot.* This is one fundamental dilemma of research methods. The very things you can do to increase one of these reduces one or both of the other two. For example, the things you do to increase precision of measurement of behavior and control of related variables (B) necessarily intrude upon the situation and reduce its "naturalness," or realism (that is, reduce C). Conversely, the things you can do to keep high realism of context (C) will reduce the generality of the populations to which your results can be applied (A) or the precision of the information you generate (B), or both.

The nature of this strategic dilemma is made clearer in Figure 3-1, which shows a set of eight alternative research strategies or settings in relation to one another. That figure shows where among the strategies each of three desired features—generalizability over populations (A), precision in control and measurement of behavior (B), and realism of context (C)—is at its maximum. It also shows, though, that strategies that maximize one of these are far from the maximum point for the other two. The spatial relations in Figure 3-1 emphasize the dilemma just discussed: the very things that help increase one of the desired features—A, B, and C—also reduce the other two. *It is not possible to maximize, simultaneously, all three.* Any one research strategy is limited in what it can do; and research done by any one strategy is flawed—although different strategies have different flaws.

The strategies listed in Figure 3-1 are in four pairs. Some are familiar ones. Field studies refer to efforts to make direct observations of "natural,"

FIGURE 3-1   Research Strategies

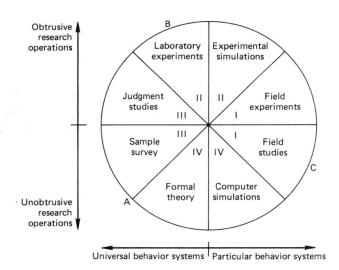

I.   Settings in natural systems.
II.   Contrived and created settings.
III. Behavior not setting dependent.
IV.   No observation of behavior required.
A.   Point of maximum concern with generality over actors.
B.   Point of maximum concern with precision measurement of behavior.
C.   Point of maximum concern with system character of context.

ongoing systems (in the present context that means existing groups), while intruding on and disturbing those systems as little as possible. Laboratory experiments are attempts to create the "essence" of some general class of systems (for the present case, groups) in a context in which the researcher can control all (or at least very many) of the extraneous features of the situation, in order to be able to maximize the essential features with precision. The two strategies in between refer to mixtures or compromises. Field experiments are field studies with one major intervention, the deliberate manipulation of some feature whose effects are to be studied. An experimental simulation is a laboratory study in which an effort is made to create a system that is like some class of naturally occurring systems (such as what are called mock juries later in this book), but which are artificial in that they are created by the researcher for study, and people perform in them for research purposes rather than for purposes stemming from their own lives.

Sample surveys are efforts to get information from a broad (and well devised) sample of actors, usually in the form of verbal responses to a relatively small set of questions. Judgment studies are efforts to get responses (usually from a very small and somewhat casually selected sample of "judges") about a systematically patterned and precisely calibrated set of stimuli. Surveys gain much generalizability over populations (A), but give up a lot in precision of measurement (B) to do so. Judgment studies have less generalizability over actors (A), but retain considerable precision of measurement (B). Both surveys and judgment studies try to deemphasize context—actually, to uncouple the behavior (judgment) from the context in which it is done. Thus, both are very low on realism of context (C).

The fourth pair of strategies are theoretical, not empirical. The term formal theory is used here to mean general theory. Such theories are high on generalizability over populations (A) because they attempt to be general; they are not very high on realism of context (C) because by being general they do not deal very concretely with any one context; and they are very low on precision of measurement of behavior (B), because, since they are theoretical rather than empiricial, they in fact involve no behaviors. The strategy called computer simulation refers to attempts to *model* a specific real life system or class of systems. Such effects are also theoretical rather than empirical; hence they are low on B because they do not involve behavior. In comparison to formal theories, computer simulations are higher in C, because they are system-specific; but they thereby lose in A, because they are limited to populations indigenous to that class of systems.

To sum up: Field studies gain realism (C) at the price of low generalizability (A) and lack of precision (B). Laboratory experiments maximize precision of measurement and control of variables (B), at the price of lack of realism (C) and low generalizability (A). Surveys have high generalizability (A) but get it by giving up much realism (C) and much precision (B). Formal theories get generalizability (A) by giving up some realism (C) and much precision (B). The other four strategies are combinations located in between those four just discussed; they have the intermediate gains and losses implied by their positions in the "strategy circle" of Figure 3–1.

Doing research is *not* to be regarded as trying to find the right strategy.

There is no right one. Indeed, they are all "wrong" in the sense that each is inherently limited, flawed. But they are all potentially useful. In considering any set of evidence, one should take into account what strategies were used in obtaining various parts of it, hence the strengths and limitations of that evidence at the strategic level.

DESIGN LEVEL ISSUES: WHAT WILL YOU COMPARE AND WHAT WILL YOU LEARN?

Any study needs a plan for what data will be gathered, how that data will be aggregated and partitioned, and what comparisons will be made within it. Such a study plan is often called a *research design*. As is evident from the preceding discussion, choice of one or another of the various strategies will limit the kinds of designs you can use. But there are also some general features of study designs, and it is those features that are to be discussed here.

Correlation versus Comparison

All research questions can be boiled down to variations of a few basic question forms. One is the *baserate* question: How often (at what rate, or what proportion of the time) does X occur? That is a purely descriptive matter, but is often a very crucial underpinning of other information. A second general form of question is the *relational* question: Are X and Y related? Do they occur together? That question has two major forms. In the correlational form, it is: Is there systematic *covariation* in the value (or amount or degree) of X and the value of Y? For example, does age covary with happiness? A high correlation between X and Y means that when X occurs at a high value, Y is also likely to occur at a high value; and when X is at a low value, Y is also likely to be at a low value. In the example from above, this would mean that older people were, by and large, happier than younger ones. The correlation between X and Y could equally well be high and *negative,* if high values of X went with low values of Y and vice versa. If that were the case for the example, then younger people would be, by and large, happier. There is little or no correlation between X and Y if knowing X doesn't help predict the value of Y. In the example, that would mean that older and younger people both vary in happiness, with some of each having high levels and some of each having less.

Given the example chosen here, of age and happiness, it certainly might occur to the reader that the highest level of happiness might occur, systematically, at some time other than in extreme old age or extreme youth. For example, happiness might increase up to age fifty, then decline. That would describe a nonlinear correlation (and, technically, a nonmonotonic one). There are statistical tools to test for such nonlinearity, although social scientists far too often do not use them when the evidence to be examined might well require them. But as the shape of the relation becomes more complicated—for example, if happiness decreased from young child to adolescent, then increased to age fifty, then decreased, but flattened out after sixty-five—our statistical tools become more cumbersome to use and many of them become less adequate to the task of assessing such complex forms of relation.

Much research in the social and behavioral sciences makes use of correlations, linear and nonlinear, that involve two, three, or more variables. Such a correlational approach requires being able to measure the presence or values of X, and of Y, for a series of "cases" that vary on X and on Y. It can tell you whether X and Y go together; but it *cannot* help you decide whether X is a cause of Y, or vice versa, or neither.

Another form of the relational question is the *comparison* or *difference* question. The difference question involves asking, essentially, whether Y is present (or at a high value) under conditions where X is present (or at a high value), and absent (or low) when X is absent (or low). For example: Do groups perform tasks better (Y) when members like each other (X) than when they do not (X' or "not-X")? You could approach this question in either of two ways. You could go around collecting measures of "liking" until you had found a bunch of groups high on it and another bunch of groups low on it (and perhaps a bunch at intermediate levels), and then compare their average performance scores. That would be, in effect, just a messy version of the correlational approach. The other approach would be to set up some groups with members who do like each other and set up some other groups whose members do not like each other; then to give both sets of groups some common tasks to perform; and then to see if the average task performance (Y) of the "high liking" groups (X) is higher than the average task performance of the "low liking" groups (X'). For the comparison to be most useful, you would need to make sure that the two sets of groups were the same, or comparable, on all the other factors that might affect task performance—such as difficulty of the task, availability of task materials, quality of working conditions, task-related abilities, experience and training of members, and the like. You might render the groups comparable on some of these factors by *controlling* them at a single *constant* value for all groups of both sets. For example, you probably would want to have all groups in both conditions do exactly the same tasks. For some other variables, such as intelligence or abilities of members, that you could not hold at a constant value for all cases, you might want to *match* the groups, on the average, between the two conditions. You might even want to manipulate a second or third variable in addition to group liking—perhaps group size, for example. But you can only manipulate, match, and control a limited number of variables in any one study. You have to do something else about all the rest of the rather large set of potentially relevant factors.

That something else is called *randomization,* or random assignment of cases to conditions. Randomization means use of a random assignment procedure to allocate cases (groups) to conditions (high liking versus low liking, or, if you were also manipulating a second variable such as size, high-liking-large-groups versus high-liking-small-groups versus low-liking-large-groups versus low-liking-small-groups), so that any given case is equally likely to be in any of the conditions.

To do what has been called a "true experiment" (see Campbell & Stanley, 1966), you *must* have randomization of cases to conditions. If you do, then you strengthen the credibility of your information about high X going with high Y (and low X with low Y); and, since *you* caused X to be high in one set of groups and low in the other, it is at least plausible that X is a cause of Y. If instead of doing such a true experiment, you had just let things vary, measured X and Y, and correlated them, then X might have caused Y, or Y might have caused X, or both X and Y might have been caused by something else that you didn't pay attention to.

You can see that true experiments are potentially powerful techniques for *learning about causal relations among variables*. But, as in all aspects of research methodology, you buy this high power at a high price in two ways: (a) a reduction in the *scope* of your study, insofar as you hold variables constant, and insofar as you make your experimental variables (the X's) occur only at a couple of levels (high or low liking, or three-person versus six-person groups, for example) so that the results of that study will be thereby limited in generalizability; and (b) a reduction in realism of context, inasmuch as your activities (rather than "nature") have created the groups, designed the tasks, and elicited behavior that served your purposes, not the group members' purposes. It has been said that such an experiment lets you learn a lot about very little, whereas a correlational study may let you learn very little about a lot.

Forms of Validity

A study needs to have high validity in regard to four different types of validity questions (see Cook & Campbell, 1979). One, to which we have been attending in the preceding description of the "true experiment," is called *internal validity*. That has to do with the degree to which results let you infer about causal relations. A second form of validity has been called *statistical conclusion validity*. That refers to the confidence with which you can say that there is a *real difference* (in Y scores) between X cases and X' cases. Internal validity deals with a logical question, how to rule out alternative explanations (such as, that Y caused X or that both X and Y stemmed from unmeasured factor Z). But statistical conclusion validity is a statistical question, usually posed in some variation of the following form: How likely is it that the difference in average Y values, between the X batch of cases and the X' batch of cases, could have occurred by *chance*? If the probabilty of such a chance occurrence is less than 1 in 100 (written $p < .01$), or sometimes if it is less than 1 in 20 ($p < .05$), the researcher may conclude that results cannot be attributed only to chance. Usually, such results are said to be "significant" at the .01 or the .05 level.

When results are significant, the researcher may conclude that the hypothesis that only chance was operating *does not* account for the results; but he or she *may not* logically conclude that the hypothesis of interest ("X causes Y") *does* account for them. It is only if the researcher can eliminate most other plausible rival hypotheses (e.g., that Y causes X; that Y is caused by factor Z that also differed between groups, etc.), by the logic of his or her study design, that he or she can continue to entertain the X-causes-Y hypothesis as a plausible—but by no means certain—explanation for the results.

A study also needs to have clearly defined theoretical concepts and conceptual relations, and clearly specified mappings (or translations) of those concepts into empirical operations. This is called *construct validity*. Finally, the researcher needs to have some basis for estimating how the obtained results would hold up if the hypothesis were tested on other populations of actors, using other measures of the same variables, in other situations and on other occasions in this same situation. Such estimates of generalizability refer to what is called *external validity*.

It will probably be apparent that the devices used to increase internal validity and statistical conclusion validity—the techniques used to gain precision—will threaten the external validity of that particular set of data. But the relation is not a symmetrical one. One should *not* leap to the conclusion that the converse is true. Things that aid external validity (e.g., large and varied samples) may either hinder or help internal validity or have no effect on it. Moreover, it is certainly *not* the case that things that *decrease* internal validity (e.g., not using randomization, or not using experimental manipulation) will somehow increase external validity. If you don't know what you found out in your study (i.e., if your study is low in internal validity or in statistical conclusion validity or in construct validity) then you cannot really determine whether or not, or how broadly, you can generalize it (i.e., what external validity it has)—but it doesn't matter anyhow. If you do know what you found out (i.e., if your study has high internal, statistical and construct validity), then it is important to try to determine how robust and general (i.e., how externally valid) those findings are likely to be.

There is much more to be said about study design, about difference versus correlation studies, about forms of validity, and about ways of dealing with plausible hypotheses that are alternatives to the hypothesis being tested—far more than can be said here. (For further reading on these questions, see Campbell & Stanley, 1966; Cook & Campbell, 1979; Runkel & McGrath, 1972). But perhaps what has been said serves to make several important points:

1. Results depend on methods.
2. All methods have limitations, hence any one set of results is limited, flawed.
3. It is not possible to maximize all desirable features of method in any one study; trade-offs and dilemmas are involved.
4. Each study—each set of results—must be interpreted in relation to other sets of evidence bearing on the same questions.

Some of these same points were made in regard to strategic issues, and some will apply, again, in the discussion of issues at the operational level that now follows.

OPERATIONAL LEVEL ISSUES: MEASURING, MANIPULATING AND CONTROLLING VARIABLES

The operational level refers to the specific instruments and procedures used to select and allocate cases to conditions, and to manipulate, measure, and control variables. There are several different types of measures, and as with design and strategy choices, each type has advantages and limitations. There was a brief discussion earlier in this chapter on some of the advantages and disadvantages of self-report measures (questionnaires, interviews, rating scales, and the like). Self-reports are the single most popular data collection form throughout the social and behavioral sciences, and there are good reasons for that. Self-reports are versatile as to both content and populations. They can be adapted to most populations (except very young children). One can ask questions that deal with any concept one can think of. Self-reports are also low cost; they have low "dross rates" (i.e., little has to be discarded, as "chaff"), and they take relatively little time. But self-reports have one major Achilles' heel: They are *reactive.* That is, the people answering them *know* that those answers will be used for research (or related) purposes. Such knowledge may bias how they respond. Respondents may try to make a good impression, to give socially desirable answers, to help the investigator get the results being sought (or, alternatively, to hinder that quest). Such biases may enter either deliberately or unwittingly. All self-report evidence is thus potentially flawed, though self-reports are a very useful form of data.

Another form of data is direct observation. This has the advantage of dealing with overt behavior, and thus seeming to bypass some of the reactivity of self-reports. But if the persons under observation know that they are being observed for research purposes, the behavior may be just as biased as self-reports. If the observer is "hidden," those problems may be lessened; but use of hidden observers poses some ethical questions. In either case, any observer, or even a physical instrument that might be used to replace a human observer, is a source of other kinds of response biases that may distort results.

A third general form of data is what Webb and colleagues (Webb, Campbell, Schwartz, & Sechrest, 1966) have called *trace* measures. They are physical evidences of behavior, left behind as unintended residue or outcroppings of past behavior. For example, trash in a garbage can indicates many features of the life style of the residents; wear on floor tiles indicates number of users of that pathway; a group's product can be examined for evidence of quality, efficiency, accuracy, creativity, conformity. Trace measures, too, have both strengths and limitations. The main strength of trace measures is their nonreactivity. They were not emitted for research purposes, but rather resulted from the routine business of living. But trace measures are far less versatile as to content then either self-reports or observations. They are simply not available for many concepts that one might wish to study, and they are often only loosely coupled to the concepts for which they are taken as indicators. For example, having a lot of wine bottles in the trash may indicate a low income (hence, no scotch bottles!), a drinking problem, a family that does a lot of entertaining, or perhaps other things.

A fourth general class of measures is *archival records.* This refers to such things as census data, production records, court proceedings, diaries, material from newspapers, magazines, radio and television "morgues," and official administrative records and contracts. Some of these are generated under the expectation that they will be examined—for administrative or political purposes, though, not for research purposes. For example, speeches in a legislature are given with the expectation that they are to be a matter of public record. Such archives may suffer some reactivity problems similar to those of self-reports and behavior in the presence of a known observer. But other archival evidence—e.g., population birth rates, weather records, obituaries—would seem to be as free of reactive biases as are trace measures and data from hidden observers. Such nonreactive archival measures have strengths and weaknesses similar to those of trace measures. But they sometimes offer "best evidence," perhaps the only reasonable evidence, for problems dealing with *times long past,* with *extended periods of time,* or with *features of very large social units* (large organizations, states, nations).

All types of measures, thus, have strengths and weaknesses. And, like strategies and designs, the strengths of one type can compensate for and offset the weaknesses of another. But unlike strategies and designs, it is not necessary to use one of them now and some other one later. It is quite feasible, and indeed essential, to get *more than one measure, of more than one type, for each key variable* in any given study.

Operational techniques for manipulating variables are not nearly as well specified as are types of measures. There are several general classes of techniques for manipulating experimental variables in the study of groups:

1. *Direct Actions by the Investigator.* For example, you can put four persons in one group, three in another, to manipulate group size; or you can give one set of groups a simple puzzle and another set a complex puzzle to manipulate task difficulty.
2. *Induction by Instruction.* For example, you can tell participants that they have been put into groups on the basis of their probable compatibility, in the hope that this will induce the participants to be positively attracted to their teammates.
3. *Induction by False Feedback.* For example, you can use false feedback in reporting results of early trials to induce some groups to perceive that they have had task success and other groups to perceive that they have had task failure.
4. *Induction by Use of Confederates.* For example, you can have some experimental confederates pretend to be participating members of groups while carrying out pre-instructed behavior, in the hope of inducing other (naive) participants to perceive them as legitimate fellow group members carrying out spontaneous actions.

As with measures, designs and strategies, each class of techniques for manipulating experimental variables has strengths and weaknesses. Direct manipulation has the advantage of delivering the result you seek with high certainty. If you decide to compare a set of six-person juries with a set of twelve-person juries, you can execute that decision by assigning a given group to one or the other of these two size conditions and be confident later that it had precisely six and only six (or twelve) members. But the price for that certainty is often a certain degree of intrusiveness, and some variables cannot be managed in that way. The other three techniques are less direct and their consequences are less certain. Instructions or false feedback may not induce what you intended. The confederate may not do what you instructed. All three involve attempts to deceive participants and doing so involves some ethical issues. It also involves the substantial risk that your deception will not succeed—that participants will not believe what you want them to believe, will feel deceived, and will react negatively to that deception. So all of these must be regarded as potentially reactive, and perhaps loosely coupled to their intended effects.

Still, studies of groups have been run with considerable apparent success using manipulation techniques of all four types. As with other methodological levels, each has some potential value, each has some serious inherent limitations. Any body of evidence is to be interpreted *in the light of* the strengths and weaknesses of experimental manipulations involved in it, as well as in the light of the strengths and weaknesses of the measures, designs, strategic choices, and theoretical concepts that it encompasses. Evidence is *always* contingent on all of those methodological choices and constraints. It is only by accumulating evidence, over studies done so that they involve different—complementary—methodological strengths and weaknesses, that we can begin to consider that evidence as credible, *probably* true, empirically based knowledge.

This chapter has presented issues of scientific method in general, as it is applied in the social and behavioral sciences. The next chapter will deal much more concretely with some methodological choices in the study of groups. Specifically, it will address the question of how one selects and/or designs groups to be the object of such study.

CHAPTER FOUR
A TYPOLOGY
OF GROUPS

As in the well-known recipe for rabbit stew, if you are going to study groups the first step is to "catch yourself some . . . ." One approach is to find some existing groups and somehow get access to them for your research activities. That approach has some obvious and important strengths; but it also has a number of serious problems and limitations, some methodological and some practical. An opposite approach is to create some groups for the purpose of studying them. That, too, has some strengths but also some serious limitations. This chapter will discuss some of the strengths and weaknesses of both of these approaches to the basic problem of gaining access to groups for study.

In so doing, this chapter will also help fulfill two other purposes: (a) to raise and consider a number of important methodological issues that play a part in research on groups; and (b) to indicate a number of kinds of groups—natural, concocted and quasi-groups—that have been used in research intended to pertain to the study of groups.

NATURAL GROUPS

The term *natural groups* refers to *groups that exist independent of the researcher's activities and purposes.* Examples include families, work crews, friendship groups, mother-infant pairs, wrestling opponents, a chorus-line, an orchestra. They are to be distinguished from *concocted groups,* groups that are created for the purpose of being vehicles for research. (Later, I also want to distinguish between such concocted groups and quasi-groups, the latter also being created for research purposes, but being not-quite-groups because they have highly artificial and constrained patterns of activity.)

The first set are called natural groups rather than "real groups." Many of the concocted groups, once created, are also quite real, from the point of view of the members and from other points of view as well. Here, the emphasis is on the fact that natural groups have an existence that does not depend on the researcher and his or her purposes.

Natural groups are all around us. Indeed, it is the very ubiquitousness of natural groups that makes the study of groups a compelling area of research interest. Why, then, not just always find, select and study such natural groups?

For one thing, you always have to have *multiple instances* of the object of your study. This usually means multiple *cases* or many different groups. The set of groups to be studied *must differ in some respects* (in those features about which comparisons are to be made) *but be alike or comparable in all other respects.* So you need to find and get access to *a set* of groups that are all of the same kind.[1]

Second, for some study purposes you may want to alter, deliberately, the values of one or more of the variables (or attributes) you plan to study. Such experimental manipulations are useful, indeed crucial, for certain methodological issues, as discussed in chapter 3. But, often, existing groups simply won't let you do that. Moreover, it is often hard, in principle as well as in practice, to make such experimental manipulations for a set of extant groups. For example, how do you change the size of a set of existing families? How could you change the educational level of members for a set of existing work groups? Furthermore, if you did succeed in making such experimental variations of some important features of a set of natural groups, in doing so you have to some degree transformed those natural groups into a set of artificial ("unnatural") groups. You have undone the very essence of their "naturalness"; their form—if not their whole existence—is no longer independent of you and your research purposes.

Moreover, a true experiment, within which the experimental manipulation of key variables is crucial, also requires random assignment of cases to experimental conditions. Often, even if it were possible to modify some natural groups on a crucial variable, it would be difficult to get a chance to assign such groups to different conditions or treatments on a random basis. It is a contradiction in terms to assign members to natural groups on a random basis; if you did, those would clearly be concocted groups rather than natural groups.

With natural groups, then, you might decide not to manipulate any variables but simply to study the groups as you find them. If you do so, it is then difficult, and often impossible, to separate the effects of the variables you are interested in from the effects of many other factors in the situation. If you found that X goes with Y, not only would you not know whether X caused Y, you would not know whether X and Y are actually related or whether both of

---

[1]It is possible to study a single group, in a so-called "case study" or ideographic approach. When you do, you still need multiple instances—multiple observations, over time and among group members. You are also limited in your generalizations to events and sets of events pertaining to *that particular* group. See the discussion of field studies in chapter 3.

them are outcroppings of some other factors that were varying among the groups you studied but that were not measured as part of your study.

Moreover, some very important features of the groups in question may not be obvious in natural groups, because they are so much taken for granted in such groups. Or, such features may appear only in confounded form in natural groups. For example, if you were to study families, drawn from average United States families of the past few decades, it would be hard to separate out the effects on power relations among the adult members that stem (a) from gender, (b) from the sex-role behavior and attitudes of those members (and of the cultures underlying those groups), (c) from the economic positions of the members, and (d) from traits such as ascendance or dominance on which individual members may vary. Sets of factors that *can vary independently* are found all in a "clump," varying together, in many natural groups. So you cannot study any one of those factors by studying natural groups in their "undisturbed" state.

Furthermore, sets of natural groups differ from one another in a variety of ways, and it is not as easy as it seems to specify which are to be regarded as "natural." Families, of course, are one kind of natural group, and they may exemplify the idea of group to an extreme degree. For one thing, families continue, with more or less the same people in them, for a very long time. For another, families deal with a very broad band of activities. In fact, in some segments of a person's lifetime, families function as *embedding systems*; they affect literally all of the person's activities, all of his or her time. They function as what have been called "total institutions."

But that is not the case for all groups, not even for all natural groups. Some groups only operate in limited spheres of activity. Work groups, for example, have only a narrow band of types of activity. Such is also the case for sports teams, activity based groups such as bridge or chess clubs, special interest groups such as Parent-Teacher Associations, study clubs, charity fund drives, and the like. Or, at least, such groups are intended to function only for a narrow band of the person's life activities.

There are some other kinds of groups that are quite broad-band, but that play a part in the person's life only for a limited temporal period. For example, the living group at a summer camp, residents of a dormitory wing, the crew of a space ship, the prisoners in a cellblock, members of a tour group on an extended (but finite) tour, the crew of a nuclear submarine on an extended mission, a wintering-over party in the Arctic—all are such broad-band but time-limited groups. These groups, *while they last,* are in some respects like families: very broad-band and embedding systems, total institutions. But they last only for a definite period of time. Moreover, the members know in advance that the group will have such a temporally limited existence (although they may know only generally, not precisely, the time of group termination).

Obviously, there is another kind of natural group, one that has limits on *both* its activity scope and its temporal scope. These are groups set up to do a specific task or mission, with the expectation that they will disband when that mission is done. Many government commissions, industrial or military task forces, and academic ad hoc committees fit this pattern. Such groups are real. They have powerful effects, on their members and on others in their en-

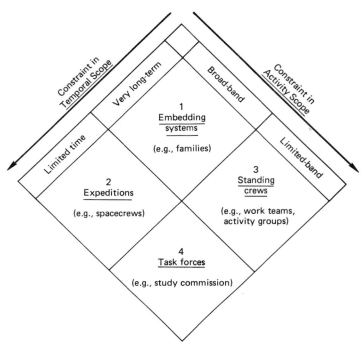

FIGURE 4-1   Types of Natural Groups

vironments. They are natural; they were deliberately created, usually by an organization of which the individuals involved are members, but for "natural" organizational purposes rather than for research purposes. (Yet they are, to some degree, "designed" groups, hence they overlap with the set of "concocted" groups to be considered later.)

So there are at least four types of natural groups, based on the temporal and activity scope that they subsume: *embedding systems* (e.g., families); *expeditions* (e.g., a space crew); *standing crews* (e.g., a sports team or a work crew); and *task forces* (e.g., a study commission). (There are, of course, perhaps hundreds of types of natural groups if we classify them on the basis of the content of the group, the source of the members, etc.) Those four types of groups are arranged in Figure 4-1, in a two-by-two "diamond" for which the axes are long versus short temporal scope and broad versus narrow-band activity scope. This natural group classification will be related to a classification of types of concocted groups in the next section of this chapter.

CONCOCTED GROUPS

There is a big difference between a one-task study commission and a person's family of origin. The task force lasts for perhaps a year, meets once or twice a month for an hour or two, and deals only with one task or topic (however large the scope of that topic might be). The family of origin lasts one's entire lifetime, meets continuously, and deals with virtually all of the tasks and topics of the business of living. Temporary but totally embedding expeditions, and continuing but limited-activity crews, are also quite different from families, from task forces, and from each other. Yet all four types of groups surely must be given the status of "natural" and regarded as important types of groups for study. Nevertheless, they differ from each other perhaps more than task forces differ from various forms of concocted groups that will be discussed next.

But task forces, and certain other forms of concocted groups, are much easier to study, in terms of various methodological problems discussed earlier in this section, than are families, expeditions and even work crews. It is possible, in principle, to design a set of task forces so that they vary from one another on some major factor but are otherwise comparable; to assign task forces on a random basis to different "levels" of that key factor; and perhaps even to assign individuals to task force membership on a random basis. It would also be possible, in principle, to get in on group activity from the group's birth, and even to have some prenatal data, so to speak, on members and surrounding conditions. So it might be possible to do a true experiment and untangle the effects of various factors using a set of task forces out of the same organization or comparable ones. Yet, the task forces are "natural," and they are carrying out tasks indigenous to that organization.

Suppose, however, that you wanted to study some features of the *task* of a set of such task forces. To do so, you might well want to alter, experimentally, some task features. Or, you might want to create, deliberately, sets of task forces to do hypothetical or simulated versions of the "natural" groups' indigenous tasks. For example, if you were studying basketball squads you might want to create a series of *practice games* or scrimmages. If you were studying infantry squads you might want to set up a series of practice battles or *training problems*. In a sense, those would still be "natural" groups. They would be the same kinds of people—indeed, the very same people—doing the same kinds of things, under many of the same kinds of conditions. But in another sense, those would no longer be "natural" groups, since the same kind of real and nonreversible consequences (lost games; dead and wounded soldiers) would not flow from the task activities, and *all participants would know that to be so in advance*. The simulated tasks would have real and important consequences—perhaps even pay and promotion consequences—but they would not have the *same* real consequences that would have followed the natural group's performance of its natural tasks.

To carry the matter one step further: Suppose you wanted to study, intensively, just some portion of the group's entire task. For example, suppose you wished to study just the running speed of the basketball squad members, or the communication skills of the infantry squad. To do so, you might want to set up some quite artificial tasks. Such tasks would not be "real" in the sense that they would not be basketball games or battles, or even simulations of those phenomena. But those tasks would still be "real" in the sense that the players would be exhibiting "real" behaviors as they performed those tasks—real sweat, real puffing, real efforts to win the coach's or commander's praises by getting fast times, errorless messages, or high ratings. Performance on these activities would be less natural than the performance of these groups doing simulations of their real or indigenous tasks. Yet the group would still have some "natural" features: it is still a naturally occurring social unit that does not exist just because of your research, even though some of its tasks are imposed for purposes of your study.

Instead of research on aspects of a natural group's tasks, suppose you wanted to study some special feature of its membership composition, or its group structure. Suppose, for example, that you wanted to test the effectiveness of task forces that did and did not have a formally appointed leader, or of task forces with same- or mixed-gender membership. To do so, you might want to *compose* two or more sets of task forces deliberately, in forms that let you make such comparisons. Instead of assigning members, hapazardly, or for organizational reasons, or on a random basis, you might want to assign two women and two men, or one faculty member each from natural sciences, social sciences, and humanities, or one congressman each from the South, the Midwest, the East and the West—or, alternatively, all members of only one of these "kinds."[2] Are these now "natural" groups?

The answer to that question is complex. These groups are composed of people from the same pool that would have been drawn upon, and they are doing the same tasks under many of the same conditions. On the other hand, they are not groups that came to be, in their present forms, independent of the research involved. However, their behavior on the tasks might be just as natural, and just as real, as the behavior of task forces set up without research intervention.

You also might want to study *both* task and composition factors. Or, you might want to study a simulation using groups with essentially ad hoc membership. Suppose, for example, that you wished to study intensively the operation of groups with certain important tasks, such as juries, but that those groups were very hard to get access to for study (with juries, it is in fact illegal to do so) and that it was impossible to get a lot of them working on the same task (e.g., multiple juries working on the same trial). You might want to set up a series of groups, getting reasonably appropriate people from a convenient source, to study how aspects of the task (e.g., order of presentation of evidence) might affect decisions. These are not real groups—indeed, they have come to be called "mock juries." But their decision processes may be quite analogous to those of real juries.

Much research on groups has been done with such concocted groups, in which the naturalness was modified either in regard to the task, or in regard to the group membership and composition, or in regard to both. Figure 4-2 displays a classification of six types of such concocted groups, showing three levels of naturalness of the task (endogenous tasks; simulation tasks; and artificial tasks) and two levels of naturalness of group composition (extant groups, and composed groups). The relation between these six types of concocted groups and the four categories of "natural" groups is shown by juxtaposition in that figure.

The types of groups shown in Figure 4-2 are progressively more concocted, less natural, as the various constraints are applied. Certainly real groups (i.e., naturally occurring social units) doing artificial tasks are less

---

[2] This does not preclude use of the randomization procedure that is necessary to a true experiment. You could determine *which* female, or male, or Southern congressman, or social science faculty member was to be assigned to *any particular* group of that composition, by selecting at random from a pool of such persons—females, males, Southern congressmen, etc..

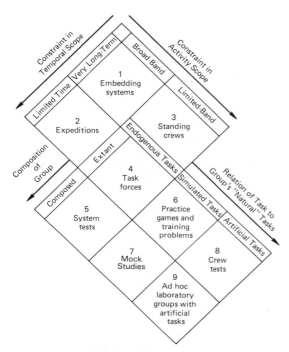

FIGURE 4-2   Types of Concocted Groups in Relation to Natural Groups

"natural" than those same groups doing tasks endogenous to them, or even do-ing simulations of those real tasks. Similarly, naturally occurring tasks being done by composed groups represent less natural conditions than those same tasks being done by extant groups. But in a similar way, one could say that short-lived narrow-band task forces, though they are "natural" or "real" groups, are somehow groups of lesser domain than are continuing crews, tem-porary but encompassing expeditions or long-term embedding systems such as families.

Ad hoc laboratory groups are the least "natural" of the types discussed so far, because they have: (a) limited activity scope; (b) limited temporal scope; (c) ad hoc composition; *and* (d) artificial tasks. Yet, they are still "real" groups, in the sense that members interact face to face, freely, through all interaction channels. The next part of this chapter examines some arrangements for study-ing social entities that use even further constraints.

QUASI-GROUPS USED
FOR RESEARCH

Let me assert the position that ad hoc laboratory groups are the *least natural* of the set of groups discussed so far; but that they, and all the other types of *natural and concocted groups* so far considered, are nevertheless *real groups.*

They are "real" in the sense that the individuals in them (however assigned) are really working together on tasks (whether endogenous, simulated or artificial) under face to face, full channel communication conditions. But the desire for precise experimental control has sometimes led group researchers to impose even further constraints on their study conditions, ending up studying what I will call *quasi-groups*. These units of study are somewhat less than "real" groups as defined above, in either or both of two ways: (1.) there can be restrictions on the task performance process, by imposing highly structured performance steps or sequences and/or by greatly restricting the form of response that groups are permitted to exhibit; (2.) there can be restrictions in the interaction pattern in the group, either by urging/training/guiding groups to use only certain communication practices (restricted communication process), or by the more drastic curtailment of communication modalities or networks (restricted communication channels). In the most extreme case, there is both a restricted set of communication channels and a highly structured task process and response, yielding a highly *stylized* form of group behavior. For example, a given group member might be allowed to communicate only with one other member, only once during each time-period or trial, and only in the form of a written note (perhaps passed on by the experimenter), with the note form only permitting one checkmark indicating which one of several alternatives that member prefers. While situations with constraints of that kind and severity have been used very often in research intended to bear on the study of groups, and while a large part of the evidence in some areas of study comes from such research (e.g., most of what we know about the formation of coalitions and responses to pay-off dilemmas), it seems to me quite reasonable to regard the social units in these highly constrained situations to be something less than "groups" in the sense in which the word groups has been used in this book and in the research literature. It is not a question of whether they are "real," but of whether they are "really groups."

At the same time, information from such studies certainly *bears on* a number of research questions about groups, and in some cases it represents the strongest body of information available. So by no means should it be disregarded by those interested in the study of groups. I have labeled the social units in these constrained situations as *quasi-groups,* to try to reflect their ambiguous position in the study of groups.

Figure 4-3 shows a classification of these quasi-groups, integrated with the prior classification of natural and concocted groups into *a matrix of forms of social units used in group research.* Figure 4-4 lists all of those forms and gives some examples of them. The examples are referred to by abbreviated names and/or acronyms. Beginning in chapter 6, there are 50 boxes, labeled *Examples of Research Technology (EXRT) Boxes.* Each provides a condensed description of one specific study paradigm used in research on groups. Each is a specific item of research technology, a technique for manipulating a particular experimental variable, a technique for observation of interaction, and so forth. These descriptions concentrate on the empirical (rather than the theoretical) side of research; and within that, they concentrate on procedures and techniques for operationalizing variables (rather than on data analysis techniques). They are presented under three main headings: *Main Study Procedures,* under

| Composed Groups | | | Natural (Extant) Groups | | | |
| Restricted Interaction | | Unrestricted Interaction | | | | |
Restricted Channels	Restricted Process	Face to Face Ad Hoc	Limited Term	Very Long-Term		
		(Natural Groups)	2. Expeditions (e.g., space crews)	1. Embedding systems (e.g., families)	Broad-Band of Activities	"Natural" Tasks Endogenous to Group
		5. System tests (not using an existing crew)	4. Task forces (e.g., study commissions)	3. Standing crews (e.g., sports teams; work crews)	Limited-Band of Activities	
(Quasi Groups)	(Concocted Groups)	7. Mock studies (e.g., mock juries; "artificial families")	6. Crew practice/training studies		Simulations	Imposed Tasks / Artificial Tasks
11. Structured communication channels studies (e.g., restricted modality studies)	10. Restricted communication process studies (e.g., communication strategy training studies; brainstorming)	9. Ad hoc laboratory groups	8. Crew tests (not on system tasks)		Free Performance Form	
14. Highly stylized constrained task & communication (e.g., PDG; coalitions; communication Nets; Delphi)	13. Structed task & restricted communication process studies (e.g., NGT)	12. Structed task studies (e.g., SJT; MAUA; concept attainment task)			Restricted Response Form	

FIGURE 4-3   A Matrix of Forms of Social Units Used in Group Research

which the primary method is described; *Main Dependent Variables of Interest,* under which is listed the main outcome or consequences that the technique has been, or might be, used to study; and *Main Variations,* under which are listed some of the more prominent independent variables that have been, or could have been, used with the technique. The EXRT boxes do not give summaries of results of studies using the technique. *References* are noted for each one, however, and some of those references are to studies that describe the technique and its use, and give results of that use. Other references are to studies that place the particular technique in a broader perspective. Most of the references cited for any technique are noted or discussed elsewhere in the text. They are not intended to be exhaustive listings of studies using or discussing these techniques.

Each of these boxes describes one "study paradigm" or item of group

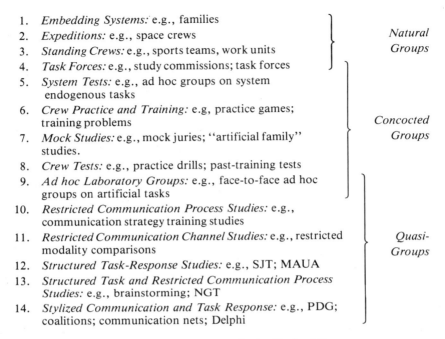

1. *Embedding Systems:* e.g., families
2. *Expeditions:* e.g., space crews
3. *Standing Crews:* e.g., sports teams, work units
4. *Task Forces:* e.g., study commissions; task forces

    Natural Groups

5. *System Tests:* e.g., ad hoc groups on system endogenous tasks
6. *Crew Practice and Training:* e.g, practice games; training problems
7. *Mock Studies:* e.g., mock juries; "artificial family" studies.
8. *Crew Tests:* e.g., practice drills; past-training tests
9. *Ad hoc Laboratory Groups:* e.g., face-to-face ad hoc groups on artificial tasks

    Concocted Groups

10. *Restricted Communication Process Studies:* e.g., communication strategy training studies
11. *Restricted Communication Channel Studies:* e.g., restricted modality comparisons
12. *Structured Task-Response Studies:* e.g., SJT; MAUA
13. *Structured Task and Restricted Communication Process Studies:* e.g., brainstorming; NGT
14. *Stylized Communication and Task Response:* e.g., PDG; coalitions; communication nets; Delphi

    Quasi-Groups

Figure 4-4   A List of Forms of Social Units Used in the Study of Groups

research technology that has had frequent use in the study of groups and that will be referred to in relation to specific topics. At this level, a *paradigm* refers to a *model or pattern of instruments, techniques and procedures* used for a given purpose, in this case, to study some given topic or problem in the group research area. Paradigms can be regarded as a set of methodological inventions, and collectively they represent the core of a *technology for group research.* Without such a technology, the vast amount of research done on groups would not have been possible. A technology represents possibilities or opportunities for study. But you should keep in mind the limitations mentioned in the preceding chapter, especially the point that the methodology of any given research area in part determines, limits, and distorts the body of evidence in that area. So the technology for group research reflected in this chapter and in the boxes throughout the book represents both the set of opportunities and the set of limitations for research on groups.

PART TWO
GROUPS AS TASK PERFORMANCE SYSTEMS

The next seven chapters deal with groups as task performance systems. One reason why there was so much early interest in the study of groups was that groups were regarded as potentially very effective vehicles to carry out a wide range of tasks. Furthermore, since much of the work of the world seems to be done by people working in group contexts, it seemed important to find out whether groups were task effective (compared to individuals); or on what kinds of tasks groups were most and least effective; and what aspects of the task performance process played a part in that group effectiveness.

The chapters of Part II deal with research done to answer those questions about group task performance. Chapter 5 traces past attempts to classify different types of tasks and to build models of group productivity. It also presents a new and comprehensive task typology that classifies all group tasks into eight related types, each with some subtypes. That classification schema is then used to structure the rest of Part II. Each of the next four chapters treats group task performance on one of the relatively thoroughly studied task types. Chapters 10 and 11 each discuss group task performance on two of the other four task types which, although relatively under-studied in group research, are tasks done by many everyday groups.

CHAPTER FIVE
A TYPOLOGY OF TASKS

If we want to learn about groups as vehicles for performing tasks, we must either (a) assume that all tasks are alike, in regard to how groups of various kinds can and do perform them; or (b) take into account differences in group performance as they arise from differences in tasks. Virtually all students of groups would reject the notion that group task performance can be studied generically, without regard to the task, just as they would reject the notion that an individual's task performance is not affected by type and characteristics of the task being performed. Yet, there has really been very little study devoted to the second alternative, namely to the analysis of task differences, in a systematic way, that takes into account how those differences affect group task performance.

All studies of group task performance, of course, use some task. Many use two or three; very few use more than that. But the choice of task is often a matter of convenience and fairly arbitrary. Even when a study uses two or three tasks, those tasks may be selected haphazardly; or, at best, they may be selected ad hoc to represent simplified classifications (such as motor versus intellectual, or easy versus difficult). If tasks really make a difference—and everyone agrees that they do—then it seems worthwhile to devote some of our efforts to analyzing and classifying tasks in ways that relate meaningfully to how groups perform them.

There have been about a half dozen notable and substantial efforts in this regard. The first part of this chapter will review those efforts, and take from them their main ideas. Then in the second part of the chapter, I will try to integrate those formulations into one coherent task classification system that seems to be very useful in understanding differences in and relations among tasks performed by groups. The task framework, called a Task Circumplex, serves as the main schema for organizing a review of empirical evidence about group task performance in the several chapters to follow.

PAST EFFORTS TO CLASSIFY TASKS AND MODEL GROUP PRODUCTIVITY

Early Task Distinctions

People studying groups have always made distinctions among different kinds of tasks. But those distinctions have often been matters of convenience, sometimes post hoc convenience to account for differences in outcome. For example, from the late 1800s into the first part of the twentieth century, researchers found major contradictions in outcomes of studies of so-called social facilitation effects. Social facilitation refers to how the presence of other people affects individual task performance. (There is a more extensive discussion of this in Chapter 17.) Some studies found that the presence of others improved task performance; others found that the presence of others led to poorer task performance. There were efforts to account for these differences in terms of different kinds of tasks. One such distinction was between intellectual tasks (for which presence of others was expected to hinder performance) and motor tasks (for which presence of others was expected to help performance). Another distinction was between simple and complex tasks. Still another task distinction, which had been shown in experimental psychology to yield systematic differences in reaction times for individuals, was between tasks with a "stimulus set" and tasks with a "response set." These ad hoc task categories did not work very well as bases for clarifying the social facilitation evidence, for several reasons. They did not clearly separate the "gain" and "loss" outcomes of prior social facilitation experiments. Moreover, even if they had, there was really no theoretical basis for expecting one of those to help, the other to hinder, so there would still have been a need for further concepts to explain the difference. But most of all, the distinctions used were oversimplified dichotomies, that could not be applied clearly to most tasks used or potentially used in group research.

Another factor hindering the development of an effective task classification is that there is some overlap and intermixing between task distinctions and group distinctions. For example, the dichotomy of formal versus informal groups implies something about the tasks those groups do, as well as about the way members of those groups relate to one another. Similarly, a dichotomy of task groups versus social groups implies a difference in what these groups do. It is not always possible to keep the two classifications—of groups and of tasks—distinct.

In one early effort, Carter and his colleagues (eg., Carter, Haythorn, & Howell, 1950) went beyond a dichotomy. They classified tasks into six types: clerical, discussion, intellectual construction, mechanical assembly, motor coordination and reasoning. These types distinguish tasks on the basis of the kinds of activities that groups (or individuals in them) must carry out in order to complete the task. In the terms to be used later, the differences have to do with the *performance processes* involved in the tasks, and with the *task as a set of behavior requirements* on the members. This set of categories does not deal with the nature of the task products, nor does it deal with the relations between members (for example, the extent to which members must work in coordination). Carter and his colleagues (e.g., Carter, Haythorn, Shriver, & Lanzetta, 1950) used these six kinds of tasks to study the degree to which leadership behavior is affected by task differences or is general across task types. (They found some of each, by the way. There was some generality of effective leadership behavior, but some specificity by task types as well. This kind of question is treated in the discussion of leadership in chapter 18.)

McGrath and Altman (1966), reviewing small group research done before the mid-1960s, argued strongly for the need for systematic conceptual analysis of tasks and their relations to group members. They suggested that tasks could be classified on any of several different bases: classification in terms of the physical/environmental properties or dimensions of tasks qua tasks (e.g., mechanical assembly; arithmetic problem); classification in terms of behaviors required by the task; classification on the basis of the behaviors usually elicited by the task (e.g., creativity tasks, or discussion tasks); classification in terms of the relations among the behaviors of individual group members—interdependencies or lack thereof (e.g., cooperation requirements); classifications in terms of the goal, or product, or criterion of the task (e.g., seeking speed, minimizing errors). All of these bases and others have been used in systems classifying group tasks.

Shaw's Classifications of Group Tasks

Although concerns about task differences have been with us always, the first really programmatic effort to lay out the different characteristics of group tasks in a systematic way did not begin until the 1960s and was carried out by Marvin Shaw (Shaw, 1973). Shaw surveyed the tasks that had been used in past published studies of small groups; he also surveyed a large number of then-active small group researchers. He extracted *six* properties, or characteristics, or dimensions along which group tasks varied—dimensions that he and other researchers thought might have appreciable effects on group task performance. Shaw's six dimensions are: intellective versus manipulative requirements; task difficulty; intrinsic interest; population familiarity; solution multiplicity versus specificity; cooperation requirements.

Shaw's six dimensions make use of several of the bases of classification suggested by McGrath and Altman (1966). The first of these dimensions (intellective versus manipulative requirements) has to do with *properties of the task qua task*. The next three have to do with *relations between the task and the group that works on it*. Difficulty, intrinsic interest and population familiarity all can vary depending on what group is to work on the group task. The fifth has to do with the *ways the outcome of the task is to be "scored,"* so to speak.

Solution multiplicity or specificity implies that *someone* knows a "correct" answer, or knows which of many kinds of answers would be good ones. The last dimension (cooperation requirements) refers to *what group members must do in relation to one another.* Many of these same distinctions are important in later, more extensive classifications.

Hackman's Task Types and Product Dimensions

Hackman took a different approach to classifying task differences and relating them to group performance (Hackman, 1968, 1976; Hackman, Jones, & McGrath, 1967; Hackman & Morris, 1975, 1978). First of all, he restricted his domain of concern to intellectual tasks, ones that yield written products. Second, he decided to concentrate on developing a classification of the *products* that result from performance of those tasks (by groups or by individuals). Third, he collected and developed a large set of tasks, had groups generate products by doing those tasks, and had a number of judges make extensive ratings of those products. He summarized those results by applying factor analysis. (Factor analysis is a statistical technique that summarizes the interrelationships among a number of properties over a number of cases. Here, the properties are the ratings and the cases are the products.)

Results suggested three types of tasks and a half dozen dimensions on which products of those tasks could be assessed. The first task type Hackman called *production.* It referred to tasks asking the group to *generate ideas* on something. It is similar to what others have called creativity tasks and is one case of what I will later call tasks requiring the Generate process. The second task type he called *discussion.* He called the third task type *problem-solving.* It referred to tasks asking the group to describe how to *carry out some plan of action.* It is similar to what I will later call planning tasks. (Hackman's problem-solving category needs to be distinguished from what many others have called problem-solving, namely, tasks that call for calculations or logical reasoning.) These three task types are based on the behavior requirements of the task, or what performance processes are needed to carry out the task.

Hackman's six product dimensions were: action orientation; length; originality; optimism; quality of presentation; and issue involvement. Note that these six product dimensions can be judged by examining the written product resulting from the task, without reference to the specific task giving rise to it or the type of that task, and without reference to who did the task (including whether it was a single individual or a group). He noted two other dimensions, creativity and adequacy, that reflect interaction between the product, as such, and the specific task giving rise to it.

Steiner's Task Types and Models of Group Productivity

The idea of task classifications has long been associated with study of questions regarding group size and group productivity. Often, these studies centered around the old question of how groups perform relative to individuals, and the related question of how groups combine skills, talents, and activities of their members into a coordinated performance of a group task. There is a relatively long history of study using formal mathematical models of group productivity. (See Davis & Restle, 1963; Lorge, Fox, Davitz, & Brenner, 1958; Lorge & Solomon, 1955; Restle & Davis 1962; Taylor & Faust, 1952; Thomas & Fink, 1961, 1963.) Much of the early work dealt with tasks of a so-called Eureka type. Eureka problems are the kind of task for which there is a correct answer so intuitively compelling that, once someone offers it in a group, the group immediately recognizes it as the correct answer.

For such tasks, one model of how groups might combine the talents of their members suggests that the probability that that group will solve the problem is equal to the probability that that group will contain at least one member who (had he or she been working alone) would have gotten the right answer. If one knows the proportion of members of some population of individuals (e.g., the sophomore class) who are "solvers" for that problem, then by fairly direct arithmetic (an expansion of the binomial equation) one can compute the probability that a group of any given size, drawn at random from that population, will get the right answer. It is then possible to compare such predictions with the actual problem-solving success for groups of various sizes. This is a "truth, if present, wins" model. A set of theoretical predictions based on such a model, when compared to performance of actual groups, systematically *overpredicts* how well groups actually do.

We could develop a contrasting model that assumes that the group will somehow "average" the inputs of all group members, whether right or wrong, and that the group's answer will be a right answer only on a probabilistic basis. Such an "averaging" model greatly *underpredicts* actual group performance. Truth lies somewhere in between these two models—"truth wins," and averaging.

Steiner and Rajaratnum (1961) formalized some of the considerations involved in the "truth wins" type of task and some others. Later, Steiner (1966, 1972) offered what he termed a partial classification of tasks that further elaborated these notions. He distinguished between tasks that are divisible and those that are unitary. Unitary tasks are ones that have a single outcome or product, into which the individual contributions of group members must somehow be combined. For example, a jury must reach a single verdict out of the disparate views of its members. As another example, a group may need to obtain a single, exact answer to a specific problem. Steiner divides such unitary tasks into types on the basis of how member contributions are combined to yield that single product. One such type is what Steiner calls a *disjunctive* task. The Eureka type problems described earlier exemplify this. In a disjunctive task, if one member of the group "does" the task, it is done for the group. So, if any one member can (and does) solve the problem, the group solves it; if any one member can fix the electric switch, the group can fix it. A second type of task is what Steiner calls a *conjunctive* task. It is the obverse of the disjunctive task; it is the kind of task implied by the saying that a chain is only as strong as its weakest link. It is the kind of task for which *all* group members must succeed for the group to be successful. For example, for a patrol to slip unnoticed through enemy lines requires that *every* member remain unseen and unheard.

The group fails that task if any one member is noticed. Obviously, whereas performance of disjunctive tasks depends on the talent and knowledge of the group's best member, performance of conjunctive tasks depends on the talent and knowledge of the group's poorest member. *Additive* tasks are those for which the contributions of group members are combined by summation to yield the meaningful outcome. Obviously, performance of additive tasks depends on the ability of the group's "average" member.

Notice that Steiner's unitary task types depend on the way in which members' contributions are combined into a final product—the way in which group performance is "scored," so to speak. They don't necessarily translate directly to relations among the behaviors of members during their task performances; nor do they depend on physical/environmental properties of the task; nor do they relate to the performance processes called for by the task (for example, mechanical versus intellectual). What type of task the group is doing in Steiner's schema depends on what aspects of its output one considers. For example, for a football game the criterion "number of points scored" might be considered an additive task; the criterion "number of penalties" is a conjunctive task; the criterion "number of touchdowns scored" might in part be a disjunctive task; while a complex criterion like "won or lost" is certainly a mix of many such "tasks." So, if the task classification is to be based on relations among member contributions, then a group is often to be regarded as doing a whole "cluster" of tasks at the same time.

Steiner's divisible tasks take into account that, for many tasks, some members of the group do one set of things while others do other things; and that task performance is related to the coordination of their efforts, rather than simply to the ability of the best member, worst member or average member. In fact, most "natural" tasks, such as the football game discussed above, are highly complex divisible tasks, requiring not so much a summing of member outputs as a complicated coordination of their efforts.

Nevertheless, Steiner's task classification is useful because it can be directly tied to productivity of groups for at least a number of tasks that have been used in studies of groups; and it can be expressed in strong mathematical form (as an expansion of the multinomial). Shiflett (1979) has shown it to be a special case of a more general mathematical model. Predictions from such models can be used to compare actual group performance for tasks of different types, and, of course, for groups of different sizes and types.

Steiner uses these models to reconsider much of the group task performance research that dealt with group productivity models. He notes that groups seldom perform up to the level of their best member. Often, the quality or quantity of their performance is about what the second best member's ability would predict. Steiner considers the combined abilities of individual members—combined according to whatever rule is suitable for that type of task, disjunctive, conjuctive or additive—as representing the group's *potential productivity*. *Actual* group productivity, he argues, falls below potential productivity because of "process losses," losses incurred in the process of performing the task. He identifies two main types of process losses: motivation losses (or, potentially, gains) and coordination losses. He goes on to show that the different degrees to which the actual productivity of groups of different sizes falls below their potential productivity (based on a combination of members' abilities) can be accounted for in terms of such motivation and coordination losses.

As we go from one individual working alone to a two-person group, a three-person group, and so forth, we are likely initially to find some increase in member motivation, reflected in feelings about and in effort on the task. Many people find working in very small groups more rewarding and more motivating than working alone. But as size of the group increases—five, six, seven. . . twenty . . . and larger—there apparently is a drop of considerable degree in the motivation (effort, morale, etc.) of individual group members. In additive and conjuctive tasks, of course, a reduction in the average member's motivation may well produce a serious reduction in group task effectiveness. The loss might be less on disjunctive tasks.

Thus, as groups get larger, there will be a larger and larger gap between potential productivity and actual productivity, even on additive tasks for which more members ought to be an advantage.

Laughlin's Group Task Classification

In reviewing the small group research of recent years (Davis, Laughlin, & Komorita, 1976), and in discussing results of some of it (Laughlin, 1980), Laughlin and his colleagues have offered a classification of group tasks that deals with both the relations among the group members and the kind of performance processes involved in executing the task. They distinguish tasks being done by cooperating groups from those being done by competitive and/or mixed-motive groups. Within the former, they make a distinction between two types of problems. For one type, there is—or is considered to be—a demonstrable right answer. The group's task is to discover that answer, so to speak. They call these *intellective tasks*. The other type consists of problems for which there is not a demonstrably correct answer. Rather, the group's task involves deciding what the right answer will be. These tasks ask for a group preference among possible answers, but not an existentially correct answer. The distinction is one between right answer as in "true" and right answer as in "moral" or "valued" or "proper" or "preferred." For the latter, the group's task is not so much to discover the existentially right answer, but to reach consensus. They call such tasks *decision tasks*. (There are some additional distinctions that are worth making in regard to demonstrability of right answer, and the intuitive compellingness of such an answer once demonstrated. These will be raised later in this chapter).

On the other side, Laughlin and colleagues offer a classification of interpersonal conflict or mixed-motive tasks that mixes two bases of classification. They distinguish the following types: (a) two-person, two-choice tasks with the prisoner's dilemma game (see chapter 9) as the prototypical case, and with an N-person two-choice game as a special case; (b) *bargaining and negotiation tasks,* with the two distinguished from each other in terms of whether conflict and its resolution is unidimensional or multidimensional; and (c) *coalition for-*

mation and resultant reward allocation. These distinctions reflect both relations between group members, who are the contending parties, and the nature
of the conflict between them.

Summary of Task
Classification Attempts

Many of these efforts, from Carter's six types of tasks to the
Davis/Laughlin/Komorita types of cooperative and competitive group tasks,
offer useful ideas on how differences in tasks may lead to differences in group
task performance. They differ but overlap in terms of their bases of classification. Some classify on the basis of performance processes; some on the basis of
task interdependencies of members; some on product differences and product
scoring or criterion differences. The Carter system, part of the Shaw classification, and one level of the Laughlin classification, deal with what kind of thing
the group members do as they are doing the task in question. Do they work with
numbers, or words, or objects? Do they calculate or compose or carry out
clerical operations? Do they solve problems with right answers or choose solutions to problems for which the right answer is "in the eye of the beholder"? Do
they cooperate toward the same goal, or try to compete with one another for
limited resources? The Steiner system, and some of Shaw's dimensions, deal
with how the results of members' efforts are combined, hence how task outcome is related to member abilities (of best, or worst, or average member). The
Hackman task types deal with the kind of performance process that is reflected
in the resultant product, and that in turn was reflected in the group's task instructions: Did they try to generate ideas? Did they discuss and try to decide
about issues? Did they problem-solve—that is, did they lay out a plan to implement action? The Hackman product dimensions reflect criterion qualities of
the group task performance outcomes. In a way, they assess how well the group
did the kind of task it was given to do.

This array of distinctions is a long way from the early "intellectual versus
motor," "difficult versus easy" and "simple versus complex" task dichotomies. Yet, no one of these systems alone provides a full classification. The next
section is an attempt to combine these into one integrated scheme.

A CIRCUMPLEX MODEL
OF GROUP TASK TYPES

The past work of Shaw, Carter, Hackman, Steiner, Shiflett, Taylor, Lorge,
Davis, Laughlin, and their colleagues, has provided important bases for a task
classification. I want to extract main ideas from several of these, elaborate on
some of those ideas, and fit them together into a conceptually related set of distinctions about tasks. Ideally, the categories of such a classification schema
should be (a) mutually exclusive (that is, a task fits in one and only one
category); (b) collectively exhaustive (that is, all tasks fit in some category); and
(c) logically related to one another. They also should be (d) useful, in that they

should point up differences between and relations among the items (tasks) that would not otherwise have been noticed. The framework offered here should be judged against those standards—especially the last one, usefulness. That framework is diagrammed in Figure 5-1, and listed in Table 5-1.

Begin by considering Hackman's three types of task: production (actually, *generating ideas* or images); discussion (dealing with issues); and problem-solving (actually, *generating plans for action*). These can be regarded as labels for the particular performance processes that are engaged by the task. In other words, they indicate what the group (or individual) is to *do*. I would like to propose that there are four general processes: to Generate (alternatives); to Choose (alternatives); to Negotiate; and to Execute.

FIGURE 5-1   The Group Task Circumplex

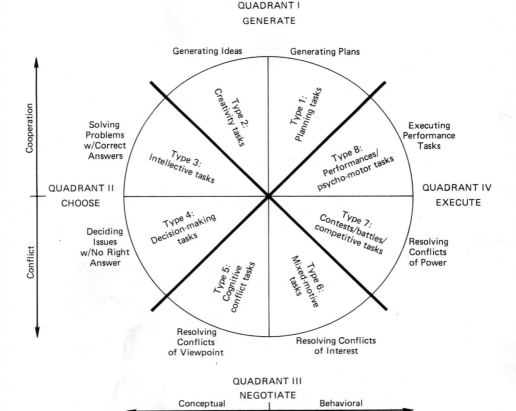

TABLE 5-1   Quadrants, Task Types, and Key Concepts of the Task Circumplex

QUADRANT I: GENERATE

> Type 1. *Planning Tasks:* Generating plans. E.g.: Hackman's "problem-solving" task type. Key notion: Action-oriented Plan.
>
> Type 2. *Creativity Tasks:* Generating ideas. E.g.: Hackman's "production" tasks; "brainstorming" tasks. Key notion: Creativity.

QUADRANT II: CHOOSE

> Type 3. *Intellective Tasks:* Solving problems with a correct answer. E.g.: Laughlin's intellective tasks, with correct and compelling answers; logic problems and other problem-solving tasks with correct but not compelling answers; tasks for which expert consensus defines answers. Key notion: Correct answer.
>
> Type 4. *Decision-Making Tasks:* Dealing with tasks for which the preferred or agreed upon answer is the correct one. E.g.: tasks used in risky shift, choice shift, and polarization studies; juries. Key notion: Preferred answer.

QUADRANT III: NEGOTIATE

> Type 5. *Cognitive Conflict Tasks:* Resolving conflicts of viewpoint (not of interests). E.g.: cognitive conflict tasks used in social judgment theory work; some jury tasks. Key notion: Resolving policy conflicts.
>
> Type 6. *Mixed-Motive Tasks:* Resolving conflicts of motive-interest. E.g.: negotiations and bargaining tasks; mixed-motive dilemma tasks; coalition formation/reward allocation tasks. Key notion: Resolving pay-off conflicts.

QUADRANT IV: EXECUTE

> Type 7. *Contests/Battles:* Resolving conflicts of power; competing for victory. E.g.: wars, all winner-take-all conflicts, competitive sports. Key notion: Winning.
>
> Type 8. *Performances:* Psychomotor tasks performed against objective or absolute standards of excellence, e.g., many physical tasks; some sports events. Key notion: Excelling.

Consider Laughlin's distinction between intellective tasks, for which there is a demonstrably correct answer, with the group's task being to find and choose that correct answer, and discussion tasks, for which the right answer *is* the group's consensus, and the group's task is to attain consensus. These represent two different aspects of the Choose process. Davis, Laughlin, & Komorita (1976) also distinguish between groups engaged in cooperative interaction and those engaged in competitive or mixed-motive interaction. When the group's task is to resolve conflicts, the process involved is not so much to Choose as it is to Negotiate. Some of these conflicts among group members are conflicts of viewpoint. Brehmer (1976) calls them cognitive conflicts. Some of the conflicts among members are conflicts of interests or motive; these are the kind Davis, Laughlin and Komorita had in mind in their competitive interaction category.

While Hackman's production and his problem-solving categories both refer to the Generate process as used here—generate creative ideas, on the one hand, and generate plans for action on the other—his work suggests another process: an implementation or action-oriented process. Hackman's work, however, was limited to tasks of a paper and pencil variety that could and did yield written products (words, numbers and perhaps pictorial displays). But much of the work of the world involves *performance of physical tasks* that require manipulations, motor behaviors and complex psychomotor activities. So an Execute (or Implement, or Perform) process is certainly needed in any task classification that aspires to completeness. Within this Execute process, at least two subsets of tasks are involved: (a) tasks for which the focal group is engaged in competition (combat) with an opposing (or enemy) group, with results of that contest (win/lose) determining the pay-offs; and (b) tasks for which the focal group is not in contest with an opponent, but rather is striving in relation to "nature," and for which pay-offs are determined by the group's performance in relation to some objective or external or absolute performance standards.

When all these distinctions are taken together, the results can be presented in a circular array that, in some usages, is called a circumplex. This Task Circumplex, presented in Figure 5–1, contains a number of distinctions and relations between types of tasks. First of all, the four quadrants are the four performance processes already discussed (a variation of the Hackman trio, plus Negotiation). Each of the processes is divided into two subtypes, using some of the distinctions noted here. Quadrant I, Generate, is divided into Generating Plans and Generating Ideas. The former is similar to Hackman's problem-solving type; it is related to the adjacent performance category in having an emphasis on action-orientation. The latter, Generating Ideas, is similar to Hackman's production type. It is the locus for "creativity" tasks; it is related to the adjacent intellective problem category in having an emphasis on cognitive matters.

Quadrant II, Choose, is also divided into two types: (3) Intellective tasks and (4) Decision-Making tasks. The terms and the distinctions are borrowed from Laughlin (1980). The former refers to tasks for which there is a demonstrable right answer, and the group task is to invent/select/compute that correct answer. The latter refers to tasks for which there is not a demonstrably correct answer, and for which the group's task is to select, by some consensus, a *preferred* alternative. For intellective tasks, at least three subsets can be identified, based on differing criteria of correctness. The first subset includes those tasks for which the demonstrably correct answer is also intuitively compelling once it is put forth (i.e., the Eureka tasks). Probably, such intuitively compelling right answers are based on very widely held cultural norms and beliefs. A second subset of intellective tasks includes those for which there is a demonstrably correct answer—in terms of the "facts," logic and criteria of some more or less technical area—but it is relatively difficult to demonstrate that logic in a way that is intuitively compelling to members of the task performing group. The third subset of intellective tasks includes those for which the "correct" answer is based on a *consensus of experts.* Such tasks have been used, for example, in studies developing models of the "accuracy" of judgments of freely interacting groups as compared, for example, to individuals, or to statisticized groups, or to groups whose interaction has been experimentally constrained. (See, for example, Eils & John, 1980; Einhorn, Hogarth, & Klempfer, 1977; Rohrbaugh, 1979.) These three subtasks represent a progression from correctness defined solely in cognitive idea terms toward correctness defined in consensus terms.

A similar but less clearly distinctive set of subtypes can be distinguished within the Decision-Making category. Whereas the correct answers of intellective tasks are based either on cultural norms, logic and broadly known facts, or on expert consensus, the "correct" answers for decision-making tasks are based on peer consensus about what is morally right or what is to be preferred. For some of these, answers draw on cultural values, presumably broadly shared in the population from which group members are drawn. Others may involve social comparison and other social influence processes operating among the particular individuals who are the group's members. Still others may involve consensus attained by sharing relevant information. Thus, decision-making tasks, like intellective tasks, have internal differentiations that shift, by degrees, from being very similar to the category adjacent to one of its "borders" (i.e., intellective tasks) to being similar to the task type adjacent to its other border (i.e., cognitive conflict tasks).

Quadrant III, Negotiate, is more or less an extension of Quadrant II, Choose, under conditions where there is intra-unit conflict. The key word here is not *solve,* but *resolve.* It, too, has two types: Resolving Conflicts of Viewpoint and Resolving Conflicts of Interest. The first refers to cases where members of the group do not just have different *preferences,* but have *systematically different preference structures.* They may interpret information differently, may give different weights to different dimensions, and/or may relate dimensions to preferences via different functional forms. Davis (1980) suggests that such differences of viewpoint may occur for subpopulations who are potential jurors, at least for certain types of cases. Hammond, Brehmer, and colleagues (e.g., Hammond, Stewart, Brehmer, & Steinmann, 1975; Brehmer, 1976) in their development of Social Judgment Theory, have induced such "judgment policy" differences experimentally and have studied their effects on group decisions. They insist that such cognitive conflicts are far more pervasive than we have recognized, because conflict is almost always construed as conflict of interest or of motive.

Such conflicts of interest form the other task types of the Negotiate quadrant. We can distinguish several subtypes, including: (a) tasks involving conflicts of both viewpoints and interests or pay-offs, and involving multiple dimensions of dissent, perhaps exemplified by labor/management negotiations; (b) tasks requiring resolution along a single, quantified dimension, such as those studied under the label of bargaining; (c) tasks in which the two (or more) parties' joint choices determine pay-offs to each, such as the prisoner's dilemma game, the N-person prisoner's dilemma, and studies of other social dilemmas; and (d) tasks in which opposing members try to establish subsets (coalitions) that can control allocation of payoffs. These subtasks range from those with an emphasis on resolution (compromise, agreement) to those with an emphasis on power. Again, these subtypes shade from one border of the category to the other.

Quadrant IV deals with overt, physical behavior, with the execution of manual and psychomotor tasks. Such tasks are very heavily represented in the workaday world and, against that baserate, are quite underrepresented in research on groups. Again, there are two types: *Contests* and *Performances*. *Contests* are tasks for which the unit of focus, the group, is in competition with an opponent, an enemy, and performance results will be interpreted in terms of a winner and a loser, with pay-offs in those terms as well. These range from "battles," where the focus is on conquest of an opponent and winner-take-all distribution of pay-offs, to "competitions," where there is a lot of emphasis on standards of performance excellence over and above the reckoning of winners and losers. The former are power based conflicts of interest that are adjacent to the *Negotiation* task type, especially the winning-coalition subtype. The latter approach *Performances,* the other adjacent task category.

Performances are those overt task executions that do not involve competition against an enemy, but rather involve striving to meet standards of excellence (or, sometimes, standards of "sufficiency"), with pay-offs tied to such standards rather than to "victory" over an opponent. These ordinarily involve complex sets of activities requiring coordination between members and over time. Much of the work of the world—lifting, connecting, extruding, digging, pushing—falls in this category, but not much of the study of small groups. These tasks can be subclassified in a myriad of ways, including type of material being worked upon, type of activity involved, intended product of the activity, and many others. Perhaps one useful subclassification is the distinction between *continuous process* and *batch process* tasks. A related distinction is between those in which the internal timing of activities is and is not crucial. Consideration of time dependent tasks brings us back to the planning tasks of Quadrant I, for which sequence and schedule are crucial parts.

Thus, not only are the four quadrants (the four performance processes) distinguished from but related to one another, each of the eight task types is related to its neighboring types on each side. Furthermore, the subtypes within each task type can be ordered, more or less, in a progression that moves, by small transition steps, from one boundary of the category to the other.

The task circumplex is a two-dimensional representation, and it is possible to describe the two dimensions of that space. If the circumplex is placed so that Quadrant I spans "12 o'clock" (with task type 1 to the right, and task type 2 to the left, of that point), the horizontal dimension reflects a contrast between behavioral or action tasks to the right (types 1, 8, 7, and 6) and conceptual or intellectual tasks to the left (types 2, 3, 4, and 5). The vertical dimension reflects a contrast between cooperation or facilitative compliance at the top (types 3, 2, 1, and 8) and conflict or contrient interdependence at the bottom (types 4, 5, 6, and 7). These two dimensions—intellectual versus behavioral, and cooperation versus conflict—are relatively familiar distinctions about groups and group tasks. Another very familiar set of concepts, the trio of cognitive, affective (or evaluative) and conative, can also be located within this circumplex space. Each of these three components of tasks reaches a maximum at a different point around the circle. The cognitive component of tasks peaks in the vicinity of task types 1 and 2. The affective or evaluative component of tasks peaks near task type 5. The conative or behavioral component of tasks peaks near task type 8.

Thus, the task circumplex seems to represent a reasonable attempt to classify group tasks. Collectively, the eight types can accommodate virtually all tasks used in group research, and many that might have been used but have not been used in that work. The crucial test, of course, is whether or not this taxonomy of tasks can be used to summarize, compare and clarify the research on group task performance, and whether that leads to new insights about the task performance process.

The next six chapters use this task taxonomy as an organizing basis for reviewing past research on group task performance. The order of treatment of task types is for convenience of presentation, and departs from the logical order implied by the task circumplex. The next four chapters will review research on tasks of Quadrants II and III, which are the most fully used task types. Chapter 6 reviews intellective tasks (type 3). Chapter 7 covers decision-making tasks (type 4). Chapter 8 reviews the relatively limited work that fits the cognitive conflict task type (type 5). Chapter 9 covers the fairly voluminous work on mixed-motive tasks (type 6). Chapter 10 reviews group task performance with regard to both task types of Quadrant IV: contests and non-competitive physical performances (types 7 and 8). Chapter 11 deals with both task types of Quadrant I: creativity and planning tasks (types 1 and 2). It is perhaps ironic that, while three of these latter four task types are relatively underrepresented in group research, they are very prominent types of tasks for groups in everyday life. This notion is certainly related to the ideas expressed in the preceding chapter, regarding the relatively high use of quasi-groups, and the relatively infrequent use of natural groups (with concocted groups intermediate in frequency), as objects of study in group-related research. Some reasons were given there, and in chapter 3, why natural groups are not only much harder to study but also offer some special limitations to what information can be gained from such study. That same relation tends to hold here, for the study of tasks of types 7, 8, and 1 (contests, performances and planning) which frequently occur in natural groups. They are probably harder to study, and they offer some limitations on what can be learned from their study, compared to the less frequently occurring, but more experimentally tractable, tasks of types 2, 3, 4, 5, and 6 (that is, creativity tasks, intellective tasks, decision-making tasks, cognitive conflict tasks and mixed-motive tasks).

CHAPTER SIX
INTELLECTIVE TASKS: SOLVING PROBLEMS THAT HAVE CORRECT ANSWERS (TASK TYPE 3)

The tasks included here are those for which there is, or is believed to be, a correct answer. I use Laughlin's term, intellective tasks (Laughlin, 1980), rather than the more familiar term, problem-solving, for several reasons: (a) to avoid confusion with Hackman's problem-solving task type (which is classified here under planning tasks); (b) to avoid the implication that the category refers only to problems requiring arithmetic and/or logical calculations; and (c) to choose a term that highlights the diversity of things intended to be included, all of which have a cognitive flavor.

I also adopt Laughlin's view that, among tasks in the Choose quadrant, there is a gradient rather than a sharp dichotomy between tasks with a demonstrable right answer and those where the choice of alternative is to be based upon a consensus of preferences (i.e., task type 4, decision-making tasks.) He points out (Laughlin, 1980) that all knowledge rests on a social consensus, at least about the logical and epistemological bases of that knowledge. What we regard now as established fact and correct logic was, at an earlier time, a set of issues to be resolved by consensus. Matters now regarded as value issues may come to be regarded as established fact in the future. People once all "knew," for example, that the world was flat and in the center of the universe; but at that time there was controversy about whether or not there were subatomic particles. Now, the state of "knowledge" on both these matters has changed.

Several steps along a gradient can be identified as subtypes within the intellective task category. First, and most "factual," are those problems for which the correct answer is not only demonstrable but is intuitively compelling once presented. This refers to what have been called Eureka type problems. Second is the subtype in which the answer is demonstrable, by culturally accepted logical and epistemological principles, but is not obvious and not necessarily easy to demonstrate convincingly to others in a task group. Such might be the case, for example, for a complex geometric or algebraic "proof." These two subtypes will be discussed together because they present a common or highly overlapping body of research. The third subtype of tasks with a "correct" answer are those for which the correct answer is the consensus of a set of judges who can reasonably be regarded as "experts" on the issue at hand. For example, one group study (see, Hall, 1971) asked groups to decide which of a list of items would be most essential for survival if wrecked on the moon; the study used the consensus of NASA experts as the criterion ranking against which the "accuracy" of group decisions was calibrated. Here, the correct answer cannot be directly demonstrated by a group member to the rest of the group, and such tasks are usually designed so as not to have an obvious and intuitively compelling correct answer. The correct answer is demonstrable only by reference to consensus of a different group. These "expert answer" tasks lie at the boundary of the intellective task category, near the decision-making task category. It is only a short step from such a task to one for which the correctness of an answer is to be defined by the consensus of the focal group itself—such as a jury—and such tasks are classified as decision-making tasks rather than intellective tasks. This classification and terminology, incidentally, does not imply that decision-making tasks have no intellective component, no "facts." Rather, it implies that for such problems the facts alone do not point to a single correct alternative. The preferred alternative depends on the way in which the facts are weighed and combined, and that in turn depends on values or points of view about the subject. Here such tasks will be regarded as decision-making tasks, and will be discussed in the next chapter. This chapter, on intellective tasks, will cover tasks with demonstrable right answers, intuitively compelling or not, and those with right answers derived from expert consensus.

EARLY STUDIES
OF GROUP PROBLEM-SOLVING

In a now-classic early study, Marjorie E. Shaw (1932)[1] compared groups and individuals on problem-solving tasks that fit the present category. She found that groups got more right answers than individuals, though often at a cost in time. She suggested that this was so because groups were more effective in checking

---

[1]This study is often referenced simply as M. E. Shaw, and thus her work is often confused with the extensive work in the small group area done by Marvin E. Shaw.

errors and eliminating wrong answers. Many other early studies got very similar results (see Davis, 1969; Laughlin, 1980, for good reviews of these studies). But there were two qualifications. First, when an index of member "manhours" was used as the time measure, groups were clearly less efficient (though more "effective") than individuals. Second, Marquart (1955) compared scores of such problem-solving groups to scores of "concocted groups." These were "statisticized groups," credited with a right answer if any member had the right answer. In these comparisons, groups were not as effective as individuals.

The latter idea, that if one member of a group knows the answer or can do the task the group can and will succeed, is a key notion in understanding how group problem-solving works. It implies that these tasks are disjunctive tasks, in terms of Steiner's classification (Steiner, 1966, 1972; see also chapter 5). It implies that group members combine their abilities and knowledge according to a combination rule (or a social decision scheme, as we will call it) that can be stated as "truth wins" (Steiner, 1972; Laughlin, 1980).

As noted in the preceding chapter, there were a number of early efforts to develop models of group productivity, and most of them involved assuming some combination rule or social decision scheme by which the abilities, knowledge and efforts of group members were combined. Taylor and Faust (1952), Lorge and Solomon (1955), Restle and Davis (1962) and Steiner (1966) have developed similar models. These models all predict the level of performance to be expected for groups of various sizes, whose members are drawn from a population for which there is a known proportion of individuals who can solve the problem. They base their predictions on formulations that involve expansion of the binomial theorum. (Later work on group productivity models, by Thomas and Fink (1961), Davis (1973), and Shiflett (1979), used more complicated formulations involving the multinomial theorum and matrix algebra.) These models imply a disjunctive task, or a "truth wins" combination rule. Sometimes, these were compared to models offering an alternative set of predictions based on an assumption of "no group effect," or of some kind of "averaging" of group members, or of some kind of majority decision rule scheme. When such predictions were compared to the problem-solving success of actual (that is, interacting though ad hoc experimental) groups, group task performance almost always was *between* the two sets of predictions. That is, group performance was superior to what would be expected if groups simply somehow "averaged" individual inputs, or solved these intellective problems on the basis of majority opinion. But group performance was lower than would be expected if the group used individual inputs in a maximally effective way—that is, if "truth," when present, always prevailed. The model assuming a disjunctive task with no process losses, where "truth wins," *overpredicts* how well actual groups do. (This model is equivalent to Marquart's concocted groups, and is equivalent to performance of the best member in each group.) On the other hand, the model assuming an additive task, where not truth but consensus prevails, *underpredicts* how well actual groups do. (This model, which has been called an equalitarian model by Davis and Restle (1963), is equivalent to an averaging model and to majority rule social decision schemes that are described in the next chapter).

LAUGHLIN'S STUDIES
ON INTELLECTIVE TASKS
USING SOCIAL
DECISION SCHEMES

Laughlin and his colleagues (e.g., Laughlin, 1980; Laughlin & Adamopoulos, 1981; Laughlin & Johnson, 1966; Laughlin, Kerr, Davis, Halff & Marciniak, 1975; Laughlin, Kerr, Munch, & Haggerty, 1976) have conducted an extensive program of research on group performance on an array of intellective tasks, including vocabulary tests, analogies, and remote associations. (See EXRT Box #1) This work drew on Davis's (1973) Social Decision Schemes (SDS) model. The SDS model will be described in somewhat more detail in the treatment of Davis's work on juries, in the discussion of decision-making tasks (see chapter 7). Briefly, the SDS model lets you test the fit of a whole family of models, or possible rules of combination, on the same set of group performance data. Laughlin and colleagues tested nearly a dozen such decision rules, including: "truth wins"; "truth supported wins" (that is, at least two group members have the right answer); majority wins; strong majority (e.g., two-thirds) wins; and a number of others. Results of these studies show, clearly and with very strong evidence, that for all but one of the tasks the best-fitting model is "truth supported wins." All of these are problems for which there is a demonstrably correct answer, but one that is not necessarily intuitively compelling. The one exception to the "truth supported wins" model is a task (Remote Associates

EXRT 1:   *LAUGHLIN'S CONCEPT ATTAINMENT PARADIGM*

Main Study Procedures: Groups (or individuals) are asked to try to find out which of a defined set of possible concepts is the right answer on each of a series of trials. A "concept" is defined as one of two or more values of each of a series of (two or more) attributes. For example, a problem might have three values on each attribute (+, 0, −) with four attributes (A, B, C, D). A particular "concept" might be +, 0, −, −, for the four attributes/positions. Subjects can be individuals or groups of any size. They are either given an instance and asked if it is the concept (or told that it is or is not the concept) (a "reception" paradigm); or else they are asked to generate an instance and then are told whether or not it is the concept (a "selection" paradigm), and/or are given feedback about what aspects of the instance match the concept (similar to the board game "Mastermind.")

Main Dependent Variables of Interest: Solutions, trials to solution, errors; inferred strategies.

Main Variations: Number of values and attributes; form of presentation and of feedback; characteristics of members (e.g., ability, gender); size, composition and type of groups; number and difficulty of trials.

References: Laughlin (1980); Laughlin & Adamopoulos (1982); Laughlin & Jaccard (1975); Laughlin & Johnson (1966); Laughlin, McGlynn, Anderson, & Jacobson (1968); Laughlin & Sweeney (1977).

test) for which the right answer, once offered, is intuitively compelling. It apparently is an "insight" or Eureka task. For this task, the best fitting model is "truth wins."

Note that in earlier studies the kinds of problems used all fit the category of having demonstrable right answers, but they varied a lot in terms of how obviously correct that right answer was. These included: the "cannibals and missionaries" task, and a similar husband-wife problem; a disk stacking puzzle; anagrams and cryptograms; jigsaw puzzles; bus routing problems; variants of the horse trading and the Luchins water-jar or gold dust problems and other logical reasoning problems; and a variation of the "twenty questions" game. (See EXRT # 2) The water-jar and horse-trading problems seem to be Eureka-like problems but turn out not to be convincingly demonstrable to many group members. Many of these tasks, such as the jigsaw puzzles and cryptograms, may be Eureka when completed; but the correctness of each step along the way (each piece of the puzzle) may be far from intuitively compelling.

So perhaps groups failed to reach levels predicted by the models tested in earlier problem-solving studies because those studies did *not* use tasks with right answers that were intuitively compelling or easy to demonstrate to group members. Groups in those studies may have operated on a "truth supported wins" basis, so that a model based strictly on a "truth wins" principle (which all the early models were) would overpredict. Groups in those studies tended to do about as well as or slightly better than their second best members, but not as well as their best member. That, too, would suggest a "truth supported wins" rule. If at least two members of the group can solve the problem, the group will solve it, though perhaps they will not do so if only one member can. So for problems with a demonstrable right answer, there is a very high probability that groups with at least two members who know that right answer will get the right answer. The group will do as well as its second best member, so to speak. If the right answer is intuitively compelling, there is a very high probability that groups with at least one member who knows that right answer will get the right

EXRT 2:   *THE TWENTY QUESTIONS TASK*

Main Study Procedures: Subjects can be individuals or groups of any size. Their task is to determine a target object by asking a series of questions that can be answered "yes" or "no," with each "no" counting as one question against their score. The aim is to determine the target object with as few "no's" as possible with the group allowed a maximum of twenty. Each trial is usually started by the experimenter indicating whether the target object is animal, mineral, or vegetable. Group members must agree on each question to be asked.

Main Dependent Variables of Interest: Number of problems correctly answered by each group or individual; number of questions needed to answer each problem; time to solution, and time-per-person to solution.

Main Variations: Size of group; difficulty level of problems; characteristics of members (e.g., gender, ability level, practice).

References: Shaw (1932); Taylor & Faust (1952).

answer. Here, groups will do as well as their best member. (It is misleading, by the way, to talk about groups doing better than their best member for this kind of task, although it makes sense to do so for some other kinds of tasks. In these problem-solving tasks, the correct answer is as "good" as you can do; so, if any member knows it, the group can't do better than that member. It is possible, of course, for a group none of whose members knows the right answer to get the right answer collectively. That turns out to be a very low probability event, for these kinds of tasks.)

It is not clear whether or not Laughlin's "truth supported wins" principle—which appears to be very robust and very general for intellective tasks—should be considered evidence of process losses in Steiner's (1972) sense. The group does less well than it *could* have done, in comparison to some idealized logical upper limit. The *best* member apparently would have done better working alone. But we need to keep in mind that most or all of the rest of the members would have done worse if working alone. This phenomenon does not seem to fit the idea of motivation losses, or even of coordination losses in the usual sense.

Alternatively, perhaps we should consider that the group does as well as it could reasonably be expected to do given the circumstances. Why, after all, should a group accept the nonobvious and not compellingly demonstrated answer of a minority of one, even though the *investigator* knows that that answer is correct? The salience of this question will become even greater as we consider group performance on tasks for which the correct answer is defined by expert consensus.

EARLY STUDIES
OF ACCURACY
OF GROUP JUDGMENTS

Early studies, by Knight (1921) and Gordan (1923), found that the average judgments of groups (what are here called "statisticized" groups) were more accurate than the single judgments of the individuals in those groups. Stroop (1932) soon pointed out that this was a statistical artifact. If errors of judgment are random in direction (just as likely to be off in one direction as in the other), then the average of a number of judgments will be closer to the true value than single judgments, whatever the source of those judgments. He showed, further, that the average of a series of judgments by the same individual also showed such an improvement in accuracy. Hence, this convergence by averaging is an arithmetic, not a group, effect. Besides, such statistical groups are not groups at all in the sense of interaction among members. Studies in accuracy of judgments of "true" interacting groups, often in comparison to "statisticized" groups made up of individuals from the same population, led to mixed results (e.g., Gurnee, 1937; Jenness, 1932; Thorndike, 1938. For reviews, see Einhorn, Hogarth, & Klemper, 1977; Eils & John, 1980; Rohrbaugh, 1979). The reasonable conclusions that can be drawn from many such studies, varying in task type, group size, and many features of methodology, are (a) that interacting groups are almost always more accurate than their average member or a statisticized group, especially for problems with some complexity (or, what Brunswick (1955) calls "intentional depth"); (b) that groups seldom do as well as their best members, or as predicted by combinatorial models based on a disjunctive (or "truth wins") principle. The difference between the accuracy of best member and the accuracy of interacting groups is usually construed as resulting from process losses. The process losses presumably come from group interaction patterns in which the contributions of members are not given weights highly correlated with those members' actual competence/knowledge on the problem at hand. Steiner (1972) suggested at least four classes of such patterns: (a) when status differences don't parallel competence differences; (b) when competent members have low confidence in their own abilities; (c) when there are social pressures for conformity by an incompetent majority; and (d) when it is difficult to judge the quality of individual contributions (that is, right answers are not intuitively compelling).

These results led a number of researchers to investigate group judgments further, by inventing various "quasi-groups" with restricted interaction. Those efforts were aimed both at exploring the bases of these presumed process losses and at trying to find ways to avoid or attenuate those losses. These efforts are summarized next.

STUDIES
OF JUDGMENT ACCURACY
USING QUASI-GROUPS

That the judgments of interacting groups are more accurate than those of average individual members, but are not as accurate as they "should" be (that is, are not as accurate as the post-hoc determined best member), had two crucial implications in the view of a number of investigators:

1. Groups offer the *possibility* of more accurate judgments than single individuals, especially on tasks with considerable complexity or "intentional depth."
2. Freely interacting groups do not live up to their potential—that is, they do not equal or exceed their best member—and that deficiency reflects process losses.

Various investigators set out both to explore where and how such process losses come about in freely interacting groups, and to develop ways to make group judgments better by avoiding these process losses (thus, a research purpose and an action purpose, respectively). Their efforts led to the development of a whole spectrum of quasi-interacting groups that fall between the freely interacting (though ad hoc experimental) groups whose errant processes are the object of inquiry, and the statisticized groups that were not groups at all but arithmetical aggregations of individual judgments. These were described in chapter 4, as part of a broader spectrum of quasi-groups, concocted groups, and natural groups. Two forms, in particular, were developed to study and try to improve accuracy of group judgments: the Delphi technique (see EXRT 3);

EXRT 3:   *THE DELPHI METHOD*

> *Main Study Procedures:* Subjects are asked to make a quantitative estimate of some phenomenon (e.g., number of miles between a certain pair of cities), or to make a quantitative prediction about some future event (e.g., the Dow-Jones closing average for next year). The members whose answers are to be combined never see each other or communicate. Member answers are averaged and/or otherwise combined, and results are given as feedback to members. They then make a second round of judgments. These are combined and fed back to members. Such a cycle may continue for any number of iterations.
>
> *Main Dependent Variables of Interest:* Accuracy of final average judgment (usually compared to the once-only group decision of an interacting group of comparable size and composition); opinion shifts of individual members toward ostensive correct answer; member satisfaction. (Accuracy is sometimes reckoned in relation to a consensus of "experts.")
>
> *Main Variations:* Size and composition of "groups"; form of comparison groups; number of iterations; type and difficulty of problem, and the basis for determining the ostensive correct answer.
>
> *References:* Dalkey (1968, 1969); Rohrbaugh (1979); Delbecq, Van de Ven, & Gustafson (1975).

and the Nominal Group technique (NGT) (see EXRT 23). Three other forms have been used in group judgment accuracy tasks, although they were developed for much broader purposes: Social Judgment Theory groups (SJT); Problem Decomposition groups; and Communication Strategy groups. (For reviews of these, see Brehmer, 1976; Eils & John, 1980; Rohrbaugh, 1979.) (Also see EXRT boxes 4, 7, 30.)

The Delphi method simply feeds back individual judgments, anonymously, with a second and perhaps third round of judgments following feedback *without any interaction.* Good research evidence on the effectiveness of Delphi method is limited and mixed, but strongly suggests that the gains in group judgment accuracy that have been claimed for it by its proponents are not always found in carefully designed studies done by other investigators. For example, in one well designed study (Rohrbaugh, 1979), although Delphi did better than average pretest individual's judgment, it did *not* do better than the second best individual judgment, and it did distinctly worse than the best member's judgments. That certainly is not much of a reduction of process losses in interacting groups.

The Nominal Group technique (NGT) is also a "voting" technique, but feedback is done publicly by having individuals announce their answers in turn; and this is followed by limited interaction—to explain and clarify judgments—before the subsequent group decision (obtained by majority vote or averaging). While this may give the individual member more of a feeling of involvement with the other people than does the Delphi method, it also clearly invites the operation of group influence processes even more than the Delphi method. If freely interacting groups perform below what they "should" on these tasks because of process losses, surely one of those hindering processes is the pressure within a group toward uniformity or agreement. There is very limited evidence on the NGT method in relation to freely interacting groups; there is by no means clear support for the hypothesis that such groups do better than either Delphi or freely interacting groups for accuracy tasks. (See Dalkey, 1968, 1969; Delbecq, Van de Ven & Gustafson, 1975; Gustafson, Shukla, Delbecq & Walster, 1973; Van de Ven, 1974; Van de Ven & Delbecq, 1971, for a view more favorable toward Delphi and NGT. See, also, chapter 11.) (See EXRT 23.)

While most uses of Social Judgment Theory (SJT) fit the cognitive conflict task type and will be discussed in a later chapter on that task type (see chapter 8), one study was used to compare accuracy of group judgments with SJT versus the Delphi method (Rohrbaugh, 1979). In that study, the SJT technique involved giving group members both outcome feedback (as in Delphi) and cognitive feedback (that is, feedback on the underlying pattern of judgments, or judgment policy) regarding initial individual judgments, and then permitting face to face interaction. These groups did not differ from Delphi groups in accuracy of judgments; and, like the Delphi groups, did better than average initial individual judgments but not better than the second best member and decidedly poorer than the best member. SJT group members did profit from the group discussion, though, increasing in accuracy from pre- to post-session on their individual judgments; Delphi group members did not show such improvement.

Note that these comparisons are not between the respective quasi-groups and freely interacting groups. Moreover, whether or not SJT equals or exceeds Delphi, neither one does any better than the freely interacting groups, whose "deficient" processes these techniques were invented to improve. In fact, it would seem that freely interacting SJT, NGT, and even the "anonymous feedback only" Delphi groups all do about the same—definitely better than a statisticized average; definitely poorer than the best member; and about equal to the second best member. While none of these studies tried to derive group decision rules such as Laughlin used, the outcomes would suggest that "truth with much support wins" is a plausible model for all of these quasi- and freely interacting groups *for this type of task.*

The Multiattribute Utility Analysis techniques (MAUA) and the Communication Strategy technique were used, separately and in combination, in one study of group judgment accuracy (Eils & John, 1980). The MAUA involves breaking the task down into a number of component parts, each requiring various rating and ranking judgments, with the group acting as a single unit while making each judgment but carrying out the task parts in a rigorous order. Group members are free to interact, but the task format to some degree dominates all the action. (See EXRT 4.) The communication strategy procedure involves instructing groups in some intra-group communication techniques designed to aid the decision-making process. These techniques are adopted from work by Hall and Watson (1971), and include instructions to group members to avoid arguments, to avoid changing position just to eliminate conflict, to expect and value differences, and so on. (See EXRT 30.) Eils and John report that groups using each of these two techniques had higher accuracy than the freely interacting groups that received neither of the two treatments; and that the groups who had *both* treatments were the most accurate of all. However, none of the communication strategy effects were statistically significant. The MAUA treatment effect *was* statistically significant; but it is unclear how substantial that MAUA effect was because data were "normalized" in a complex way. The authors draw much stronger conclusions about the efficacy of the two techniques than I think are justified by the data. They point out, correctly, that the communication strategy was not designed for use in combination with highly analytic procedures such as the MAUA, or on such highly quantitative tasks. Hence, its full potential is probably underestimated by the data of this study. It is proper to conclude, I think, that both the communication strategy and the MAUA technique are at least as accurate as (and perhaps more accurate than) freely interacting groups for tasks defined in terms of "accuracy" in relation to expert consensus. It is also the case that these two techniques are designed to structure or channel group process, not to constrain or eliminate such processes. In a sense, they "add to" rather than "subtract from" normal process in ad hoc groups, by providing aids and strategies that place little *explicit* constraint on free interaction. Eils and John (1980) hold that the MAUA technique works by focusing group members' attention on relevant factors, and that the communication strategy works by diverting group attention away from interactions tangential to the task. These two techniques should perhaps be considered, along with the

EXRT 4:   *THE MULTIATTRIBUTE UTILITY ANALYSIS (MAUA) TECHNIQUE*

Main Study Procedures: Individuals are formed into groups and are asked to make a series of complex judgments of the same type (e.g., a series of job application decisions or graduate school admission decisions). The problems are "decomposed" into a series of subtasks or stages, and groups are required to carry out the stages in a specific sequence. For example, a problem might have the following set of stages: (1) an initial listing of the set of alternative courses of action to be evaluated (or alternative "cases"); (2) specification of a set of attributes with respect to which each alternative can be evaluated; (3) numerical assessment of the value of each alternative with respect to each attribute; (4) ranking and rating each attribute in terms of its importance; and (5) deciding what combination rule (e.g., additive, multiplicative) to use to combine judgments across attributes into a single judgment of the alternative (or "case"). All stages are carried out by the group in open, full channel, face to face communication; but the steps and their order are experimenter-determined.

Main Dependent Variables of Interest: Speed and accuracy of group judgments (compared to judgments made by groups under some other set of task procedures); member satisfaction; improvement over trials.

Main Variations: Size and composition of groups; nature and difficulty of problem; extent and type of training in MAUA procedures.

Reference: Eils & John (1980).

strategy priming and brainstorming techniques discussed in a later chapter, as techniques for augmenting rather than constraining group process.

GROUP PROBLEM-SOLVING UNDER MEDIATED COMMUNICATION

With the proliferation of electronic media (telephone, television, teletype-writing), there has developed a body of research on effects of such media on group task performance. (For a review, see Williams, 1977). One part of that literature deals with groups working on tasks for which there is a demonstrably correct answer. For that literature, results seem strong and clear:

1. Written media (such as remote handwriting, teletypewriting) differ from voice media (such as audio only, video, face to face). Voice media get faster solutions, though using more messages.
2. There are few differences among the written media. There also are few differences among the voice media, even though that set included such vastly different conditions as audio only and face to face.
3. Apparently, for these tasks, nonverbal cues are of little consequence for task solution.

The body of research on task performance under mediated conditions, and Williams's (1977) review of it, also covers conflict tasks, creativity tasks, and some aspects of group interaction process. These will be discussed in appropriate places elsewhere in the book. (See, especially, chapter 13.)

SUMMARY

The evidence on groups performing intellective tasks seems strong and clear. When the task has an intuitively compelling right answer, groups perform as if they were working on a "truth wins" principle. But relatively few tasks have such intuitively compelling right answers. When problems have a clearly demonstrable right answer, but it is not easy to demonstrate the correctness of that answer convincingly within a task group, group performance reflects a "truth supported wins" principle. For tasks where there is a less demonstrable right answer—for example, where the criterion of accuracy lies beyond the knowledge of the task group in a consensus of experts—task groups seem to operate as if they were on a "truth with much support wins" principle. (As we will see later, solutions to decision tasks seem to require not truth with some minority level of support, but rather majority—often strong majority—support.)

Two points should be noted about the "accuracy of judgments" tasks. First, results of these studies imply process losses only under the assumption that groups "should" attain the level predicted by a disjunctive or "truth wins" model. Remember that in intellective problems with demonstrable right answers, "truth wins" is accurate only if the correct answer is also intuitively compelling. Otherwise, even when there is a demonstrable right answer, "truth" needs at least some support to prevail. At the end of that discussion, I posed the question of why we should expect groups to accept the answer of a single member just because the investigator knows that the member's answer is correct. Note, for accuracy of judgment tasks, the correct answer is *not* demonstrable on logical or factual grounds available to the group members. Rather, it hinges on a consensus of experts—whose views and premises are totally unknown to the group's members. The question of why we should expect the group to accept the "accurate" answer of its best member, when the bases of "accuracy" are quite extrinsic to the group, must be raised even more strongly for these tasks. The results seem to support a "truth with much support wins" decision rule, which is a not unreasonable rule for solutions where accuracy is defined by a consensus of experts unknown to the group.

The second point to note is that many of the problems used in these accuracy of judgment studies do not have "right answers" at all, not even right answers defined by expert consensus. Some of them ask for predictions of future events (e.g., the date of an armistice; who will win an election). Some call for judgments of conditions that are for all practical purposes unknowable by anyone, except by assumption (e.g., the distribution of some personality traits among children, the credit-worthiness of hypothetical customers). Even for tasks for which there is an "accurate" answer in principle, such as judging the number of beans in a bottle or evaluating the artistic merit of paintings, there is no way for a member to make his or her answer demonstrably correct. It is no wonder that such "truth" doesn't always prevail! Some of these tasks fall more readily into the decision-making task category, to be discussed next.

CHAPTER SEVEN
DECISION–MAKING TASKS: DEVELOPING GROUP CONSENSUS ON ISSUES THAT DO NOT HAVE CORRECT ANSWERS (TASK TYPE 4)

Much of the world's work involves not so much seeking or calculating a right answer as deciding what to do when there is no right answer, and no shared formal logical criteria for establishing one. Furthermore, a sizeable proportion of such decision-making tasks get done by groups rather than by individuals. Juries decide many criminal and civil cases. Legislatures debate and pass laws. Committees decide policy on many matters and at many levels of governmental, industrial, educational, religious, medical, and recreational organizations. Groups would seem to have three natural advantages over individuals in regard to such "no right answer" decision tasks. First, by sheer numbers, they are more likely than any one individual to include a broader range, and therefore, perhaps, a more fitting range, of skills and knowledge pertaining to the task. Second, the total amount of information to be acquired and processed may be vast, and a group provides the opportunity for an effective division of labor. Third, decisions reached by a group are more likely to be regarded as legitimate, as worthy of being followed, than decisions by most individuals.

But groups may also have some natural disadvantages, as we have seen in discussing performance on intellective tasks. They may not utilize fully or efficiently the range of knowledge they contain. Some members may have more influence than others, and more than their knowledge or task competence would warrant. There may be pressures to agree, tending toward quick rather than good decisions. And the very diversity of knowledge among members may carry with it a diversity of views and values, some of which may be hard to reconcile into a single group decision. So questions about the efficiency of groups as systems for performing decision tasks have been prominent in the literature of small group research.

We have already begun considering evidence in this task category because some of the judgment accuracy studies reviewed under expert consensus tasks really include problems with no correct answer. From that subtype of task, really on the border between the intellective and decision-making task categories, we will proceed to a subtype of task for which the consensus draws upon the norms and values of the embedding culture. That is exemplified by the tasks of one major group of studies, known as the "risky shift" studies. Then, we will consider a subtype of task where the consensus draws upon the views of members of the particular group in regard to a particular topic. This subtype is exemplified by studies of juries. We will then consider some special topics related to jury studies, including effects of size and some aspects of composition. That latter topic raises several questions about the application of social science. It also points up that, in some groups, members differ from one another in fundamental viewpoints, not just in opinions or alternative preferences. That, in turn, brings the discussion to the next major task type (cognitive conflict tasks), the topic of the next chapter.

RISKS, CHOICES, AND POLARIZATION IN GROUP DECISION-MAKING

For many years, both the social science literature and the popular press "knew" that groups were predominantly conservative, even reactionary, instruments for deciding things. (See, for example, Whyte's *Organization Man,* 1957.) After all, group judgments tended to "average out" individual differences in opinions among group members. Furthermore, groups generated strong pressures for uniformity, for conformity to group norms. Moreover, religious institutions and many totalitarian industrial and political institutions had, for many years, deliberately used group forces to keep potential deviates in line, to maintain the status quo. Groups are likely to make more conservative decisions than individuals, since in a group one can avoid personal responsibility for inaction.

Such was the conventional wisdom when Stoner (1961) reported on results of his master's thesis, which showed that on a series of questionnaire items with alternatives differing in riskiness, individuals shifted to riskier decisions when working in a group. This finding, counterintuitive at the time, was virtually pounced upon, by a bevy of investigators, as a phenomenon worthy of research attention. A very large number of studies poured forth, almost all of them using Stoner's Choice Dilemma (CDQ) items as well as his "within-subjects" design, (e.g., Wallack, Kogan & Bem, 1962). (In a within-subjects design, the same persons are tested as individuals, then in groups. In a between-subjects design, different though randomly assigned people would be used in "individual" and "group" conditions.) The specific finding was that, when all items of the CDQ are averaged together, there is a shift toward risk from pre-discussion average

EXRT 5:   *THE STONER–KOGAN–WALLACK RISKY SHIFT PARADIGM*

Main Study Procedures: Subjects are asked to indicate what risk level (expressed in odds levels, from 1 in 10 to 9 in 10) they would need in order to adopt the riskier of two alternatives, for a series of choice dilemma items. The items involve advising someone about relatively desirable-but-not-certain courses of action, rather than less-desirable-but-certain courses, for life events such as job choices, decisions about medical treatments, and the like. Subjects are then placed into groups and asked to discuss the issue, to provide a group decision, and then to provide post-group individual responses.

Main Dependent Variables of Interest: Whether, how far, and in what direction, the group as a group, and the individuals in the group, shift in the risk levels they choose for the choice dilemma items.

Main Variations: Types of items and distribution of prediscussion choices on them (risky versus cautious items); whether or not there is a group discussion (versus other kinds of information about the issue or about other's views on it).

References: Cartwright (1973); Dion, Baron, & Miller (1970); Lamm & Myers (1978); Myers & Lamm (1976); Stoner (1961); Wallack, Kogan & Bem (1962).

individual judgments both to group decisions and to post-group average individual judgments. That specific finding turned out to be extremely robust. And theoretical "explanations" for it bloomed like dandelions in the spring. (See EXRT 5.)

Among the earliest and most tenacious of those theoretical explanations of the risky shift was that groups allowed a diffusion of responsibility. (Ironically, such a diffusion of responsibility had been part of the earlier explanation for why groups were so conservative in their decisions.) Still another explanation was that the group discussion simply increased individuals' familiarity with those somewhat esoteric issues, and that such increased familiarity led to shifts toward increased risk. A third, and very tenacious, explanation was the "risk as value" hypothesis. This position asserted that risk is positively valued in our culture, and that therefore everyone feels himself or herself to be *relatively* risk taking. When group discussion reveals that others are not nearly so cautious as one had thought, one is obliged to shift toward risk (to keep up with the Jones's, so to speak, or perhaps to keep slightly ahead of them). A fourth early explanation was that relatively risk-taking individuals were likely to be more persuasive and, hence, have more influence, than persons who took more cautious positions.

The "familiarity" and "persuasive risk taker" explanations were relatively easy to test, and they were soon disconfirmed and discarded, at least in their original forms. The diffusion of responsibility and risk as value hypotheses, however, were not readily testable. Hence, they could not be disconfirmed. They were retained as plausible hypotheses, not so much because of any evidence directly supporting them, but because none of the evidence could disconfirm them.

While the specific finding was very robust, it turned out not to be very general, over task or even over items of the CDQ. For example, equivalent findings were not obtained on "risk" in gambling tasks. Furthermore, even though the *total set* of items consistently showed a risky shift, not all items of the CDQ showed risky shift. Some showed no shift; and one repeatedly showed a shift toward the "caution" end of the scale. Moreover, it became evident that items could deliberately be designed so as to give a cautious rather than a risky shift. This replicable and robust finding no longer had such a clear and counterintuitive (hence interesting) meaning. Furthermore, the remaining theoretical formulations needed either to be abandoned or to be radically modified to account for these choice shifts in both directions.

The risk as value hypothesis was simply elaborated: the culture valued risk for some matters, but caution in others. The rest of the rationale remained intact. The diffusion of responsibility notion now had to account for why diffusion should lead to risk sometimes and to caution on other matters.

But one additional regularity in the vast body of data on this topic now was noticed. Each CDQ item had a characteristic degree, as well as direction, of shift. These were very stable over studies. Furthermore, the best predictor of the direction and degree of shift of an item was its characteristic pattern of initial (that is, pre-group individual) judgments. Those items with the strongest pro-risk initial distributions were the items with the largest shifts toward risk; similarly, items with initial judgments loaded toward the cautious pole showed the largest shifts toward caution. This is counter to all of the statistical artifacts likely to occur in repeat testing. We expect extreme scores to "regress" toward the middle on repeat testing. Instead, here, the larger the departure from "neutral" at the outset, the greater the shift in that same direction, risk or caution, after group discussion.

This latter description of the phenomenon is now referred to as polarization, or group polarization, or group induced polarization. (This is a somewhat unfortunate choice of terms. The term polarization usually denotes shifting of two subsets toward opposite poles. The phenomenon under discussion here refers to shifting of the entire group further in the direction of the pole toward which it already tended. "Accentuation" might have been a more accurately descriptive term.) It is this shift—not toward risk as such, but toward the already preferred pole—that is so very robust. Moreover, polarization appears to be very general over tasks and measures. (For reviews of the risky shift and polarization research, see Cartwright, 1973; Dion, Baron & Miller, 1970; Lamm & Myers, 1978; Miller, 1978; Myers & Lamm, 1976.) And we seem to have made effective progress toward sound theoretical explanations of that polarization effect.

The theoretical field has been more or less narrowed down to two main contenders. One, which is a decendant of the risk as value hypothesis, is the *social comparison theory*. The other, which is a distant relative of the old familiarity hypothesis, is the *persuasive arguments position*. Both are related to the risk as value hypothesis. The social comparison position argues that it is the normative pressures resulting from learning about the position of other members—and learning, thereby, that you are not as good an example of the culturally valued position, risk or caution, as you thought you were—that produces the polarization effect of group discussion. Presumably, such an effect could be produced by feedback without group discussion. The persuasive arguments position builds on the premise that the group discussion provided arguments for the two poles that are distributed in proportion to the distribution of pre-decision positions of the members, and that these are both distributed in a way that reflects the cultural value for that item. For this position, group discussion is regarded as a crucial condition, although such arguments could be provided without a group discussion.

The first of these positions corresponds to the idea of normative influence and the second corresponds to the idea of informational influence, both long established aspects of persuasion in individuals and conformity in groups. It should now be clear that polarization is not really a group task performance phenomenon. It is a phenomenon related to group effects on members— specifically, polarization effects on the opinions of members *after, and perhaps because of,* group discussion. This phenomenon will therefore be discussed again under group effects on members (chapter 17). It will not be discussed further here, except to close with the comment that there is considerable evidence in support of both social comparison and persuasive arguments positions, and it seems likely that *both* are causes of, or contribute to, polarization effects.

MOCK JURIES
AND SOCIAL DECISION
SCHEMES

There is a very large and still growing body of research on juries. Almost all of it is on social units that have come to be called mock juries (see discussion in chapter 4). These are studies of ad hoc experimentally-concocted groups (often college students), who are presented with the key information (written, or audio, or video) from a trial (often a condensed version of a real trial), and are then asked to discuss the case *as if they were a jury* and to render a verdict. A few of the mock jury studies have used participants drawn from the juror rolls of a jurisdiction; but even when that was the case, they were still acting in the study as research participants, not real jurors. There is one overriding reason why jury research has not been done on real juries deciding actual cases: it is illegal. But as was pointed out in chapter 4, with real juries there is an inevitable confounding of jury (and juror) factors with the particular case. Any one jury hears only one case; and any one case is heard only by one jury. Experimentally concocted mock juries can, in principle, yield several advantages for research. You can (a) assign participants at random to different comparison conditions (e.g., different sized juries; different orders of testimony; different kinds of evidence); (b) have many juries "try" the same case, under comparable conditions, thus averaging out the impact of factors peculiar to the individual jurors of any one jury; and (c) have the same juries—or the same jurors in different combinations—try several different cases, so that case peculiarities can also be ruled out. (In fact, most mock jury studies do not take advantage of that third possibility.)

Jury research has addressed questions such as:

1. How do juries combine diverse opinions to yield a verdict; or, more generally, what is the relation between the distribution of individual (post-evidence, pre-discussion) views and the resulting group decision?
2. What effects do variations in the judge's description of the "reasonable doubt" criterion have on jury verdicts?
3. What effect would modification of the unanimity rule (e.g., to permit a two-thirds majority decision to hold) have on jury verdicts?
4. What effect would changes in jury size have on jury verdicts?
5. What effect do variations in order, style of presentation, and content of evidence have on jury verdicts?
6. How are any or all of these matters affected by characteristics of the individual jurors, and of the type of case?

(For reviews of this work, see: Berment, Nemeth, & Vidmar, 1976; Bray & Kerr, 1981; Monahan & Loftus, 1982; Nemeth, 1981; Penrod & Hastie, 1979; Tapp, 1976, 1980).

Davis and his colleagues (Davis, 1980) have developed a comprehensive conceptual framework for considering a number of these questions, and have carried out an extensive program of research on them. Davis's (1973) Social Decision Scheme theory (SDS) extends his own earlier work (Davis & Restle, 1963; Restle & Davis, 1962) and the work of others (e.g., Lorge & Solomon, 1955; Thomas & Fink, 1961; Smoke & Zajonc, 1962; Steiner, 1966) on formal mathematical models of group productivity. Davis's SDS theory asks how group members' inputs (in this case, juror pre-discussion judgments) get combined into a single group output (in this case, a jury verdict). SDS theory applies, in principle, to any kind of group decision or product, and Laughlin's (1980) use of it for intellective tasks was noted in the preceding chapter. When applied to jury research, it requires data on individual jurors' judgments about the case, after hearing the trial but before jury deliberations. These data are then used to compare actual (mock) jury verdicts with what would be predicted under each of a variety of social decision schemes. Examples of some social decision schemes are (a) unanimity, the standard rule for juries; (b) a two-thirds majority; (c) a bare majority; (d) for decisions with more than two alternatives, a plurality; or (e) in the kinds of "right answer" problems discussed under intellective tasks, a correct minority of one or two (i.e. "truth wins" or "truth supported wins"). The SDS is then applied by comparing actual results with predictions based on every one of the set of decision schemes, to see which (if any) are acceptably close fits to actual verdicts, and which (if any) is the best fitting social decision scheme. (See EXRT 6.)

When this scheme is applied to results of mock juries in a number of studies (e.g., Davis, Bray & Holt, 1977; Davis, Kerr, Atkin, Holt & Meek, 1975), with a variety of conditions (e.g., different jury sizes, instructions, etc.) results are quite consistent. They show that (mock) juries operate as if they used a "two-thirds majority wins" rule. Predictions from the two-thirds majority schema consistently are a very close fit, and it is often the only SDS that is an acceptable fit. So, while the jury system assumes that juries work on a unanimity

EXRT 6:   *DAVIS'S MOCK JURY, SOCIAL DECISION SCHEME (SDS) PARADIGM*

Main Study Procedures: Individual subjects are randomly assigned to juries (of twelve, unless some other jury size is to be studied). They view a videotape in which a brief version of a simulated trial is displayed. The enactment presents the key testimony of an actual legal case (e.g., an alleged rape); key evidence may be added, strengthened, or deleted, when the nature, strength and order of presentation of evidence is being studied. After viewing the testimony but before group discussion has taken place, subjects are asked to make an individual verdict (guilty or not guilty) and perhaps to answer other questions about their memory for and perceptions of the evidence. Groups then deliberate, as if a jury, and reach a verdict (guilty or not guilty), or report that they are unable to do so (i.e., a hung jury).

Main Dependent Variables of Interest: Distribution of verdicts of a set of juries, compared to distributions of judgments of the set of individual jurors; the "decision scheme," or rule by which a set of individual judgments are combined into a group decision, as inferred from the pattern of individual/group differences.

Main Variations: Type and difficulty of case; amount, type, balance, and order of evidence; size and composition of juries; effects of instructions (e.g., regarding decision rule, or regarding meaning of "reasonable doubt").

References: Davis (1980); Davis, Bray, & Holt (1977); Davis, Kerr, Atkins, Holt, & Meek (1975).

---

rule, these results suggest (and studies using post-trial interviews with actual jurors tend to confirm) that jury decisions are much more accurately depicted by a two-thirds majority scheme.

Recall that, when Laughlin applied the SDS to an array of intellective tasks, in most cases the most viable SDS was "truth supported wins," with "truth wins" a good fit only for the one task with an intuitively compelling solution. So, while groups do not use "truth wins" when the logical structure of the problem would seem to make such a strategy the most efficient one, they similarly do not use a unanimity schema when the legal structure of the problem makes such an SDS the most salient one. In each case, groups seem to operate on a decision rule that is one step *less stringent,* and that makes somewhat less extreme assumptions about the nature of the problem, than the formal structure of the situation would suggest. Perhaps such an amelioration of extremes toward a more practical decision rule has some generality in group task performance. In this light, perhaps we ought not regard differences between actual group performance and the extreme or "ideal type" principle of "truth wins," in the case of intellective tasks as process losses due to "faulty" group process. Perhaps we should not regard differences between actual group performance and the extreme or "ideal type" principle of unanimity, in the case of juries (and other groups doing decision-making tasks), as deviations from expectations of the legal system due to "faulty" group process. Instead, perhaps we should regard both cases as groups placing a *pragmatic boundary* on the extreme solution rules, and thereby achieving *more effective practical* solutions that approximate the ideal extreme but yield a practical resolution much more often. If no one ever modified his or her pre-deliberation views, and juries actually operated on a unanimity rule, a huge majority of all cases would result in hung juries—a condition that would probably destroy the jury system. On the other hand, if problem-solving groups slavishly accepted the answer of any one member who purported to have the "truth," even when no one else in the group could directly verify that answer, such groups would soon be useless as task performance instruments. So, a "truth supported wins" criterion in the latter case, and a "strong majority wins" (e.g., two-thirds majority) criterion in the former case, may reflect very rational and pragmatic principles for those kinds of task groups to use.

I am not trying to make a case that, if groups do things in such and such a way, that must be a good way to do them. Rather, I am trying to differentiate between "ideal performance" as viewed from the perspective of the researcher—who "knows" the right answer because he or she designed or selected the problem, and who therefore knows which members who offer solutions are offering "correct" ones—and effective task performance, as viewed from the perspective of the group trying to do the task without being privy to which answer is correct or to which member is the group's "best" member. In these terms, the "truth supported wins" SDS for intellective tasks, and the "strong majority" SDS for decision-making tasks, may both be cases of *groups doing the best they can from their point of view.* In this light, groups may be very effective task performance instruments indeed.

JURY RESEARCH AND THE LEGAL SYSTEM

A number of studies have been done comparing juries of different sizes, from the standard twelve-person form down to six-person juries. Virtually none of these studies found significant differences between juries of different sizes. A few court jurisdictions have cited these "no difference" findings in declaring legal, and using, juries smaller than twelve. Such actions by the courts have been criticized by a number of jury researchers, who argue that action should not have been taken on such incomplete research, and that the studies finding no difference were methodologically flawed. Davis, applying his SDS model as a tool for extrapolating, makes a series of stunning logical points about this jury size issue (Davis, 1980). First, he shows that, if juries of different sizes operate in the same manner (i.e., use the same decision rule or SDS)—and all of the evidence seems to agree that they do—then it is *logically inevitable* that the *distribution of verdicts will differ* for juries of different sizes. Such differences have not been detected in the mock jury studies, or in studies using data on verdicts from actual cases in jurisdictions that permit juries smaller than twelve, for two reasons. First, the differences are relatively small, so that it would take far more groups than any experimenter would ever be able to run to show those differences by conventional statistical means. (In one set of circumstances, Davis estimated that it would take over two thousand mock jurors to do so.) Of course, even very small differences in probability of conviction, if they are systematic in direction, are of enormous importance if you are the defendant in the case, or the victim. The second reason is that the direction of difference depends on the pre-deliberation distribution of judgments. That is, assuming a two-thirds majority SDS (or any majority SDS), when the predominant view in a population is pro-conviction, a twelve-person jury is more likely to convict than a six-person jury; but the reverse is the case if the predominant pre-deliberation view in the population is pro-acquittal. So, when you aggregate data from juries of two or more sizes, hearing a variety of cases, presumably with different distribution of juror opinions, it is very unlikely that such aggregated data will show large differences in one direction (unlikely even if you did have several thousand cases).

Several lessons can be learned from this set of considerations. First, it points up the complexity of the relation between research and application (in this or any other content area). Second, it shows one of the major advantages of having a strong theoretical formulation underlying empirical evidence: one can use a strong theory to make reasonable extrapolations/predictions to conditions not yet studied. Third, it shows the importance of taking distributions of outcomes into account, because a lot of crucial information can be lost when we aggregate and average over a lot of data. Finally, it points up that, on the one hand, we should take social science research (collectively) quite seriously; on the other hand, we should not take any one piece of social science evidence too seriously.

Davis (1980) also applied SDS as a tool for extrapolation on another question: the effects of composition (that is, the distribution of individual characteristics of jurors), and therefore the effects of juror selection procedures (preemptory challenges; *voir dire* questioning; etc.). Overall, the evidence from post hoc studies of attributes of members of real juries in relation to jury verdicts, and from mock jury experiments, does not show a strong and clear pattern. But there are some juror-by-type-of-case interactions. For example, Davis (1980) has found a sharp difference between males and females in probability of conviction for the rape case that he and his colleagues have used in many of their studies; but there does not seem to be consistent male/female differences across cases of different types (for example, murder, theft).

Davis proposes that the problem of juror composition effects could be addressed by assuming that juries are drawn from two or more subpopulations, with different pretrial predispositions regarding guilt (either for that particular case or for cases in general). He develops some additional SDS variants to predict the possible size and limits of such effects. In that exposition, Davis (1980) suggests that it is not unreasonable to expect that different "batches" of potential jurors—different in terms of gender, age, race, political orientation, social class or the like—may not only have different "opinions" on given cases even after hearing the same evidence, but may also have different viewpoints, different perspectives, in their judgments on a whole set of questions underlying the judgment of guilt or innocence. The idea of groups composed of persons with sharply different cognitive viewpoints not only gives additional salience to practical questions of jury selection and composition, it also foreshadows the next task type to be considered: tasks requiring resolution of cognitive conflicts.

CHAPTER EIGHT
COGNITIVE CONFLICT TASKS: RESOLVING CONFLICTS OF VIEWPOINT WITHIN THE GROUP (TASK TYPE 5)

Hammond, Brehmer, and associates (e.g., Brehmer, 1976; Hammond, Todd, Wilkins, & Mitchell, 1966) have developed a program of research referred to as Social Judgment Theory (SJT). It builds on Brunswick's (1955) lens model and probabilistic functionalism in human perception. Hammond, Brehmer and colleagues argue along lines similar to Davis's suggestion for juries, described at the close of the previous chapter, namely, that coworkers attempting to reach a joint solution often differ in their underlying cognitive views of the problem, as well as in their specific opinions. Such differing viewpoints, such cognitive conflicts, are often very difficult to resolve—precisely because we tend to misunderstand them. On the one hand, we recognize that people disagree on issues; and we recognize the need for discussion, sometimes for compromise, to achieve a consensus. On the other hand, we tend to think of conflict in terms of conflict of interest or of motives (a category of tasks that will be the topic of the next chapter). But the cognitive conflicts to which social judgment theory (SJT) points lie between these two: they are more than just disagreement on position; they are disagreement on the underlying judgment pattern or *judgment policy* (that is, the relevant information cues, their weights, the functional form by which these cues connect to the criterion events, etc.). But such disagreements are *cognitive conflicts*. All parties share the same goals and purposes. They are *not conflicts of motive or interest*. The SJT theorists argue that such cognitive conflicts are much more pervasive in human affairs than we realize.

SOCIAL JUDGMENT
THEORY

Proponents of SJT have developed a set of techniques by which group members are given public feedback about the pattern of their own and others' judgments (that is, their *judgment policies*), as the context within which they try to reach agreement using more or less free interaction. They have conducted an extensive, systematic program of research to develop and apply their techniques and to explore the findings they yielded. (See Brehmer, 1976, for an excellent review of this work.) The social judgment theory model, derived from Brunswick's (1955) lens model, construes judgments of complex environmental patterns or events in the following way: complex environmental events or patterns "give off" or are indicated by a variety of cues, but only probabilistically. For example, if a certain set of cues is present, a certain environmental condition is *likely*, but not surely, going to occur. (Where there is smoke there is *probably* fire.) People use the cues when they make judgments of the events, but again, only probabilistically. The social judgment model involves a set of criterion events; a set of cues; and a set of judgments about those events, based on observation of those cues, by a set of judges.

The model implies four components: (a) an *organizing principle* by which cues (stimuli serving as indicators of those environmental events) are combined (often assumed to be linear or additive); (b) *weights,* reflecting the relative importance of various cues as used in various people's judgments; (c) *function forms,* referring to the form of actual relation between cues and the criterion environmental events, and between cues and judgments; and (d) *consistency* or predictability with which cues predict events and judgments, given the proper function form.

When two or more judges are trying to arrive at agreement on a common problem, their disagreement may be based on underlying differences in the *structure* of their judgments—the way cues are weighted, the organizing principle, and the function form—even with the same cues (e.g., the same evidence in a trial). This pattern or structure of judgments is called the judge's *judgment policy;* and SJT proponents call these differences *cognitive conflicts.* (See EXRT 7.)

Research on these cognitive conflicts is done either (a) by training individuals in different judgment policies (e.g., by training them to give high weights to different cues, or to relate cues to criteria by different functional forms), and then bringing them together to reach a group decision on problems of the same class; or (b) by finding people who already are using different judgment policies and bringing them together for group decisions. The SJT researchers argue that although the real world offers a vast supply of persons and tasks for which such cognitive conflicts exist, manipulating differences in judgment policy by training seems a more efficient research strategy. For one thing, the investigator can know in advance the nature, form and extent of the conflicting policies, and can replicate the same pattern of cognitive conflict for many sets of individuals. While SJT could, in principle, be applied to groups of any size, much of the research has used two-person groups.

EXRT 7:   *THE HAMMOND–BREHMER SOCIAL JUDGMENT THEORY (SJT) PARADIGM.*

Main Study Procedures: Subjects are assigned to groups (usually two-person) and are asked to make a series of decisions that require them to make inductive inferences from a set of available information (i.e., a set of cues), each piece of which is imperfectly correlated with the criterion. For example, they may be deciding on the suitability of a set of job candidates, or a set of graduate school applications. A test score, or grade average, is information related to probable success, but imperfectly. The members of each group differ from each other in terms of how they view the specific judgments involved—the importance of various cues, how those cues should be combined, and so forth. These differences arise either because they have received differential training in an earlier stage of the study, or because they were selected in terms of their different viewpoints (or judgment policies). The subjects are asked to make a set of judgments individually. The experimenter may then give each individual feedback on own and partner's "judgment policies" (i.e., weights assigned to different cues; combination rule for combining cues, etc.). They then work together in a group, discussing each case until they reach a joint decision on it. The experimenter then gives them the correct answer (in terms of some "outside expert" criterion in most cases), and the group moves on to the next problem.

Main Dependent Variables of Interest: Agreement among group members; changes in aspects of members' judgment policies (attribute weights, cue-attribute correlations, etc.); interpersonal trust.

Main Variations: Patterns of differences in judgment policies; selected versus trained differences; actual (ecological) pattern of relation among cues, attributes, and so forth.

References: Brehmer (1976); Hammond, et al. (1966, 1975).

In the group part of the study, for each criterion item (environmental event), subjects are asked (a) to study the case (i.e., the evidence); (b) to make individual judgments of the criterion (environmental events), presumably following their different pre-study or pre-trained judgment policies; (c) to communicate to each other; and, (d) if their judgments don't agree, to discuss the case until they reach a joint judgment acceptable to both (or all) of them. Then, they are informed of the correct answer, and another "case" of the same general type is presented.

Brehmer (1976) points out that such differences of viewpoint represent a very benign form of conflict. Subjects have no differences of interest; neither can profit at the other's expense. Yet disagreements in such cases apparently are very difficult to resolve. One basic finding of early studies in this program (Hammond, et al., 1966) was that there seemed to be little or no reduction in disagreement over a twenty-trial sequence. But when these authors used their full model (their application of Brunswick's lens model) to analyze the underlying structure of those judgments, a different picture emerged. Apparently, subjects are very quick to reduce systematic differences between their policies. But shifts from their prior (or well practiced) policies led to increased *inconsistency* in applications of the newly adopted policy. By the end of the sessions, there was little change in the *amount* of disagreement (as noted above) but there was a dramatic change in the *structure* of disagreement. At the outset, disagreement arose because the subjects used (experimentally trained) different judgment policies, but used them consistently. By the end, subjects had shifted to reduce or eliminate policy differences, but they used their new policies inconsistently, and that inconsistency produced as much disagreement as there had been before. This finding is apparently quite robust; Brehmer (1976) notes a number of studies under a variety of conditions for which it held. These include studies done in nonlaboratory settings using natural groups. This counterintuitive finding suggests that one result of group interaction process in these cases is a shift toward uniform judgment policy (which increases agreement), but a simultaneous decrease in consistency of application of judgment policy (which decreases agreement).

Further explorations of these matters led to another nonintuitive finding, namely, that subjects abandon their prior policies too rapidly, rather than hang on to noneffective policies too long. The problem arises because they abandon the old, nonworking policies before they have learned new policies. The new policies are those that will both yield agreement with partner *and* yield success against the outside criterion values (that is, the "correct" answers, as known to the experimenter). This situation apparently arises because people respond more rapidly to a decrease in validity of a cue than to an increase in validity of a cue. If there is a decrease in validity of a cue to which a participant is giving a lot of weight, this leads directly to error feedback. But if there is an increase in validity of a cue to which S is not giving much weight, this change must be inferred from the *lack* of a shift in error feedback. For the same reasons, a person can detect what cues the other is *not* using faster than he or she can detect what cues the other is using. SJT theorists argue that this expresses a general principle of change in judging probabilistic environments.

Brehmer (1976) further argues that these results suggest a new way of considering why groups often suffer serious disruption, and sometimes disintegrate, when environmental conditions change. Such outcomes are usually discussed either in terms of motivational forces (i.e., conflicts of interest), in terms of systematic differences in policy, or in terms of members' inability to change previous ways. The results discussed here suggest that the reason for disintegration may be that the process of change produces inconsistency, and that the unpredictability arising from inconsistent use of shared policies is more difficult for group members to deal with effectively than was the more predictable situation of consistent use of differing policies. When two group members are using consistent but differing policies, verbal interactions can and usually do lead to clarification of why the differences occur, to an understanding of the other's judgments, and sometimes to a resolution of those differences in cognitive views (policies). But when two group members are *inconsistently* making judgments based on *explicitly similar* policies, verbal interaction leads to a distrust of, and a reduction in understanding of, the other.

Why do participants change their prior judgment policies so readily in this situation—to increase accuracy or to reduce conflict? In many studies the two cannot be distinguished. Brehmer, Hammond and colleagues conducted a series of studies that let the two be assessed separately (by training one S in a valid policy and the others in invalid ones). Results show the following: (a) participants change policy to achieve increased accuracy, not to reduce conflict (since only the participant with the "wrong" policy changed), in tasks for which predictability is high (i.e., where the *best* use of cues predicts criteria well); (b) when the task has low predictability, both change, but this may occur because the participant with the "right" policy may not be able to tell that it is correct under these low predictability conditions, and therefore may still be changing to attain accuracy; (c) when participants get no feedback (hence, can't judge accuracy), they "compromise" much as they do when each has equally valid policies. This may again be because, in the absence of feedback, they try to increase accuracy by learning from each other, or it may be because, in the absence of feedback, they compromise to reduce conflict. Brehmer (1976) goes on to point out that, in most real cognitive conflict tasks there is liable to be low predictability and little feedback, and in many instances the criterion for the task is determined by the intentions of the participants.

Brehmer (1976) explores the effect of task differences on such cognitive conflicts. *Substantive* differences in tasks (e.g., admission policies, or stock choices, or budget allocations) apparently do not yield different effects. But differences in *formal* characteristics of the task have major effects. Brehmer offers seven formal properties of these tasks. The first three are surface characteristics, referring to characteristics of the task that are directly observable by the participants: (a) *number of cues;* (b) *metric level of cues* (i.e., is the information in quantitative or qualitative form?); and (c) the *intercorrelations among the cues.* The other four are called system characteristics, and refer to the relations between the cues and the criterion: (d) the *distribution of validities of the various cues,* that is, are all cues equally important, or are some very good and some very poor predictors? (e) the *function forms* relating cues to criterion (e.g., linear or nonlinear); (f) the *organizing principle* (additive or configural) by which the weighted cues are combined; and (g) the *predictability of the criterion,* given the optimal organizing principle and function forms. All of the SJT research thus far has used additive organizing principles (task characteristic f). Several studies indicate that results are consistent over one, two, three, or four cues (task characteristic a) and for nonmetric (qualitative) as well as quantitative cues (task characteristic b). Judgments are less consistent—hence, there is more disagreement—on tasks with low predictability (task characteristic g), that is, on tasks with high uncertainty. Consistency is also lower on tasks with nonlinear function form (task characteristic e), apparently because nonlinear function forms (actually, nonmonotonic as well, in these studies) are harder to use than linear functions. (They are also harder to learn.) Policy similarity is not affected by distribution of validity of cues (task characteristic d) but judgment consistency is affected by that factor. Judgments are more consistent if only one cue needs to be used (that is, if one cue is highly valid and the others are not). Differences in cue intercorrelations (task characteristic c) pose several interesting points. If cues are positively correlated with one another, then two judges can *agree, and be equally accurate,* using different cues and judgment policies. This lets agreement on the individual instance mask disagreement in principle. It also lets an individual have a high level of "accuracy" using invalid cues. So, with tasks where there is high positive intercorrelation among cues, we would expect participants to show judgment agreement but less change in policy and less policy agreement. Studies following up this prediction support it. They also show that low policy shift occurs because these cue intercorrelations yield a high level of accuracy without policy change, rather than just because there is a high degree of judgment agreement between persons. As with other aspects, these task differences suggest that *policy changes are in the service of increasing accuracy, not reducing conflict.*

Several studies of real cases of conflict (labor management; community groups and municipal agency; within-organization conflict) using the SJT approach indicate that these findings are not artifacts of the lab. (See Brehmer, 1976, for a review of those studies.) The cognitive conflicts could reasonably be described in terms of the SJT model. Disagreements could be attributed to inconsistency, which increased after communication that reduced policy differences. Participants, on their own, could not identify the true nature of the differences; but cognitive aids developed within SJT theory helped resolve these differences. These aids involve detailed feedback to participants of the structure of judgment policies being used by themselves and by the other participants.

OTHER CONFLICT-OF-VIEWPOINT TASKS

The tasks that would logically fit into this cognitive conflict task category are not limited to those studied by SJT methods, which require a very elaborate problem structure, usually quantitatively expressed. As previously noted, Davis (1980) suggests that some jury problems might well be regarded as involving populations with conflicting viewpoints as well as specific judgment disagreements.

There are many real world decision problems that are made by groups under conditions where there are major differences among the members in cognitive viewpoints or judgment policies. Legislatures, for example, at city, state, national and international levels, often deal with issues for which such cognitive conflict holds. It is certainly the case that legislatures sometimes operate under conflict of interest conditions (e.g., what is good for one party is bad for an opposing party). But it is also the case that, very often, members of a legislature do *not* have differing and conflicting interests; rather, they share the same goals (e.g., helping the country reduce inflation) but have major differences in their beliefs about how to attain that goal (i.e., they have different judgment policies). One of them might give much weight to tax cuts; another might view budget balancing as crucial; still another might stress low unemployment; still another might want aggressive international monetary policies. They might all agree on the general merit of certain features—who can be against a balanced budget, or in favor of high taxes or high unemployment?

But they might disagree sharply (and even unknowingly) on how important they thought each of those to be in terms of achieving the common goal.

Such is often the case, as well, for groups trying to plan a variety of kinds of programs. On a board of directors of a company, for example, the fiscal officers might give great weight to cost and cash demands in regard to every issue on the agenda; the production specialists might view every issue in terms of how much it might help or overburden the production facilities; the personnel specialists might try to treat each issue in terms of its impact on company/union relations. All have the same goals. None can profit at the expense of the others. Yet they might profoundly disagree, not only on what is the best alternative for each of a series of agenda items, but more fundamentally, on what are the important criteria on which to base company policy.

It can be argued, of course, that in some sense such board members, or legislators, do have conflicting interests. If they can prevail, they will have gained some immediate power. If their view turns out to be correct (successful) they can gain some longer-run credibility, while those who supported different (and losing) views will have lost power and credibility. It can even be argued that there is always some degree of competition among members of a group, under all kinds of tasks and situational conditions. In that view, members of all groups, even those trying to solve intellectual problems together for a common pay-off (as in task type 3), are in both cooperative and competitive relationships with one another. Whether that is a useful perspective to take depends, in part, on one's purposes. For purposes of this book, it seems to me much more useful to distinguish between tasks that themselves do not *force* a competition between members (such as the intellective and decision-making tasks already noted, and the planning and creativity tasks to be discussed later), whether or not individuals nevertheless "compete" for prominence and status within the group; and those tasks that directly pit the interests of different group members against one another (as in the negotiation tasks of type 6, and contests of type 7, to be discussed in the next two chapters). It seems useful, moreover, to recognize that there is a middle ground or grey area where there is conflict among members, more fundamental than just different content positions on an issue, but nevertheless common interest and agreement on common goals. The task type here considered is in this grey area. In the next chapter, attention shifts to tasks for which the mixed-motive and conflicting interest of group members are center stage.

CHAPTER NINE
MIXED-MOTIVE TASKS: RESOLVING CONFLICTS OF INTEREST AMONG GROUP MEMBERS (TASK TYPE 6)

While the preceding task type dealt with problems for which group members had conflicting cognitive viewpoints (judgment policies), it was presumed throughout that discussion, as it had been for discussions of decision-making and intellective tasks, that all parties shared common interests/goals/motives. The pay-off structure of the situation (at least for the experimental laboratory studies) was such that members could not profit at one another's expense, nor did they have any stake in their own "policies." Yet those tasks led to conflicts that were very hard to resolve even under favorable conditions. We turn now to a category involving tasks based on conflicts between members' interests, motives, pay-offs—tasks that potentially yield much more disruptive disagreements.

The tasks of this category have received extensive research attention. They can be divided into four subtypes. As was the case for some previous task types, these subtypes shade in a step by step progression from some tasks near the cognitive conflict boundary (with the conflict involving a considerable cognitive as well as motivational component) through some purely motivational or mixed-motive conflicts, to tasks approaching the unbridled competition of the next task category (contests). The four subtypes, in order of that progression, are:

1. *Negotiation tasks.* These involve disagreements between two or more parties on a complex set of factors, such that resolution can involve trade-offs on multiple dimensions of pay-off and need not be "zero-sum" (that is, what one wins the other loses).

2. *Bargaining tasks.* These involve disputes regarding the positions of two or more parties on a single dimension—usually quantified, often in dollars or other pay-off units, and necessarily zero-sum.

3. *Dilemma tasks.* These involve tasks where the *choices* made by the two or more parties—usually simultaneously or at least independently of one another—*jointly* determine the outcomes of each of them, so that each one's pay-offs depend on one's own *and* the other's choices (i.e., the parties are interdependent in outcomes).

4. *Winning Coalition and Pay-off Allocation tasks.* These involve tasks in which subsets of members can form a *winning coalition* that totally controls pay-offs, and thereby deny any positive pay-offs to persons excluded from the coalition, while at the same time *allocating pay-offs* among members of the winning coalition in ways that may reflect their relative power or strength or resources.

These four subtypes are listed in an order in which, increasingly, the members stand in greater and greater conflict of motives with one another. This order reflects both an increase in the degree to which *others' actions* affect one's own outcome, and an increase in the degree to which *others' outcomes* affect one's own outcomes. They shift, in other words, from differences in values or preferences for alternative resolutions (similar to the preceding task category) to flatout pay-off disputes to be resolved on the basis of power differences (similar to the next task category).

While the first two—negotiation and bargaining—are worth separating for conceptual purposes, in fact the research literature of the two overlaps a great deal, and the terms are used interchangeably by many researchers. So they are discussed together. There is somewhat less overlap in literature between the dilemma tasks and bargaining and negotiation tasks; and the literature on coalition and allocation tasks is quite separate from the others.

Note that in shifting from the previous task type to this one, we have shifted from conditions where we assume that all group members share the same goals and motives, at least with regard to the focal task (although it is understood that members might have some additional goals, not necessarily tied to success on the group's task). Specifically, all task types considered previously presume that all group members *want the same outcome for the group*—the "correct" answer, the "right" verdict, and so on. The tasks about to be discussed are designed so that what is the best outcome for one member is not the best outcome for one or more other group members. Members' interests are pitted against each other. Yet, the tasks are such that each member's behavior affects his or her own *and* others' outcomes—in other words, members are interdependent regarding outcomes. No one can achieve good outcomes by his or her own unilateral actions; each needs the cooperation of the other(s) to get desirable outcomes (or avoid undesirable ones). So, besides putting members' interests in conflict, these tasks are also designed so that members are motivated to cooperate. They are sometimes referred to as mixed-motive tasks, in contrast to the tasks of the previous categories that are assumed to evoke purely cooperative motives; and in contrast to the tasks of the next category (contests) and perhaps even of the last subtype in this category (winning coalition and pay-off allocation tasks), that are designed to arouse purely competitive motives.

BARGAINING AND NEGOTIATION TASKS

One form in which conflicts of interest have been conceptualized and studied is in terms of tasks that require individuals to bargain or negotiate with one another. These are tasks where two or more persons (parties) representing two or more different sets of interests (proposed outcomes) have to resolve differences and agree upon an outcome. (If parties don't agree to some outcome, the bargaining or negotiation is stalemated and the rewards involved are withheld from all parties. "No resolution," here, is akin to a hung jury in certain ways, but usually it has much more negative consequences.)

Bargaining and negotiation tasks differ from each other in certain ways. Although the two terms are used interchangeably by some researchers, and differentiated from each other in a variety of different ways by other researchers, I want to distinguish between bargaining and negotiation in terms of whether the parties are trying to resolve their disagreement (by bargaining) along a single dimension (often quantified, usually in monetary terms); or whether they are trying to resolve differences (by negotiation) on multiple issues and/or along multiple dimensions. This distinction treats bargaining as a limiting (one-issue-one-outcome-dimension) case of negotiation. Obviously, within a set of negotiations between two or more parties, the participants may choose to separate out one issue and "bargain" about it on one dimension, in isolation from the rest of the negotiation agenda. Conversely, they may try to resolve their position differences on one dimension or issue by trading it off against other issues (a practice called logrolling in the political arena). So, two important features of these tasks are (a) whether the task involves only one or many issues or dimensions of dispute (that is, whether it is a bargaining or a negotiation task); and (b) whether the issues or dimensions are dealt with one at a time in isolation (bargained), or collectively as a set (negotiated). Three additional important features are (c) the strategy of the opponent; (d) whether the negotiators are working solely for their own interests or are representing a broader constituency; and (e) whether a third party has intervened or might intervene to help resolve the task, and if so, what degree of control (e.g., as observer, mediator, arbitrator) does that third party exercise. (See EXRTs 8 and 9.)

One critical problem in negotiation and bargaining is how to get each party to give up some of its ideal solution (i.e., to make concessions) in order to reach agreement. There are two quite different theoretical views about how B's strategy affects A's willingness to make concessions. Siegal and Fouracker (1960) propose a model based on level of aspiration, which assumes that concessions by one party, A, raise the level of aspiration (expectations) of the other party (B), which in turn will evoke a tougher stance by B. Hence, one should "bargain tough" if one wants to induce concessions from the other. Osgood's GRIT model (e.g., 1962) arrives at a distinctly different conclusion. (GRIT stands for Gradual, Reciprocal, International Tension-reduction). Osgood argues that, *if negotiations are deadlocked,* one side must initiate a small concession and wait for the other to reciprocate. It is assumed that such reciprocated concessions will gradually be increased until an agreement is reached.

EXRT 8:   *MCGRATH'S NEGOTIATION PARADIGM*

Main Study Procedures: Subjects are drawn from separate pools of "constituents" of different "parties" or interest groups. They are put into negotiation groups made up of one or more negotiators from each party to the conflict of interest (e.g., labor versus management groups; different religious groups). A third-party representative may also be included, drawn from a constituency that is neutral or nonpartisan with respect to the issues/topics of concern. Each negotiator is charged with serving as a representative of a particular party to the dispute, and with attaining the best outcome for that party that he or she can from the negotiations. Negotiation topics are issues on which the parties disagree, and on which a multi-party agreement or decision is necessary for any outcome (otherwise, the negotiation is aborted). But outcomes are not necessarily zero-sum games nor are all the dimensions along which bargaining can take place specified in the problem materials.

Main Dependent Variables of Interest: Quality of negotiation solutions, as evaluated by each party and by third parties; time to solution and whether one is obtained; interpersonal relations among negotiation group members; evaluations of negotiators by their constituents.

Main Variations: Number of contending parties; presence and role (e.g., as arbitrator, as mediator) of third-party representatives; relation of negotiators to their constituents (e.g., formal members; holders of common attitudes; legal representatives); characteristics of negotiators and their relations to each other; complexity of negotiation tasks.

References: McGrath (1966); McGrath & Julian (1963); Morley & Stephenson (1977); Vidmar & McGrath (1970).

There is some support for both theories (e.g., Pilisuk & Skolnick, 1968). But the support for the Siegal and Fouracker "bargain tough" model comes from studies where there was not a decided deadlock, whereas studies tend to support Osgood's GRIT model as applicable *after* such a deadlock. It is not at all unreasonable that *both* theories have some validity—one before, and presumably preventing, deadlock; the other after, and presumably because of, such deadlocks. (Some of the discussion of third-party mediation later in this section will relate to these same issues.)

In many negotiation situations, the persons in the negotiation groups are representatives of a party, or group, or constituency beyond themselves. This is the case for labor/management negotiations, for international negotiations, and for many kinds of inter-organization agreements on economic and political matters. When the negotiators are representatives, in this sense, they can be actual members of the represented constituencies or merely outsiders serving as agents. For any one person, there are really two groups involved: (a) the group whose interests are to be represented, the constituency; and (b) the negotiation group itself. The first is a standing group; the second, with mostly different members, is an acting group. In some cases, the negotiator is agent for, but not

EXRT 9:   *THE BARGAINING PARADIGM*

Main Study Procedures: Two subjects are assigned as opponents to bargain about how much pay-off each of them will receive, under conditions in which there is a fixed total pay-off (that is, it is a zero-sum game, except that, if there is no agreement, no one receives any pay-off). They may or may not be asked to represent a hypothetical or simulated organization.

Main Dependent Variables of Interest: Absolute and relative gains of individuals over a series of trials; interpersonal perceptions of opponents; responses to different bargaining strategies; frequency of no-solution trials.

Main Variations: Size of pay-offs; number of trials; characteristics of bargainers; instructions and prior training and experience.

References: Morley & Stephenson (1977); Siegal & Fouracker (1960); Swingle (1970); Walton & McKersie (1965).

---

member of, that standing group. In some cases there is interaction between the constituents and the negotiator (the constituent group becomes an acting group) in a first stage, followed by a negotiation between representatives of the contending parties in a second stage. (See Table 9–1).

When people negotiate as representatives of a constituent group, and feel role-obligated to and accountable to that group (cases III, IV, V, and VI, as opposed to cases I and II, in Table 9–1) they are apt to be more competitive; likely to make smaller (fewer) concessions; less likely to accept offers that depart from the constituent group's positions; and, perforce, less likely to reach agreement. If negotiators meet with constituents to discuss the issue (cases III and V) and/or form a prior commitment (cases I, III, and V), they are likely to take an even more extreme and more competitive position. This has been attributed to a "group-induced shift"; and that would be compatible with the group-induced polarization effects discussed in chapters seven and seventeen. It has also been attributed to a "social categorization" that yields a "pro-ingroup, anti-out-

TABLE 9-1   Types of Relation of Negotiator to Represented Position

	NEGOTIATOR IS REPRESENTING ONLY SELF	NEGOTIATOR IS REPRESENTING A CONSTITUENCY:	
		AS A MEMBER OF IT	AS AN OUTSIDER
Negotiator meets with constituents and/or forms position prior to negotiations.	Case I	Case III	Case V
Negotiator does not meet with constituents nor form position prior to negotiations.	Case II	Case IV	Case VI

group'' bias. Brewer (1979), in a review, suggests that such ingroup-outgroup biases derive largely from increases in positive feelings toward the ingroup, rather than negative feelings toward the outgroup. That would not seem to lead, necessarily, to increased competitiveness. But Brewer also suggests that the mere fact of ingroup "categorization" may lead to competitiveness with an outgroup.

Negotiators are also more competitive when any of the following conditions hold:

1. they think they are distrusted by constituents;
2. they were elected;
3. they are being observed by a superordinate in the organization, or by constituents;
4. they have a prior commitment;
5. their constituents are competitively oriented; and/or
6. their constituents are a highly cohesive group.

A few studies have been done on the effects of being represented by a negotiator who is not a member of the constituency group (see Breaugh & Klimonski, 1977; Klimonski & Breaugh, 1977). Negotiators who are members of the constituency group (case IV), especially if they have helped develop a pre-negotiation position (case III), experience more difficulty in negotiating than do outsiders (cases V and VI). Constituents react more favorably to outsider negotiators when they have obtained favorable results, and when their outcomes hew closely to the group's position, compared to outsiders who have had less success and whose solutions have departed more from the group's stand. But constituents tend to *reject outsiders,* and to *fail to ratify* agreements they reach, compared to member-negotiators who have obtained the same "objective" degree of success. So, outsider-negotiators feel (or act) free to maneuver in the bargaining, but are less often supported by the constituents. Or, alternatively, member-negotiators feel more committed to the group's prior position and less free to vary from it, but they and the agreements they reach more often receive group support.

There has been a lot of research on how agreements are affected by intervention of a third party, the anticipation of such intervention, and the kind of intervention. Those studies often compare third-party intervention of various degrees of control. They may compare, for example, no third party; intervention by a mediator (who tries to facilitate a solution but does not impose one); intervention by various levels of arbitration (a third party that imposes a solution). Rubin (1980), in an excellent recent review, presents three "strands" that he believes run through this fairly large literature, and that seem to make a sensible interpretation of it. The first "strand" is that third parties provide a mechanism for negotiators to make concessions without loss of face. This seems to occur even if the third party has a very passive role. This permits deadlocked negotiations to get unstuck, as Osgood's GRIT does, and keeps concessions from being interpreted as weakness. Rubin's second strand states that certain frequently used third-party intervention techniques (such as increased inter-party communication; negotiating the whole set of problems at once rather than one at a time; and procedures for identifying the underlying issues) seem to work well when conflict is relatively low but may backfire under more intense conflict.

Rubin's third strand has several parts. First, parties regard third-party intervention as an unwelcome intrusion and will resolve issues without it if they can. It turns out that under relatively low levels of conflict, the *anticipation* of a threat of intervention leads to progress toward resolution—the more so, the more "controlling" the type of threatened third-party intervention. At the same time, under high levels of conflict, when negotiators anticipate third-party intervention, they tend to freeze into their positions—the more so, the more controlling the form of anticipated intervention. This is interpreted as being an attempt to save face by turning responsibility for the problem over to the third party. Once such intervention occurs, however, third-party intervention lets the negotiators make more concessions than they otherwise would, especially under high conflict conditions; and this tends to be more so the more controlling the form of third-party intervention. Some of these strands, or related notions, will arise in discussion of the other subtypes of conflict tasks, later in this chapter. (For other good reviews and analysis of the negotiation and bargaining area see Morley & Stephenson, 1977; Rubin & Brown, 1975; Walten & McKersie, 1965; Swingle, 1970.)

DILEMMA AND MIXED-MOTIVE GAMES

This task subtype is exemplified by, and a very large proportion of the research in this category was conducted within the mixed-motive matrix game known as the prisoner's dilemma (and several variants of it). The game gets its name from an anecdote about two alleged criminal partners who were arrested, placed out of communication with each other, and propositioned by the sheriff as follows: "The state has a pat case for convicting both of you on a serious charge, but perhaps not on the most serious of the charges against you. If *one* of you turns state's evidence, we will let that one off on a lesser charge with a minor sentence, but throw the book at the other. Of course, if *both* confess and turn state's evidence, both will be given a heavy sentence." While the sheriff in this anecdote probably violated the prisoners' rights, he nevertheless posed a serious dilemma for each of them. The dilemma faced by each prisoner is as follows: If both refuse to cooperate, each will suffer a serious sentence (call this R). If one confesses, but the other doesn't, the one who confesses gets off easy (outcome T) but the partner will get a very serious sentence (outcome S). But if both confess, both will be heavily sentenced (P).

This dilemma is displayed in 2 x 2 matrix in Table 9–2, first in terms of the prisoner's dilemma, then in a general form (using R, S, T, and P as pay-offs), and finally with a set of specific pay-off numbers as an example.

It turns out that when two experimental subjects "play" such a game, for a series of trials, there is a very strong tendency for them to end up in the P/P cell where both lose. From each player's point of view, to choose C (cooperate with the other player) could lead to a favorable outcome (R) but risks being double-crossed, yielding unfavorable outcome S. On the other hand, to not

TABLE 9-2   Mixed-Motive Game Matrix

A. THE PRISONER'S DILEMMA MATRIX

Prisoner A's Choices

		STAND FAST	CONFESS
Stand Fast		A gets medium sentence R / B gets medium sentence R	A, very heavy sentence, S / B, light sentence, T
Confess		A, light sentence, T / B, very heavy sentence, S	A, heavy sentence, P / B, heavy sentence, P

Prisoner B's Choices

B. THE GENERAL PDG MATRIX

		PLAYER A	
		COOPERATE	DEFECT
PLAYER B	Cooperate	R / R	S / T
	Defect	T / S	P / P

C. AN ILLUSTRATIVE PDG PAY-OFF MATRIX

		PLAYER A	
		C	D
PLAYER B	C'	5 / 5	-10 / 10
	D'	10 / -10	-5 / -5

Top entry, A's pay-off; lower entry, B's pay-off. T>R>P>S for prisoner's dilemma. For "maximizing difference" game R>T>S>P. For "chicken" game: T>R>S>P

cooperate (to choose D—used for the idea of "defecting") could lead to the highest individual pay-off (T), if the partner stays "faithful," but risks a very poor outcome (P) if the partner also chooses D. What is the highest potential pay-off for A, considered alone, is not only not best for the joint A and B outcome, even if B "cooperates" (that is, T plus S is less than R plus R); but it is an undesirable outcome for A as well as B if B also goes for his or her best individual gain alternative. (See EXRT 10).

EXRT 10:   *THE PRISONER'S DILEMMA GAME (PDG)*

Main Study Procedures: Two players, A and B, are asked to choose one of two alternatives, under conditions where the pay-off that each receives depends on the pair of alternatives chosen. Alternatives are often labelled C (for cooperate) and D (for defect). Pay-offs are arranged so that if both choose C, each gets a favorable and equal pay-off; if one chooses D and the other chooses C, the player choosing D gets a highly favorable pay-off and the one choosing C gets a very negative pay-off; and if both choose D, both get equally negative pay-offs.

Main Dependent Variables of Interest: Pattern of A and B choices over trials; individual and joint pay-offs over trials; response strategies used and reactions to specific strategies or patterns of response by the partner.

Main Variations: Size and pattern of pay-offs; number of trials; characteristics of players and of partners; experimentally imposed strategies of the partner; instructional sets (e.g., to maximize own gain, to maximize own relative gain, to maximize joint gain).

References: Komorita (1973); Pruitt & Kimmel (1977); Rapoport (1967); Rapoport & Orwant (1962); Shubik (1964).

The prisoner's dilemma game (PDG) is one of a family of mixed-motive games that have been developed within mathematical game theory (see, Rapoport, 1967; Rapoport & Orwant, 1962; Shubik, 1964) and "imported" into social psychology for the study of social conflict in groups. To both game theorists and group researchers, this matrix game seemed to capture much of the *strategic* complexity of many aspects of real life conflict, while at the same time avoiding many of the substantive particulars that confound research evidence. For example, it is not an international conflict, nor a family conflict, nor a labor/management dispute, but it is *like* them, in some strategic ways. But the PDG (and its cousins, the "maximizing difference" game and the game of "chicken") have served two different purposes in mathematical game theory and in group research. For the game theorists, the PDG pay-off matrix was a device designed to help specify the player's best (that is, most rational) strategy. They are interested in what players *should* do—assuming their only motive is to maximize their own gain. (This is called a *normative* model, a model of what *should* occur.) For group researchers the PDG was a device to pose dilemma choices for individuals, to try to determine what people *do,* and what conditions (e.g., what variations in pay-offs, in instructions, in relations of the partners, etc.) will alter what they do. Group researchers are seeking a *descriptive* model rather than a normative model. This difference becomes important, for example, when persons in the two fields try to generalize from experimental studies to "real" situations.

Is the PDG a group situation? Yes and no. It does not represent the interaction of a set of two or more people with "past history of and expectation for future interaction." But, then, neither do many ad hoc experimentally concocted groups—including some "real" groups, such as actual juries. It is not a group in the sense that the members have a common goal—that there is one outcome that they all prefer. But, then, this may also be true of groups with cognitive conflict, or decision-making groups such as juries (real or mock). Persons in a PDG are a group in the sense that they are *interdependent*. The outcomes of each depend on the actions of both. And they engage in *interaction*. Each takes into account the behavior and situation of the other, and the behavior of each is responsive to prior behavior of the other. PDG players are not a group in the sense that they don't have a desired common product; but they are a group in the sense that the group must produce a *joint* outcome for any member to have an outcome. We might say that, for the PDG, there is no standing group but there is an acting group. In terms of the discussion in chapter 4, it is a quasi-group with both communication and task structure restricted.

There has been a torrent of research on dilemma tasks since the early 1960s. Most of it has used the PDG or a close variant; used two players; used "points" as pay-offs; and used college students as subjects in a laboratory setting. Apfelbaum (1974) and Pruitt and Kimmel (1977) present good reviews of group research on dilemma games, and also offer some theoretical generalizations about that work. I draw heavily on their reviews in the following summary of major findings:

1. Under normal conditions, most PDG groups will gravitate toward the DD' choice. Each player will make more D than C choices.

2. Instructions (e.g., to seek maximum joint pay-off; to beat the other player; etc.) will shift the proportion of C choices in the expected direction.

3. Female pairs play PDG *more competitively* than male pairs—but males and females do not differ in mixed-gender pairs. This is a counterintuitive finding, considering the gender differences found in social influence studies and in coalition studies (see later part of this chapter). It is also counterintuitive considering the general stereotypes about male and female behavior in our culture.

4. Shift in the relative sizes of pay-offs (among R, S, T, and P) will shift the proportion of C choices as expected. Players will "defect" more if there is more to gain by doing so. Komorita (1973) calls this the "temptation to defect." There is little evidence that shifts in absolute sizes of pay-offs have effects, but the range of such pay-offs is limited in experimental games. There is evidence that the use of money rather than points increases cooperation at least somewhat.

5. Opportunity to communicate with the partner, and sometimes even visual presence of the partner that provides eye contact, as well as pre-game observation of other pairs playing a PDG, all increase the proportion of C choices, and the joint pay-offs obtained. (Remember that the sheriff who posed the prisoners their dilemma kept them incommunicado!)

6. In general, *situational* factors—pay-offs, instructions, strategy or behavior of the partner—have much more powerful effects on the proportion of C choices than do *personal* factors (e.g., gender, status, personality characteristics, even pre-game preferences for competition or cooperation). Moreover, there is not a high correspondence between how cooperative a given person is in PDG and in other mixed-motive tasks.

7. The most crucial factor influencing the PDG player is the strategy of the partner. A consistently competitive strategy by B (always choosing D') leads to consistently competitive choices (D) by A. But a consistently cooperative strategy by B (always choosing C') apparently invites exploitation, also leading to a high level of D choices by A. A *contingent* strategy by B (often called a tit for tat strategy) in

which B imitates A's response of the preceding trial, induces maximum C choices by A, and leads to maximum joint pay-offs by the pair.

8. The proportion of C choices shows a U-shaped function over a long series of trials. After the first few trials, while players are presumably still exploring the game, the proportion of C choices drops and stays low; after many trials (thirty or so) the proportion of C often climbs to a higher level and stays there.

9. The proportion of C choices is higher when the partner is a real and present person than when the partner is known by the subject to be a computer, or a preprogrammed set of responses.

10. Having a partner who is a friend (or someone similar to self), compared to having a stranger (or someone dissimilar to self) as a partner, does not affect the proportion of C choices immediately, but does increase the proportion of C choices later in the trial series.

Apfelbaum (1974) and Pruitt and Kimmel (1977) integrate and interpret these and other findings in ways that seem quite compatible. Both see the partner's responsiveness as crucial. Pruitt and Kimmel argue that, as a first step, player A must adopt a *goal of mutual cooperation*. Presumably, this happens after a costly period of mutual noncooperation, during which each player learns that the partner can't be exploited, and that mutual noncooperation is mutually costly. The second step is for A to develop the expectation that B also has adopted a goal of mutual cooperation. A then may *initiate cooperation* with the expectation that B will reciprocate. (See discussion of Osgood's GRIT in an earlier section of this chapter). Apfelbaum deals with these same phenomena in terms of B's responsivity to A's choices, and A's perception of B's responsivity. If A perceives (correctly) that B is reactive to A's choices, that means that B is willing to be cooperative, but cannot be exploited; and that B's behavior is predictable and controllable by A. Hence, A's best course is to respond so as to induce C choices from B. Hence, A and B end up in the CC' cell, and thereby increase joint pay-off.

Pruitt and Kimmel (1977) summarize the conditions that favor the development of the *goal of mutual cooperation* as (a) experience with the PDG over time, involving mutual noncooperation; (b) time to think about the pay-off matrix; (c) being shown the PDG pay-offs in a form that enhances the perception of interdependence (what are called decomposed prisoner's dilemma matrices; see, e.g., McClintock, Messick, Kuhlman & Campos, 1973); (d) when temptation to defect is low; (e) when pay-offs in CC' are equitable outcomes to A and B; (f) when decisions can be reversed; (g) when A and B communicate; (h) when B uses a tit for tat or highly contingent and responsive strategy; (i) when A sees B as stronger and self as dependent on other for pay-offs. Pruitt and Kimmel list the conditions that favor development of the *expectation that the other will cooperate* as:

1. when A knows that B has recently or consistently cooperated;
2. when A has sent or received a message requesting or assuring cooperation;
3. when A knows that B's pay-offs or instructions favor cooperation;
4. when A sees B as dependent;
5. when B uses a tit for tat or other highly responsive strategy; and
6. when A sees B as similar or as a friend.

OTHER MIXED–MOTIVE TASKS

While the PDG has dominated the research in this problem area, there is some research done in each of three other paradigms: (a) a "trucking" game; (b) a many-person dilemma game; and (c) models of social traps. The "trucking game" was developed to study interpersonal conflict (see Deutsch, 1949a, 1949b; Deutsch & Krauss, 1962). In this task, players represent two trucking companies (Acme and Bolt), each with the task of moving truckloads of material from warehouse to destination at maximum profit (or minimum cost). Cost is figured in time and distance. The dilemma arises because the direct route for each of them uses a section of one-lane road over which only one can travel at a time. There is a longer, separate alternate route for each, so that each can carry out the task independently of the partner—but at a cost. On the other hand, if they do not cooperate at the one-lane section, they can stalemate each other into extreme costs (in delay time). (See EXRT 11.) The trucking game has been especially valuable in the study of effects of threats. One, both, or neither player can be given a "gate" that can be used to block the other's trucks, but not one's own. Such a device can hurt the other's success, but not directly help one's own profit. Threat of using the gate gives power to the player who has that capability. Groups do *worse* when both have high power—both have the threat of the gate—than when only one does; and groups do best of all when neither one has high power (i.e., gate, threat). This comes about because, if available, threats tend to be used, and both players then use their longer, alternate routes. If the alternate routes are removed—hence, if players cannot es-

EXRT 11:   *DEUTSCH'S TRUCKING GAME*

Main Study Procedures: Two persons (or two teams) are assigned to be two competing trucking companies, Acme and Bolt. They each must make delivery trips from their own company headquarters to a destination, with cost corresponding to travel time, and profit corresponding to number of deliveries minus costs. One portion of the most direct delivery route for each player is over a common path, on which only one of them can travel at a time. Each also has an exclusive path, though it is longer and hence more costly. One, both or neither may be able to impose a barrier, that blocks the opponent's but not one's own truck, along the common path.

Main Dependent Variables of Interest: Each company's total profit, costs, delay times; use of barriers, and threat of such use; amount, pattern and content of inter-player communication when permitted.

Main Variations: Barriers available for one, both or neither player; relative cost of delays/longer path; presence of alternative routes; characteristics of players.

References: Deutsch (1949a, 1949b); Deutsch & Krauss (1962).

cape their interdependence—they tend to learn to cooperate even under high power (high threat) conditions. Under these conditions groups seem to use the gates as a signal, or communication, rather than as a threat. (See discussion of Osgood's GRIT, earlier in this chapter.)

Studies of effects of direct communication between A and B have also been conducted with the trucking game. When partners were given intercoms and *permitted* to communicate, they did not improve their performance and, generally, they *did not communicate*. When *forced* to communicate, they hurled insults and threats at each other—essentially increasing the intensity of the conflict. So, while under some circumstances (e.g., in the PDG) communication gives "insight" into the game and improves performance, communication is by no means a panacea for resolving conflict. Under some conditions it makes matters worse. (See the review by Rubin, 1980.)

The essential conflict involved in the prisoner's dilemma game has been generalized to situations involving three or more "players" (though still with a two-category choice) in what is called an N-person dilemma (or NPD). Komorita (1976) argues that this is much more representative of real life situations, such as problems of energy conservation, ecology, and overpopulation. As in the PDG, each player in the NPD is faced with a binary choice—C for cooperation and D for defection, or noncooperation, or self-gain. Pay-offs depend on how many of the N players give the C choice—from none to all—and are designed so that (a) any person "defecting" will get *more* than those who cooperate in that same case; (b) any person who cooperates will get more the more others there are who cooperate (the fewer who defect); (c) any person who defects gets more the fewer others there are who defect. So, from an individual point of view, the best pay-off is when one is the only defector; from a group point of view the best total pay-off is for all to cooperate and the worst is for all to defect. This is displayed in Table 9–3, both in terms of example numerical values and in terms of a variation of the R, S, T, and P symbols used for the PDG.

Research using NPD is limited and fairly recent, but the technique seems to offer promise for expanding the study of conflict to groups larger than two. Another recent development, the idea of "social traps," has both inspired further use of NPD models and led to the development of new models for studying group performance on conflict tasks. That set of developments grew from two contributions: Hardin's (1968) paper on the "tragedy of the commons" and Platt's (1973) paper on social traps. The tragedy of the commons can be described as follows: When a community has a common resource to which all members have free and unlimited access (such as a commons, where villagers may graze their herds free), it is to each person's advantage to increase his or her use of that free resource (to increase the size of the herd). But if all act in that individually-rational way, eventually the common resource will be depleted/destroyed (that is, the commons will be overgrazed and destroyed as a resource), to the extreme disadvantage of all. The dilemma, of course, is that if each acts in his or her own short-run best interest, it leads *inevitably* to a long-term result that is contrary to the interests of the group *and* of each individual. The problem is how to get people to act collectively against their own short-run

TABLE 9-3   Example of Pay-off Matrix for an NPD Game

ILLUSTRATIVE PAY-OFF MATRIX FOR NPD, FIVE PLAYERS	NUMBER OF (FIVE) PLAYERS WHO COOPERATE (C)					
	5	4	3	2	1	0
Each C chooser gets:	10	8	6	4	2	X
Each D chooser gets:	X	12	10	8	6	4
Group Total Pay-off:	50	44	38	32	26	20

SYMBOLIC PAY-OFF MATRIX:	R	S4	S3	S2	S1	
		T4	T3	T2	T1	P

PATTERN OF PAY-OFF MATRIX:

$R > S4 > S3 > S2 > S1$;
$T4 > T3 > T2 > T1 > P$;
$T4 > R > S4$; $T3 > S4 > S3$;
$T2 > S3 > S2$; $T1 > S2 > S1$;
$P > S1$.

best interests—by agreeing on limitations or whatever. The parallels between this dilemma and some of our current ecological, population, and energy problems are obvious.

Platt (1973) pointed out that the commons tragedy is just one type of a broader class of problems that he called social traps. The essence of all of them is a conflict of interest between individual and group interest, or individual short-run and long-run interest, or combinations of these. He discusses, for example, the "missing hero" class of problems. Suppose a mattress has fallen off a truck and is blocking the northbound lane of a two-lane road on a busy Sunday. If each motorist avoids the mattress by going out into the other lane—allowing for southbound traffic—all motorists (both north- and southbound) will be slowed down (and, indeed, endangered). If any one motorist would absorb the individual cost of stopping to remove the obstacle, the problem is solved for all at no cost to anyone else. (This is related in some ways to the "disjunctive" tasks discussed earlier, and could be formulated as "one pay, all win." It is also related to the "bystander" phenomenon that will be discussed in chapter 17.) Another type of social trap is the problem faced by a person who is recruited to join (and pay dues to) an organization designed to provide benefits to all members of some public—whether dues-paying or not (e.g., a union, or a lobby group, or a charitable or health organization). If everyone except A joins and pays, and the organization is effective, A will benefit at no cost. But if no one joins, or not enough join and pay for it to be an effective force, *all,* including A, will lose the potential benefits. This type of social trap is related to the NPD case, already described. (See also Dawes, 1980, for a description and analysis of social dilemmas.)

COALITIONS
AND THE ALLOCATION
OF REWARDS

The resolution of conflict has been studied in still another format: the formation of coalitions, that is, of agreements among subsets of members, who then allocate pay-offs among themselves, with zero pay-offs to members who are excluded from the winning coalition. Mathematical game theorists, social psychologists and political scientists have all been attracted to the general problem area, though they have emphasized different aspects of the problem in their work. (See Murnighan, 1978, for a review of models from the three fields. For other reviews, see Gamson, 1964; and Komorita, 1974.) From the point of view of group research, the key question is: How will the group deal with the problem of allocation of limited resources among group members? This includes the question of which, if any, coalitions will form, and what allocation principle (distributive justice principle) will be employed. Two bodies of research are relevant here. The first is research on "coalition games" dealing with the twin questions of which coalitions will form and how pay-offs will be allocated within the coalition. There has been considerable research on these problems, from which a number of formal theoretical models have been developed and tested. It is the topic of the next several pages. The second body of research has to do with the more general question of principles of distributive justice, by which groups allocate rewards, and of how these operate in group interaction process. Here, too, there have been many theoretical ideas—reciprocity, equity, reward/cost maximizing, and the like—and some empirical research. But those matters are much more concerned with group interaction process than they are with group task performance. So, although some of these theoretical ideas are pertinent to the coalition theories to be discussed here, and will be noted briefly when they apply, these "principles of social interaction" will be treated more fully in chapter 15 dealing with interdependence in group interaction.

Theoretical interest in coalitions dates from the early work of sociologist Georg Simmel (1950), and was furthered by the work of Mills (1953) and Caplow (1956). But the biggest impetus for the study of coalitions came from the invention, by Vinacke and Arkoff (1957), of an elegant and manageable paradigm for empirical research. They developed an adaptation of the game of pachisi, in which each player's piece is assigned a weight, and moves are made by multiplying the results of the roll of a pair of dice by that weight. In one frequently studied three-person version, players A, B, and C are assigned weights (resources) of 4, 3, and 2 respectively. Players are allowed to play alone or to combine with *one* of the other players (that is, play one piece and add their weights) if they can agree to do so, and agree on a division of the prize. Obviously, a coalition of any two is a winning coalition. One question of interest is Which of the possible coalitions will tend to form, over a series of trials? Another question is How will the winning coalition split the prize? (See EXRT 12.)

EXRT 12: *THE VINACKE-ARKOFF COALITION PARADIGM*

Main Study Procedures: Subjects are placed in groups, usually of sizes three or four, on a random basis. Each is assigned a weight, ostensibly and sometimes actually on a random basis. For example: Players A, B, and C might be assigned weights of 4, 3, and 2 respectively. They are then asked to play a pachisilike board game, under the constraints that (a) a single roll of the dice is used to define one move for each player; (b) each player multiplies that dice roll value by his or her own assigned weight to determine how many spaces he or she can advance. Players are told that they can form coalitions, and that a coalition can act as a single player, adding the weights of its individual members to determine the coalition weight, and moving the joint marker that amount. But the coalition must decide in advance how it will split the prize, and players are not allowed to form the grand coalition (of all players in the game) nor to make side payments to players who are not members of a winning coalition. The distribution of weight is usually designed so that no one player can win alone, and various different coalitions can win. (Since these rules make it the case that any coalition with a simple majority of the weights will always win, the game need not actually be played out once some players decide on a coalition and on the allocation of the prize among them.)

Main Dependent Variables of Interest: Which coalitions form, what division of outcomes they agree upon, and how this shifts over trials.

Main Variations: Parameters of the game (e.g., number of players, distribution of weights, number and sizes of possible winning coalitions, size of prize, characteristics of players—e.g., gender, game experience).

References: Caplow (1956); Gamson (1961, 1964); Komorita (1974, 1979); Komorita & Chertkoff (1973); Murnighan (1978); Vinacke & Arkoff (1957).

It has become customary to refer to the "weights" assigned players as the "resources" that players can bring to a coalition. In the form of the game most often studied (technically called "characteristic function game"), the prize remains constant no matter what coalition forms; side payments (e.g., to persons excluded from the coalition) are not allowed; no communication is allowed among members except for coalition "offers" and responses; and the "grand coalition" of all members is not allowed. Some studies have been done using another form, called "quota games." In quota games, the "prize" varies with coalition membership, and the "grand coalition" is permitted. Of course, some studies of coalitions have used techniques other than the Vinacke and Arkoff paradigm, but that procedure has dominated the coalition area as much as the PDG has dominated the dilemma choice area.

Several theoretical models have been developed to predict which coalition will form, and/or to predict how the prize will be divided. Gamson (1961) proposed a "minimum-resources" theory. It assumes (as do all coalition theories) that players will try to maximize their own gain. It further assumes that players will expect to split the prize according to the principle of parity. Parity, here, like the term equity as used elsewhere in this book, means that pay-offs are split proportionally to contributions (i.e., resources brought to the coalition). These assumptions lead to the prediction that the coalition most likely to form is the one with just enough resources to win. Thus, in the 4-3-2 game, for example, this theory predicts the BC coalition (with 5, a bare majority). It also predicts that the members of the coalition will split the prize in the ratio of three to two (or 60 percent to 40 percent).

An alternative "minimum-power" theory is based on a parity or equity principle in another way. It assumes that what is crucial is not resources, but "pivotal power"—that is, being *essential* to the winning coalition. In the 4-3-2 case, all three players are pivotal to any two-person coalition—but that would not be so for many other coalition games. So, in the 4-3-2 case, minimum power theory can not predict which coalition will form. But it predicts that the prize will be split *equally among pivotal members;* hence 50-50. In fact, in very many studies of the 4-3-2 coalition, the BC coalition does predominate (thus supporting the minimum resources theory); but pay-offs tend to be 55-45, which is half way between parity and equality, thus not supporting either of these theories.

Komorita and Chertkoff (1973) offered a "bargaining" model of behavior in coalitions. They build on the idea, from Thibaut and Kelly (1959), that members value a given coalition, and a proposed split, in relation to the attractiveness of the alternative coalitions they could join. (See discussion of Thibaut and Kelly's "comparison level for alternatives" in chapter 16.) Furthermore, the bargaining model assumes that players will use alternatives as threats during coalition bargaining. In this model, the allocation values will shift over time (i.e., over trials). It assumes that the player with the higher resources of a given potential coalition will call upon the *parity or equity* norm, whereas the player with the lower resources of that potential coalition will call upon the *equality* norm. In the first trial, they will tend toward a "split the difference" level (which is in part what happens for the BC coalition in the 4-3-2 game). On subsequent trials, coalitions will form and pay-offs will be divided so that for each player there is a minimum discrepancy between that pay-off and that player's maximum expectation from alternatives. Thus, the game approaches the state where there is minimum temptation to defect for each player of the coalition (though not, of course, for those excluded from the coalition).

Komorita (1974) has offered another model, called the "weighted probability" model, mostly applicable to groups larger than three (whose minimum winning coalitions can have two or more players), which assumes that probability of a particular minimum winning coalition is an inverse function of its size.

There are also several models of coalitions, developed out of political science, that predict on the basis of minimum winning size, either in number of members or votes (i.e., resources) (see Riker, 1962), or in terms of a minimum number of parties (i.e., minimum players) (see Leiserson, 1968). Other models out of political science, though, focus on the homogeneity of ideological positions of members of a coalition (e.g., Axelrod, 1970; Leiserson, 1966; Rosenthal, 1970). They argue that members of winning political coalitions seldom represent strange bedfellows, ideologically speaking.

Research studies that test these models tend to support the following propositions:

1. For tests of the social psychological models, there is a strong tendency toward the formation of coalitions of minimum winning resources; and, for groups larger than three, toward coalitions with a minimum number of players.

2. Such a minimum size effect does not seem to hold for tests of the political coalition models, but rather there seems to be a decided tendency toward coalitions of minimum ideological distance. (Of course, the Vinacke and Arkoff paradigm, most often used to test the social psychological theories, has no meaningful ideology—only "points" as resources. So "ideological range" cannot be tested in studies using that paradigm).

3. At least in the Vinacke-Arkoff paradigm, there appears to be a consistent tendency for females to play the coalition game more accomodatively, and for males to play it more exploitatively. This was especially so for females in high power positions in the coalitions—they tended to demand a lesser share of pay-offs than males in comparable power positions, and often included "unnecessary" members in the coalition. Moreover, *all* of the theories predicted better for males than for females. Such a difference is in line with (and probably helped shape) the general notion that gender differences in behavior reflect learned sex-role differences toward "instrumental" and "social-emotional" roles. But they are *not* in accord with even more consistent gender differences for the PDG, where female pairs play *more* competitively than male pairs.

4. As to pay-off allocations, the predictions of the bargaining theory seem to receive the strongest support. They imply dynamic balancing between the parity norm and the equality norm, with a comparison to gains anticipated from possible alternative coalitions providing the instrument for such dynamic balancing. So, the winning coalition will tend to be the one with least resources and fewest members needed to win; at the outset, allocations will split the difference between parity and equality; and over trials, allocations will tend toward the level where each member has a minimum temptation to defect, because that pay-off is as good as he or she can get in alternative coalitions. Over a series of trials, allocations tend to approach equality.

There is some relation between the idea of a minimum winning coalition—either minimum resources (e.g., votes) or minimum parties (i.e., players)—and the idea of a bare majority or even a plurality social decision scheme. That basic notion comes through in almost all the models, usually yoked to the idea that the fewer members there are in the winning coalition the larger the share of rewards each will have. In group tasks involving conflicts of interest or motive, the "struggle" has to do not with what is "correct" in an intellective sense, or what is "right" in a value or preference sense, but who will win or lose, who will get how much. Perhaps in such power struggle or pay-off conflict tasks, the dominant social decision scheme is "barest possible winning plurality" (which for many practical cases becomes "barest possible majority"). Then, for allocation, the dominant rule becomes "divide the prize to give each (essential) member the least temptation to defect."

SUMMARY

The span of group tasks considered in this chapter progresses from negotiation and bargaining tasks, that sometimes have substantial cognitive aspects as well as motivational/pay-off aspects of the conflict; through mixed-motive dilemma tasks that put members in motivational conflict by pitting a member's own gain against joint gain; to coalition/allocation tasks, that are mixed-motive at the individual level (a member has to cooperate with some members, while competing against others) but purely competitive at the group level (gains of some members are necessarily at the expense of other members, and there is no "mutual cooperation" outcome, at least when side payments and the grand coalition are prohibited). This progression has moved the discussion from tasks involving cognitive conflict to tasks involving a pure power struggle for pay-offs. The latter is the nature of the tasks in the next category of the task classification.

CHAPTER TEN
CONTESTS AND PERFORMANCES: GROUP PERFORMANCE ON COMPETITIVE AND NONCOMPETITIVE PHYSICAL TASKS (TASK TYPES 7 AND 8)

The next quadrant in the Task Circumplex contains the two task types that refer to *physical,* as opposed to symbolic or intellectual or verbal or numerical, tasks. There are two main task types in Quadrant IV. The first type is *Contests,* tasks in which one group is trying to conquer the other—metaphorically as in football games, or literally as in military combat. The second type is *Performances,* tasks in which the group is trying to carry out some physical task, not in battle against another group but striving against external standards of excellence (or of sufficiency). This chapter addresses these two types in turn.

CONTESTS: GROUP TASKS INVOLVING COMPETITIVE PHYSICAL PERFORMANCES (TASK TYPE 7)

Contests are quite near the conflict tasks of the prior type, especially the coalition/allocation subtype which has a winner-take-all flavor. Contests differ from tasks of the prior type in that they are no longer mixed-motive but sheerly competitive. Groups are no longer trying to "resolve" a conflict of interest with another group—by negotiation, or bargaining, or implicit mutual cooperation in a dilemma, or even by bargaining for pay-off allocations in a coalition. The group is trying to *beat* an opponent. To be sure, one can argue that there is a kind of implicit cooperation provided by the structure and rules of the game, even in completely competitive games like football and rugby; and, indeed, that even wars have "rules" through which the opponents cooperate even as they compete. Such a viewpoint may provide an interesting analytical or conceptual position for some purposes, but for present purposes—from the point of view of the focal group—it seems sensible to regard the group's task as solely competitive.

Performance of tasks of this type (and even more so, tasks of the other type in this quadrant, to be discussed in the next section of this chapter) constitute a large part of the time and energies of a large number of actual groups. Considering that, the amount of attention given to such performance in small group research is rather limited. Psychology and social psychology have often been accused of being "the scientific study of the college sophomore." It may be even more cogent to accuse social psychology, and within it, the group research area, of being "the scientific study of verbal behavior." Not only is there an extremely high preference for questionnaires and other self-report instruments as sources of data (see chapter 3), but even when "overt" behavior is the object of study it is very often verbal behavior that is studied. There are some very good reasons for such a preference. Verbal behavior often allows inferences about norms, attitudes, values, intentions, expectations, and so forth, more readily than does motor behavior. Verbal behaviors are more likely than motor behaviors to occur in comparable forms across different groups, tasks, and situations. The sheer mechanics of recording and storing information is so much more efficient for verbal "messages"—already predigested, in a sense,—than for physical performance accomplishments. Perhaps still another reason is that many researchers may regard the tasks done in the verbal/symbolic domain (choosing, deciding, bargaining) to be more important, more interesting for study. One could make a case that most of the crucial tasks formerly done by humans have either been automated (as in computer-controlled systems) or transformed into symbolic form (as in negotiations, or chess). But for whatever set of reasons, much less group research has been done on physical tasks than would reflect the baserate of those tasks in nature.

Still, there is a substantial body of research on groups performing such competitive tasks. Groups that have been studied include athletic teams, such as high school basketball teams (Fiedler, 1954) and little league baseball teams (Lowe & McGrath, 1971; McGrath, 1976); military units such as infantry rifle squads, armored reconnaissance squads and tank crews (e.g., Goodacre, 1953; Greer, Galanter, & Nordlie, 1954; Havron, Fay, & Goodacre, 1951; Havron & McGrath, 1961); and laboratory groups engaged in tug of war or similar physical contests. Some of these studies used real groups working on their real tasks (the basketball and little league studies, for example). Some obtained both group and individual performance measures. Virtually all of the studies of military combat units were simulations (see chapter 4), sometimes with a live "enemy" but blank ammunition, sometimes with live ammunition but a hidden "enemy" simulated by means of explosives and visual and auditory effects. There also have been studies using archival outcome measures, both for military combat and for athletic teams (e.g., Fiedler, 1954). (See EXRT 13, 14, 15.)

EXRT 13:   *THE ROUND ROBIN TOURNAMENT PARADIGM*

Main Study Procedures: Each of N teams plays each other team an equal number of times, under an equal pattern of situational conditions (e.g., home team versus visitor; early season versus late season). Sequence of pairings are either systematically counterbalanced or randomized. Data on each "contest" are gathered by investigator by observation.

For Example: Lowe and McGrath made observations of all batters of all four teams of a little league baseball league, for all games of a season (36 total games; 18 games by each team; 6 games for each pair of teams).

Main Dependent Variables of Interest: Team performance (e.g., games won, runs scored); individual batter performance (e.g., hits, outs, walks, runs scored, bases advanced); pitcher performance (e.g., games won, earned run average); situation and game criticalness; batter stress or arousal (e.g., pulse rate).

Main Variations: Number of teams, games; characteristics of tasks/game/situation; characteristics of players; coaching styles.

References: Lowe & McGrath (1970); McGrath (1976).

EXRT 14:   *THE PROGRAMMED OPPONENT (AGGRESSOR TEAM)*
PARADIGM

Main Study Procedures: Focal groups perform as teams in competition with an ostensive opposing team whose performance is under experimenter control. The opponent makes a series of preplanned moves or attacks, and responds to the focal group's moves or attacks in preplanned, semi-standardized patterns.

For Example: Havron and associates designed a set of field problems to test effectiveness of army squads. A pre-drilled squad (or "aggressor army") attempted to present each test squad with an equal-difficulty "battle" in each of a series of missions (e.g., attack of a hill, defense of a position, a reconnaissance patrol, and so forth).

Main Dependent Variables of Interest: Indices of group and individual task performance effectiveness (e.g., rounds fired, accuracy and rate of fire, communication errors, tactical errors); indices of leader effectiveness; interpersonal relations among group members.

Main Variations: Size, composition and type of group under study; nature of tested performances; difficulty level and complexity of missions/tasks tested; degree to which opponent group has its actions preprogrammed in detail.

References: Goodacre (1953); Greer, Galanter, & Nordlie (1954); Havron, Fay, & Goodacre (1957); Havron & McGrath (1961).

These tasks pose a special set of conceptual problems for group research. One must distinguish between *how well the focal group performs* (how hard they hit the ball, how accurately they shoot, how rapidly and effectively they move, etc.) and *how the contest comes out* (who wins the game or the battle).

EXRT 15:   *SEASON RECORD COMPARISON OF COMPETING TEAMS*

Main Study Procedures: Data are gathered for a set of teams over a series of contests of a season. The data are archival records or secondary data. They may not have been gathered by direct or indirect observation by the investigator of either individual or team performance in individual contests. All teams do not necessarily play each other in a systematic round robin fashion, although some pairs of teams may play one another once or twice. Investigator does not assign pairings or otherwise control schedules. It is assumed that all teams have played roughly comparably difficult schedules.

For Example: Fiedler used team performance records (win-loss) of a set of high school basketball teams, and also gathered data about perceptions of self and teammates from members of those teams.

Main Dependent Variables of Interest: Team win-loss records; intra-team attraction, interpersonal perception; styles of team leader(s).

Main Variations: Number, level of competence, and range of competence, of teams studied; nature of the game/context/tasks involved; size, composition of the teams; degree of detail of performance data available (e.g., individual versus team scores only; trial by trial versus game versus whole season only).

Reference: Fiedler (1954).

The two are only loosely coupled. The outcome of any performance—individual or group, verbal or physical, cooperative or competitive—must be conceptually distinguished from the quality and quantity of that performance. Many factors, quite beyond the control of the performing group or individual, affect *outcomes*. These include external events in the environment within which the endeavor is taking place (e.g., weather, shortages of material, breakdowns in surrounding systems) and probabilistic or chance factors. Such is the case for *all* performances; but for contests there is an additional major class of factor tending to uncouple the linkage between performance level and outcome level: There is a human (or human-managed) *opponent* actively trying to prevent group performance from leading to good outcomes for the focal group. So, any group performance task that involves competition against an opponent (enemy, opposing team) must somehow take into account the level of effectiveness of performance of that opponent in assessing the level of effectiveness of performance of the focal group. Studies using simulated opponents—for example, studies of military combat units—try to assess performance level against a "standard" task, or an opponent of "standard" ability. Studies of athletic competition have tried to take opponent effects into account by getting game outcome data on an entire season (e.g., Fiedler, 1954) or by means of a balanced, round robin schedule (e.g., Lowe & McGrath, 1971; McGrath, 1976). Perhaps the difficulty of taking opponent level into account is another reason for the relatively low frequency of such tasks in group studies.

Notice that for tasks in this task category (contests), unlike the preceding task category (mixed-motive), all members of the focal group are on the same side (i.e., have shared interests) rather than being in conflict with one another.

The conflict is sharper, but the conflict is with an opponent. One prominent feature of inter-group conflicts is that they often enhance positive feelings within groups, sometimes at a cost in increased hostility toward the "out-group," the "enemy." Much of the research that has been done on inter-group competition has focused on the development of and changes in such positive and negative feelings (see Brewer, 1979, for a good recent review of some of those issues); or else they have focused on how to go about reducing inter-group hostility, usually by altering the competitive interaction situation so as to require mutual cooperation between groups (see Sherif, Harvey, White, Hood, & Sherif, 1961, for a classic study of this kind, using relatively realistic group tasks. Also see EXRT 16.) But none of these studies have to do with *how well the focal group performs its task(s)* under conditions of inter-group competition, which is the topic of this section.

Regarding task performance under these conditions, we can draw relatively few firm conclusions:

1. Inter-group competition increases within-group attraction (or cohesion) under a broad range of conditions, but it may or may not affect the level of group performance.
2. Success in a competitive task also increases within-group cohesion, but the reverse is not necessarily so.
3. Groups do not always distinguish between good performance and winning in their evaluations of own and others' performance. In both athletics and combat, it *does* matter whether you win or lose, and it is precious little consolation to know that your group performed well but lost. The criterion for the task—understood by all parties—is winning; and so outcome level affects members and the group much more than performance level.

EXRT 16:   *SHERIF'S INTERGROUP COOPERATION PARADIGM (THE ROBBER'S CAVE STUDY)*

Main Study Procedures: A set of pre-teenage boys, selected to be homogeneous and unaware that they were participating in a research study, spent three weeks at an isolated summer camp near Robber's Cave. They were divided into two separate living and activity groups (the Eagles and the Rattlers). They were put into competition by means of a tournament of games (baseball, tug of war, etc.) Later, they were placed together for a series of activities (e.g., meals, movies). Then, they were placed in a series of "crises" (e.g., a breakdown in the camp water supply) in which the two groups had to work together to resolve the crisis.

Main Dependent Variables of Interest: Friendship choices, aggressive or friendly behavior, activity-companion choices, between and within groups; changes in those behaviors and choices over different phases of the study.

Main Variations: Size, composition of groups; types of activities; degree and forms of interdependence.

References: Sherif, Harvey, White, Hood, & Sherif (1961).

Many aspects of athletic and military contests involve divisible tasks that require complex coordination (i.e., teamwork). Some aspects are additive, but others are conjunctive (one player's or soldier's mistake can cost the whole unit), and a few are disjunctive (as in the heroic deed of the single player or soldier). Many of the tasks involved could not be carried out at all by individuals—all of the team sports, for example, and many of the military crews that need multiple persons to operate key equipment (e.g., a tank or plane crew). So the idea of individual versus group performance is not really applicable to those tasks, and there is no straightforward way to use any of the group productivity models to predict group performance levels. There is a great deal of anecdotal evidence and some systematic evidence that, for competitive tasks, both the competition with the opponent and the cooperation with teammates are likely to lead to motivation gains, rather than losses, at least for relatively small groups. It is also evident that performance of the complex actions that many of these tasks involve requires much coordination, and that there are likely to be serious coordination losses unless offset by extensive practice. And it is the case that such groups—military and athletic—are notable for spending a very large portion of their total resources (mainly time) on extensive training in situations as much like the actual performance situations as possible.

In previous chapters I have noted that the dominant combination rule or social decision scheme that seems to underlie or characterize group task performance for various types of tasks, shifts as our focus moves around the Task Circumplex. For intellective tasks (type 3) it starts as "truth wins" for tasks with demonstrable and compelling right answers, and progresses through "truth supported wins" for tasks with demonstrable but hard to demonstrate answers, to "truth with lots of support wins" for tasks based on a consensus of expert opinion. The dominant combination rule for decision-making tasks seems to be "two-thirds majority wins" or, more generally, "strong majority wins." In mixed-motive tasks (type 6) the rule seems to be "majority wins," but the majority is one of power/resources, not just a headcount. In the coalition forms of that task type, the rule seems to be "minimum majority wins" and allocation of rewards among coalition members according to a balance of both parity and equality rules.

There has not been any work directly on such combination rules for tasks of the contest type, partly because a single individual cannot perform many of these tasks (such as team sports or the operation of a piece of combat equipment), and hence one cannot apply the usual individual-to-group comparisons of SDS theory (see chapters 6 and 7 and Davis, 1973). But there is at least some anecdotal evidence that suggests that for tasks of the contest type, involving competition against an opposing group, task success may follow a conjunctive rule. That is, success may depend on the performance of the poorest member of the team. To formulate it in a rhetoric to match that used for the other types, this might be called "error avoided wins." Several sets of ideas would seem to support this hypothesis. First, it is obvious that many military missions rely heavily on the effective performance by every team member. For example, an inept bombardier, or an inaccurate navigator, can negate the efforts of even the best pilot and crew. The same is probably the case for many team sports. A first baseman who can't catch the ball negates the best pitching, fielding and batting.

Moreover, it is common practice, and part of the conventional wisdom of many sports, that successful teams know how to exploit the weaknesses of the opposing team (e.g., to pass to the area covered by a rookie cornerback; to run plays to the region where a slow or injured linebacker will have to cover; and so forth). It is also part of the lore of many team sports that, quite often, championship teams are not the teams with the truly superstar players on them. Some of the best running backs in professional football were never on championship teams (e.g., Simpson, Sayers, Kelly, Brown, Peyton, and many others). *Balanced* teams win games and championships. And, perhaps, balanced units win battles and wars. But balance in this context implies that not having major weaknesses, hence minimizing errors, may be more important than having some brilliant features along with some major limitations. I am hypothesizing that, for physical competition against an opposing team, successful group task performance is based on the "errors avoided wins" combination rule.

PERFORMANCES: GROUP TASKS
INVOLVING PHYSICAL PERFORMANCES
AGAINST EXTERNAL/ABSOLUTE/NONCOMPETITIVE
STANDARDS (TASK TYPE 8)

The other task type of Quadrant IV, Performances, includes most of the physical behavior of most groups: group tasks that require physical performance, against standards of excellence (or sufficiency) that are not tied to competition against an opponent. As with the preceding category, there is a relatively small amount of research on task performance of such group tasks, at least compared to the central role such tasks play in everyday affairs. That relatively low research effort is doubtless due to many of the same reasons noted for the previous category: cost, cumbersomeness, and a methodological and conceptual bias toward verbal behavior processes. While there is no opponent involved, it is still the case that many factors can operate to uncouple level of performance from level of outcomes. Those factors may pose even more problems for research because the presence and effects of such factors as chance, material shortages, and the like, are less obvious than the presence and effects of a human "enemy." (See EXRTs 17, 18, 19.)

One of the early, and now classic, series of studies in social psychology was carried out on a group performing such a physical task. These were done at the Hawthorne plant of the Western Electric Company during the Depression. (See Mayo, 1933; and Roethlisberger & Dickson, 1939, for reports of the studies.) The studies were originally designed in the spirit of the "time and motion" studies of that era (Taylor, 1911), to test the effects on productivity of improvements in lighting and other physical conditions of the environment. What they seemed to find was improvement in production whether lighting conditions were improved, degraded, or left constant. These unexpected results were accounted for by examining certain conditions of the study.

To carry out part of the studies, the researchers moved individual subjects from a large, open-floor factory operation into a separate room, where they worked beside the same coworkers day after day, with an experimenter present

EXRT 17:   *WICKER'S OVERMANNING/UNDERMANNING PARADIGM*

Main Study Procedures: Subjects are asked to perform a group task involving slot-car racing. Each group is given a complex task—driving a slot-car around a track as rapidly as possible, without going off the track, while circumventing various obstacles. The task can be arranged so that it requires different numbers of members for efficient performance (by varying the number and location of required task activities such as lifting barriers on each pass of the car, replacing cars that fall off the track). Tasks and members are assigned so that some groups have too few, some have the right number, and some have too many members to carry out the required tasks efficiently.

Main Dependent Variables of Interest: Task performance indices (speed, errors); member satisfaction (with the task, with the group, with own role).

Main Variations: Simultaneous countervariations in number of members and task roles, to separate out effects of group size and over- or undermanning levels; variations of specific features of the task and situation; characteristics of members (ability, task experience, gender).

References: Barker (1965); Barker & Wright (1955); Wicker & Kirmeyer (1976).

EXRT 18:   *THE TASK PROCESS (OPERATING EFFICIENCY) PARADIGM*

Main Study Procedures: Groups (natural or concocted) are asked to perform a complex group task (one that is indigenous to that group, or a simulation, or an artificial task), and the group's and members' performances are observed (directly, or by instrument, or indirectly by ratings). Data are gathered on the trial by trial, step by step or time by time performance, as well as on overall results.

For Example: Torrance observed the "survival" performance of a series of air crews who had to find their way back to base after "crashing" in a wilderness location. While crews would not have been allowed to fail, hence die, focus of evaluation was on efficiency of the process.

Main Dependent Variables of Interest: Indices of effectiveness, cost and efficiency of performance; evidence of performance level changes over time; indices of interpersonal relations among group members, and of group and member relations with the surrounding system (e.g., to managers of the larger organization).

Main Variations: Type and composition of groups; type and difficulty of tasks; degree to which performance units are finegrained (e.g., trials or part tasks, games or whole missions versus sets of missions or whole seasons).

Reference: Torrance (1954).

to keep track of flow of materials, units produced, and the like. The aim, in making these changes, was to increase experimental control and to improve measurements of productivity. But one unintended side-effect of these procedures was, apparently, to allow the workers to build a "group feeling" in the experimental work room, and, in general, to react favorably *to the fact of their being* studied rather than to the conditions being studied.

EXRT 19:   *THE TASK OUTPUT (PRODUCTIVITY LEVEL) PARADIGM*

Main Study Procedures: A set of groups that have been in a common situation, hence have performed a given task under natural and more or less comparable conditions, are studied in terms of the *results* (outcomes, productivity levels) of those performances. Only the products or results of those efforts (e.g., number of units produced per time; sales per year) are observed, as archival or secondary data. No data on the performance process is gathered and no observations of performance are made.

For Example: Fiedler studied accuracy of results of land surveys by a series of engineering student survey crews, doing a comparable set of field problems.

Main Dependent Variables of Interest: Indices of production level (e.g., number and quality of units produced per time); indices of personal motivation and satisfaction, and of interpersonal relations.

Main Variations: Size, type and composition of groups; type and difficulty of tasks; aspects of productivity; characteristics of members.

Reference: Fiedler (1954).

This study was a landmark. It had three important effects on the behavioral sciences. First, the importance of nonintended effects of research activities themselves was highlighted, and given a name—the Hawthorne effect. The need for making control comparisons, and the need to take account of the likely reactivity of experimental arrangements and procedures, are now a standard part of the concern in designing *any* study of human behavior.

The second major effect was to highlight the importance of interpersonal relations in the work place. This recognition played a key role in the development of what came to be called the "human relations" movement in industry. This movement served as a counterforce to the then-growing effect of industrial engineering and other efficiency oriented conceptualizations of industrial management. A key premise of the "human relations" movement was that changes in human relations aspects of the job—increased social interaction, increased interpersonal attraction—could affect productivity on tasks.

It was evident from the outset, however, that increased interpersonal interaction among workers didn't always lead to *higher* productivity. Companion studies in the Hawthorne-Western Electric program found that, under some circumstances, the very features that made a set of workers a cohesive group could and did work to keep productivity down (to a group determined "norm"). Groups applied negative sanctions to members who were "rate busters," and effectively kept members from producing either too little or too much, even under an incentive system in which pay was based on units produced. Many later studies—some laboratory experiments (e.g., Schachter, Ellerton, McBride, & Gregory, 1951) and some correlational studies in real industrial settings—have made it clear (a) that groups influence their members toward conformity with the group's norms or standards; (b) that more cohesive groups have more powerful influences on members; and (c) that such influences can serve to raise or lower member productivity, depending on what the norms of the group are. (See EXRTs 20 and 21.)

EXRT 20:   *SCHACHTER'S PRODUCTIVITY-NORM MANIPULATION*

Main Study Procedures: Subjects are asked to work, ostensibly as part of a three-person group, on a three-part checkerboard construction task. The parts are cutting out squares, pasting them onto a board, and painting them. All subjects are actually assigned to the same part of the task (cutting cardboard squares). Their alleged group mates are presumed to be performing the other two parts of the task (painting and pasting) in adjacent rooms. Communication between group members is done only by written notes, delivered by the experimenter. During task performance, the experimenter delivers a series of preplanned notes to the subject. These notes either (a) urge the subject to keep his or her production rate down, so that the subject's output doesn't stack up too much work for the groupmates; or (b) urges the subject to have a high production rate so that the group can produce many checkerboards.

Main Dependent Variables of Interest: Subject's rate of production and changes in that rate over time (before and after receipt of the production rate messages).

Main Variations: Simultaneous manipulation of group cohesion (see cohesiveness manipulation paradigm, EXRT 43).

References: Schachter, Ellerton, McBride, & Gregory (1951).

EXRT 21:   *THE COCH-FRENCH PARTICIPATORY DECISION PARADIGM*

Main Study Procedures: Given a company that plans to institute changes in the production system, some of the workers are assigned to a condition in which they hold a series of meetings with management production experts to help decide on specific changes in work methods; other workers are asked to select representatives who would take part in such decision meetings; while still other workers would have new work methods imposed upon them (as would be the case in the usual procedure of such a company in the absence of a research activity).

Main Dependent Variables of Interest: Production rate and changes in production rate over time, before and after changes in work methods; absenteeism and turnover; worker satisfaction.

Main Variations: Application in different cultures and task settings; degree of flexibility permitted in the new work methods, or degree of worker decision scope; characteristics of the workers and of the jobs.

References: Coch & French (1948).

The third impact of the Hawthorne studies was a negative one in my opinion. The Western Electric studies were taken not only as *evidence for* experimental effects and for group interaction effects, but also as evidence *that physical variables* (such as lighting) *did not have effects* on group performance. This is, of course, a serious logical error. One cannot "prove" the negative via the empirical evidence from a study. It is also a gross empirical error. Clearly, physical variables can have enormous effects on human performance (a whole subfield of environmental psychology has grown up in recent years to study those effects). But the Hawthorne studies provided an implicit rationale for *not* studying physical environmental variables. And that rationale held for nearly thirty years. This had the additional bad effect of a kind of abdication of interest, on the part of group researchers, in group performance of many physical tasks in industrial organizations. Instead, these problems have been pursued by engineering psychology, industrial psychology and environmental psychology. This, in turn, has meant that group and interpersonal relations aspects have been downplayed.

Another feature of tasks of this category in industrial organizational settings is that they are often "decomposed" into a series of relatively isolated individual or person-machine subunits. Indeed, the assembly line systems in industrial production tend to "disassemble" the interpersonal relations that can grow up in work groups under other physical arrangements. There is some evidence that this can have adverse effects on performance, as well as on interpersonal relations (e.g., Trist & Bamforth, 1951). Moreover, most technological changes have the effects of both (a) "decomposing" multi-person units into single person-machine units; and (b) putting the physical part of the performance task into the machine's role, and allocating peformance of the decision-making aspects of the task to the human part of the person-machine team. There is at least some evidence, then, of a tendency for task performance of physical tasks not to be done by groups.

There is a body of research literature on organizations that deals with the effects of both organization size and dominant technology on organizational structure (Blau, Falbe, McKinley & Tracy, 1976; Keller, 1978; Woodward, 1965). While that work deals with a social unit larger than a group, and while most of it deals with structure rather than performance, it sheds some light on questions of group task performance on physical tasks. Three types of technological systems have been identified: unit or small batch processing (such as hand-crafted furniture); mass production or large batch processing (such as auto-assembly lines); and continuous processing (such as oil-refining systems). Continuous processing systems, which tend to be smaller than the other two and to be the most technologically advanced, seem to require less hierarchically organized, more participative, management structures for best performance.

Organizational research has also addressed the issue of how employee performance and satisfaction can be increased by changes in the nature of the job, particularly changes in the perceived meaningfulness and responsibility of the job and knowledge of results of job performance (Hackman & Oldham, 1975, 1980). This work has dealt with a variety of types of tasks including the performance type (type 8) dealt with here. But it has mainly dealt with individual, rather than group, task performance. Both this job redesign/job enrichment, and the work on forms of technology, may be further evidence of my earlier supposition: That technological advance brings with it a tendency to "disassemble" group tasks of the performance task type into a series of individual-machine, or operator-computer-machine units, with the physical task performances assigned to the machine and decision/judgment aspects of the task alloted to the human.

CHAPTER ELEVEN
PLANNING AND CREATIVITY: GROUP PERFORMANCE OF TASKS REQUIRING GENERATION OF PLANS AND IDEAS (TASK TYPES 1 AND 2)

The last task types to be discussed—though in quadrant I of the task circumplex—are the two types that embody the Generate process: Planning tasks and Creativity tasks. Note that these two task types fit between the Execute quadrant and the Choose quadrant in the task circumplex. Planning tasks are adjacent to the performance task type, discussed in the preceding chapter. They are related to tasks of that type in that they are descriptions of how to carry out some action. Creativity tasks are adjacent to the intellective task type, and are related to tasks of that type in that they share an emphasis on cognitive aspects.

Interestingly, these two types exemplify two of Hackman's three task types. He called them problem-solving (describing *how to implement* some course of action), and production (the generation of ideas and images). (Hackman's third task type, discussion tasks, would pretty much fit decision-making task type 4 of the task circumplex.) In Hackman's development of those task types, he found the products of production (i.e., creativity) tasks to be characterized by an "originality" dimension; and he found the products of problem-solving (i.e., planning) tasks to be characterized by an "action orientation" dimension. (The discussion or decision-making tasks were characterized by an "issue involvement" dimension.) These task types also yielded differences in the interaction process of groups working on such tasks (see Morris, 1966). (See EXRT 22.)

Hackman and Morris (1975; 1978) and Hackman (1968, 1976, 1977) have built upon these results to develop an extensive research program around several basic notions: (a) the importance of task differences; (b) the importance of group interaction process in mediating relations between input variables

EXRT 22:   *HACKMAN'S PLANNING TASKS (PROBLEM-SOLVING TASK TYPE)*

Main Study Procedures: Subjects, as individuals or groups, are given a goal and asked to develop a written plan for carrying out the steps needed to reach that goal. Such a task, for example, might ask the group (or individual) to plan a fund raising campaign to raise a certain amount for a specific cause or purpose.

Main Dependent Variables of Interest: Indices of task performance effectiveness (e.g., quality, speed, practicality); indices of group interaction process.

Main Variations: Size and composition of groups; specific planning tasks; characteristics of group members.

References: Hackman (1968); Hackman, Jones, & McGrath (1967).

(such as member skills, group composition and task types) and group task performance; (c) the need to examine more closely *how* group interaction process functions to mediate those effects; and (d) the need to consider how these produce process losses and how they might be modified to produce process gains. Some of this work fits more appropriately in the discussion of group interaction process, and will be considered in later chapters. Furthermore, this work is not specifically limited to tasks of the Generate quadrant, the topic of this chapter. It relates in part to tasks in other quadrants as well, although it is to some extent especially pertinent to the creativity and planning tasks of this quadrant. In any case, since I believe this work can play a key role in advancing our understanding of group task performance effectiveness, I will describe at least some of the basic ideas of that work in the last section of this chapter. Before that, the chapter contains a discussion of the two tasks of Quadrant I, namely, planning tasks (type 1) and creativity tasks (type 2).

PLANNING TASKS: GENERATING PLANS TO CARRY OUT ACTIONS (TASK TYPE 1)

The planning task type lies between performances of physical tasks (type 8) and creativity (type 2), and is related to each of them. Planning tasks share with creativity tasks the same task performance process: Generate. Creativity tasks involve generating ideas or alternatives, whereas planning tasks involve generating plans to carry out already chosen alternatives. Planning tasks are related to performances because both focus on implementation. In Hackman's (1968) terms, both have an action-orientation. But performances are the actions; planning tasks are the preparations for those actions. The distinction is more than just between one step and another in a performance sequence. Often, different groups make the plans and carry them out (e.g., military missions are typically carried out by lower echelon personnel than those who made the plans for the mission). Certainly, different performance processes are involved.

The term planning has been used with widely varying me... been used with qualifiers such as strategic, tactical, programmatic, ... administrative. It has been used to refer to organizational, group, an... ual level activities. It has been used to refer to long-range, short-range, a... on-the-spot or ad lib. activities. Considerable attention has been given to d... opment of schemes proposed as optimal tools for planning in particular ind... trial, military and educational contexts. Some that have received relatively wid... use and recognition are PERT (program evaluation and review technique); PPBS (planning-programming-budgeting system); cost/benefit analysis; and MBO (management by objectives). These schemes have two limitations for present purposes. First, most of them include what would here be termed generating alternatives/objectives, and executing actions, and thus include the two adjacent task types as well as planning proper. Second, these are generic schemes for planning—templates that might be used by any group faced with a planning problem of the particular content for which the scheme applies. There has been relatively little concern with studying *how well groups do planning tasks,* and what factors influence their performance on such tasks.

A planning task, as I will use the term here, is one that requires the group to lay out a course of action by which it (or another group or individual) can attain an already chosen objective. This limits the term more narrowly than some uses. It does not include, for example, the search for objectives or criteria for organizational policy. It does not include the generation of *alternative goals or policies,* but it does include the generation of *alternative paths or actions.* Planning, as used here, also does not include performance of the actions thus planned, nor monitoring and evaluating that performance. Planning includes both the laying out of routines or procedures for what Simon (1960) calls "programmed" decisions—those for which there is consensus on goals and a known technology or "best path" to attain them. It also includes plans for those less clearly understood cases that Simon calls "heuristic," and Delbecq, Van de Ven and Gustafson (1975) call "judgmental." For these, the goal is set, at least in a general way; but there is considerable uncertainty about the best path, or perhaps about any path, to reach those goals.

In many ways planning tasks, as used here, are analogous to "programming" as that word is used in the computer field. The computer programmer starts with a prescribed goal—to develop a program that will carry out a certain set of calculations or alpha-numeric manipulations on batches of data with certain characteristics. In principle, there are many ways to attain that goal. Some ways are easier to do (for the programmer). Some ways are more efficient, or more effective, or cheaper. Some ways may be more salient, perhaps because of recent exposure or frequency of past use. For certain cases, one way may so dominate everyone's thinking, because of its use, prominence and popularity, that it is applied more or less automatically, is the only one considered, and its choice is taken for granted (hence, not seen as a choice). At the other extreme, there may not be any readily available programs, or programming techniques, to reach some preestablished goals. So the programmer has to invent the "plan," from scratch.

A plan, as used here, is like a computer program in several of these ways. A plan is also like a recipe, or an algorithm. It does *not* refer to a goal, or a

ers to a description of a time-and-function-linked
ecuted, will (it is supposed) lead to a specific

d that little research attention has been given to
nning tasks. In Hackman's (1968) study of prob-
ng tasks), written products for those tasks were
han products for tasks of other types, were less
isks (here, decision-making tasks), and were less
(here, creativity tasks). Those products did not
...tasks of other types on length, quality of presentation, ef-
...ctiveness or other dimensions. Nor did performance on them differ for
groups of differing sex-compositions (Kent & McGrath, 1969).

Delbecq, Van de Ven and Gustafson (1975) argue for the value of Delphi,
and especially of the Nominal Group Technique (NGT), as methods to improve
group performance of planning tasks. Most of what they deal with, though, involves either generation of goals (hence, the creativity task type 2) or choosing
among alternative goals or policies (hence, the decision-making task type 4).
Some of it does deal with planning as here used, but mainly the "judgmental"
or "heuristic" or nonroutine forms rather than the programmed or routine
forms of planning. They also claim some gains for Delphi and substantial gains
for NGT over interacting groups. (See EXRTs 3 and 23.) Drawing on a large
study by Van de Ven (1974), they posit a series of process characteristics that
yield such differences. Although they regard all of these as benefits, one can
question whether some are not mixed blessings.

EXRT 23:   *THE NOMINAL GROUP TECHNIQUE (NGT)*

Main Study Procedures: NGT involves a two-stage process. Individuals work
separately in the first or elicitation (i.e., generation) stage, then work as an interacting group on the second or evaluation (i.e., choosing) stage. NGT can be used
for tasks of the first three quadrants: for tasks requiring generation of plans (type
1), for tasks requiring generation of ideas (type 2), and/or for tasks requiring
choosing correct (or consensus of experts) answers (type 3). The elicitation stage,
correspondingly, involves generating alternative means, generating alternative
goals, or deciding on the best answer. The second stage involves the group collectively listing, and then evaluating, the plans, ideas or judgments (for the three
types respectively) that were generated in the elicitation stage.

Main Dependent Variables of Interest: Number and quality of solutions; agreements; costs in participant hours, researcher hours, and other resources; member
satisfaction compared to interacting groups and to groups or quasi-groups
operating under other sets of procedures.

Main Variations: Size and composition of groups; type and difficulty of tasks;
number and timing of iterations of the elicit-list-evaluate cycle; characteristics of
members.

References: Delbecq, Van de Ven, & Gustafson (1975); Gustafson, Shukla,
Delbecq, & Walster (1973); Van de Ven (1974); Van de Ven & Delbecq, 1971.

1. Interacting groups get involved in social relations to the detriment of task efforts; Delphi eliminates social relations altogether, leaving members uninvolved with the group and its efforts and reducing clarity of communication. NGT has a balance of the two.

2. Interactive groups search "reactively," and with less focus on the problem; they also tend to get into a rut on certain alternatives. Both Delphi and NGT groups search "proactively" and extensively, without getting hung up on one or a few alternatives. The latter methods also show less variability from group to group than do interacting groups. (Note that Delbecq and colleagues consider low variability between groups desirable; but that is a matter on which one could disagree for many instances.)

3. Interacting groups show strong evidence of social influence and conformity. NGT and Delphi do not.

4. Participation is very unevenly distributed over members in interacting groups (see later chapters on interaction patterns), but is more equally distributed among members in NGT and Delphi groups. (Note that this also is considered desirable by these authors; but one can question its desirability in many cases. See later comments.)

5. Such uneven participation for interacting groups is exacerbated as group size increases. NGT can handle groups up to about nine without such negative size effects, and Delphi is essentially unaffected by size (except in terms of cost, see below).

6. Interactive groups tend to avoid conflicts between members' ideas, or smooth them over, and spend most of their time discussing noncontroversial issues. When they do deal with conflict, the issues become personalized. NGT groups confront disagreements, but depersonalize them (Delphi, of course, allows no interaction; hence, the question of how conflicts are dealt with is moot).

7. Interactive groups report less closure and satisfaction than NGT groups, with Delphi in between.

8. Delphi groups take far less time per participant, but far longer calendar time and far more research administration time and cost per group, than either interactive groups or NGT groups (whose time and costs are about equal).

In considering these differences, the reader should keep several things in mind. First, these results really apply to groups generating alternatives (strictly, the creativity task type 2) but some of the tasks used in relevant studies could be regarded as generating *alternative paths*—hence, planning tasks. So they have some relation to the present discussion. Second, while quite strong claims are made by the NGT proponents (Delbecq, Van de Ven, & Gustafson, 1975; Van de Ven, 1974), those claims are not supported when tested by others (e.g., Rohrbaugh, 1979). Third, as noted, there is no compelling reason to regard all of these differences as desirable benefits. For example: Why is equal participation—with its unstated accompaniment, equal weight in the decision—by all members of the group a desirable thing? That is equivalent to an "averaging" rule, and for the most part, interacting groups do much better than that (presumably, by unequal participation by the most competent members). Fourth, the interacting groups to whom the Delphi and NGT are compared in these studies are, themselves, what this book terms ad hoc laboratory groups, and relatively unstructured ones at that. The groups had no past or future, members had no stake in one another nor in the experimenter-imposed artificial tasks.

We have no way to estimate how natural groups would perform on tasks endogenous to them. Still, even with these limitations, these NGT studies do provide a portion of the very limited research on planning tasks. The need for much more research on group performance of planning tasks is clear, for both theoretical and practical reasons.

There is one other body of work bearing on group planning tasks, namely, work that studies how groups deal with task performance strategies (see Hackman, Brousseau, & Weiss, 1976). This is addressed in the final section of this chapter.

BRAINSTORMING AND GROUP CREATIVITY (TASK TYPE 2)

"Brainstorming" refers to a group interaction technique that was developed in the mid-1950s (Osborn, 1957), and spread, fad-fashion, to many work organizations. Group members are asked to generate as many ideas as they can on a given topic within a certain time interval. They are admonished *not* to evaluate or criticize their own or others' ideas; sorting out is to be done later. But they are allowed, indeed encouraged, to build on ideas that are proposed (called "piggybacking"). (See EXRT 24.)

Proponents of brainstorming (e.g., Osborn, 1957) claimed that use of brainstorming techniques could increase creativity, particularly for groups. But subsequent studies (e.g., Taylor, Berry, & Block, 1958; Dunnette, Campbell, & Jaastad, 1963) have cast doubt on those claims.

In the present context it is important to make one distinction that is often overlooked. The brainstorming rules can be and have been applied to task performance by individuals as well as by groups. Most of the comparison studies have compared groups using brainstorming techniques to individuals also using

EXRT 24: *OSBORN'S GROUP BRAINSTORMING PARADIGM*

> *Main Study Procedures:* Individuals are trained in techniques designed to facilitate the generation of creative ideas and to minimize barriers to the expression of such ideas in groups. For example, group members are not allowed to evaluate or be critical of their own or others' expressed ideas, although they may offer ideas that build upon an idea previously expressed (by self or others). These techniques together are called "brainstorming."
>
> *Main Dependent Variables of Interest:* Number and originality/creativeness of ideas/solutions produced by the group working under such brainstorming conditions (versus groups not under such instructions/conditions).
>
> *Main Variations:* Number and composition of groups; types of problems; conditions of the brainstorming sessions.
>
> *References:* Dunnette, Campbell, & Jaastad (1963); Osborn (1957); Taylor, Berry, & Block (1958).

brainstorming techniques. For this comparison, the evidence speaks loud and clear: *Individuals working separately generate many more,* and *more creative* (as rated by judges) *ideas than do groups,* even when the redundancies among member ideas are deleted, and, of course, without the stimulation of hearing and piggybacking on the ideas of others. The difference is large, robust, and general.

However, to assess the effects of brainstorming as a technique to help groups overcome process losses (or attain process gains) the appropriate comparison is between groups using brainstorming rules and *control groups,* otherwise comparable but uninstructed as to their intercommunication process or task performance strategy. There is much less research on this comparison; but it is such research that has given some positive credence to the claims for brainstorming. And while that research is far too limited and equivocal to settle the issue, given what we know from other research areas it seems likely that the nonjudgmental constraints of brainstorming rules can help a group generate more ideas, perhaps more creative ones, than a group operating with "normal" (and inefficient) idea-evaluating processes. Such attempts to develop techniques to *enhance* group process, rather than to try to reduce or offset supposedly inevitable process losses, are discussed in more detail in the final section of this chapter.

The rules of brainstorming, like NGT, Delphi, and some other techniques, are designed to try to do two separate things:

1. To make sure that the creativity of each individual is not stifled by various social influence processes that operate in groups: fear of social embarrassment, conformity pressures, status systems that inhibit participation by low status members, and the like.
2. At the same time, to take maximum advantage of whatever creativity-enhancing forces operate in groups: social support and reinforcement for contributing, cross-stimulation of each other, and so forth.

This implies that, in groups operating under "normal" (i.e., uninstructed) conditions, those two forces might well offset each other, whereas in groups operating under brainstorming rules, the first set of forces—the inhibiting ones—is mitigated by the instructions, while the second, facilitative set would continue to operate. By the same token, individuals trying to do this kind of task, working alone and under "normal" (uninstructed) conditions, might have a parallel but somewhat less strong set of inhibiting forces, self-critical or self-evaluative in nature, but would not have the positive social support forces at all. But individuals operating under brainstorming rules should be free of those inhibiting forces, though still lacking the positive ones. These notions are represented in Table 11–1. If we regard the forces as combining algebraically, these relations clearly predict the (slight) dominance of brainstorming groups over uninstructed groups claimed by the brainstorming protagonists. But they would also predict either a tie or a slight advantage of brainstorming groups over brainstorming individuals—a prediction that is contradicted by very robust empirical findings. This suggests either that a third set of forces is involved, or that the question needs rephrasing.

Consider an alternative formulation of what goes on in such groups. Suppose (a) that the set of facilitative forces posited for groups is really not very powerful; (b) that individuals are just better than groups at such tasks, on a participant hour basis; (c) that both individuals and groups have inhibiting forces, but groups more so; (d) that brainstorming instructions do reduce those inhibiting forces, hence helping groups more than individuals; but (e) that individuals within brainstorming groups are more creative than the uninstructed groups. This would leave open the question of whether uninstructed individuals do better, poorer, or equal to brainstorming groups; that question has not been tested, perhaps because answering it does not seem to have any direct theoretical import.

The "search for alternatives" uses of NGT, as discussed under planning tasks earlier in this chapter, really apply to these creativity type tasks. NGT would seem to combine the power of individual generation of ideas with the power of group support/stimulation and with the group's effectiveness in selecting among alternatives. Groups using the NGT technique may very well be superior to brainstorming groups, normal/uninstructed groups, and even brainstorming instructed individuals, in their ability to: (a) generate alternatives; and then (b) select among and/or shape those alternatives. Brainstorming groups do not do the first of those as well as individuals; brainstorming individuals do not do the second of those at all, by definition. In this light, we can regard the NGT as being a system that *couples brainstorming individuals to decision-making groups,* in an attempt to get the best of both formats.

What, then, can we say about the combination rule that applies for these creativity (i.e., generate ideas) tasks? Member contributions would seem to combine as in Steiner's (1966) additive tasks: Any nonredundant idea by any member adds to the group's total number. Furthermore, each nonredundant idea adds equally to the group's output. The total number of ideas, the total output, then ought to increase as a negatively decelerated function (i.e., a diminishing returns shaped curve) as group size increases. Hence, a ten-person group should have more ideas than a five-person group (but not twice as many). If those groups are operating under brainstorming rules, the number would be higher for both five- and ten-person groups but in the same relation. If those people were working alone, with their (nonredundant) ideas to be combined

TABLE 11-1   A Summary of Empirical Findings re Brainstorming

PERFORMING UNIT	NATURE OF THE TASK INSTRUCTIONS	
	"NORMAL" UNINSTRUCTED	BRAINSTORMING INSTRUCTIONS
Individuals	IN	IB
Groups	GN	GB

IN > GN	Implied by findings.
IB > GB	Very robust empirical finding.
GB > GN	Brainstorming advocates claim some support.
IN > GB	? Undetermined on basis of present evidence.

later into a "group" product, the numbers would still be higher, but still be in the same relation (i.e., a diminishing returns shaped curve over changes in group size).

If the combination rule for groups seeking correct answers to intellective tasks is a "truth supported wins" rule, or even a "truth wins" rule when the correctness of the answer is compelling once stated; and if the key feature of the creativity tasks here discussed is the need to *generate* ideas freely, without the inhibiting forces of self-criticism or social pressures, hence without any attempt to evaluate the quality of the ideas; then the combination rule for tasks of the creativity type might be stated as "any idea is truth," or "any truth is welcome."

THE HACKMAN-MORRIS PROCESS ENHANCING APPROACH

Summary Variables

Hackman and Morris (1975), working out of a framework resembling the model presented in chapter 1, argue that one can represent all of the ways in which group interaction process can affect group task performance in three *summary variables:*

1. *Task performance strategies:* The collective choices that group members make about *how they will go about performing* the task. (These are, in effect, *plans* for doing the task.)
2. *Member efforts:* How hard group members work on the task.
3. *Member knowledge and skill:* The level, range and distribution of task-relevant knowledge and skills among group members, and how these are brought to bear on the group's task.

They argue, further, that each of these summary variables can be affected by group interaction process in two different ways, corresponding, more or less, to potential process losses and potential process gains.

Strategy. Group interaction process can affect the group's task performance strategies by locking the group into preexisting strategies, shared by the members on the basis of prior cultural norms, without examining how such strategies fit the task at hand. This, in fact, seems to be the usual case. When groups are given any of a wide range of tasks, they almost never spend time talking strategy (see review by Hackman & Morris, 1975). Such behavior may work well when, in fact, the assumed or implicit strategy fits the task. But when such is not the case, groups plunge ahead using performance strategies that may be dysfunctional. Such a situation can be one major source of process losses.

But group interaction process could, *in principle,* be a focus for reformulating existing strategies or generating new ones, to execute a task at hand more effectively. When groups do talk about strategy such discussion *improves* group performance. But left to their own devices, groups almost never "waste time" considering strategy. So, Hackman and colleagues (e.g., Hackman,

Brousseau, & Weiss, 1976) took advantage of another fact about task groups: In both field and laboratory settings, groups will almost always perform whatever tasks are assigned to them, provided the assignment comes from sources they see as legitimate authorities in the setting. Hackman and colleagues (1976) inserted a "preliminary task" that instructed groups to plan their strategy for the main task. They also tested, along with a "no treatment" control, an "anti-strategy" group whom they instructed *not* to waste time on talk, and exhorted to work hard on the task. The strategy primed groups performed better under task conditions designed to let members decide about and work on the task independently of one another. So, under conditions where the task can benefit from strategies other than the routine, obvious one, group process can lead to exploration of new strategies that lead to process gains. (See, also, Herold, 1978.)

Member effort.   Group interaction process can affect member effort in two ways. First, it can affect the degree to which member efforts on the task are coordinated—members do the same, or coordinated, things at the same, or appropriately synchronized, times. Imperfections in such coordination (e.g., not all pulling at the same time in a tug of war, or not all moving at the exact instant the ball is centered in a football game) are undoubtedly a source of the coordination losses postulated by Steiner (1972). But group interaction process can also affect the *level* of effort of group members. This corresponds to Steiner's (1972) motivation losses, but Hackman and Morris (1975) argue that group interaction process can also be a basis for increased motivation, hence process gains.

Member knowledge and skill.   Group interaction process can affect how groups utilize members' knowledge and skills on the task in two ways. First, the group interaction process is a focus for assessing and weighing members' knowledge and skills—for deciding which members have the most to contribute on a task, which have the right answer on an intellective task, which are most accurate. Such assessments and weighings of contributions often are done imperfectly for a variety of reasons. Such imperfections lead to more or less inevitable process losses. But group interaction process also can affect the level of knowledge and skills that group members have and can apply to the group's task. Presumably, group members can learn to use one another as resources, not just to share knowledge, which doesn't increase the total available to the group, but also to enhance individual competence, interpersonally and task instrumentally. This is a potential source of process gains, although Hackman and Morris (1975, 1978) note that research developing such techniques is only just beginning (e.g., Argyris & Shoen, 1974; Herold, 1978; Delbecq, Van de Ven & Gustafson, 1975).

Input Factors

Each of these three summary variables reflects two ways that group interaction process can influence group task performance, one leading almost inevitably to process losses, the other leading, potentially, to process gains.

Hackman and Morris (1975) also suggest one class of input variables that, if changed, would be likely to have the most influence on each of these summary variables. Group use of effective task performance strategies is most likely to be affected by altering *group norms* about strategy planning. Member efforts on the task are most likely to be affected by altering *task design*. Member knowledge and skills are most likely to be affected by altering *group composition*.

The Hackman and Morris (1975, 1978) approach goes a long way toward integrating the input-process-performance linkages of their model (and of the model described in chapter 1), with Steiner's (1966, 1972) analysis of tasks and group productivity models. It offers another level of consideration of group process effects—arguing for potential gains as well as losses. It is quite compatible, I believe, with the suggestions made at several points in earlier chapters of this part of the book, that we ought not too readily assume that group productivity is hindered by inevitable process losses just because group products don't match those predicted from some "ideal" model of frictionless and errorless group interaction process. Those earlier suggestions have proposed that we consider typical results of group task performance on intellective tasks ("truth supported wins"), on decision-making tasks ("very strong majority wins"), and even on coalition tasks ("minimal majority wins"), and subsequent allocations in which parity and equality principles are honored, as *pragmatically effective*. They each "back off" one notch from the very stringent demands of "ideal" models (such as "truth wins," unanimity, or a maximization of some one allocation principle, equity or equality). They thereby greatly increase the effectiveness of results (by avoiding accepting idiosyncratic "truths," by avoiding hung juries). Hackman and Morris (1975, 1978) propose that we can invent interventions (e.g., to alter composition, group norms and task design) that will permit groups to perform tasks even more effectively than one would predict from direct combination of members' abilities by any of the combinational models (disjunctive, conjunctive, additive, etc.). Collins and Guetzkow (1964) talked of groups attaining an "assembly effect bonus," that is, performances better than what the average member could do and perhaps even better than what the sum of members working alone could do. Hackman and Morris (1975, 1978) seem to be postulating the possibility of what might be called *interaction enhancing* models of group productivity. In those, the group interaction process leads not to inevitable process losses through faulty coordination and reduced motivation, but rather to enhanced task performance, because conditions (of task design, group norms and composition) are arranged so that group members increase their efforts/motivations, their performance strategy effectiveness, and their task competence by interacting with one another in the group interaction process.

Not What Is but What Could Be

Hackman and Morris (1975, 1978) are not talking about a description of how "most" groups behave, but rather about demonstrating possible ways groups *might* be able to perform. Theirs is a normative rather than a descriptive model in that sense. They argue that using natural groups may be the worst possible way to seek out evidence for these enhancement models. Natural groups are likely to be doing tasks with effort-reducing designs; to use ready-made but inappropriate strategies; and/or to have inappropriate skill composition or ineffective skill utilization procedures. Ordinary ad hoc laboratory groups are not effective either, unless the investigator gives thought to how the summary variables will be treated. Tasks given to many ad hoc groups are not particularly well designed to enhance group effort. In experiments, the intrinsic interest of the task is usually hostage to the search for experimental precision and control. Furthermore, ad hoc groups, having no past history on this or any other task, usually draw, *tacitly,* on norms broadly shared in the culture about how such problems are to be handled. Finally, most lab groups are not designed to maximize the fit of the distribution of group member skills to the requirements of the task. Indeed, unless the study is specifically interested in effects of group composition, the possibility of systematic study of the pattern of member knowledge and skill is likely to be set aside in deference to the experimental need for random assignment of subjects to groups. So, neither natural groups nor "normal" experimental groups are useful vehicles to search for *interaction enhancement* effects.

Instead, Hackman and Morris (1975, 1978) argue, research is needed on groups deliberately designed to maximize their potential for obtaining process gains. The Hackman, Brousseau, and Weiss (1976) *strategy priming* approach is one such tactic. The brainstorming techniques, "synectics," and other techniques for creative problem-solving (see Stein, 1975) represent other means to try to enhance group process. The communication strategy techniques and, for a limited range of problems, the Social Judgment Theory and MAUA approaches (EXRTs 4, 7, and 30), are still other possibilities. But, these authors caution that such intervention techniques must affect performance processes in a way that is congruent with demands of the task (Hackman, 1977; Hackman & Morris, 1978; also Herold, 1978). Effort enhancing techniques won't help on tasks for which effort differences are not important; inducing groups to talk strategy won't help on a simple task for which the optimal strategy is obvious; and teaching members to help each other enhance their task skills won't help increase performance effectiveness on a task for which members' skills are already more than adequate. Research that attempts such very complex "fits" between group composition, group norms, and task design, on the one hand, and group task demands on the other, is very difficult to design and carry out. It is also, however, very likely to lead to advances in our understanding of how groups perform tasks of various types, and how they could be modified to perform them better.

PART THREE
GROUPS AS SYSTEMS FOR STRUCTURING SOCIAL INTERACTION

Groups are many different things, depending on what aspects of them one considers. Groups are often viewed as vehicles for task performance, and the preceding chapters have concentrated on the study of groups as task performance systems. Groups are also important in human affairs because they provide the locus for social interaction, and to some degree shape or structure it. The several chapters of Part III will focus upon those aspects of the study of groups that view groups as systems for structuring social interaction.

That consideration begins, in chapter 12, with general discussion of group interaction process, a description of some of the early efforts to observe group interaction process, some key facets of that process, and some regularities in the patterns of interaction over participants and over time. Chapter 13 then deals with the communication process as the form or *pattern* of interaction, and with effects of restrictions in channels, modalities and strategies on verbal and nonverbal aspects of communication. The next three chapters deal with the attraction or acquaintance process, that is, with the *content* of interpersonal interaction. Chapter 14 treats interpersonal attraction; chapter 15 deals with interdependence and exchange in interaction; and chapter 16 deals with the process of development of interpersonal intimacy and regulation of privacy. The final chapters deal with the influence process; that is, with the *consequences* of interaction for the members and for the group. Chapter 17 discusses some of the effects of group interaction on members. Chapter 18 treats the development of group structure, in the form of patterns of norms and roles in groups, including that special set of influence relations we call leadership. That chapter ends with a discussion of the interplay of group structure and interaction process in families, the prototypical and most ubiquitous form of group.

CHAPTER TWELVE
GROUP INTERACTION
PROCESS: THE
ACTING GROUP

Group interaction process is at the heart of the study of groups. The arrangement and logic of the model in chapter 1 implies that the acting group is the focal point of all of the forces or inputs; and that all of the effects or consequences also flow from it. Group interaction process, as used here, refers to all of the behavior of *all of the members of an acting group,* in relation to each other and in relation to the task / environmental aspects of the setting, *while that group is in action.* The acting group is a summary term for all the behavior that is to be subsumed under the group interaction process term. The first main step in considering groups as systems for structuring social interaction will be to examine the general concept of group interaction process, how it has been observed, and what those observations have shown. That examination is the task of this chapter.

THE OBSERVATION OF
GROUP INTERACTION

The dynamics of interaction of people in groups has been a topic of major concern for students of groups for a long time. One of the earliest analyses that stressed such interaction was Simmel's (1950) concern with how two- and three-person groups operate internally. But his analysis was mainly theoretical and speculative, based on his own experience rather than on systematic observation of such groups actually interacting. Another early contribution to interest in group process was Whyte's (1943) detailed case study of an adult male street corner gang during the Depression. Whyte's work provided a number of key insights about the nature of interaction, about leadership, about group structure and status; all of these were drawn from intense observation of a single group over a long period of time. Many other early efforts dealt with changes in group structure, or shifts in members' attitudes (e.g., Newcomb, 1943; Lewin, 1953), from which inferences were made *about what processes must have intervened* between prior factors and subsequent changes. But such studies did not really observe interaction per se; rather they used it as an "intervening variable" in interpretations of data about input-output relations.

Bales's Interaction Process Analysis

While there were a number of early efforts to chart group interaction empirically (e.g., Chapple, 1942), the first really effective and extensive attempt to observe group interaction directly, and to do so in terms of systematic observation categories, was the work of R. F. Bales and associates (e.g., Bales, 1950a, 1950b, 1953; Bales & Slater, 1955; Bales & Strodtbeck, 1951; Borgatta & Bales, 1953). Bales developed a system of interaction process analysis (IPA) that combined both a structured set of categories for observation and a set of theoretical concepts underlying those categories. While we will touch upon some other observation systems elsewhere, Bales's IPA so dominated the field for several decades that a review of its basic premises, its successes, and its problems, provides a reasonable view of the waxing and waning of research that attempted direct observation of group interaction.

The basic theoretical ideas underlying IPA are as follows. Problem-solving groups (groups with a purpose, or a goal, or a task—but quite broadly construed) are continually faced with two distinct but related sets of concerns: *instrumental* or task oriented concerns associated with the effort to deal with the group's task; and *expressive* or social-emotional concerns associated with the interrelationships of the members. Both instrumental and expressive concerns operate continually. Group attention and effort devoted to one of these is not devoted to, and may produce strains for, the other. A given group will give emphasis to one over the other at various times. In fact, one of the facets of Bales's theoretical structure is the idea that there is an orderly series of *phases* involved in the instrumental activities of problem-solving groups, and a parallel cycle of phases of expressive behavior. The instrumental phases focus first on *orientation* (gathering information), then on *evaluation* of that information, and then on *control* and decision-making. Concentrating on such instrumental activities will produce strains in the social-emotional aspects of the group. These strains increase as the three task phases continue; but efforts to counter these social-emotional strains also increase. Hence, there is an increase in both positive and negative aspects of social-emotional activity as the group progresses through its task activity phases.

Bales built an observation system based on a set of twelve intricately interrelated categories. (That set of categories is shown in Table 12–1). (See, also, EXRT 25.) The twelve categories cover task instrumental (4 through 9) and

TABLE 12-1   The Categories of Bales's Interaction Process Analysis Observation System

POSITIVE SOCIAL-EMOTIONAL / EXPRESSIVE

1. Shows Solidarity
2. Shows Tension Release
3. Agrees

ACTIVE TASK / INSTRUMENTAL

4. Gives Suggestion
5. Gives Opinion
6. Gives Orientation

PASSIVE TASK / INSTRUMENTAL

7. Asks for Orientation
8. Asks for Opinion
9. Asks for Suggestion

NEGATIVE SOCIAL-EMOTIONAL / EXPRESSIVE

10. Disagrees
11. Shows Tension
12. Shows Antagonism

CATEGORIES	FUNCTIONS
6 and 7	Orientation
5 and 8	Evaluation
4 and 9	Control
3 and 10	Decision
2 and 11	Tension Management
1 and 12	Group Identification

social-emotional (1 through 3 and 10 through 12) areas. The six task categories are further divided into three passive (asking or question categories, 7, 8 and 9) and three active (giving or answer categories, 4, 5 and 6). That set of six categories is also paired in relation to the three problem-solving phases mentioned previously: orientation (asking and giving information, categories 6 and 7); evaluation (asking and giving opinion, categories 5 and 8); and control (asking and giving suggestions, categories 4 and 9). The six expressive categories are also divided into two sets, three positive (1, 2 and 3) and three negative (10, 11 and 12). Within these, categories are again paired, in terms of a set of expressive "phases": statements of agreement and disagreement (3 and 10); indication of tension build-up and tension release (2 and 11); and expressions of group solidarity and antagonism (1 and 12).

These categories provide a systematic framework for making observations pertinent to Bales's theoretical ideas regarding instrumental and expressive acts, and phases in group interaction. Indeed, the theory and the observation system were developed together, so to some degree the categories of

EXRT 25:   *BALES'S INTERACTION PROCESS ANALYSIS (IPA) PARADIGM*

Main Study Procedures: Subjects (usually male college students) are assigned to relatively small groups to discuss and decide upon an issue (often a human relations problem). No leader is designated; each member has some but not all the information needed to deal with the problem. Groups are expected to complete the problem within the session (usually 40 to 120 minutes). One or more observers divide ongoing (verbal) interaction into unit acts and categorizes each into one of 12 mutually exclusive, exhaustive, highly interrelated categories: three active task or instrumental categories (gives orientation, opinion, suggestion); three passive or reactive task or instrumental categories (asks for orientation, opinion, suggestion); three positive social-emotional or expressive categories (agrees, shows tension release, shows solidarity); and three negative social-emotional or expressive categories (disagrees, shows tension, shows antagonism).

Main Dependent Variables of Interest: Distribution of acts over time, categories and participants; shifts in distribution over categories-by-time (process phases); shifts in distribution over categories-by-persons (roles); post-session judgments of members about influence, participation.

Main Variations: Types of problems and groups (e.g., therapy groups, labor/management negotiations); size of groups; prior group experience; characteristics of members (gender, status, assertiveness, etc.).

References: Bales (1950a, 1950b, 1953); Bales & Slater (1955); Bales & Strodtbeck (1951); Borgatta (1963); Borgatta & Bales (1953); Carter, Haythorn, & Howell (1950); Landsberger (1955); Morris (1966).

the system determined the terms of the theory and vice versa. Bales's interaction observation system requires that every action fit one and only one of the 12 categories. Hence, each act has to be *either* task instrumental or social-emotional; and each task instrumental act has to be either active or passive, and has to be about orientation, evaluation or control. So the categories themselves, and the application rules for their use, guarantee that the observations will fit the terms of the theory pretty well, and therefore permit tests of its propositions.

By the same token, although Bales's IPA is widely regarded as a *generic* process observation system, one that could be used for a variety of groups doing a variety of tasks (limited mainly to tasks involving talking), and although IPA can indeed be used for groups engaged in a variety of kinds of verbal behavior, nevertheless the category system is so closely linked to Bales's underlying theoretical structure that data derived from its use can seldom be used to test propositions from any other theory of interaction. While it has been used to test many parts of Bales's theory, the IPA turns out to be theoretically barren as a system for testing any other theory.

Bales's IPA can be used to illustrate two other problems faced by all observation systems: choosing a perspective from which to make observations, and deciding on the unit act. Every observation system requires that the observer take some stance or perspective from which to make the observations.

Some ask observers to judge the meaning of the act from the point of view of the actor, a very difficult thing to judge in ongoing interaction. Bales avoids this problem. Instead, IPA asks the observer to consider what impact the act would have on "the group." Bales's system defines a unit act as the smallest segment of behavior that is meaningful in terms of the category system. An act always ends as soon as it would require a category change to code it. Consequently, unit acts in IPA vary a lot among themselves in size (e.g., number of words, number of seconds) but tend to be at a micro-level, often a single sentence or less.

These features are related to two other aspects of the Bales IPA. The twelve categories are regarded as mutually exclusive and collectively exhaustive. That is, any act fits one and only one category. Hence, there is no multiple coding, and there is not an "other" category for actions difficult to place in one of the categories. Although such characteristics are very useful features of a classification system from a practical and methodological point of view (e.g., McGrath, 1968) they imply certain theoretical premises. For example, they imply that every action serves either a task instrumental or a social-emotional function; no behavior serves any other function; and no behavior serves both of those functions. Not all theoretical views and observation systems make those assumptions.

Problems and Limitations

The Bales IPA system both stimulated and dominated the study of group interaction process for some time. Many studies using Bales's category system (e.g., Bales & Slater, 1955; Bales & Strodtbeck, 1951; Landesberger, 1955) and using variations of it (e.g., Borgatta, 1962; Borgatta, Couch & Bales, 1954; Morris, 1966), were carried out in the 1950s and early 1960s. They constituted the lion's share of work on interaction. The set of features that characterized the system (generic, contentless categories, a group perspective, a micro-level unit act, single categorization, etc.) were both its strengths and the seeds of its limitations. Its very generality, purchased by being "content free" in the sense that it wasn't tied to the content of any group task or group activity, made it very difficult to apply IPA to test any content based hypotheses (for example, about the effectiveness of various task strategies). Furthermore, IPA's tight ties to Bales's theoretical view were both a boon and a bane. On one hand, these ties made IPA automatically useful to provide support for that position (e.g., every act *had* to be either task instrumental or social-emotional). On the other hand, these same theoretical ties made it difficult to use IPA in relation to any other theoretical view.

Moreover, the complex and abstract (i.e., contentless) character of the categories, the difficulties of making observations from a "group" perspective, the requirement for singular categorization, and the problems arising from using a small unit of action, all increased the difficulty of the observation task. While Bales's own work reflected high levels of observer reliability, that reliability was obtained by extensive observer training. Other users of the IPA schema were not always willing to make such a training investment. Sometimes, too, investigators recorded the audio portion of the interaction, both to avoid putting an observer into the group's meeting room and to make it easier to assess and improve coder reliability. In many uses, the audio record was then transformed into a written transcript, with coding done from that typescript. It is very difficult for the observer to take the group's perspective when working from a written transcript or even from an audio record, both of which lose all of the richness of the nonverbal activity that helps us "interpret" the meaning of communications in an actual group.

Decline and Resurgence

These problems raised both theoretical and practical difficulties for the use of IPA. As studies using IPA accumulated, so did the burden of those difficulties, so that by the early 1960s use of IPA began to decline. This decline had two consequences. On the one hand, a number of investigators tried to develop alternative systems. Many of these were very specialized for specific classes of groups or of group activity. For example, observation systems were developed to code in-classroom behavior of students and teachers (e.g., Medley & Mitzel, 1958). Others were less comprehensive than IPA, less general, less systematic. Each had its own set of solutions to the problems of unit definition, observer perspective, multiple coding, observer reliability, and so forth, and each set of such solutions had its own advantages and limitations. But no one system proved sufficiently broadly attractive to be used beyond the research of the program within which it was developed.

Along with the search for alternative systems for group interaction process observation, especially as those efforts met only limited success, there came a major decline in research involving the direct observation of group interaction. That decline had a number of consequences. First, it encouraged researchers to do studies designed to test input-output links directly, hence to ignore the mediating effects of (group) process. At the same time, it encouraged a shift in interest and emphasis from process to structure (hence, from the dynamic to the static), and probably also a shift in emphasis from behavior to its outcome or consequences. But in many studies, it became clear that input-output relations needed to be *interpreted* in terms of intervening processes. So group interaction process, instead of being center stage and the focus of behavior observation (as it had been in Bales's work), was shifted to the status of *unobserved* intervening process, amenable to speculation in the absence of empirical data, but not subjected to systematic observation. The *study* of group interaction, in that empirical sense, waned, but the conceptual use of hypotheses about such processes did not.

That decline in study of group interaction process extended for over a decade. There is evidence, I believe, that a resurgence has begun (e.g., Dabbs, 1980; Gottman, 1979a. See also McGrath & Kravitz, 1982). The decline was triggered because the research had reached the limits of the technology available at the time. It also had "used up" or reached the limits of the theory available at the time. The resurgence, in turn, was triggered by the availability of some new technology, both for data collection (e.g., sophisticated videotaping systems) and for data analysis (e.g., some applications of Fourier analyses and other complex mathematical techniques for studying cycles). It remains to be seen whether advances in theory will also come about, or whether the resurgence in study of interaction can be sustained long without them. The resurgence stemming from this new technology is discussed in the last section of this chapter.

One basis of optimism that such theoretical advances will be forthcoming is in some work by Bales and colleagues (Bales & Cohen, 1979). That work offers an entirely new interaction process observation system, called SYMLOG. Among other changes, SYMLOG codes each unit in terms of three bipolar dimensions: up-down (dominance-submissiveness); right-left (positive-negative); and forward-backward (task-conforming versus deviating). It also can be used either for act by act recording or for rating larger segments of interaction. The SYMLOG system is far more flexible, but also far more complex theoretically, than the earlier IPA. It has had little use, as yet, beyond the Bales group; so it is hard to assess its impact or its effectiveness at this time.

This brief history of the study of group interaction process sets the stage for an examination of patterns of interaction that have been hypothesized and observed using such interaction observation systems.

THE MORPHOLOGY OF INTERACTION: REGULARITIES IN THE PATTERN OF INTERACTION OVER MEMBERS AND TIME

To refer to group interaction is to imply that two or more people are communicating to one another about something. In the early days of use of Bales's Interaction Process Analysis (IPA), a number of researchers gave considerable attention to seeking regularities in the pattern of such communications, for groups doing "typical" problems. They were seeking clues as to how such patterns varied over types of tasks, types of groups, and time; and they were trying to establish how such interaction was distributed among members of the group. (See, e.g., Bales, 1950a, 1950b, 1953; Bales & Slater, 1955; Bales & Strodtbeck, 1951; Borgatta & Bales, 1953.) Many of these regularities can be stated in rather direct forms, and some of them are among the most consistent and robust findings in the field.

Distribution of Participation Among Members

Some people talk more than others, and do so consistently. This is an extremely general and robust finding, for amount of participation in a wide array of groups under a wide array of conditions (e.g., Bales, 1953; Borgatta & Bales, 1953). Furthermore, *persons who talk more get talked to more.* There is substantial correlation between the rank order of interaction initiated and the rank order of interaction received. This, too, is robust and general (e.g., Bales, 1953; Stephan & Mishler, 1952).

The person who talks most (the top initiator) *addresses most of his or her communications to the group as a whole,* and is the only member of the group to do so. All other members of the group address most of their communications to specific individual group members, with the top initiator receiving more than anyone else. If members of a group of any given size are ranked in order of the total communications each initiates, the proportion each initiates can be represented very accurately by a downward-tending diminishing returns type curve. A decreasing exponential function provides an imperfect but rather good fit. (See Horvath, 1965; Nowakowska, 1978; Stephan, 1952; Stephan & Mishler, 1952; Tsai, 1977.) The top initiator may initiate about 40 to 45 percent of the communications, the next highest about 23 percent, the next about 17 percent, and so on. *As the size of the group increases, the proportion of communications initiated by the top initiator increases while differences in amount of communication among the other members tend to decrease.* The downward curve falls much more sharply from top to next highest initiator, then tends to flatten out (to become asymptotic) to near-equality among the other members.

Individuals seem to have relatively consistent rates at which they would interact *if they were under hypothetical "free running conditions."* Bales (1953) calls this a "basic initiation rate" for the person. But the actual amount of a given individual's interaction, and its contents, will vary as a function of the time available, the task, the situation and the interaction tendencies of other group members. *It is as if any given time-task-situation set an upper limit on the total communication for the group as a whole during that time period.* That total is "allocated" among the group members, as a function of the group size and the appropriate exponential curve for that size, and as a function of the individuals' basic interaction rates. An individual's amount of interaction relative to other group members in a given group interaction situation is highly predictable. It is (a) a direct or positive function of that individual's "basic initiation rate" (estimated, for example, from previous sessions in other groups); and (b) an inverse or negative function of the "basic interaction rates" of the other group members (Borgatta & Bales, 1953).

But there seems to be an upper bound for each individual's interaction rate, even if not constrained by competition with other group members for "floor time." Individuals tend toward that *limit*, but do not exceed it even if the situation permits them higher rates. So, while the absolute initiation rates of high initiators will be much reduced if they are placed in a group with other high initiators (given that the situation poses a fixed task and time limit), the interaction rates of low initiators will increase far less if they are placed in groups with other low initiators. Even so, you can raise a low initiator's rate somewhat by removing high initiators from the group. It can also be raised if the group's leader (or its norms) urges participation by all.

Any given individual's rate of interaction will also be affected by the individual's "position" in the group. The term position is used here very broadly, to refer to several different aspects of the individual's situation vis-à-vis other members. The individual's interaction rate, initiated and received, will be higher or lower, respectively, (a) if he or she is in a central as compared to a more peripheral position in the group's communication network (see chapter 13); (b) if he or she is seated in a prominent position (e.g., head of the table, or front of the class) as compared to a less prominent one (e.g., corner of a rectangular table, or back of classroom); (c) if he or she is high or low in terms of status in the group (that status being based on any of a number of ways in which groups in general, or any particular group, reckon status); (d) if he or she is highly motivated to perform the group's task (as compared to less motivated) or highly attracted to the group (as compared to less attracted); and/or (e) if he or she is in some way especially valuable to the group (e.g., a content expert on the task) or negatively valued by it (e.g., a deviate from group consensus on some matter important to the group).

Distribution of Interaction Among Categories (of IPA)

In the typical group interaction, the distribution of actions over types of acts, as defined by sets of categories of the Bales system, is an extremely orderly pattern. Typically, about half of the interactions of a group are "proactive" attempts to deal with the group's task. The other half are "reactive." In terms of Bales's IPA system, categories 4, 5, and 6, giving orientation, opinion, and suggestions, are the proactive categories. (Actually those three categories typically include about 56 or 57 percent of the acts. Of this total, some 6 or 7 percent are considered reactions. See below.) About half of the reactive half of the acts, or about 25 percent of the total, are positive reactions (Bales's categories 1, 2, and 3). Bales (1953) and Hare (1976) regard these as completing the cycle of activity (or the "disturbance of equilibrium") begun by the proactive event. About half of the remainder, or about 12.5 percent of the total, are negative reactions, Bales's categories 10, 11, and 12. These can be regarded as rejections of the proposed solution; hence, they recycle the interaction back to a "new" attempted solution. About half of the remainder, or about 6 or 7 percent of the total, are questions (Bales's categories 7, 8, and 9). Direct answers in reaction to these questions (the "reactive" 6 or 7 percent of attempted answers, over and above the proactive 50 percent) make up the rest.

Alterations in that pattern occur as a function of type of group and type of task. Therapy groups, for example, may show higher proportions of positive and negative reactions and fewer attempted answers. Jurors show high proportions of agreement (their task requires it). Groups drinking beer and brandy show high rates of disagreement and antagonism, whereas groups under the influence of LSD show high rates of tension release and solidarity.

The distribution over categories can also be altered by reinforcing, positively or negatively, one or another of the categories (see Hare, 1976, p. 81, for a list of many studies showing this). The general reluctance to transmit bad news is a specific case of this (see e.g., Rosen & Tesser, 1970). Presumably, giving bad news has been negatively reinforced in the past. So, that "category" becomes less frequent in future interactions. But the positive and negative categories are themselves "reinforcements," as well as positive and negative reactions. Such reinforcement effects, and feedback and other effects, can be examined by considering the way in which group interaction varies over time.

Distribution of Interaction over Time

Bales (1953) postulates several kinds of changes in interaction pattern over time. Some of these deal with "equilibrium" on an act-to-act basis; some deal with phase movement within sessions; and some deal with development of the group over sessions. Before examining those postulations, it is worth noting that most data used by Bales (and others using the Bales system) to test these distribution questions, and to establish baseline data or "norms" for interaction rates, were done with ad hoc laboratory problem-solving groups. (Regrettably, moreover, almost all of these were groups of *male* college students.) These groups were dealing with what Bales considered "full-fledged" problem-solving tasks, requiring the group to carry out a complete task (usually discussion of a human relations case) within one relatively short session of forty minutes to two hours. Many other kinds of groups might have tasks that really extended over many meetings (e.g., therapy groups). Still others might deal with tasks for which early problem-solving stages (e.g., gathering information) had already been completed by others (as is the case with many management meetings). One would not expect the same pattern over time to occur in groups with such truncated tasks.

The Basic Equilibrium Problem.   Bales (1953) argues that two types of patterns take place within a session of groups dealing with "full-fledged" problems. The first is a series of continual shifts, to reestablish equilibrium, between task efforts and social-emotional efforts. Such shifts occur at a micro level, perhaps at an act-to-act level and certainly between "strings" of successive acts within the ongoing group interaction session. (The second pattern is a phase-to-phase pattern, through the course of the session. That pattern will be discussed in the next part of this chapter.) According to the equilibrium idea, task activity itself produces strains in the social-emotional relations among group members. Even successful task activity produces strains, from the results of inattention to social-emotional matters; but task failure or task difficulties amplify these strains. These tensions build up until a point is reached at which the group must put the task aside, so to speak, and turn its attention to these social-emotional strains. But while these strains are being dealt with, there is no further progress on the task. So, when the high level of tension is "bled off" sufficiently by social-emotional activity, the group can set aside its social-emotional efforts and return its attention to task activity. This process continues until the task is completed, or interrupted by time running out (or, one would suppose, until the group "breaks up" due to unresolved social-emotional strains—although that is not permitted to happen in the ad hoc laboratory groups upon which most interaction research has been done).

Act-by-act patterns.   Such an equilibrium-seeking pattern ought to be visible in the sequence of actions within the interaction of problem-solving groups. Bales (1953) examined two sets of "act to act" matrices. One, a "reactive" matrix, plots how acts are distributed over categories when one person's act is followed by an act by another person, that is, when there is a change of speaker. The other, a "proactive" matrix, plots the act to act distribution when a speaker keeps the floor for more than one act. The patterns in these two matrices bear on the equilibrium problem.

Keep in mind that, overall, interaction rates are highest for attempted answers (56 percent), then positive responses (25 percent), negative reactions (12 or 13 percent) and questions (7 percent). Within these, *relative* rates differ as a function of the preceding act. (Acts can, of course, be influenced by acts earlier in the sequence than the one just preceding; but such analyses have been too complex for detailed treatments. See later discussion of some sequential analyses employing more complex mathematical forms by Gottman, 1979a).

The reactive pattern (one speaker followed by another) shows that attempted answers are typically followed by positive reactions, especially agreements. There are weaker tendencies to reply to a suggestion with a suggestion, and to reply to attempted answers with negative reactions (disagreements especially), and with questions, in that order of frequency.

Positive actions by one member of an interacting pair, A, generate both positive reactions (especially of the same kind—agree for agree, solidarity for solidarity, tension release for tension release), and also attempted answers (especially orientation and opinion) by the other member of the pair, B. Questions follow in relative frequency, with negative reactions very unlikely. Negative actions by A show an opposite pattern. They generate both negative reactions (especially "in kind") and attempted answers (especially orientation and opinion) by B. Questions by B follow in frequency, with positive reactions very unlikely. Questions by A generate attempted answers (again, in kind) by B, and there is some tendency for questions by A to generate questions (ask for orientation, especially) by B. Both positive and negative reactions to questions are infrequent.

Looked at from the other side of the matrix, reacting with an attempted answer is most often "induced" by the prior speaker asking for such answers, and/or giving either positive or negative responses. Giving positive responses is most often induced by the prior speaker being positive, or attempting an answer. Giving negative reactions is most often induced by the prior speaker being negative; and disagreement is also induced by the prior speaker offering an attempted answer. While questions are low rate in all cases, B's asking for orientation is induced by A's asking for suggestion; B's asking for opinion is induced by A's positive or negative responses, and B's asking for suggestion is induced by A's giving suggestion.

When person A initiates two acts in a row (the proactive matrix), attempted answers are most often continued (in kind) with further attempted answers. Questions, also, are usually continued (in kind) with further questions, but questions also generate attempted answers (orientation and opinion), indicating that they may have been more or less rhetorical. Asking for suggestion is often followed by disagreement.

A's positive reactions are most often followed by attempted answers (opinion and suggestion). Solidarity is often followed by agreements; but agreements are often followed by disagreements, and tension release is often followed by antagonism and tension (first the good news, then the bad news). These varying forms of continuation after a positive response (presumably to a prior speaker) suggest that the positive response may have any of several meanings or functions. This idea will be discussed later.

A negative reaction by A is followed most often by tension reduction and next most frequently by further antagonism, then by giving opinion or showing solidarity. Both tension and disagreement are followed by giving suggestion or opinion.

Looked at from the other side of the matrix: A's acts of attempted answers can be induced by virtually any type of A's own prior act. A's positive acts are likely to have followed a prior positive or negative act by A. This is especially so for tension release, which tends to follow expressed antagonism, expressed solidarity, or other tension release. A's negative acts are likely to have followed positive or negative prior acts by A. (This is especially so for antagonism following antagonism and for prior tension release.) A's questions tend to have been preceded by other questions of the same kind.

A brief summary of all this may point up some patterns. If A initiates an act, the most likely category is an attempted answer. If A keeps the floor, the next act is likely to be another attempted answer, of the same kind. If another speaker, B, assumes the floor, B's most likely first act will be a positive response. Less likely would be a negative response (disagreement), or an attempted answer of his or her own. But whichever of these was B's first act, B's next act, if he or she keeps the floor, is very likely to be an attempted answer, with one exception. Acts of antagonism and tension release "provoke" themselves and each other, as well as provoking "gives opinion". So some subcycles of this sort are quite possible. (Bales suggests that such cycles also occur for solidarity and tension release.)

The only other sequence that is very likely to occur would be A's single (or multiple) attempted answer, followed by B's positive (or negative) single act response, which is then in turn followed by A as a speaker. If B gave a positive response, then A is likely either to give another positive response (followed by more attempted answers), or to respond to B's positive response immediately with an additional attempted answer. If B gives a negative response, then A is most likely to give another attempted answer (at least orientation or opinion), or to give back a negative response (disagreement or antagonism). The first of these, disagreement, is likely to be followed by more attempted answers. The second, antagonism, is likely to lead to an antagonism-tension release subcycle, that eventually "breaks out" into the "gives opinion" category, which in turn leads to further attempted answers.

Equilibrium versus punctuated sequences.   Such examination of the act to act sequences does not give a picture of simple two- or three- step action/reaction sequences, with each "proaction" creating a disturbance in equilibrium and each "reaction" resolving or rejecting or reducing it. Rather, the pattern suggests that there is a focal thrust to solve the task; that so-called attempted answers are efforts toward that goal; and that responses to those task attempts are not so much distinctive reactions as they are one or another (or several) of the following:

1. reinforcements, encouraging or discouraging further development of the same "line" of task effort;
2. devices to help "seize" the floor, so as to offer one's own task effort;
3. the offering of nonevaluative feedback ("uh huh"; "go on") to facilitate the flow of interaction (a regulatory function);
4. the fulfilling of social rituals of courtesy (agreement even if that is to be followed by disagreement).

This process generates mostly *strings of attempted answers,* some of which are proactive but some of which are really reactive to one's own or another's immediately prior (or almost immediately prior) task actions. Bales (1953) cites Murray's term, "serial programs," for those strings. *Such strings or serial programs of task events are punctuated with positive and negative reactions* (agreements and disagreements) *by others.* These reactions serve as feedback, reinforcement, courtesy, flow regulators, tactics to get the floor, and the like. These strings of task events are also punctuated, though infrequently, with questions. Questions also may serve feedback functions, and perhaps floor-taking or other functions.

Occasionally, a strong form (or a more interpersonal form) of negative reaction (antagonism) will move the string into a temporary negative "reverberation": antagonism generates further antagonism, tension, or tension release; tension release generates antagonism or further tension release. That reverberation persists until the tension is reduced (according to Bales, 1953) or until it shifts over into the task area (since "gives opinion" is also a relatively probable response to tension release). A similar positive reverberation, of solidarity and tension release, can also occur, though this is more likely to "exit" quickly back into the task area. These results suggest that task activity, once started, tends to persist for an extended time (Bales, 1953). They also suggest that cycles of social-emotional activity occasionally get started and, once started, tend to reverberate for a time; but that they get "spent" through tension release relatively soon. In summary, then, one can regard this whole process not so much as a continuous see-sawing, task/social-emotional equilibrium process, but rather as a *straightforward problem-solving* (i.e., task) *process punctuated by social-emotional activities that reinforce, guide, and regulate the flow of essentially task-oriented behavior.*

Bales (1953) also regards positive and negative reactions as involving reinforcement. He argues that such positive reinforcements must exceed negative ones by a substantial amount (as they characteristically do) for a group to be successful or even viable over an extended period. He argues that if there were *no* reinforcements the behavior rates would reduce or cease as motivation waned. Positive and negative reactions serve two purposes: to reinforce (positively or negatively), and to guide toward or away from the behavior just exhibited. But a negative reaction is, in itself, a reducer of motivation and satisfaction. So you need at least one positive act to counteract each negative one. But that would only overcome the friction of operation of the group's own controlling system (Bales, 1953). If positive equals negative, then task motivation would run down, the task would not get completed, and task satisfaction would be less. A group needs positive reactions in excess of negative ones in order to get its tasks successfully completed, hence, to get satisfaction from task performance itself. (This holds even without considering the pleasure and satisfaction that come from the interpersonal domain when more positive than negative interactions occur.)

It follows that groups with higher positive to negative ratios should have higher satisfaction (and they do, with correlations from .6 to .8, says Bales, 1953). Furthermore, individuals who receive higher positive to negative ratios of feedback from fellow group members should have higher satisfaction. There is no direct evidence of this, but several sets of indirect evidence bear on it:

1. Higher status members get higher positive/negative ratios and also have higher satisfaction. (This is evidence based on covariation, and not direct evidence of a relation between positive/negative ratio and satisfaction.)
2. Members who are rejected reduce communication (Dittes & Kelley, 1956) and communication to them is also reduced (Schachter, 1951).
3. Members who get support from others communicate more (Pepinsky, Hemphill, & Shevitz, 1958).
4. Members in more active places in the communication net of the group also are more active and have more satisfaction (Leavitt, 1951; Shaw, 1959).

Even more indirect evidence lies in results showing that members communicate more with those whom they like and dislike (and far more with the former than the latter) than with those toward whom they are neutral, and receive communications from those whom they perceive as liking them or disliking them more than from those they perceive as being neutral toward them (Festinger & Hutte, 1954). Similarly indirect evidence is the finding that members of highly motivated groups communicate more; that highly motivated members of groups increase communication rates over successive sessions whereas members of low-motivation groups decline in their interaction rates over time (Bass, Pryer, Gaier, & Flint, 1958).

All of these findings represent indirect evidence that positive and negative reactions within group interaction serve as reinforcements; and that these reinforcements facilitate and regulate the flow of interaction, affect and are affected by the motivation of members for task performance, and (along with task success) affect the satisfaction members get from the group interaction. This evidence does not directly discredit the idea of a continual task/social-emotional equilibrium process, but it does not support it either. It is at least as plausible to view the process as an extended, task oriented "serial program," punctuated, reinforced and guided by positive and negative reactions, partly of an interpersonal nature (solidarity, antagonism), partly task-related (agreement and disagreement), and partly a mixture of personal, interpersonal, task and situational aspects (tension and tension release). The matter of groups as equilibrium-seeking systems will arise again in several other chapters of this book, and will be discussed in terms of the perspectives of those chapters.

Phase Movement in Groups

Bales (1953) also postulated a series of shifts in the relative rates of different categories of interaction as the group moves through its session (hence, as it executes a "full-fledged" problem). He concentrated on three problem-solving steps: orientation (gathering information and clarifying what the task is); evaluation (assessing that information); and control (deciding what to do). These three stages, incidentally, deal only with Quadrants I and II of the Task Circumplex: Generate and Choose. These phases might or might not include activities pertinent to Quadrant III, Negotiate. They do not include Quadrant IV, Execute (see Part II, especially chapter 5).

These three phases correspond to the three pairs of categories at the center of IPA: 6 and 7 (ask for and give orientation); 5 and 8 (ask for and give opinion); and 4 and 9 (ask for and give suggestions). As the group moves through its task efforts, Bales hypothesizes, the relative rates of acts in these three pairs of categories shift as follows: (a) orientation is highest at the outset and declines as the session progresses; (b) evaluation rises from the beginning to the middle of the session, then declines; and (c) control is low at first and rises to its highest at the end. (Note that these are *relative* rates within categories.)

At the same time—to reintroduce the idea that there is a continuing task / social-emotional equilibrium process—as the group progresses on the task from the relatively unemotional orientation to the more controversial evaluation, and especially control, there is a corresponding increase in tension. This increased strain is reflected in an increase in negative reactions; efforts to deal with this strain bring an increase in positive reactions through the course of the session. As a consequence, both positive and negative reactions increase from beginning to end, although they still remain a small proportion of all acts, and although positive reactions have much higher rates than negative ones. Both positive and negative reactions reach their highest level in the last phase; but positive reactions, in the form of tension release and expressions of solidarity, predominate at the very end.

These descriptions of phase movement are fairly good representations of several sets of group data that have been examined in this regard (e.g., Bales, 1953; Bales & Strodtbeck, 1951). They did *not* hold up for a large set of sessions of therapy groups studied by Talland (1955). But such groups are definitely not carrying out a "full-fledged" problem in each single session, and they differ in many other ways from the kinds of groups studied by Bales and others for baseline IPA data. Therapy groups are to some extent searching for "the problem" and, if anything, solve the full-fledged problem only over many sessions, perhaps extending for years. Furthermore, Psathas (1960) analyzed data from a set of groups in therapy by comparing early versus middle versus late *sessions* (over a nine-month course of therapy), rather than comparing beginning versus middle versus end periods within a single session. Those therapy groups apparently went through the problem-solving phase sequence once over the entire course of the therapy. Talland's groups were all taken from early sessions, when they were still concentrating on the problem of orientation. Landsberger (1955) also found the phase sequence in a series of labor negotiation groups. He suggests that the phase sequence holds for all groups, but is sharper for the more sucessful groups. So, within the limitations involved in the IPA categories and data, most of it from ad hoc laboratory groups with full-fledged tasks, there seems to be a reasonable body of evidence supporting the proposed phase sequence.

BASIC FUNCTIONS OF
THE GROUP INTERACTION
PROCESS

What is going on when a group is interacting? To borrow an example from the physical sciences, when chemicals are interacting (i.e., when a chemical reaction is taking place) at least two things may be occurring: Some particles may be uncoupling and recoupling in new combinations; and some matter-to-energy conversions may be occurring, often evidenced by accompanying heat exchange. The outward forms of the substances involved may undergo dramatic changes, including shifts to either far more stable or quite unstable substances. What comparable kinds of occurrences take place when a group of people is in interaction? In other words, what are the group interaction equivalents of bonding and energy exchange in chemistry?

Bales's Two-Process Schema

Many past studies using systems for observation of group interaction process, as well as studies not observing group interaction but making inferences about intervening processes from input-output relations, have tried to hypothesize about such underlying processes or have tried to discern them from results of observation. Bales posited two fundamental processes: task oriented or instrumental, and social-emotional oriented or expressive. Except for some highly unusual limiting cases, both these processes are always in operation when group interaction is taking place. For Bales, though, they are mutually exclusive at the action level. Any unit act serves one or the other function but not both. The two processes are interrelated, and to some extent in opposition, within a general group equilibrium. For example: Attention to task creates social-emotional friction. Attention to social-emotional concerns detracts from task efforts. Too much attention to either process leads to system breakdown because of failure of the other process (i.e., either social-emotional disruption of the group or group failure to do the tasks necessary to its goals).

Many other theoretical efforts have posited two underlying processes similar, in many respects, to Bales's instrumental and expressive processes. The distinction between task concerns and interpersonal (social-emotional) concerns also underlies several historically important distinctions between types of groups: Simmel's (1950) *gemeinshaft* and *gesellshaft* (often translated as community and society); Cooley's (1902) primary versus secondary groups. In the leadership area, this same distinction underlies Hemphill's (1949) initiating structure-in-interaction versus consideration; and Fiedler's (1967) task oriented versus interpersonal oriented leadership styles. It is also one of the key distinctions made in the interaction framework presented in chapter 1.

The Bion-Thelen Interaction Theory

Contemporaneously with Bales's pioneering work, Bion was formulating a theory of group process (Bion, 1961) in the context of group therapy. Thelen subsequently used the concepts of that theory to develop a group observation system. (Stock & Thelen, 1958; Thelen, 1956; Thelen, Stock & others, 1954). It, too, posits a "work" versus "emotion" distinction, but unlike IPA it assumes that every act is *both*. Work is coded at four levels (effort concerned with personal goals; routine group work; active problem-solving; and creative, integrative work). The emotional categories are: fight/flight; pairing among group members; and dependence on the leader. Thelen separated fight and flight into categories, scored degrees of the emotions, and added an "other" category for coding acts clearly emotional but not clearly fitting one category or the other. Thelen also used a larger "natural unit" of group interaction, by trying to identify points when a shift occurred in the particular subgroup involved in the discussion. That tended to divide "sessions" into four to twenty "natural" units, ranging from three to eighteen minutes. (Bales's IPA would divide a session of the same length into hundreds of acts, each lasting, on the average, only a few seconds.)

Stock and Thelen (1958) applied this system to a series of training groups at the National Training Laboratory at Bethel, Maine. They did not find a dominant phase movement of the type Bales posits. Bion was more interested in the swings between various emotion/work states than any specific developmental pattern. But Dunphy (1964) inferred a developmental scheme implicit in Bion's concepts: (1) dependence on leaders; (2) attack on leader (fight) followed by scapegoating others (flight); (3) pairing; (4) effective work with little emotionality. That is a sequence similar to several that will be discussed later under group development.

The Thelen observation system shared with Bales the basic task/social-emotional distinction, but it contrasted sharply with Bales in several other respects. First, rather than being mutually exclusive alternatives, task and emotion are treated in the Bion-Thelen system as *independent, crossed* dimensions; every act is scored on both. The observer takes the perspective of the actor (what he or she is *really* doing). Thelen uses a more macro-level unit, with boundaries based on participation patterns rather than on categories of the system. While their theory and observation scheme gained some following, it never was very broadly used in the study of groups.

Steiner's Analysis of Process

An earlier chapter provided a description of Steiner's (1972) task typology and model of group productivity. A central idea of that model is that a group's actual productivity is often below its potential productivity because of *process losses.* Steiner talks about two general types of process losses: those due to shifts in member *motivation* (usually losses, but sometimes increases for groups of very small size); and those due to the need for *coordination* of actions of different members (always losses). One could regard these as results of shifts in force (motivation) and in integration (coordination), not unlike the energy exchange and bonding of chemistry. But these really label the results of the process losses, rather than the nature of the processes themselves. Furthermore, they are at least somewhat related to Bales's task (coordination) and social-emotional (motivation) processes.

The Hackman-Morris
Summary Variables

An earlier chapter also described, though briefly, a three-factor approach to analysis of the relation of group interaction to task performance, by Hackman and Morris (1975). In that analysis, the authors propose that all of the ways that group interaction process can affect group task performance can be reflected in three summary variables: task strategy, member effort, and member knowledge and skills. Note that this analysis is explicitly concerned with summarizing and labelling the *effects* of group interaction process, rather than specifying the fundamental *processes* themselves. So, as with Steiner's analysis, the terms label outcomes of group interaction, but do not specify processes. Note also that this analysis, as well as Steiner's analysis, is concerned primarily with groups as task performance systems. So, quite naturally, the "task" aspect of group interaction process is heavily reflected here. Both the first (task strategy) and the third of the summary variables (member knowledge and skills) refer directly to aspects related to the group's task. Member effort, on the other hand, like Steiner's motivation, refers to what might be regarded as the social-emotional aspect—though the concern is also with how such individual effort affects group task performance.

Hare's Four-Dimensional System

Hare (1973, 1976) has drawn upon some theoretical ideas of Parsons and his colleagues (e.g., Parsons, 1961; Parsons & Shils, 1951) to identify four basic needs or functions of groups. He argues that all groups, to survive, must meet four basic needs:

1. The members must share a common identity and have a commitment to the values of the group. (This is termed L, for latent pattern maintenance and tension reduction.)
2. They must have or be able to generate the skills and resources needed to reach their goal(s). (A for adaptation.)
3. They must have rules (norms) to coordinate their activities and enough solidarity (cohesiveness) to stay together to complete their goals. (I for integration.)
4. They must be able to exercise enough control over members to be effective in reaching their common goal(s). (G for goal attainment.)

Hare (1976, p. 15) argues that these can be viewed as categories of a 2 × 2 matrix. Two of the needs have a referent *external* to the group (A and G) while two have an *internal* referent (L and I). Two refer to *instrumental* processes (L and A), and two to *consummatory* processes (I and G). These four distinctions are drawn from Parsons' structural-functional theory of social systems. Hare (1976) has related them to major social subsystems (A-economic; L-familial and religious; G-political; and I-legal), and to different system levels (A-organismic; G-personality; I-social system; L-culture).

Hare (1976) ties these four functional needs to sets of dimensions used by other researchers to characterize interpersonal relations in groups. Chapple (1942) used a single observation category (action/silence), hence had a single behavior dimension (dominance/submissiveness). Bales's IPA had two, as did the Bion-Thelen scheme, Leary (1957), and several others. These two-dimensional systems essentially added a positive/negative dimension to the dominance/submission one. Couch and Carter (1952) postulated a three-dimensional system, adding "individual prominence" to group sociability and group facilitation dimensions. Borgatta (1963) had three similar dimensions.

Schutz (1958) also had three: inclusion, control and affection. Bales, too, in his later work, added a third dimension (up/down or dominance/submission; positive/negative; and a task oriented and conforming versus deviant dimension).

Hare (1976) maintains that the set of three dimensions obscures a fourth. He postulates four dimensions of interpersonal relations in groups, and relates them to Parsons' four functional needs of groups, as in Table 12-2.

It is not clear in all cases why these functional needs map to the interpersonal dimensions in the fashion proposed by Hare. For example, why doesn't G fit the third dimension just as well as A? But Hare's efforts to align all of the systems proposed by Parsons, Bales, Couch, Carter, Borgatta, Leary, Schutz, Bion, Thelen, and others, is heroic. And his integration of them is by far the most comprehensive yet developed, even though some portions of the rationale for it are not entirely clear.

Hare (1976, p. 15) also orders the four Parsons functions in terms of what he calls the "cybernetic hierarchy of control" (that order is L/I/G/A). Moreover, he uses those four needs as the basis for a theory of group development (for which the order is L/A/I/G/L). That latter use is discussed in a later section, in the context of changes in the pattern of interaction over time.

While the labels used by Hare for the four group functions derive from and are sensible within Parsonian theory, they seem to add jargon unnecessary for the purposes and focus of this book. I want to substitute for them some terms drawn from the concepts used elsewhere in this book. For Adaptation, substitute Abilities and Resources. For Goal attainment, substitute Group Task Performance. For Latent pattern maintenance, substitute Values and Goals. For Integration, substitute Norms and Cohesiveness. In these terms, the four basic problems can be stated as:

(V) Developing or adopting fundamental values and goals for the group.

(A) Developing or having abilities and resources needed to do the tasks necessary to achieve those goals.

(N) Developing or having norms to guide behavior toward the goals, and cohesiveness to support and enforce conformity to those norms.

(P) Performing effectively the group's tasks in pursuit of the common goals.

When the four are presented in this form, it is clear that Bales's IPA system (and most of the other two-dimensional systems) focused more or less on task execution (P here, G for Hare) and on interpersonal relations (N, or I). Those two functions are the two that Hare calls consummatory. They are the

TABLE 12-2 Functional Needs and Interpersonal Dimensions

HARE'S INTERPERSONAL RELATIONS DIMENSIONS	PARSON'S FUNCTIONAL NEEDS
I Dominance versus Submissiveness	G Goal attainment
II Positive versus Negative	I Integration
III Task-serious versus Expressive	A Adaptation
IV Conforming versus Nonconforming	L Latent pattern maintenance

TABLE 12-3   Four Fundamental Group Problems. A Reformulation

REFERENT OF ACTION	LEVEL OF EXPRESSION	
	MANIFEST	LATENT
EXTERNAL TO GROUP	P Group Task Performance (Hare's G, Goal attainment)	A Abilities and Resources (Hare's Adaptation)
INTERNAL TO GROUP	N Norms and Cohesiveness (Hare's I, Integration)	V Values and Goals (Hare's L, Latent pattern maintenance)

explicit aims of action in groups. The other two, that Hare calls instrumental, are more or less implicit or latent. They *underlie* the two consummatory ones. Abilities (A) underlie and are essential to task performance. Values and goals (V or L) underlie and are essential to interpersonal relations. So it may be worth considering that the four functional needs are really *two needs* (task-external and interpersonal-internal), *at two different levels of expression*. That would cross Hare's internal-external distinction with manifest-latent, rather than with instrumental-consummatory (see Table 12–3).

Still another way to view these is to regard them as functionally linked in terms of what underlies or logically precedes what. In that view, consensus on values and goals (V) is fundamental to all else. Then come both insuring abilities and resources to carry out those goals (A), and developing norms to guide behavior and cohesiveness to support those norms (N). Both A and N, then, serve as preconditions for effective group task performance (P) (see Figure 12–1). This formulation has the advantage of displaying basic group needs in a functional order that relates to, but doesn't presuppose any specific order of, group development. At the same time, it separates out what is latent (hence, not directly observable) from what is manifest though instrumental. In a sense, values and goals set the purposes for group action; abilities and norms provide the means; and group task performance *is* the action (consummatory).

GROUP DEVELOPMENT: PATTERNS OF INTERACTION OVER SESSIONS

Considerable attention has been given to the question of how the distribution of activity shifts over periods of time longer than the single session. Much of this has been provided under the rubric of "group development" (e.g., Bales, 1950a; Bion, 1961; Hare, 1976; Schutz, 1958; Bennis & Shepherd, 1956; Dunphy, 1964; Tuckman, 1965; Mills, 1964; Mann, Gibbard, & Hartman, 1967; Slater, 1966). There are two striking features of IPA profiles taken for the same group over several sessions, when the group is solving a "full-fledged" problem at *each* session. First, there is a reduction in relative proportion of group interaction that is devoted to task activity as the group progresses through a series of problem-solving sessions. This reduction is paralleled by a rise in positive social-emotional activity. But that rise in social-emotional activity includes a slight drop in agreements along with a large increase in tension release and solidarity, especially in the final meetings. The second striking feature of those session to session IPA profiles is a sharp rise in negative reactions during the *second meeting*. Negative reactions are typically low (around 12 percent) in the first session, and return to that level in the third, fourth and later sessions. But they rise to over 18 percent in the second session. This feature has occurred in data from other studies, not using IPA, and it is made much of in several theories of group development that are described later in this chapter.

It has already been pointed out that Bion's theory does not postulate a series of phases within a session nor a fixed sequence of developmental stages for the therapy groups about which he theorized. Thelen's empirical use of Bion's concepts (Stock & Thelen, 1958) also did not find any dominant developmental sequence for training groups. (Training groups, or T-groups, refer to one of the earliest forms of experiential groups discussed in Chapter 2. Later forms are called sensitivity groups, encounter groups, and the like). But Dunphy (1964) derived a developmental sequence from Bion's categories (first dependence, then fight, then flight, then pairing, then task efforts low in emotion). Bennis and Shepherd (1956) offered a theory of development for training groups. It postulated two major phases: dependence, or concern about relations to authority; and interdependence, or concern about intimacy and personal relations. Each phase had three subphases that reflect a dialectic sequence of thesis, antithesis and synthesis. In phase I, the subphases are dependence on the leader, then counterdependence and attack (the rise in negative reactions!), then resolution. In phase II, the subphases are enchantment, disenchantment and consensual validation.

Schutz (1958), too, posed a theory of group development, working mainly from laboratory problem-solving groups. He posited three interpersonal needs: inclusion, control, and affection. He asserted a universal sequence of group development: interaction dealing with inclusion, then with control, then with affection. That cycle recurs until the final three time-intervals before the group expects to terminate. In the last three time-intervals, the sequence is reversed: group members break their ties of affection, then stop controlling one another, then stop interacting and feeling identity with the group.

Tuckman (1965) developed his theory of group development on the basis of an extensive review of work done with therapy groups, and later applied it to development in training groups, laboratory groups, and groups observed in natural settings. He posits four major stages, each with two aspects: group structure and task behavior. Stage I involves testing and dependence for the group structure aspect, and orientation and testing for the task behavior aspect. Stage II involves intra-group conflict and emotional response to the task demands (the rise in negative reactions at the second stage again!). Stage III involves the development of group cohesion, and open discussion of self and other group members (the latter being work on "the task" for therapy groups). Stage IV involves development of functional role relatedness and the emergence of insights (i.e., successfully "solving" the therapy group's task). The essence of Tuckman's four stages has been paraphrased as: I, *forming;* II, *storming;* III, *norming;* and IV, *performing.*

Several other theories of group development, based on training groups, use four or sometimes five stages similar to Tuckman's (e.g., Dunphy, 1964; Mann, Gibbard, & Hartman, 1967; Mills, 1964; Slater, 1966). Hare (1976) argues that these can, in large part, be described in terms of Parsons's (1961) functional theory of groups. Hare postulates that the following sequence of the four functional problems posited by that theory (see the previous section) constitutes a developmental sequence for groups: latent pattern maintenance (L), adaptation (A), integration (I), and goal attainment (G). The sequence ends with a return to L, a reorientation of the group after completion of the cycle of development.

When those four functional needs were discussed earlier, I offered substitute terms more closely fitted to the concepts of this book, namely: values and goals (V); abilities and resources (A); norms and cohesiveness (N); and group task performance (P). Tuckman's and Hare's stages are laid out along with those terms in Table 12–4. It is clear that there is a good fit for stages I, III and IV, but a misfit for stage II. Tuckman's storming stage is simply not comparable to the Hare-Parsons adaptation (which we have termed abilities).

The three-level representation of the four fundamental problems, offered in Figure 12–1, may provide a clue about the misfit. Tuckman's stage I is clearly related to the most fundamental latent function: developing consensus on values and goals (my V, Hare's L). Tuckman's stage III, norming, is clearly related to the middle level—the manifest-instrumental needs for task abilities and resources (A) *and* for group norms and cohesiveness (N). Tuckman's stage IV, performing, is clearly related to the final consummatory phase of group task performance (P). But the three-level functional chain formulation simply does not include an equivalent to Tuckman's phase II, storming. One possibility is that the storming stage is spurious. But it reflects the much-touted rise in intragroup conflict and negative reactions in the second developmental stage. Such a

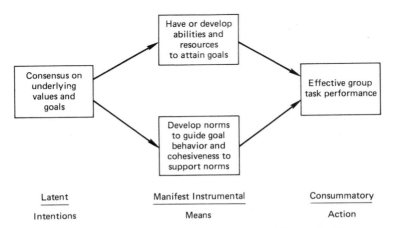

FIGURE 12-1   A Functional Chain of Fundamental Group Problems

conflict stage is found in IPA profiles, in Tuckman's review of therapy groups, in Schutz's laboratory groups, and by Bennis and Shepherd, Mills, Dunphy, Slater, and Mann and colleagues, with training groups.

It was noted in chapter 10 that the full-fledged problems used in Bales's ad hoc laboratory groups dealt only with two of the four quadrants of the Task Circumplex, namely: Generate and Choose. Not only did they not deal with Quadrant IV, Execute (a natural consequence of using verbal group tasks), they also did not deal with Quadrant III, Negotiate. That quadrant deals with the resolution of conflict within the group. Suppose, then, that we imagine that the full-fledged or *total* task of a group, over its development, subsumes all four quadrants of the Task Circumplex: Generate, Choose, Negotiate, and Execute (see chapter 5). Let us further imagine that those four quadrants or segments of the generic group task are in some way related to the stages in the development of the group. Retaining Tuckman's labels to identify the four stages, and recognizing that each stage involves *both task and interpersonal activity,* perhaps the developmental sequence can be represented in a manner similar to Figure 12–2.

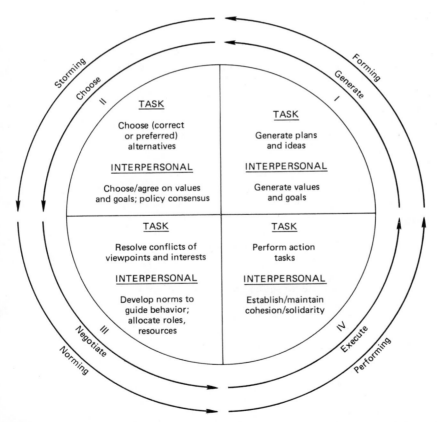

Figure 12–2   An Integrated Circumplex: Task Performance Processes, Interpersonal Processes, and Stages of Group Development.

TABLE 12-4   Developmental Stages Compared

HARE/PARSONS	TUCKMAN	THIS BOOK
L Latent pattern maintenance	I Forming	V Values and Goals
A Adaptation	II Storming	A Abilities and Resources
I Integration	III Norming	N Norms and Cohesiveness
G Goal attainment	IV Performing	P Group Task Performance

The possibility of fusing the extensive theoretic integration of Tuckman regarding stages of group development, the Hare-Parsons functional theory of group interaction and group development, and the Task Circumplex presented in the earlier chapters of this book, makes the exploration of this set of relations worthwhile.

SOME NEW TECHNOLOGY FOR STUDYING INTERACTION PROCESS

As indicated in the first section of this chapter, research involving the direct observation of group interaction process waned for over a decade, beginning in the 1960s, except for work with specialized systems tailored to specialized group situations such as classroom behavior. But there has been a resurgence in such work, triggered largely by the availability of some new technology for collection of observation records, for analysis of data, and for modelling interaction processes. A few examples of each of these are discussed here.

Data Collection Technology

Gottman (1979a, 1979b) has pioneered the use of split-screen presentations of video recordings of dyadic interaction. He displays, side by side on the same screen, the face and even upper bodies of the members of a dyad. In Gottman's work this is often a husband and wife dyad. In that way, there can be direct observation of both the visual and verbal responses of A and B to each other's inputs, and it can be done either with A and B's simultaneous behavior being examined or with either partner's behavior "lagged" by any given amount of time. With this technique and some complex analysis methods to be noted below, Gottman is able to study the cyclicality of behavior of the couple and of both of its members, the lead-lag relations (i.e., temporal intervals) involved in their interdependence, and especially the *dominance* relations between them. Gottman defines dominance of A over B as the degree to which B's behavior is predictable from A's simultaneous or prior behavior. If the probability that B does X is higher when A has just done behavior Y (compared to B's doing behavior X in general, or when A has not just done Y), to that extent and in regard to those behaviors and that situation, A can be said to dominate B.

Obviously, such a definition of dominance will, in many cases, lead to the conclusion that A dominates B *and* B dominates A. More specifically, it could lead to the conclusion that A's behavior X dominates B's behavior Y, while B's behavior P dominates A's behavior Q. Dominance, in this sense, is what we will later call influence. Such *mutual influence* or *complementary influence* between interacting partners is the rule rather than the exception in group interaction. Gottman uses these techniques, among others, to help identify and clarify bases of marital conflict.

Data Analysis
Techniques

On the data analysis side, both Gottman (1979a, 1979b) and Dabbs (1980) have made use of Fourier analyses and spectral analysis to treat interaction data. These techniques have long been used in the physical sciences and in some areas of psychology (e.g., audition) but seldom in social psychology or in the study of groups. They help to find cycles and subcycles within continuous data, and to identify the periodicity of those cycles. Gottman has used them to identify cycles of behavior in husband-wife and other dyadic interactions, and to study lead-lag relations of dominance in those cycles. Dabbs (1980) has used Fourier and spectral analyses to try to identify the "cognitive load" of different kinds of dyadic interactions, and to examine patterns of talking, silence and gaze. Specifically, he has compared temporal patterns of talking, pauses, interruptions, and floor shift pauses for dyads engaged in intellectual discussions as against social conversation. He also examined those patterns of verbal behavior in relation to the temporal patterns of gaze.

Dabbs (1980) argues that pauses *during* a floor turn (but *not* the silence just before a floor shift) are evidence of cognitive load (thinking, searching for the right word or for an elusive fact). He hypothesizes that there will be a reduction of visual input (gaze by the speaker) during such cognitive work. Dabbs defines a "turn" as a period of time during which one participant has the floor. It includes pauses in that person's speech, and it includes the silence after he or she stops speaking until the next speaker starts. Such turns last longer in intellectual conversations than in social conversations. Dabbs suggests that such turns may be organized into "megaturns" in such high-cognitive-load conversations. A megaturn is a period of time during which *one* of the interactants has the floor a very large proportion of the time, usually having a number of relatively long turns punctuated by a partner's very short responses (perhaps the reactive acts suggested from Bales's profiles, discussed earlier in this chapter). Dabbs finds that such megaturns are characteristic of dyadic conversations involving intellectual discussions, and that the "cycle length"—from the predominant talking of one to the predominant talking of the other and back again—generally took 32 to 128 seconds in dyads having such conversations. In contrast, dyads engaged in social conversation typically had cycles of a length of two to four seconds, indicating that the cycles were single turns rather than megaturns. (Dabbs also found interesting relations between the vocalization cycles and patterns of gaze. Both Dabbs's and Gottman's work offer techniques for studying patterns of nonverbal behavior as well as, and in conjunction with, studies of verbal behavior. Some of these are discussed in chapter 13, dealing with nonverbal behaviors.

Modelling Group Interaction
Patterns

Tsai (1977) applied an exponential model, similar to the one by Stephan and Mischler (1952) discussed earlier, to examine the pattern of participation of a rather large, natural group (the eighteen-member Economic and Social Council of the United Nations). Incidentally, he found very high correlation of participation rates using three quite different definitions of a unit act: (a) Bales's IPA unit, rather micro and based on category of the act; (b) number of sentences, a unit based on semantic rather than interaction content categorization; and (c) number of floor turns, regardless of length of speech. So the rate phenomena discussed in this section are not artifacts of the way the unit act is defined.

Tsai found a very good fit of the exponential model to actual participation rates, but he also found some significant deviations. Specifically, the model underestimated rates for the highest participators while overestimating them for the middle-participators. Nowakowska (1978) offered a stochastic (probabilistic) model to try to account for such deviations. It supposes that the total group is composed of two "factions" (but it could be extended to more than two such subgroups); that participation *within* each faction is distributed in a manner similar to the downward exponential curve of the other models; but that the two curves may differ in starting level (reflecting between-faction differences in the rate of the faction's highest participator) and in slope (reflecting such factors as faction size, leadership structure, basic initiation rates of individuals).

It is worth noting that each of these models is built upon certain hypothesized psychological processes. Descriptions of those processes, by researchers developing the models (e.g., Horvath, 1965; Nowakowska, 1978; Tsai, 1977) sound pretty unrealistic. For example, Horvath's model (and subsequently both Tsai's and Nowakowska's) was built on the assumption that each member of the group has the same constant probability of trying to initiate the next act if given the opportunity, but that group members are arranged in a hierarchical order in terms of each person's reaction time in responding to a pause in the conversation. So, the probability of each person's actually getting the floor varies inversely with that response speed. It is as if each person waited to see whether each person higher in the hierarchy was going to speak, and if and only if none did, to then themselves initiate speech (or not to do so, and thus to pass the opportunity on to the next member in the group's hierarchy) as a function of that uniform probability of a member talking if given the chance.

It is important to make the point that *the value of the mathematical model,* as a basis for *describing and predicting the phenomenon* (in this case, the distribution of participation in a group), *does not rest entirely on the validity of the psychological processes hypothesized as underlying the phenomenon.* The model can provide a very accurate description, and be very effective in predicting the pattern for some groups not yet observed, even if what the model builder hypothesized about underlying processes is incorrect, even unrealistic. The model maker may have described an unrealistic process that happens to correlate highly with the (as yet unappreciated) real underlying process. Such seems to be the case for the topic at hand. The models accurately describe and predict the pattern of interaction in groups, but we are yet a long way from appreciating just how that pattern comes about, and why it varies as it does over group size, task and situation differences, and the like.

Thomas and Malone (1979) have examined and compared a series of formal mathematical models for analyzing the time course of two-person interaction. They concentrated on what are termed discrete-state, discrete-time, two-person models. Each person's behavior at any instant of time can be classified as in one or the other of two states (i.e., a given behavior is or is not being exhibited). Therefore, the two-person system is in one of four states at time t (A is or is not doing the key behavior, and B is or is not doing it at time t). Those models also assume (a) that A's behavior at time t is independent of B's behavior at time t, but may be dependent on B's behavior at the prior time interval (t-1); (b) that the state of the system at time t depends on its state at time t-1, but not at any earlier times; and (c) that the set of probabilities of the system going from each given state to each other given state (i.e., transition probabilities) remains constant throughout the interaction. (Readers with appropriate backgrounds will recognize that this describes a set of stochastic models that are Markov chains with stationary transition probabilities.)

The main parameters of each of the models divide into three sets; (a) bias, or the individual's tendency to do the key behavior; (b) sensitivity to own prior behavior; and (c) sensitivity to other's prior behavior. The models differ in terms of whether they focus on the behavior itself or transitions in behavior, and in terms of whether they allow for asymmetry between the interacting persons (as we would expect, for example, in mother-infant pairs). Applications of these models to several sets of interaction data, from vastly different kinds of groups (e.g., mother-infant pairs, college student strangers on the telephone, subjects in a face to face laboratory group), lead Thomas and Malone to offer several *general* results. For example, there is evidence of interdependency between members of a pair, but in all cases that tendency is much weaker than the dependence between successive acts of the same person. As another example, in mother-infant dyads, the mother's smiling and gazing behavior depends on the infant's prior behavior, but the converse does not hold. It may well be useful to try to connect these mathematical models of the interaction process with the data analysis models used by Dabbs and Gottman, and to connect both of these with some substantive theories about interaction.

There are some other models of group interaction process, more or less recent and more or less mathematical, that also promise to serve as bench marks for future work. Most of these deal with what we are here regarding as the content of interaction, rather than its pattern. Some (e.g., Altman, 1975; Altman & Taylor, 1973; Altman, Vinsel, & Brown, 1981; Huessman & Levinger, 1976; Levinger, 1980) deal with the acquaintance process and are treated in chapter 16; others (e.g., Adams, 1965; Kelley & Thibaut, 1978; Thibaut & Kelley, 1959) deal mainly with interdependence and allocation of resources and are treated in chapter 15. Still others, dealing with the task performance process, have been discussed in the chapters of Part II. There are some further comments about the functions of models and theories at appropriate places later in the book.

CHAPTER THIRTEEN
THE COMMUNICATION PROCESS: EFFECTS OF RESTRICTIONS IN COMMUNICATION NETWORKS, MODALITIES AND STRATEGIES

In the previous chapter, the discussion focused on patterns of interaction in groups in which the usual channels of communication were more or less left alone. What happens to communication patterning when the channels of communication are deliberately modified? Several factors that have a constraining effect on communication patterns have already been considered. One can regard changes in such factors as group size, task type and difficulty (hence, in what communication is required, useful and possible), and even the distribution of abilities or status among group members, as antecedent conditions that produce (as one of their multiple effects) what amounts to a biasing of the communication channels. Such biasing alters the amount, the distribution, the timing, and/or the content, of communication within the group.

But there has also been considerable research in which the potential patterns of communication within the group have been deliberately modified or eliminated, in order to study the effects of those communication constraints. Major alterations of communication can be done (a) by altering who can communicate to whom, that is, by changing the *communication network* of the group; (b) by altering the modalities by which members of the group can communicate (e.g., audio only versus face to face); and (c) by modifying the communication *strategies* and tactics that are used by group members. Those three methods, progressively less drastic in their control of group communication patterns, are discussed in that order in this chapter. The first section describes the now-classic body of studies using *experimentally restricted communication nets*. The second section deals with some nonverbal features of communication. The third section deals with the body of literature concerned with communication effectiveness of face to face groups compared to groups for which various *modalities* of communication have been eliminated (e.g., audio only, as in a telephone discussion; written communication). The fourth section deals with studies of the effects of using different communication strategies.

STUDIES OF COMMUNICATION NETWORKS

One of the early methods for experimental study of groups was the use of experimentally-concocted communication networks. What happens to group interaction process and task performance when only some of the possible communication "connections" between group members are possible? What happens, for example, if group communication is centralized, so that all of it must flow through one specific member (or, the member at one specific location in the group's communication network)? What happens if it is decentralized, so that all members (or, members at all positions) are equally central in the communication flow?

Bavelas (1948), then Leavitt and colleagues (e.g., Leavitt, 1951), and subsequently many other researchers (for review, see Shaw, 1964, 1978; and Glanzer & Glaser, 1959, 1961), ran a number of experiments using three-, four- and five-person groups, comparing them in communication networks in which only certain channels were possible. One key comparison network has been the "wheel," a highly centralized pattern in which all other members can communicate only to one central member, hence, all messages must pass through the person at the "hub" position in the wheel. Another comparison pattern has been the "circle," in which each member is connected to two other members, but no one member is more central than any other. Still other patterns, such as a Y, a chain, an all-channel or "comcon," and so forth, were used in various studies; but the wheel and circle define the extremes of the main network variable studied: centralization versus decentralization. (See EXRT 26.)

Literally hundreds of studies have been conducted using the communication net approach. The main findings, for present purposes, can be summarized rather directly. First, centralized communication nets are more efficient in transmitting messages. Hence, when the task only requires transmission of information (as the tasks used in some of the early studies did), the highly centralized *wheel* is the most efficient net. The task gets done faster, with fewer messages (and fewer errors, in studies where there are any errors at all). But as the task becomes more complex or difficult, requiring reasoning or problem-solving as well as information transmission, then the wheel loses its relative task efficiency advantage. In a sense, the group's task performance in the wheel depends on the ability of the person in that central position to "solve" the problem, once all pertinent information has been routed to that node. The *circle,* on the other hand, cannot route all information to any one node as efficiently as the wheel, but the information can be routed to, and the nonroutine aspects of the group's task (e.g., reasoning to a solution) can be done by, *any* group

EXRT 26:   *THE BAVELAS–LEAVITT–SHAW COMMUNICATION NET PARADIGM*

Main Study Procedures: Subjects are placed in groups in which only an experimentally predetermined subset of communication links between members is permitted. Those networks of communication vary in pattern. One pattern, called a *wheel,* has each member connected only to one central member, c. (That is, communication links a-c, b-c, d-c, and e-c are the only ones that are operative. It is called a wheel because c is a hub and all the connections are spokes.) Another commonly used pattern is the *circle,* in which each member is connected to only two others. (The communication links a-b, b-c, c-d, d-e and e-a are the only ones operative.) Still others are the *chain* (with a-b, b-c, c-d and d-e the only links); the *kite* (with a-b, b-c, c-d and c-e the only links) and the *star* or "comcon" (in which each member is connected to every other member). Such groups are asked to perform tasks for which the task solution requires that all information, initially distributed among the members, is assembled in some one place in the network, and that the person who has all the information is able to select the correct answer.

Main Dependent Variables of Interest: Task performance indices (errors, time to solution, number of messages); member satisfaction indices; leadership nominations by members.

Main Variations: Number of members; types of networks; types of problems; distribution of information; inter-trial planning communications.

References: Bavelas (1948); Berkowitz (1956); Glanzer & Glaser (1959, 1961); Leavitt (1951); Shaw (1959, 1964, 1978).

---

member equally easily. So a circle group in effect can use its best member as its key member in the central node.

On the other hand, satisfaction of members with the group activity differs for members in central nodes as against those in less central ones. The person at the hub of the wheel, and all members of circle groups, have relatively high satisfaction, while peripheral members of wheels (and other centralized nets) are dissatisfied.

Shaw (1964, 1978), has reviewed many of those studies, and has provided much conceptual clarity for interpretation of their findings. He suggests that the idea of degree of centralization of nets, or positions in nets, is not as useful as the ideas of *independence* and *saturation* of the positions. *Independence* of a position has to do with the degree to which the person in a given position can carry out his or her part of the task autonomously, rather than depend on (one or more) others in the group. *Saturation* of a position refers to the total load—task and role demands as well as message transmission demands—that the person in that position must handle. In principle, positions can vary independently on the two, although they often vary in opposite directions in practice. Both are affected by the nature of the *task,* and by the pattern of the *network.* Satisfaction derives primarily from high independence, but also from moderate saturation. Task performance may be *aided* by independence, and is *seriously hindered* by saturation. Independence is generally higher in decentralized nets, regardless of tasks. Saturation is lower in centralized nets for simple tasks (few messages need be sent in the efficient net on the simple problem); higher in centralized nets for complex problems (because the task requires more messages, and they flow through a centralized position, while peripheral members tend to demand more information feedback on such problems). Hence, centralized nets should be more efficient on simple tasks, less on complex ones, compared to decentralized nets; networks should not differ in satisfaction on simple tasks (though central and peripheral members differ), while on complex tasks decentralized networks (all of whose members are fairly independent, but not saturated) should have higher satisfaction than centralized nets (whose peripheral members have low independence, and all of whose members are likely to be saturated). The evidence, in general, supports these expectations. However, in a more recent update of communication net research, Shaw (1978) finds increased support for the *saturation* concept but suggests that the *independence* concept may need modification.

Shaw's review also examines the other sets of variables, besides task difficulty, that have been studied in relation to network differences. Increases in group size increase saturation and decrease independence, hence would be expected to reduce both performance and satisfaction, though equally for all communication nets. The data support that expectation. Opportunity to organize for task performance (by communication between trials) increases independence and decreases saturation, hence should improve performance and satisfaction, and does so for groups that actually plan an effective organization. Changes from one communication network to another increase saturation and reduce independence (hence reduce performance and satisfaction) if the new organization forces the group to change the pattern it had developed (and it does so); but such changes should have no effect if they permit continuation of the previous pattern (which, under these conditions, would be expected to perseverate, and does). There is very little evidence that attributes of the members (personality traits, for example) affect network performance. There is one study (Berkowitz, 1956) showing that when a high ascendent person is put in a peripheral position in a centralized net, or a low ascendent person is put in a central position, the rate of communication reflects the person's ascendent tendency (a basic initiation rate) on the *first* trial, but shifts to reflect the communication requirements of the position on subsequent trials. Unequal distribution of information tends to help performance if a peripheral person has the high amount, but it tends to hurt performance if the central person has the high amount, presumably because in the latter case it increases already high saturation. Introducing *noise* in either the channel or the message acts like an increase in task difficulty. It increases saturation, hence decreases performance, for all nets, particularly for centralized ones.

None of these findings are very surprising. *Of course* more difficult problems are harder and take longer. *Of course* performance is poorer when a position has more load than the person can handle (saturation). *Of course* people like it better if they control their own work (independence) than if they must depend on others. But the value of carefully researched findings does not depend on whether they seem to fit common sense, or fly in the face of it. The whole body of work on communication nets supports certain self-evident results, such as those just noted. But it also *refutes* a lot of "facts" that would be viewed as equally self-evident—except that they are *not* found in the evidence. For example, centralized (hence efficient) nets are *not* better for all problems. Moreover, *fully-connected* nets (called "comcon" in these studies) are not best for all tasks. Furthermore, while it is "self-evident" that differences in personality characteristics of members affect how people communicate and how effectively they solve problems, there is virtually no evidence in support of that idea and there is a lot of evidence that task type and network type—probably operating by processes such as saturation and independence—*overwhelm* whatever individual differences there are in determining communication patterns, satisfaction and task effectiveness. (There is further evidence of the strong interactive effects of tasks and communication constraints in the studies of communication under modality restrictions, to be discussed later in this chapter.)

NONVERBAL ASPECTS OF COMMUNICATION

The first line of an old song says: "Every little movement has a meaning all its own." While that is a bit of an overstatement, except perhaps for the young lovers to whom the song refers, it is certainly the case that there is a lot more communication going on when people interact than what is contained in the semantic meanings of the words they say. Not only are there many nonsemantic aspects of the verbal activity itself (e.g., loudness and tone of voice, hesitations and speech disturbances, rate and temporal patterning), sometimes referred to as paralinguistic aspects. There is also much nonverbal communication by means of the visual modality and, sometimes, by touch, heat and even olfactory cues.

Among the nonverbal aspects that play a part in interaction are: (1) *distance* between the interactants; (2) body *orientation* (vis à vis the co-interactants); (3) body *posture;* (4) physical *contact* (touch); (5) the operation of *cues from thermal and olfactory* modalities; (6) *visual orientation* (eye contact, looking behavior); (7) *facial expression* (especially smiling); (8) bodily *movement;* (9) patterning of *vocalizations in time.* Argyle and Kendon (1967) distinguished between (a) *standing patterns* that change relatively little during the course of an interaction, and thus serve as backdrop for the interaction (distance, orientation, posture, touch and olfactory and heat cues); and (b) *dynamic patterns* that change continuously and that are part of the flow of the interaction itself (visual orientation, facial expression, body movement and the temporal patterning of sounds and silences).

Interpersonal Distance Zones

E.T. Hall (e.g., 1966), with an anthropologist's perspective, was one of the first social scientists to bring attention to these matters. He identified four "distance sets" at which interaction can take place: *Intimate* (from touching to about eighteen inches); *Casual-Personal* (from eighteen inches to about five feet apart); *Social-Consultative* (from five feet to about ten or twelve feet); and *Public* (beyond twelve feet). These differ in what sets of cues are operating. In the closest distance (intimate), for example, thermal, touch, and olfactory cues operate fully, while the visual mode is not very effective and language serves mainly a regulatory function. By the outside edge of the casual-personal distance (about five feet), the thermal, touch, and olfactory cues are no longer operating and only visual cues and hearing are important. These distance sets also differ in terms of what activities are appropriate for them. The near half of the intimate distance has been called the distance for lovers and wrestlers. The second zone, two to five feet, is still rather personal and is for close and informal social relations (a family at dinner; friends talking). The third zone, social-consultative, is for the conduct of more formal social activities, including such things as job interviews, social conversation among casual acquaintances, and so on. The fourth zone, public, is for the very formal interactions, such as lectures, public speeches and the like. Hall cautions that cultures vary widely in the way in which they use interpersonal distances. For example, the normal distance used for standing conversation by adult males in some Mediterranean area cultures (very close, often touching) is much too close for comfort for males raised in the United States; while the distances used in some Middle Eastern cultures for seated social conversation between adult males (fifteen to twenty feet) are far too great for comfort for U.S.-raised males. In a recent review of a very large number of studies done on these distance sets, Altman and Vinsel (1977) conclude: (a) that when allowance is made for a standing versus sitting difference in interpersonal distance, the distances Hall postulated for these four zones hold up remarkably well over all studies; (b) the distances associated with the four zones hold across cultures, as we would expect if they are tightly tied to the operation of cues from different modalities; while (c) there are cultural differences in which distance zones are regarded as appropriate for various activities.

Intimacy as reflecting a pattern of interaction features.   Hall, Argyle and Kendon (1967), and others, hold that the different nonverbal features of interaction operate as components of a pattern. Furthermore, some have argued that the different components operate in a *compensatory* fashion to maintain an *equilibrium*. For example, Argyle and Dean (1965) regarded eye contact, distance and body orientation as operating in a pattern to reflect the level of intimacy of the interaction. When one feature changed to increase intimacy (e.g., a reduction of distance), something else would change (e.g., a reduction of eye contact) to counter-balance the reduced distance and restore the prior level of intimacy.

The empirical evidence on this question is mixed. In some studies, changes in the direction of increased intimacy were reacted to by intimacy-reducing changes, as one would predict from the idea of a compensatory equilibrium. But in other studies, shifts toward increased intimacy by one person are *reciprocated* by the partner with further shifts toward intimacy, and so on. Equilibrium as an offsetting or *compensating* reaction is quite different from, and somewhat contradictory to, an intimacy-increasing reciprocity that shifts the equilibrium (or set point). But the two are not always distinguished in the research literature, so that explorations of equilibrium sometimes get needlessly confused.

Equilibrium, compensatory action, and reciprocity. Since the ideas of equilibrium, compensatory responses and reciprocity will occur again at several other places in this book, it is worth a brief digression here to try to clarify them. Consider the equilibrium represented by the relation between a furnace and a household. Compensating equilibrium operates when, with the thermostat in a given setting, someone opens a window or otherwise lets in cool air. The thermostat senses a discrepancy between the temperature called for by the situation (i.e., the thermostat setting) and the temperature actually existing. It signals for a change. The furnace comes on to compensate for the decreased temperature. When it has reduced the discrepancy, the thermostat senses that and signals the furnace to shut off. This is sometimes called a *negative feedback cycle,* and it is what is usually meant by an equilibrium-maintaining system.

But suppose someone in the household raises the thermostat setting. That signals the furnace to turn on even though there is no change in ambient temperature. The relations between the furnace and the household is a temperature-equilibrium-seeking system, with the thermostat serving as controller/coordinator. But the relation between the *householder* and the furnace is a *signal-response* system, not an equilibrium-seeking system in the usual sense, with the thermostat serving a mediating function while the householder serves the control function.

To put this in social interaction terms, suppose that certain kinds of actions are regarded (by the interactants) as *signals of a change in desired state of the system.* For example, suppose a couple is sitting side by side in a theater and one takes the other's hand. The partner is likely to regard this as an invitation to increase the level of intimacy. The partner might decide *not* to accept that intimacy-increasing move, and show a compensatory—distancing—response (moving further away, pushing the hand away, shifting body orientation, etc.). On the other hand, the partner might decide to accept that invitation. In that case, the partner is likely to respond with an intimacy-increasing move of his or her own, such as putting an arm around the other, moving closer, and so on. The initiator is then likely to take further intimacy-increasing actions, with the partner responding, and so forth. That describes a *positive feedback cycle.* It might continue until a point is reached at which one or the other partner is not willing to permit further increases in intimacy (or the situation will not permit such further increases). A new equilibrium is then established at that much more intimate level of relationship. At that new level (or at any other level) different features of interaction can compensate for or offset one another. Distance, smiling, touch, and so on, may be equipotential ways to regulate intimacy. *Intimacy in interaction is an equilibrium system* in the sense that these features can compensate for one another. But the *interacting partners* are *not an equilibrium-seeking system* regarding intimacy; they do not necessarily compensate for, i.e., offset, intimacy shifts initiated by the other. A *may offset* or compensate for B's shift in features of the intimacy pattern. Instead, A *may accept* B's shift as a *signal to change the meaning of the* situation—a change in the set point of the thermostat, so to speak—and consequently may reciprocate by generating further shifts in features of the intimacy pattern in the same direction.

Biologists and biological psychologists who study thermoregulatory systems use the concept of "set point" to refer to the level at which the thermoregulatory system is set to maintain body temperature at a given time. It is very similar to what we mean when we refer to the setting of a household thermostat; and, like a thermostat setting, it can be changed for different conditions. For example, aspirin treats a fever not by changing body temperature but by shifting the thermoregulatory set point. Moreover, the body's temperature set point varies over circadean (near daily) and subcircadean cycles in quite regular fashion, in conjunction with diurnal and shorter cycles of activity and rest.

An analogy to interaction may be useful. It is *as if* each person had an intimacy regulation device and that different situations called for different set points on that device. Some situations call for considerable distance and low intimacy (e.g., those in the public zone). Other situations call for much more intimacy (e.g., informal socialization among close friends). The conditions that establish the social meaning of the situation define an intimacy set point, so to speak, for that situation. Chapter 16 discusses the dynamics of regulation of intimacy and changes in intimacy in some detail. Here, intimacy is merely used as an example to clarify equilibrium and reciprocity. When actions or events occur that violate the situation-definition (e.g, when some interactants move closer than they "should" for that situation; or when intimate topics are introjected into a social-consultative level situation), that produces a disturbance of, or a negative feedback discrepancy with respect to, the intimacy set point of that social situation. The participants can take either of two directions of action. They can carry out discrepancy-reducing compensatory action; in other words, they can reestablish equilibrium at the level specified by the set point. Or, they can take the event to be a signal inviting a change in definition of the situation, hence calling for a relocation of the intimacy set point. Consequently, they can *reciprocate* with actions that further shift intimacy in the same direction, until an equilibrium is established at a new level, which establishes a new set point appropriate to the new definition of the situation.

Functions of Some Key Features of Nonverbal Interaction

The look, the touch, and the smile are of special importance in interaction. So says folklore, and so says much empirical research. But the ways in which touching, looking and smiling function in interpersonal interaction turn out to be not quite what folklore would suggest. Certain other features of interaction—posture, body orientation, body movement—are also part of the communication pattern, but these are both less prominent and less thoroughly studied than the touch, the smile and the look.

Touch. We all know that touching is a sign of intimacy (and that striking is a sign of hostility). But patterns of touch observed in actual interaction often show a somewhat different function. To touch is a sign of having higher status than the touched one; to be touched is a sign of lower status than the toucher. In interaction, males touch females substantially more often than females touch males. Males virtually never touch other males of the same age and status, but interacting females do touch each other. So females receive more touching, by far, than males. Furthermore, adults touch children much more than the reverse; and, in general, persons of high status touch those of lower status much more often than they are touched by them.

Another way to consider these results is to relate them to the previous discussion of equilibrium and set points. Perhaps touch functions as a signal inviting change in the intimacy level of the situation; and, perhaps, persons of higher status are much freer to initiate such situation-redefining signals. They are less likely to have their overture rejected; and they may be less sensitive to the negative interpersonal message of such rejection when it does occur.

Looking and smiling.   There has been much study of gaze (interpersonal looking) and eye contact (mutual simultaneous interpersonal looking), as well as much folklore about the potency of looking and the meaning of the "look in the eye" (e.g., the "evil eye"; seductive glances; calculating or menacing gazes). Similarly, much meaning has been attached to smiling and other facial expressions in folklore, and there also have been some studies of smiles. While the matter is by no means totally resolved, it is clear that both the look and the smile serve several important functions in interaction.

One such function is expressive. To smile is to express *friendliness*. Smiling, however, is *not* an accurate indicator of the *happiness* of the smiler. At the start of an encounter, a smile serves as a form of social greeting, and also helps define the intimacy set point for the interaction. Later on, it serves as a form of positive feedback to the other. (This is sometimes called a "backchannel" function in communications jargon.) Such feedback serves information functions, reinforcement functions, and regulatory functions aiding the flow of interaction.

Gaze, too, serves many functions. First, it is worth distinguishing between one person looking at another (gaze, or looking behavior), and eye contact, which implies mutual and simultaneous looking by the two. Individuals differ from one another in their tendencies to look at interacting partners, and they are pretty consistent about it. It is as if each individual could be characterized by a "basic gaze rate," analogous to the idea of a "basic initiation rate" for verbal interaction (Bales, 1953; see previous chapter). This rate is modified by characteristics of the situation and of the person's role in it, just as the individual's basic initiation rate for verbal interaction is modified by such situational and interpersonal factors. It is clear that *mutual gaze* (eye contact) can be accounted for by the *chance occurrence of individual gaze behavior* by the two persons at the same time, given the basic gaze rates of those two persons (e.g., Rutter, Stephenson, Lazzarini, Ayling & White, 1977). So gaze or looking, rather than eye contact or mutual looking, is the factor to be examined.

Second, certain features of the interactors and their relation alter gaze rates. There is a gender difference: females look more and longer at their partners than males do, and are generally more observant about the gaze behavior of the other. Furthermore, people look more at other people whom they like, or seek approval from. Individuals talk more and longer to people they look at (e.g., Mehrabian 1971). It was noted earlier that people speak more to those they like. So speaking to, looking at, and liking, apparently all go together.

Third, the listener has a much higher gaze rate than the speaker. To look at the speaker may be expressive behavior, indicating attention and openness to influence. It certainly is an important source of information and feedback to the looker, providing information about the meanings and intentions of the speaker. It also offers the opportunity to regulate and facilitate the smooth flow of conversation, as will be apparent in the next part of this discussion.

Fourth, the speaker looks much less at the listener(s) than the converse. Furthermore, in two-person interaction, the temporal pattern of gaze by the speaker reflects the "cognitive load" of the speaker at that time, and also helps regulate the flow of conversation. Typically, when a person starts to speak, he or she glances away from the other, then gazes intermittently as the conversation proceeds. Overall, the speaker will look much less than the listener. The speaker will look more or less, depending on how much thinking is required for the conversation. At pauses, which may indicate cognitive work, the speaker often averts his or her gaze. But when the speaker gets to a pause that is to be the end of his or her turn—hence a shift in who has the floor—the speaker will gaze at the other (or, in multi-person cases, will look at the presumptive next speaker—perhaps a chairperson, perhaps a person whose ideas or interests are particularly at stake in the topic under discussion.) That other person, the presumptive next speaker, will have been looking at the previous speaker a lot of the time, but will now avert gaze as he or she takes over the floor.

Dabbs (1980) and others interpret looking by the speaker as his or her acceptance of a high level of visual stimulation. Another human face is, after all, a very rich source of stimulation. When the cognitive load of the conversation gets heavy (at the outset, and at spots along the way), the speaker may pause or hesitate in speech; during such pauses, the speaker is very likely to *reduce stimulus input by gaze aversion.* But increased gaze by the speaker near the end of a turn is interpreted as a flow-regulating message to the listener/next speaker. Gaze by the speaker during interaction, directed at a particular person if the interaction involves more than two, is interpreted, also, as giving status to, or attention to, the other. The high level of gaze by the listener is interpreted mainly as information-gathering, and to a lesser degree as regulatory and as expressive (of status, liking and attention).

In summary, then, touch implies intimacy, indicates relative status, and may signal the toucher's invitation to increase the intimacy of the definition of the situation. Smiling expresses friendship, but not necessarily happiness, and serves as informing and reinforcing feedback and as an aid to regulation of conversational flow. Looking by the listener expresses interest, status and attraction, provides informational feedback to the listener, and helps regulate transitions of speaking turns. Looking by the speaker is an indication of low cognitive load, signals a floor transition, and may express attraction and give status. Mutual looking by speaker and listener is a chance coincidence of individual gaze behaviors.

Other features of interaction.   Changes in posture, body orientation, and body movements all serve as regulators of the interaction process; patterned movements of the head and body accompany the temporal patterns of gaze in interaction. Body movements and facial expressions also are considered to serve expressive functions. Apparently, people can judge emotions pretty accurately from facial expressions, although they can do it better for some emotions than for others, and some people are better at it than others. The main feature expressed by posture is tension as against relaxation.

Angle of orientation is perhaps the most important of the remaining features of nonverbal interaction. There are essentially four angles of orientation at which two interactors can sit or stand with respect to one another: face to face, at right angles, side by side, and back to back. These angles, in combination with distance, are used to adapt to different situations calling for different interaction patterns. When two persons are in the same place but coacting rather than interacting, as two students studying in the same area of a lounge or library would be, they choose seats at a distance and not face to face. When they are in informal conversation, or working on a cooperative task, they tend to sit at right angles. When they are working on a competitive task, they tend to sit facing each other. Close and side by side is the preference for very intimate situations. Sommers (1959) interprets these preferences as being determined by the way the angle facilitates or inhibits visual communication (or, in the intimate, side by side case, communication in other modalities such as touch).

The visual communication aspects of orientation angles are also reflected in seating positions and consequent communication in larger groups. People tend to talk more to people *across from them rather than beside them* (Steinzor, 1950; Bass & Klubeck, 1952), although this did not hold for a study of training groups in "trainer-dominated" conditions (Hearn, 1957). Differences in roles and status among group members are often reflected in the patterns of positions that members take in the group. For example, the lecturer or formal leader usually faces as many members of the audience as possible, often sitting at the head of the table or standing in the front of the room. But positions affect communication initiated and received; and communication affects status in the group. So, these three sets of factors—status, communication and position in the group—form another subsystem of interdependent variables within the interaction process.

Concluding Comments

Features of interaction other than the meanings of the spoken and written word are part of the communication pattern resulting from group interaction. Interpersonal distance, posture, orientation, looking, touching, and smiling all affect, and are affected by, the meaning of the interaction situation and of the individual's role in it. There are consistent differences—individual differences, gender differences and differences arising from both physical and social position in the group—in the basic rates for gazing, smiling, talking, and for "decoding" such nonverbal behaviors by others. All of these differences seem to play a part in the communication pattern of the group interaction process.

This ends the discussion of nonverbal communication in the present context. But concern with the role of such communication in group interaction will arise again, in several places, later in this book. Many of these features of nonverbal interaction will be brought up in the context of the discussion of the *content* of communication, and especially in regard to the regulation of interpersonal privacy. Before that, though, some effects of formal and informal constraints on the *modalities* of communication are examined. Some of those effects put nonverbal communication in a different perspective, tying it more effectively to the process of interaction.

STUDIES OF COMMUNICATION WITH RESTRICTED MODALITIES

The early communication network studies were concerned with patterns of communication in which each specific person (or position) in the group could communicate only with persons in certain other positions. The communication itself was sometimes by written note, sometimes by voice; the channel from A to B was sometimes only one-directional, though it was usually two-way; and only messages with task-relevant information were permitted. This amounts to a very drastic reduction of communication, one that is not nearly as representative of interaction in small groups as it is of interaction within formal "channels" of larger organizations. But more recently, there has been a substantial body of research on communications in groups—some ad hoc laboratory groups, some "real"—in which the effects of restricting one or more communication modalities (permitting auditory communication only, versus visual plus audio, etc.) in otherwise unrestricted communication nets. Much of that work has been carried out in England, by Stephenson, Morley, Rutter, Robinson, Williams, Argyle, Cook and their colleagues. (See Argyle & Cook, 1976; Cook & Lallijee, 1972; Rutter & Robinson, 1981; Williams, 1977, for reviews). That work has two important goals: a theoretical one, to help understand both the role of nonverbal cues and the basic interaction processes in groups; and a practical one, to see how communication is affected by interaction through media (e.g., telephone, videophone) that restrict various communication modalities. The pattern of the research has been to compare groups interacting face to face with otherwise comparable groups interacting on the same tasks under one or more modality restrictions: visually screened but physically present; audio-visual but electronically mediated; audio only; written only. Results of that work raise some doubts about previous interpretations and offer some new insights about group interaction. (See, especially, Williams's, 1977, review; and Rutter & Robinson's, 1981, report of their research program on teaching by telephone.) (See, also, EXRT 27.)

First, this work suggests that despite past research indicating that various functions are served by nonverbal (especially visual) cues—expressive, informational, and regulatory functions—visual communication may be much less important in regard to task performance than we have supposed. Or, it may have its effects in less direct ways. There are major differences in task performance between conditions allowing only written communication and those allowing audio communication. Written communication takes longer but uses fewer messages. But there are far fewer differences among different audio conditions that we might expect, considering that the audio conditions include audio only, audio plus visual, and face to face.

EXRT 27:   *THE RUTTER-STEPHENSON-MORLEY COMMUNICATION MODALITY CONTROL PARADIGM*

Main Study Procedures: Subjects are asked to work together as two-person or relatively small groups to complete a task or solve a problem. The modalities available for communication among group members are experimentally varied, including full modality and physical presence (i.e., face to face groups); visual and auditory accessibility but not physical presence (e.g., video, in adjacent rooms); auditory only (e.g., telephone or intercom); auditory but physical presence (e.g., screens between members); written only (e.g., teletype).

Main Dependent Variables of Interest: Speed and effectiveness of task performance; quality of group solutions; amount, pattern and content of communications; members' satisfaction.

Main Variations: Type of task; prior acquaintance and individual characteristics of group members; other variations of communication modalities.

References: LaPlante (1971); Rutter & Robinson (1981); Rutter, et al. (1977, 1978); Wichman (1970); Williams (1977).

Furthermore, the differences among the audio mode conditions seem to depend on *task type*. There are virtually no differences by modality for brainstorming tasks (i.e., creativity tasks, Quadrant I), or for tasks requiring simple problem-solving (intellectual and decision-making tasks, Quadrant II). There are differences, however, for tasks involving conflicting views or conflicts of interests (Quadrant III). For example, negotiation groups, under audio only, were more likely to settle the issue strictly in terms of the "merits of the case," but also were more likely to "abort" the negotiations. In contrast, groups under face to face conditions were more likely to reach a solution, and to do so as a "split the difference" compromise (Morley & Stephenson, 1969, 1970, 1977). Moreover, people are more competitive, less cooperative, in prisoner's dilemma situations under audio only conditions, compared to face to face conditions (Wichman, 1970; LaPlante, 1971). They apparently perform better in bargaining, under instructions to disregard the opponent's position, when visual access is restricted; but such visual restriction has no effect when the bargainers are under instructions to consider their opponent's position (Lewis & Fry, 1977). Modality differences seem to vary with tasks on a simple to complex or degree of difficulty continuum. For very simple tasks, there either are no differences or, occasionally, the more restricted (audio only) condition is more efficient. For more complex tasks, the face to face groups are better; but those are also the tasks involving conflict, so the task difficulty and task type differences are not totally separated in these studies.

Second, many of the earlier studies comparing audio only and face to face confounded visual communication with physical presence. Many nonverbal cues—sounds of movements, breathing, perhaps some additional voice cues—are available when two persons are in one another's presence but not when the communication is electronically mediated. Rutter and Robinson (1981) report a series of studies attempting to separate the effects of visual access and physical presence. Typically four conditions are used: face to face; face to face but visually screened; audiovisual presentation, electronically mediated with interactants in different rooms; and audio only presentations, electronically mediated with participants in different rooms. They found differences in *style, content* and *outcomes* (see below). Some portion of the differences was due to visual accessibility and some portion was due to physical separation. Face to face and audio only were always the conditions most different from each other; and both screened and audiovisual conditions were always in between.

From these results, Rutter and Robinson (1981) conclude that differences between communication under face to face and restricted modality conditions arise not so much from a loss of visual cues per se, but from a loss of social cues of various kinds. They refer to this as "cuelessness," though others have talked about "social presence," "immediacy" and the like. Furthermore, they argue that the differences are in *content,* with *style* and *outcome* differences following therefrom. The main *content* differences are a relatively increased attention to the task, and relatively impersonal communication, as the situation becomes more and more cueless (i.e., as the communication modalities become more restricted). These content differences are accompanied by *style* differences in a pattern that they interpret as reduction in spontaneity. They are also accompanied by *outcome* differences, the pattern of which suggests that results are more task-based and less influenced by interpersonal factors. It was noted above, for example, that negotiation outcomes are more in line with "merits of the case" for audio only, but are more likely to deadlock; whereas face to face negotiations seldom deadlock, but usually compromise.

Rutter and Robinson (1981), and Williams (1977) discuss several conceptual bases for interpreting these differences. One is essentially an *efficiency* argument. The relatively cueless conditions (the audio only condition, for most studies, but even more so for the written only conditions of a few studies) are relatively narrow-bandwidth channels, and are relatively efficient forms for transmission of pure task information. The more cueless, the less distraction from other cues (e.g., interpersonal cues) that are not task-relevant (hence, are noise). But the limiting condition is that the channel must not get so narrow that cues necessary to the task will be eliminated, with a consequent decline in task performance. More complex or more difficult tasks may need broader-band channels. Moreover, some kinds of tasks (e.g., negotiations and other conflict tasks) may require information about the other persons (their positions, attitudes, moods, etc.) as well as about the task narrowly defined. For these, the cueless conditions provide *too* narrow a bandwidth, one that eliminates important interpersonal cues.

An alternative way to view this is to regard the effective continuum on which these modality-restricted conditions differ as one of *rich versus lean interpersonal information.* Several features of the evidence suggest this kind of approach. For example, participants virtually always *prefer* the socially rich, face to face condition, even though in some cases they admit that the other conditions are more task efficient. Furthermore, they like the other interactants more in the richer conditions. Moreover, there are a number of indications that the normal development of patterns of interpersonal relations does not take place in the leaner conditions. There is less role differentiation and less leadership exhibited. The correlation between amount of communication and amount of influence in the group is much lower in the restricted than in face to face groups. The hierarchical pattern of distribution of communication among members (the exponential curve) does not develop; communication amounts tend to be equal for all members. In short, *it is as if a patterned set of interpersonal relations did not develop,* or developed far less thoroughly, in the relatively lean or cueless conditions, than it normally does when groups interact under unrestricted, face to face communication conditions.

Recall the model of group interaction process discussed at the end of chapter 1. That model suggests that every communication act carries both task and interpersonal "messages," hence has an effect on both the task performance pattern and the interpersonal relations pattern. These two patterns, in turn, have influences on each other and on the participants. It is as if the restriction of communication modalities dampened or eliminated the *interpersonal aspects* of the communication acts, leaving the *task aspects* much more prominent. This is perhaps what is reflected in the greater task orientation and impersonality of content that Rutter and Robinson (1981) find for the relatively cueless conditions. If the interaction in the "lean" conditions carries task messages but not interpersonal ones, then the *outcomes* should also reflect that bias. For example, we would expect *task products* to be based on "pure" task information (as in the "merits of the case" effects for negotiation groups), and not to be "contaminated" by the operation of interpersonal forces (hence, negotiation groups breaking off, not compromising; prisoner's dilemma groups not cooperating). At the same time, we would expect a less well articulated structure of interpersonal relations. Not only does the group fail to develop a communication pattern reflecting role differentiation, leadership, and so on, in the leaner conditions, but members are less happy and less attracted to group and groupmates.

It is, of course, the case that under many circumstances the interpersonally rich conditions provide "noise" that may distract from the task, that certainly doesn't directly help on the task, and that may direct group time and effort from the task (as in Bales's equilibrium-maintaining conceptions, discussed earlier). Under these conditions, the relatively lean modalities may deliver more efficient task performance—provided the leanness does not eliminate necessary cues—but at the end of it there will be no pattern of interpersonal relations, no interpersonal attraction, and members will not be very interpersonally satisfied. (This is the pattern found in the centralized communication nets on relatively simple tasks.) But it is also the case that some tasks require interpersonal information (e.g., some of the conflict tasks of Quadrant III), and some tasks are facilitated by smooth interpersonal coordination. These may require communication through channels that carry richer interpersonal information. Furthermore, most "real" groups are "in business" for more than one task performance session. Work on tomorrow's tasks, and the next day's, will flow much better if the group has a stable pattern of interpersonal relations, a stable set of functional roles. Such structure reduces "saturation," to use Shaw's term. Besides, it is more pleasant and satisfying to develop, and maintain, patterns of interpersonal relations. Thus, group members *prefer* relatively rich communication modes, need them for some tasks, and do better in them for some—but not all—tasks.

If we regard the modality restrictions as affecting the *social richness* or *interpersonal richness* of the information, some other studies bear on this matter. In a series of studies of obedience, Milgram (1965) showed that individuals were less willing to harm a third party when the potential victim was *closer* (in both physical distance and channel "richness") than when the other was distant. Conversely, people were more willing to obey the experimenter's instructions to harm that victim when the experimenter was closer (in those same senses) than when the experimenter was further away. (See EXRT 28.)

Williams (1977) reports studies (by LaPlante, 1971) which indicate that the richer modalities emphasize the affective content (positive and negative interpersonal communications) of the other's behavior. Members like those who gave positive reactions more and dislike those who gave negative reactions more under *rich* rather than under lean conditions.

It is as if the *richness of social cues in a situation*—including physical and social-psychological distance, and availability of interpersonal cues via visual and other nonverbal modalities—*operates as an enhancer of the potency of the other person(s)* in the situation. Or, to put the matter conversely: it is as if reduction of the richness of social cues, including increases in the effective distance of the others, *muted the impact of the others as persons,* made them more non-persons, more machine-component like, more object-like, and so on.

Indeed, it is possible to consider that a whole panel of factors, in addition to communication modality restrictions, operates in this fashion. Group size, the physical positioning of members, status and role differentiations among members, including formally designated leaders—all of these may have effects on the richness of social cues transmitted during interaction, as well as on the efficiency of transmission of task information. These communication, task and

EXRT 28: *MILGRAM'S OBEDIENCE PARADIGM*

Main Study Procedures: Two ostensive subjects are brought to an experimental room where one (the actual naive subject) is assigned (ostensibly on a random basis) to be "teacher," with the other (actually a confederate of the experimenter) assigned to be "learner." The teacher is set at a keyboard with a series of switches labelled as successively strong and dangerous levels of electric shock. The subject is instructed to administer a shock each time the "learner" makes an error, and to increase the level of shock each time. The "learner" makes an experimentally predetermined pattern of errors.

Main Dependent Variables of Interest: How strong a level of shock the subject will deliver (with the experimenter urging the subject to continue when the subject expresses doubt or hesitancy).

Main Variations: Demographic characteristics of subjects and learners; differences in prestige of different settings; visual, auditory and even tactual closeness of learner to the subject.

Reference: Milgram (1965).

EXRT 29: *KELLEY'S DIFFERENTIAL STATUS MANIPULATION*

Main Study Procedures: Subjects are placed in one of two groups (presumably on a random basis), and groups are assigned to one of two roles or sides in a game (ostensibly on a random basis). The one group always has the dominant and high status role in the game; the other group always has the low status subservient role.

Main Dependent Variables of Interest: Amount, content and target of communication, within and between groups; attraction judgments within and between groups.

Main Variations: Whether or not members could "locomote" to either the higher or the lower status level, and, if so, on what basis (e.g., merit, task performance, experimenter preference, chance); attraction of subject for others in own and other group (see cohesiveness manipulations).

References: Kelley (1951).

---

interpersonal patterns, in turn, influence all of the outcomes of group interaction. (See EXRT 29.)

EFFECTS OF MODIFYING
COMMUNICATION
STRATEGIES

A number of the techniques used to concoct groups for experimental study (see chapter 4) are designed to restrict communication not by eliminating links (as in the communication net studies examined in the first part of this section) nor by restricting modalities (as in the studies just discussed) but rather by requiring, training or otherwise trying to induce various strategies for communication within the group. The different strategies impose various restrictions on the content and style of both task and interpersonal aspects of communication. For example, the brainstorming technique (see chapter 4 and chapter 11) urges group members not to criticize or evaluate one anothers' ideas during the "creative" or idea-generating period. Similarly, in the eliciting phase of nominal group technique (see chapter 4 and chapter 11), members are forbidden to criticize or evaluate ideas, are permitted to discuss them only for clarification, and are encouraged to depersonalize their origins. (One could regard the Delphi technique, also discussed in chapter 4 and chapter 11, as the limiting case of restricted communication strategy, in which members' ideas are communicated to one another only in a form mediated by the experimenter and transformed into written, often numerical, summary. Or, one could regard it as more a case of modality restriction, to "written only" form.) Notice that in all of these there is an attempt to reduce the richness of social cues, by permitting only tasks messages and by eliminating or attenuating affect laden, evaluative comments—even on the task.

Several other types of concocted groups place far less drastic constraints on the flow of interaction. In one, referred to in chapter 4 as MAUA (multiattribute-utility analysis), a highly structured sequence of problem-solving steps is imposed on task activity, but the group is allowed to carry out those steps with unrestricted communication networks and modalities (i.e., it is face to face interaction). In another technique, that is referred to in chapters 4 and 8 as the Social Judgment Theory technique, the experimenter asks each group member for complex task judgments, then gives highly complex feedback to all on each others' responses; but those task-structured steps are followed by a period of unrestricted face to face communication in an effort to reach a joint decision. Finally, another technique used in concocted groups, described in chapter 4 as "communication strategy training" groups, involves exhorting group members to use certain communication techniques, to avoid others, and to adopt certain attitudes about the communication (e.g., never to argue; never to change just to reduce disagreement; to expect differences in opinion, make them explicit, and explore the underlying reasons for them, rather than try to suppress them). This encourages (though it does not absolutely require or prevent) certain communication patterns intended not so much to reduce the interpersonal aspect of communication, but to shape it so that it is less affect laden and evaluative (especially negatively evaluative) and *will not interfere with* task performance—usually, on complex problem-solving tasks of the intellective or decision-making types of Quadrant II. (See EXRT 30.)

Two implicit assumptions underlie all of these techniques: (a) that groups *can* attain better levels of task performance on these tasks than can individuals, provided that all that they transmit and process is "pure" task information; but (b) that much if not all interpersonal activity or communication will distract from, interfere with, or perhaps downright distort and disrupt, the "accurate," "effective," "efficient" performance of the group's task.

It is interesting that most of these techniques have been used for tasks of Quadrant I (Generate) and Quadrant II (Choose). These are also the types of tasks for which the lean modalities work well. They are apparently tasks for which information about interpersonal aspects is not useful in the task itself (or

EXRT 30:   *HALL'S COMMUNICATION STRATEGY TRAINING TECHNIQUE*

Main Study Procedures: Prior to working as a group, subjects are trained in a series of communication techniques designed to produce more efficient and effective intra-group communication on group discussion tasks. For example, trainees are taught to expect and to value members' differences in views on the topic; to encourage expression of such differing views; not to agree or to change views just to reduce conflict; not to make ultimatum-like statements of positions. Members are encouraged to practice these techniques during group discussions, but otherwise those discussions are carried out without experimental intervention.

Main Dependent Variables of Interest: Speed, accuracy and effectiveness of group task resolution; member satisfaction.

Main Variations: Forms of group tasks; initial distribution of views on the discussion tasks; number and characteristics of group members.

References: Eils & John (1980); Hall (1971); Hall & Watson (1971).

even would be dysfunctional for the task). Most of these techniques have been used only in conditions in which the *group does not have a tomorrow*—hence, it has no need for a functional role pattern, a stabilized status system, a developed communication pattern. None of these techniques has been used in groups that have substantial temporal continuity and only Social Judgment Theory techniques have been used in groups dealing with conflict tasks. Note that it is the conflict tasks (negotiations, and other tasks of Quadrant III) for which the rich and lean modalities gave striking task performance differences. Apparently, in such conflict tasks, effective task performance itself requires interpersonal information; hence, modalities that provide extreme leanness of social cues yield different task outcomes than do the richer modalities. But most of the communication strategy techniques (e.g., Delphi, NGT, brainstorming, MAUA) probably could not be applied to such conflict tasks. Two of them—Social Judgment Theory and communication strategy training—are designed for tasks including conflicting views (type 5), not conflicting interests (type 6). They structure some parts of the task communication. But they both also use full channel, face to face communication for the conflict-resolving stages.

It is interesting, also, that the main experimental techniques for studying conflict of interest tasks—the prisoner's dilemma game and other dilemma tasks, and coalition formation tasks—*all use very highly constrained communication networks, modalities and strategies*. In many cases, only written notes are used. In all of them, communication is controlled by the experimenter as to content (only task-relevant acts allowed), modality, frequency and temporal pattern. Only in a few negotiation studies (e.g., McGrath & Julian, 1963; Morley & Stephenson, 1977; Vidmar & McGrath, 1970) were participants allowed full channel, face to face interaction with one another. So even though the research testing modality restrictions suggests that conflict tasks may *need* interpersonal, as well as "pure," task communication, most of the research designed to study conflict tasks has imposed communication modalities and strategies that are extremely lean in social cues and virtually preclude transmission of interpersonal information. The research paradigms used to study conflicts of interest also typically make use of groups with little temporal continuity—hence, with less need for patterned interpersonal activities. One can only speculate on how results of conflict studies might differ if they were done using groups having temporal continuity, and using conditions permitting broad-band communication channels rich in interpersonal as well as task information. For better or worse, that is how real groups, solving real conflicts of viewpoint and conflicts of interest, do communicate with one another. Perhaps experiments permitting richer communication channels on such complex and difficult tasks would provide new insights about conflict and its resolution.

CHAPTER FOURTEEN
INTERPERSONAL ATTRACTION: THE ACQUAINTANCE PROCESS

The previous chapter ended with a consideration of how communication under conditions of restricted modalities seemed to contain, at the same time, pure task information and very lean interpersonal relations information. It was noted that this leanness of social information affected both task performance and interpersonal relations patterns. This chapter begins with questions about how communication of information about a hypothetical other person—a minimum kind of interpersonal contact—is related to positive interpersonal attitudes (attraction) to that person. It will consider, progressively, attraction and acquaintance at various stages of involvement of the parties, ending with consideration of factors affecting maintenance and disruption of long-term relationships such as marriage.

Interpersonal attraction has been a topic of major concern to a broad group of social psychologists, including group researchers, for a long time. Unfortunately, much of the work in the past several decades involved studies of quite artificial groups and highly superficial kinds of interpersonal relations. In a review covering a fairly recent period of years, Huston and Levinger (1978) found that over 35 percent of the studies of interpersonal attraction were studies of first impressions of a hypothetical stranger gleaned from experimenter-supplied descriptions or lists of traits. Another third were experimental studies of attraction judgments following very brief, and often experimenter-arranged, interpersonal contacts. Only about a third of the studies were of persons whose relations to one another extended prior to and/or subsequent to the brief data gathering session. So one might characterize much of this research as dealing with attraction among strangers. But there are a few studies of persons in "real" and continuing interpersonal relations. These can provide a check on the findings from studies of very limited relationships, to see if the same kinds of factors seem to be at work.

These studies are limited in another way. Almost all of the studies of interpersonal attraction have been done on pairs consisting of same-gender peers, or on dating heterosexual couples and married couples. Huston and Levinger point out that relationships in many other pair populations (homosexual couples, age-differentiated same- or opposite-sex pairs, cross-gender friendship pairs, work setting pairs, boss-employee pairs) are hardly ever studied.

Huston and Levinger (1978) note that close relationships between persons are characterized by positive attitudes, behavioral involvement, and joint belongingness. These three factors seem quite close to Schutz's (1958) three, affection, control and inclusion. It is the first of these—positive attitudes, or attraction—that is the topic of this chapter. Behavioral involvement is the main feature explored in the following two chapters. Joint belongingness is touched upon in all three chapters.

FACTORS AFFECTING ATTRACTION AMONG STRANGERS

While much of the research bearing on these questions could hardly be considered research on groups, it nevertheless has bearing on the question of attraction among individuals in social interaction, including groups. Furthermore, there are several remarkably robust findings that provide a set of bench marks for later discussion of interpersonal relationships in more interactively dynamic situations.

Physical Attraction

Social scientists did not get around to studying physical attractiveness as a correlate of interpersonal attraction until quite recently. (See review by Bersheid & Walster, 1975.) There were probably two main reasons for such delayed consideration of what is perhaps the first panel of information that people usually receive as they meet and get to know a person. For one thing, the preference for attractive others was probably considered by many as so self-evident that no study was needed (even though, as in some other areas of social science study, the particulars turn out not to be quite as self-evident as would have been supposed). Another possible reason for delayed treatment is the general acceptance of the idea that "beauty is in the eye of the beholder," with standards of beauty varying among cultures, over time, and over situations, and with judgments of beauty varying from one individual to another. No one has yet been able to specify the features of a face or figure that are the necessary or sufficient conditions for it to be "beautiful"; it is quite likely, in any case, to be a gestalt or pattern rather than a specific, precisely-defined set of features. But when people drawn from a given culture and subculture are asked to judge the attractiveness of a set of photographs, or a set of specific individuals, there is remarkably high agreement among them. So, rather than trying to specify and measure degree of "objective beauty", researchers in this area have dealt with "judged attractiveness." (See Bersheid & Walster, 1975.)

People are more apt to be attracted to others who are physically attractive (in terms of such consensus judgments). This holds for either sex, in relation to targets of either sex, although it is especially strong for male judgments of female targets. (Keep in mind that most data in this area is from college student populations in our culture.) These results seem quite robust, although there are some complexities to be noted.

While those general findings hold fairly broadly, they have been elaborated in a number of studies. When judging attractiveness in the context of potential partners for a date, there is an interaction between the attractiveness of target and the judge's expectation about whether that person would be willing to go on the date if asked. That latter factor has been studied in several ways. It has been experimentally manipulated by the researcher telling the judges just how probable it was that a given target would accept the date if offered. Other studies have asked the judges to make such estimates themselves. In still other studies, the experimenter manipulated judges' self-esteem, on the presumption that this would alter the estimated probabilities of being accepted or rejected. There is also some indication that a female's judgments of attractiveness of male targets may interact with her own physical attractiveness. Specifically, attractive females know that they are attractive, and therefore set the odds on not being accepted for a date quite low.

Physical attractiveness continues to play a part for males in their interpersonal attraction judgments in actual relationships (e.g., couples computer-matched for a date) including ones that continue over time (e.g., actual dating couples). The physical attraction of the male partner becomes less important to the female as the relationship becomes more long-lasting (or, perhaps, as it gets more "real").

Similarity

The most studied factor related to attraction has been similarity, and a wide variety of kinds of similarity have been considered. The strongest evidence about similarity effects for *actual relationships* (as opposed to judgments of hypothetical persons) has to do with similarity of demographic factors: socioeconomic status, education, occupation, age, race, ethnic background, and gender. But the demographic factors related to attraction are often viewed as bases of selective-encounter differences, rather than as bases of differences in selective-attraction-given-encounter.

There is also strong evidence, both from impression-formation studies and from a few field studies of actual relationships, that attraction is a positive function of perceived similarity of attitudes and values. (See reviews by Byrne, 1971; Byrne & Clore, 1968; Clore, 1976; Huston & Levinger, 1978. Also see Newcomb, 1961). (See EXRTs 31 and 32.) In the impression-of-hypothetical-strangers studies, there is a direct, linear relation between the proportion of items on which the stranger (ostensibly) agrees and the degree of positive attraction that the judge expresses in his or her ratings of that stranger. In the studies of natural setting pairs, Newcomb (1961) found strong association between the

EXRT 31:   *THE BYRNE-CLORE SIMILARITY/ATTRACTION PARADIGM*

Main Study Procedures: Subjects are asked to answer a series of questions about themselves and their views. They are then shown the ostensive answers of their hypothetical partners-to-be in the interaction. The experimenter manipulates the number and pattern of ostensive agreement of the hypothetical partner-to-be's answers with those of the subject.

Main Dependent Variables of Interest: Interpersonal attraction expressed by subject toward hypothetical partner, as a function of extent and pattern of perceived similarity.

Main Variations: Content areas (e.g., demographic, attitudes, personality characteristics) of similarity; objective characteristics of subjects.

References: Byrne (1971); Byrne & Clore (1968); Clore (1976).

EXRT 32:   *NEWCOMB'S ACQUAINTANCE PROCESS PARADIGM*

Main Study Procedures: A group of seventeen male college transfer students, no two of whom were from the same home town or had attended the same college, were selected to occupy a residence house at a Midwestern university, rent-free in exchange for their participation in the study. (The study was replicated the following year, with a second group of seventeen students selected by the same procedures.) Subjects were required to (a) respond to a battery of questionnaires and interviews, weekly for a semester; (b) attend a weekly house meeting, at which specific topics and issues were sometimes placed on the agenda by the experimental team; and (c) manage the house themselves, by deciding how to deal with meal preparations, food budgets, and purchasing, house cleaning and maintenance, and the like.

Main Dependent Variables of Interest: Interpersonal attraction, attitudes and agreement on them, perceptions of others; changes in those patterns over time.

Main Variations: Attitude change attempts; the posting of group house-centered problems to solve; variations in backgrounds of members.

References: Newcomb (1961)

---

friendship networks that developed among the male students in an experimenter-managed college residence house, on the one hand, and patterns of pre-study attitudes and values, on the other. But he found the strongest association of all between attraction to others and agreement by those others on that most important matter: the other members of the house. As one might expect, the findings from the real life setting were both more complicated (and more interesting), and showed more robustness over time, than did the findings from the much more artificial studies of impression of strangers.

There also have been a lot of studies of attraction in relation to similarity of personality characteristics. Here, results are disappointing. A few studies have found some relation between similarity on some personality dimensions and attraction judgments; but a very large number have found no relation, for studies of a very large list of personality traits. (See Huston & Levinger, 1978 for a list of such studies.) Moreover, what few positive findings there are regarding personality traits and attraction were obtained in the more artificial impression-of-hypothetical-strangers studies. None have held up in studies of actual pairs.

Complementarity of Needs

While it is widely held in folklore that "birds of a feather flock together"—as in the very robust similarity-attraction findings—it is perhaps equally widely held that "opposites attract." One version of the latter proverb in the interpersonal attraction literature is the idea that relationships develop and persist between persons who have complementary needs and hence can make reciprocal contributions to each other (Winch, 1965). There is really no empirical support for this maxim at all, in regard to studies of impressions of hypothetical strangers, or even in studies of actual but brief interactions (e.g., encounters in a laboratory session, under experimental control). But there seems to be at least some support for this idea of complementarity of needs for pair relations that persist over the long run—as in continuing relationships between dating couples and in marriages. (See Huston & Levinger, 1978, for a review of this evidence.) One treatment of this issue proposes a successive filter model, with socio-demographic factors acting as an initial filter (perhaps mainly affecting the probability of encounter); with perceived similarity of values and attitudes providing a second filter, relatively early in the relationship; and with need complementarity providing still a further filter as the relationship continues and perhaps becomes permanent. By this view, one would expect need complementarity rather than value similarity to predict which couples continued and perhaps married (Kerckhoff & Davis, 1962). One would also expect the effects of value similarity to decrease or vanish for very-long-run relationships. That is what has been found by Levinger and colleagues (Levinger, Senn, & Jorgenson, 1970) and by Hill, Rubin and Peplau (1976).

Note, though, that as more realistic and more long-run relationships are discussed, the focus also tends to shift from sheer "judged attraction" to a number of other considerations, centering around the continuation of the pair relationship. People get married, and stay married, for a lot of reasons other than the interpersonal attraction between them, at least in the limited senses of interpersonal affect or liking that are usually the substance of impression-type measures. In *Fiddler on the Roof*, the wife's answer to the protagonist's twenty-fifth anniversary query, "Do you love me?" is a detailed and poetic testimony to the complex meanings that interpersonal relationships have in real life.

Theoretical Interpretations

Interpersonal attraction, and especially the similarity-attraction relation, has been explained mainly on the basis of two somewhat competing theoretical formulations. One is the Byrne-Clore affect-reinforcement explanation, which is couched in terms of traditional learning theory (e.g., Clore, 1976). Such theories assume that people learn the stimulus-response connections that have received reinforcements in the past. People learn to associate positive affect with the presence and activity of other humans, especially others with certain similarities to self. The other theoretical formulation is a "balance theory" view. It assumes that certain patterns of perceptions or cognitions are "balanced" and rewarding, and that other patterns are "imbalanced" and bring about a strain to reduce that imbalance. Heider (1958), Newcomb (1953) and Festinger (1957) have all presented such balance theory views. Newcomb's is more inter-person oriented than the other two, and is described briefly here.

Newcomb proposes that when two persons, A and B, interact, they *co-orient* to each other and to some focus of interaction, X. The X can be any topic of conversation, any attitude, including attitudes about each other and about the A-B relationship. Newcomb assumes that reciprocal liking between A and B is a desired and stable state; that reciprocal disliking is undesirable but somewhat stable; and that a nonmutual A-B attitude (A likes B but B dislikes A, or vice versa) is an imbalanced state and highly unstable. Newcomb also proposes that, given a positive A-B relation, in the absence of other information A will assume that B agrees about any important X. Furthermore, disagreement about an X with a positively attracted other is an imbalanced state, and there is a *strain toward balance*. If A dislikes X, he or she will assume that a liked B also does. If it is really the case that A and B disagree about X, then when A and B communicate about X, argues Newcomb, they may come into a state of imbalance. If so, there is a strain toward change to reduce that imbalance by persuading the other about X, by changing one's own judgment about X, by changing one's judgment about B, or by various substrategies (such as distorting the communication, devaluing X, redefining X as not germane to the A-B relationship, etc.). But agreement with attractive others on values and attitudes, especially attitudes about important matters such as the other people in the group, reflects a balanced state, hence an absence of strain. It is also assumed to be rewarding.

Reinforcement-learning theories and balance theories are often considered alternative ways to "explain" the similarity-attraction relation, (and many other facets of social behavior). In principle, they can lead to somewhat different theoretical derivations, hence to comparative experimental test. In practice, though, both are relatively hard to pin down in operational terms; hence it is hard to design an experiment that could definitively *disconfirm* either one of them. But they may really be more or less complementary theories, rather than mutually exclusive competitors. They can most usefully be viewed as heuristics. That is, they are *potentially useful* descriptions of phenomena that help clarify those phenomena. But they should not be regarded as either true or false in any literal sense. These two theoretical preferences are also applicable, probably as complements, to several other substantive areas discussed in this book.

FACTORS AFFECTING ATTRACTION
AMONG INTERACTING PAIRS

Some research has been done on attraction for pairs in actual interaction, though often in brief encounters. Physical attraction continues to play a role, especially for males in judging females in the context of heterosexual dating relationships. It is likely that physical attraction has quite powerful effects for both males and females in other contexts, too. There are a number of studies that suggest that the physically attractive receive all sorts of preferential treatment. Good-looking people are seen as more responsible for good deeds and less responsible for bad ones. Their evaluations of others have more potent effects on third parties. Their task performances are over-rated. Others are more responsive to them, more willing to help them, and more willing to work to please them. An exception appears to be for juries (or, strictly speaking, for mock juries). Attractive defendants who either appear to use their physical attractiveness to get away with something, or who don't have justifiable reasons for their (criminal) behavior, receive especially harsh treatment from such mock juries.

Perceived similarity of values and attitudes, though not necessarily actual similarity, continues to affect attraction for pairs in brief encounters. Personality traits, and similarity on them, are ineffective as predictors of attraction. Moreover, some additional features, that are not applicable to the impression-formation context, come into play.

Proximity heightens the probability of interaction or encounter, and interaction tends to enhance familiarity and liking. This may further increase proximity, or at least probability of encounter, which in turn may further promote attraction. Such a spiral—closeness-interaction-attraction-closeness-interaction-attraction—has been shown in field studies of attraction among neighbors in housing units in several settings (e.g., Festinger, Schachter, & Back, 1950. See Huston & Levinger 1978, p. 129). In housing units in which all residents are initially strangers, for example, friendship patterns develop along lines predictable from a notion of functional proximity—actual distance, modified to take account of certain architectural features (such as locations of mailboxes and stairs) that alter the probability of contact between people who use particular facilities and the people who live very near those facilities.

The literature on mate selection also shows a strong effect of proximity. Spouses are very likely to have lived within blocks of one another before marriage. Again, the proximity effect is undoubtedly one of increasing probability of encounter. We don't marry everyone we meet. But we certainly don't marry anyone we have not met, and the odds on meeting are much much higher if two people live in the same community, the same neighborhood, the same campus. So, proximity can perhaps best be viewed as an *enabling* condition, with encounter a necessary but not sufficient condition for attraction, subsequent acquaintance, and in some subsets, of cases, continuing friendship or marriage.

Too much proximity can have negative effects on attraction, when it becomes transformed into perceived crowding. Whether or not any given degree of physical closeness is perceived as crowding, and hence as unpleasant, depends on the persons and the situation, and on the sex composition of the group involved. Patterson (1976) suggests that crowding, along with a number of other factors, functions as a basis for arousal. He and others (e.g., Shiffenbauer & Schiavo, 1976) suggest that arousal of this kind serves to *intensify* whatever feelings are already present in the situation. Thus, closeness can increase positive attraction for liked others, and can also increase negative attraction for already disliked others.

Two other sets of factors have been related to judged attraction in brief interpersonal encounters. One is a set of nonverbal factors, including eye gaze, touch, distance, body orientation, and so on. Those were discussed in chapter 13, in relation to the problem of reciprocity versus compensatory response to increased intimacy. The other set involves self-disclosure of verbal content in relation to attraction. Attraction generally increases self-disclosure. Self-disclosure generally increases attraction, provided it is not inappropriate to the role or situation. The question of reciprocity of self-disclosure in interaction is more complicated. Altman (1973) holds that strangers are more likely than are acquaintances or more intimate friends to show reciprocal self-disclosure. These matters are discussed much more extensively in chapter 16 in the context of development and regulation of intimacy and privacy in interpersonal interaction.

MOVING TOWARD PERMANENCE: FRIENDSHIP, ROMANCE, MARRIAGE

Relatively little has been established empirically about how friendships develop or how they operate. It is clear that friendship networks differ during the life-span, being much more important and extensive for young and older persons than for middle-aged persons. Presumably this occurs because persons in their middle years are much more extensively tied up in family relationships, and thus have both less opportunity and less need for development and maintenance of many friendships. It is also clear that the nature of friendships varies among cultures and subcultures, and that the behaviors included in intimate relationships have varied widely over history. In U.S. culture, nonkin friendships are mostly pairs of the same age, gender and race. There has been little study of cross-age, cross-gender or cross-race friendships, although it is clear that these are relatively low frequency occurrences in present day America, and that they are facilitated by opportunities for informal interaction under equal status conditions.

Two features stand out in descriptive accounts of friendships. Friends are people who do things together; and friends are people whom you can count on for support. There is some evidence that men tend to emphasize the former, women the latter, in their descriptive accounts. Friends also are characterized as "irreplaceable," and as people who respond to each other as unique individuals.

There have been some laboratory studies of friends, in comparison to pairs of acquaintances. Morgan and Sawyer (1967) propose that friends interact so as to *maintain solidarity and status equality*. For example, friends tend to try to allocate rewards equally, are less likely to compete and more likely to cooperate in laboratory dilemma games. Friends are seen as more responsible for positive behaviors and as less responsible for negative behaviors, compared to acquaintances. Spouses receive even more extreme attributions. Note that such over-favorable attributions were also typical of judgments of *physically attrac-*

tive people. Such over-favorable attributions may result from increased attraction from any source.

Romantic Love

Research on relations involving sexual attraction has been limited entirely to heterosexual premarital couples and to heterosexual spouses. Virtually no research has been done on homosexual relations or extramarital relations, and very little on other nontraditional patterns. Moreover, very little research was done even on heterosexual dating couples or married couples until fairly recently. There has been some study of precursors to romantic love. Bersheid and Walster (1975) using Schachter's two-factor or "labeling" theory of emotion (Schachter, 1964) argue that explaining "passionate love" requires two conditions: intense physiological arousal, from any of various sources; and situational cues indicating that love is an appropriate label for those feelings. (See EXRT 33.) In general, in studies of attraction among dating couples (early in the relationship) physical attraction has strong effects, attitude similarity has smaller effects, and personality characteristics have no effects. "Role-fit," or the degree to which the partner fits the desired role for that gender, also plays a part; but the specific role expectations that represent "fit" depend on the gender-role stereotypes of the people being studied. Such gender-role attitudes also are related to behavior of seriously dating couples in laboratory studies. Women who hold traditional sex-role attitudes perform less well when competing against their boyfriends than when working together with them; the opposite pattern holds for women with nontraditional sex-role attitudes (Peplau, 1976).

As such cross-sex relationships develop, the partners increase in interdependence and affection. Partners similar in social characteristics are more likely to escalate involvement, and to marry (as well as more likely to encounter one another and become acquainted in the first place). Similarity of attitudes does *not* predict escalation of the relation, except for similarity in degree of in-

---

EXRT 33: *SCHACHTER'S FEAR–AROUSAL AFFILIATION TECHNIQUE*

Main Study Procedures: Subjects are brought to an experimental room, in which they are told that they will be undergoing a painful experience (e.g., a painful injection; a painful shock). They are told to wait, and permitted to do so in either of two rooms, one of which has no one in it and the other of which has other persons in it, ostensibly waiting to take part in the same experiment.

Main Dependent Variables of Interest: Whether the subject chooses to wait alone or with others.

Main Variations: Number of others; whether the others are ostensibly waiting for the same painful experience or waiting for another purpose; whether the anticipated experience is painful or embarrassing.

Reference: Schachter (1959, 1964).

volvement in the relation and in its "definition." Another factor that does *not* predict pair continuation is whether and how early in the relationship the couple engages in sexual intercourse. One factor that *does* intensify romantic attraction is parental interference. The lesson Shakespeare teaches us about the Montagues and Capulets apparently applies to modern romances as well.

Marriage

Social scientists have given marriage far less study than one might expect. Some features are clear. Mate selection is strongly influenced by proximity, probably via probability of encounter. It is also strongly influenced by similarity on socio-demographic factors, including socio-economic level of families, with wealth, occupation and education all playing a part; education level of the partners (as well as of their parents); race, ethnicity and religion; and age. Similarity on these same socio-demographic features predict *continuation* of marriages as well as their occurrence. Within that matrix of constraints, physical attraction continues to play a part, especially for the male; similarity of values and attitudes plays a much lesser role than in early stages of the relationship; and complementarity of needs begins to play a more prominent role in pair-continuation and permanence than it had in earlier stages of the relationship.

People get married, or do not, for a lot of reasons besides romantic attraction. Various factors more or less external to the pair-relationship either constrain or facilitate the transformation of a romantic pair into a married couple. These include socio-economic factors, importance of the kinship network, time in partners' life-cycles, employment situations, and many other social forces. Likewise, people stay married—or they do not—for many reasons. The same factors that increase probability of marriage can function as barriers to the dissolution of marriages. Both the increase in divorces and the increase in cohabitation by unmarried pairs in recent years may reflect, at least in part, the weakening of such pulls toward marriage and the weakening of such barriers against marriage dissolution.

The dissolution of marriages, like their instigation, depends on a lot more than interpersonal attraction. As already noted, similarity (or lack of it) on certain socio-demographic factors functions to alter (a) the probability of encounter, hence acquaintance of a couple; (b) the probability of persistence of a relationship and of its leading to marriage; and (c) the probability of that marriage continuing. Certain socio-economic conditions also can be regarded as putting the marriage pair under stress: low income; unstable employment; unplanned children. Positive interpersonal attraction is likely both to serve as a buffer against pair-dissolution in the face of such stressors, and to suffer as a consequence of such stressful circumstances.

Still other stressors arise from features of the couple's interaction patterns. Some of the work of Gottman and his colleagues (Gottman, 1979a, 1979b; Gottman, Notarius, Markman, Banks, Yoppi, & Rubin, 1976), discussed in chapter 12 as related to the temporal patterning of interaction, is pertinent here as well. They found differences between "distressed" couples and "nondistressed" couples not only in the content and sequence of verbal messages but also in nonverbal behavior and accompanying affect. Partners in such distressed and nondistressed pairs were asked to indicate (continuously, by use of a set of response keys) both the *intended* impact of their own behavior and the *received* impact of their partner's behavior. Distressed and nondistressed couples did not differ in intentions; but members of distressed couples perceived their partner's behavior more negatively than intended by its originator, while members of nondistressed couples did not. Gottman calls this a "communication deficit." Such malfunctions of interaction should be viewed as factors *causing* marital distress and as interactive *consequences* of such dissatisfaction. Some other aspects of behavior of marital pairs will be noted in a later chapter in the context of discussion of families.

CHAPTER FIFTEEN
INTERPERSONAL INTERDEPENDENCE: SOCIAL INTERACTION AS EXCHANGE

Close relationships are characterized by behavioral involvement and mutual interdependence, as well as by positive, often intense, affect. Behavioral involvement with another person implies the need to coordinate and synchronize plans, intentions and activities with that person. Increases in such involvement and coordination imply increased mutual interdependence and predictability. Increased predictability and interdependence, in turn, imply increased mutual interpersonal control. This cycle of interdependence underlying the development of social relations has been analyzed as an exchange relationship, by several authors (Homans, 1958; Blau, 1968; Foa & Foa, 1975), but most effectively by Thibaut and Kelley (1959).

INTERACTION AS EXCHANGE

Thibaut and Kelley (1959) regard social interaction as an exchange relation. Unlike economic exchange, social exchange does not involve a common "coin," money, but rather involves a multitude of types of positively and negatively valued "goods and services." Their scheme supposes that people can somehow translate all of these valued things into a common "medium of exchange." They call the positive aspects "rewards," the negative aspects "costs," and hinge their theoretical ideas on a reward minus cost (or "profit," or net, or "pay-off") relation. Much of Thibaut and Kelley's work deals with pair or dyadic relationships. In principle, their theories can be extended to larger social units; but in practice, very little work has been done in that direction.

The Basic Matrix

Consider people interacting under conditions in which results for each of them depend not only on their own behavior but on the other's behavior as well. If two people, A and B, are engaged in a common task, or even behaving in a common space, the results A will get from whatever he or she does will be affected by what B does—and, of course, vice versa. Thibaut and Kelley use a 2×2 matrix to represent this interdependence (see Figure 15–1). In that figure, A and B are the interactors; i and j and k and 1 are the pairs of alternatives available to A and to B, respectively. (The limitation to two behaviors, like the limitation to two actors, is a practical simplification rather than a theoretical limitation.) The cells of the matrix show the net values of the pay-offs that B (lower, left-hand number) and A (upper, right-hand number) would receive if the *joint A and B choice* were in that cell.

FIGURE 15–1   The Thibaut and Kelley Social Exchange Matrix

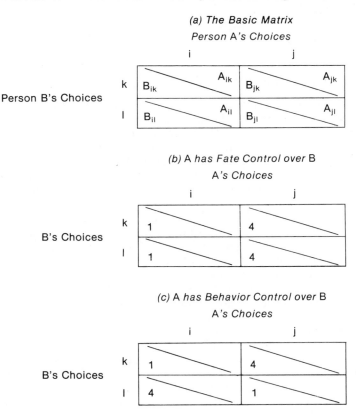

(a) *The Basic Matrix*

Person A's Choices

(b) *A has Fate Control over* B

A's Choices

(c) *A has Behavior Control over* B

A's Choices

This is obviously a "game matrix" similar in format to the prisoner's dilemma game discussed in chapter 9 on mixed-motive games. But Thibaut and Kelley put it to quite different uses. Consider Figure 15-l(b). Pay-offs for B are given such that B's outcomes depend entirely on A's behavior, with his or her own behavior making no difference. Thibaut and Kelley call that condition "fate control" of A over B. Consider Figure 15-1(c). In this matrix, pay-offs for B are so arranged that B gets the most favorable pay-offs by choosing k if and only if A chooses j; but B would get low pay-offs from k, better ones from 1, if A were to choose i. Under these conditions, in Thibaut and Kelley's language, A is said to have "behavioral control" over B. A can probably "induce" B to choose response k if that were to A's advantage, by consistently choosing response j. Person A also can convert "fate control" into such behavior control by making response j (favorable to B) contingent on person B giving the response that A prefers (perhaps in this case, k).

Most human interaction involves people who each have some degree of potential behavioral control of the other's behavior. This holds, in the general case, because gaining satisfaction (or other pay-offs) from an interaction usually requires some degree of cooperation and coordination of behavior by the others involved in that interaction. It often holds even in the limiting case in which the partners share only the interaction space, because noncooperation by others can raise the costs of the interaction and thus reduce the reward-cost net. It may even hold in the limiting case of the total despot, whose pay-offs require certain kinds of responses by others.

Rewards, Costs, and Pay-offs

When two people interact over a period of time, exchange theory supposes, each of them wants to *maximize his or her own "pay-off"* (i.e., the degree to which rewards exceed costs). There are at least three problems with this proposition. First, it may imply more self-centeredness than is evident in human affairs. That need not be a major drawback. It is possible to build features into the exchange theory model by which the "other's" receipt of rewards is rewarding to oneself (as is presumably the case for intense loving relationships). Indeed, Huessman and Levinger (1976) have built a model of interpersonal relations that has just such a feature (see chapter 16).

A second objection to the pay-off-maximizing proposition is that there is considerable evidence, mostly regarding economic behavior, that people very often *do not* try to maximize but instead use other criteria for making choices. For example, they may try to minimize loss rather than maximize gain. Or they may "satisfice"—that is, choose as soon as they find an alternative that surpasses some threshold value—rather than continue the process in order to maximize. This is also not a terribly limiting condition for exchange theory, since one could just as well deduce many of its other postulates on the basis of a minimizing, a satisficing or any other choice criterion.

A third objection to the pay-off maximizing proposition is based on the departure of that proposition from phenomological experience, from common sense. Introspection about one's own choice behavior does not lead one to the inference that choices are based on elaborate *calculations,* however rapid, of gains, costs, differences and alternatives. Furthermore, far from there being a readily available value-metric, into which the various kinds of positive and negative events and consequences can be translated, we often find ourselves facing comparisons of things we cannot compare, seeing certain behaviors or events as both pay-offs and costs, and otherwise facing anything but a simple and unidimensional pattern of positive and negative values.

As with other theories already discussed, one should not regard exchange theory as an attempt to give a literal description of the actual internal behavior involved in choice. Thibaut and Kelley, rather, suggest that choices get made *as if* they were based on such reward/cost calculations. The content of our introspective experience is really not to the point. (After all, we don't "experience" neural firings, patterning of recovery periods, hormonal flow variations, cell division or dozens of other physiological processes. But we seldom regard that nonexperiential quality as a sound basis for questioning the existence of such processes.) What is germane is whether the proposed processes provide a *useful* description that would predict the kinds of patterns of choice actually observed.

Behavior Sequencing
Under Mixed-Motive Conditions

If two people have potential behavioral control over each other, hence each must cooperate with the other, yet each wants to maximize his or her own pay-off (higher rewards, lower costs), they are in what is often called a mixed-motive situation. Each is motivated both to cooperate with and to compete against the other. Such situations were discussed in an earlier chapter, in the context of some conflict tasks involving such mixed motives.

One can make a reasonable case that all human interaction, to some degree, involves mixed-motive situations. The comment was made earlier that there is probably no such thing as a "pure" conflict situation; even wars have "rules" guiding the behavior of the parties. It is apparent, in the present context, that there may be no such thing as "pure" cooperation. Even love and altruism may have self-serving elements.

How can people behave sensibly in such mixed-motive situations? Thibaut and Kelley describe the process by which people learn to coordinate and synchronize their behavior so as to get the best pay-offs they can in the situation. For one thing, it *sometimes* is the case that the same joint response is the highest pay-off for both A and B. This poses no problem in the short run—assuming that both recognize that situation, both have some notion of the other's pay-off picture, and/or both communicate their preferences to the other effectively. But, Thibaut and Kelley argue, every behavior has some cost, and costs increase as a function of fatigue. Furthermore, every reward has a diminishing returns or satiation aspect to it. So even if A and B initially have a joint response that is the highest pay-off for each of them, if they keep repeating that same response the costs will increase and the rewards will decrease, so that that response will eventually have a lower pay-off than other options. Thus, even if there were a "mutual best response" at the outset, the pair A-B would want to vary their responses if they keep on interacting.

In many other conditions, there is no "best for both" response in the first place. One joint behavior is preferred by A, a different joint behavior is preferred by B. If A and B are mutually interdependent—that is, if each needs the other's cooperation to get into the desired state—and if each of them has potential behavior control over the other, they must devise some strategy so that they each get at least "pretty good" pay-offs out of it. Otherwise, they will stop interacting (if they can do so).

One main strategy for such interdependent pairs is sequential alternation; taking turns. (We'll go to the movies tonight, as you prefer; then we'll go dancing tomorrow as I prefer!) Use of such turn-taking requires trust in partners, and confidence that the "rules of the game" will not change (or be changed) before the tit for tat equation has been balanced. Behavior in the prisoner's dilemma game and in the "trucking game" (discussed in chapter 9), so often noncooperative and mutually destructive, shows what can happen in such mixed-motive situations when the development of mutual trust is undermined by (a) the reward structure of the task and situation; (b) the interpersonal relations structure (or lack of such patterning); and (c) constraints on the communication pattern. It was noted in chapter 13 that, while the evidence shows that negotiations and conflict resolution are affected by the richness of the communication modalities (hence the richness of interpersonal information), most studies of conflict tasks (such as PDG) have used highly restricted communication, yielding very lean interpersonal information. The Thibaut and Kelley matrix formulation, on the other hand, implies face to face full channel interaction between the mutually interdependent parties. It is under such conditions that strategies requiring effective communication of future intentions and expectations, and the development of mutual trust, have a good chance to be generated and sustained.

Development of Norms

When turn-taking or some similar sequential pattern of interactive behavior is developed between two people, it becomes a "habit" for them, so to speak. In Thibaut and Kelley's terms, they develop, and become mutually aware of, a *norm* for such behavior. In this context, a norm is a set of expectations about what someone, self or other, *ought* to do under a given set of conditions. (The term, norm, is sometimes used to refer to expectations about what people *will* do. I will try to limit the meaning of norm as used in this book to the *ought* meaning.)

Norms, once developed, take on a kind of life of their own. Violation of them is negatively sanctioned, at least to the extent that the other may object to the behavior *on the grounds that it violated what ought to be done.* Either party to the interaction can call upon the norm as a basis for arguing for the appropriateness or fairness of a certain outcome. In effect, it is as if norms became third-party moderators of disagreements between the interacting individuals.

If each party has potential behavioral control of the behavior of the other, to exercise that control requires what Thibaut and Kelley call use of personal power. To do so involves some cost, in any case, and the cost increases with repeated use of such personal power to force or induce the partner to make a certain behavior choice. It is much more efficient, much lower cost (hence higher pay-off), not to use personal power but instead to substitute reference to a shared norm—to argue, for example, that under a certain range of conditions, A is supposed to do x while B is supposed to do y.

Norms are thus ways of cutting costs, thereby increasing profit. They are ways of "institutionalizing" or "routinizing" behavior sequences that have been strategically valuable within that interaction in the past. Norms, therefore, are *rules for appropriate behavior* in a given situation and under a given set of circumstances.

As described here, norms are rules for behavior developed and used by a particular interacting dyad in a particular class of situations. But there also are norms of much broader scope and generality. Particular dyads develop some norms for all of their interactions. Groups develop some norms that apply in many situations. There are even culture-wide or society-wide norms for certain features of social behavior. Moreover, there are norms (i.e., rules for appropriate behavior) of several different types. For example, sets of interactants (dyads, larger groups, organizations) develop norms for appropriate allocation of rewards/resources. These are norms of distributive justice. Some of these (equity, equality, etc.) are discussed later in this chapter. As another example, norms develop about the proper division of labor or activities, about who should do what. Such norms or expectations for functionally differentiated sets of behaviors among the members of an interacting group are usually talked about in terms of roles, role expectations and role systems. Role expectations are norms that not only specify *what* should be done, but specify *who* should do *what, when* and *how.* Role differentiation in groups is discussed in chapter 18, as part of a discussion of structural patterns of interpersonal relations. Still another species of norms that develop as a result of social interaction are norms about what is *true,* and about what people should *believe and feel* about various matters. These norms are specifications of the values, attitudes and beliefs about reality that others—or specific others—*should* hold. All cultures, organizations, groups and individuals hold such expectations, for self and others. When people with different sets of such beliefs about reality interact, considerable cognitive conflict can result. Such conflicts of viewpoint (not of pay-offs) are represented as one task type discussed in chapter 8. These varieties of norms are listed here:

1. *Interactional Norms:* Rules for appropriate behavior specific to a dyad and a class of situations. ("In situation X, you should do a, and I should do b.")

2. *Situational Norms:* Rules for appropriate behavior specific to a class of situations, held by members of a group, subculture or culture. ("In situation X, people should do c.")

3. *Role Expectations:* Rules for appropriate behavior for an encumbant of a specific role in relation to the incumbent of a specific related role. ("Parents should X their children.")

4. *Allocation Norms:* Rules for fair distribution of rewards/resources (e.g. equity, equality).

5. *General Interaction Norms:* Generalized rules for appropriate interpersonal behavior. ("People should respect one anothers' privacy.")
6. *Social Reality Norms:* Broadly shared beliefs, attitudes and values about reality: What is *true,* what is *right* (moral), what is *valuable.* ("The world is round." "Time is scarce.")

Comparison Levels, Satisfaction, and Dyad Stability

What determines whether the members of a dyad continue to interact, or cease to do so? One answer for exchange theory is that the dyad will continue so long as it yields high pay-offs to both members. At this point Thibaut and Kelley introduce two additional concepts. The first is the Comparison Level (CL) which is a kind of "average" level of pay-offs that the person has come to expect in this kind of interaction situation. It is an adaptation level. Person A compares the pay-offs being received (or anticipated) from the present relation (say, level X) to this comparison level (CL). To the extent that CL exceeds present level X, A is dissatisfied. To the extent that X exceeds CL, A is satisfied. But since CL is an adaptation level that changes as a function of experience, if A were to stay in the relation for a long time, at X level of pay-off, CL would approach X. There is an old expression that you can get used to hanging if you hang long enough. We also recognize adaptation in the other direction, that one gets jaded, bored, by previously stimulating and satisfying experiences.

The other concept is the Comparison Level for Alternatives (CL_{ALT}) This refers to A's expectation about the pay-offs he or she *could* be receiving in the best of the *available* alternative relationships, including being alone. The relation between X and (CL_{ALT}) specifies not A's satisfaction, but A's probability of leaving or staying in the A-B relationship. If (CL_{ALT}) greatly exceeds X, A is likely to leave the relationship—even if X greatly exceeds CL, hence, is highly satisfying to A. Thus, a person might leave a good job if an outstanding job opportunity arose. Conversely, if X exceeds (CL_{ALT})—if the relation has better pay-offs than any *available* one—then A will stay in it even if X is below CL (i.e., even if A is dissatisfied). If we take into account the costs of the actual termination of an established relationship (e.g., a marriage) as part of the costs of the contemplated alternatives, this description is similar to the idea of barriers against marriage dissolution discussed in the preceding chapter. Even dissatisfying relationships can be better than available alternatives, especially if one takes into account the costs of changes.

In one sense, social exchange theory represents a useful account of how people's behavior becomes shaped by the pattern of interpersonal relationships—that is, how people become mutually interdependent with one another—and of the distinction between the satisfaction of a relationship and its probable continuation. It is less than complete and, although useful, it has some limitations. Some of those limitations have already been noted. One further limitation is that it does not reflect the fully dynamic "flow" of interpersonal relations. The models described in the next chapter address that limitation.

Exchange theory is based on the premise that individuals are motivated by interpersonal pay-offs, a very broad idea intended to subsume rewards and costs of various kinds. The nature of such rewards and costs—the "resources" that people exchange with one another when they interact—is the topic of a later part of this chapter. Before that, there is a discussion of allocation norms, i.e., the norms that people develop about what is a just distribution of such resources and costs. That discussion deals, first, with the widely studied principle of equity, and then considers other allocation rules and some nonallocation rules that shape interactive behavior.

NORMS FOR ALLOCATION OF REWARDS / RESOURCES

The matter of rewards and costs, and their distribution among members, becomes even more complex when one considers multi-member groups that remain "in business" for an extended period of time. Groups develop norms about sequences of behavior that lead to particular patterns of outcomes judged as being "right" or "fair" or "just" or "proper." But there is more than one way to view distributive justice; hence, there are several potential norms or rules that a group may adopt. Leventhal (1976) provides a broad review of many of these, which will be drawn upon at several points in this discussion even though Leventhal approaches these matters from the point of view of a single, powerful allocator (e.g., a boss) rather than from the point of view of a group as a whole.

Equity

One obvious principle for allocation of rewards, and the one most widely studied by social psychologists, is the norm of equity (or parity). Equity of allocation means that pay-offs are distributed in proportion to contributions, or inputs, or costs. If person A contributed twice as much effort, or talent, or "investment" to a group endeavor as did person B, then A should receive twice as much reward or pay-off as B. What is equitable in this matter is not some fixed relation between A's inputs and A's outcomes (which is Thibaut and Kelley's idea of net pay-off) but rather a fixed relation (equality) of A's and B's input-output ratios (in Thibaut and Kelley's terms, A and B obtaining *equal net pay-offs,* not necessarily highest net pay-off). (See EXRT 34.)

Whenever A's ratio (pay-off to A/inputs by A) becomes discriminably different than B's ratio (pay-off to B/inputs by B), there is a state of inequity between A and B. Of course, inequity, like many other features of interpersonal relations, is largely "in the eye of the beholder." Inequity between A and B, from A's point of view, is really a question of whether A perceives his or her own pay-off/input ratio as equal to, greater than, or less than, what A perceives B's pay-off/input ratio to be. If A perceives those ratios as equal, then A and B have equity from A's point of view. If A sees B as having a higher ratio, then A will feel inequity in the direction of disadvantage, will experience dissatisfaction, and will be motivated to do something about it. (This statement makes

EXRT 34:   *ADAM'S INEQUITY PARADIGM*

Main Study Procedures: Subjects perform a task with coworker(s), are given feedback on each person's contributions, and are then assigned the task of allocating the group's pay for the task to the individual members, including self. In a variation, the subject is told the level of pay that the experimenter has allocated to each (along with information on the contributions of each). In another variation, the subject is asked to allocate pay-offs among a set of workers not including self, after being told of their relative contributions to the group's task.

Main Dependent Variables of Interest: Relative amounts allocated to self and others, in relation to members' relative inputs; degree to which allocations approach equity (pay in proportion to contribution) or equality (equal pay to each); reactions of subject to receiving over-equitable pay, and to receiving under-equitable pay.

Main Variations: Form of allocation task (as above); size of pay-off; size of discrepancies in member contributions; ambiguity of sizes of contributions; characteristics of members (gender, status, prior preferences for equity/equality).

References: Adams (1965); Walster, Walster & Bersheid (1978).

---

clear that equity theory is an interesting blend of exchange theory, based on ideas about rewards, costs and pay-offs, and balance theory, based on ideas about dissonance or strain toward reduction of nonbalanced sets of perceptions or cognitions. Those two—reinforcement and balance—are usually regarded as different and more or less competitive theoretical principles of social motivation. But, as noted in an earlier chapter in the discussion of similarity and attraction, reinforcement and balance theory may well provide complementary perspectives rather than mutually exclusive ones.) In the case where A is inequitably disadvantaged, he or she can do many things: work less hard, hence make the pay-off/input ratio more favorable; reassess the value of own and other's contributions; try to get higher pay-offs. One interesting feature of equity theory is its prediction that A will also *feel distressed* (guilty) if own pay-off/input ratio is *higher* than B's and will also do something to reduce that advantageous inequity. The "something" includes working harder (so as to "deserve" the higher pay-off), and reassessing own and other's inputs. While some studies have found that over-rewarded persons work harder, the "reassess contributions" option is so very attractive, and permits such painless reduction of the guilt of advantageous inequity, that it tends to dominate. ("My own contributions must really be more exceptionally valuable than I thought, and this must be recognized by others, because I received such high pay-offs for them.") It is not nearly so easy to reduce disadvantageous inequity. Efforts to increase pay-offs may face an intractable allocation schema. Reassessment of inputs to view one's own as less important runs counter to one's own interests. Reducing one's efforts may lead to further reduction in one's own pay-offs.

The reason that equity is considered a "just" rule for allocation—when, indeed, it is so considered—is based on the idea that persons *deserve* pay-offs in amounts clearly related to how much they contribute to the group's endeavor.

But in actual operation, the idea of equity is fraught with complexities. First is the matter of assessing the contributions of each—and somehow translating different kinds of contributions (labor, planning, capital investment, special talents, etc.) into a common measure. The same is so if there is any notion of pay-offs that extends beyond a simple hourly wage to include values such as task achievement, self-fulfillment, and the like. There is the further problem that A's and B's perceptions and translations of one another's pay-offs and inputs are likely to differ.

What is to be the basis of contribution: effort, task ability, capital investment, or other kinds of input such as status, popularity, power? Leventhal (1976) argues that groups use equity allocations because that increases group task productivity; the high producers are highly rewarded, hence are motivated to be even more productive; while the low producers receive little, hence are motivated to work harder so as to get a bigger slice next time. Leventhal recognizes that the equity principle, carried to the extreme, can have quite negative effects. The low paid members are likely to rebel, rather than to increase effort. They may leave the group. Under some conditions, the costs of recruiting and training replacements would make that unprofitable for the group. Moreover, members often cannot easily leave the group. We are members of some groups on a more or less permanent basis—families, for example—and leaving the group is a last, not a first, resort. Members of some groups are "entitled" to continued membership, and to a "fair share" of what that group has to allocate. This is so for families, and also for work groups whose members hold tenured, or seniority based, or elective positions. In the Thibaut and Kelley formulation, our leaving the group depends on the *attractiveness of available alternatives* (X versus CL_{ALT}), *not on the attractiveness of the pay-off of the present situation* (X versus CL).

When low pay-off members remain in a group, they tend to be dissatisfied and to manifest that dissatisfaction in various ways that can lead to reduction of group morale, uncooperative task behavior, dissension in the group, formation of hostile cliques, and outright rebellion. So, while an all-out equity norm may increase group task productivity under some circumstances, it is also likely to reduce intra-group cohesion or solidarity. To deal with those interpersonal relations problems, the group often turns to other criteria of just allocation.

Effort

One alternative to a pure merit system, in which pay-offs are distributed wholly in proportion to resultant task productivity or task effectiveness, is to base pay-offs on each individual's own ability. Instead of rating A by comparing his or her productivity to B, C, D, . . . N, this approach would compare A's output to what one can expect from a person of A's ability. In recent decades, for example, many public school systems have talked of "underachievers" and "overachievers." This requires that you be able to measure ability—potential achievement—independent of actual attainments. It may or may not imply that to do better than you "should" is dismeritorious, but it certainly implies that to do worse than you "should" is dismeritorious and probably the result of lack of effort. This kind of criterion would reward those who work hardest to live up to their full potential, without regard to how task effective they actually are. When contribution is measured solely in terms of task effort (or *apparent* task effort), this tends to undercut the group's overall productivity. It may motivate poorer performers to try harder and, *if* trying harder actually increases productivity, to thereby increase group productivity. But it is far from clear that it will motivate high-ability people—who get less in relation to the quality or quantity of their performance than do their lower producing but hard working groupmates—to increase their efforts and productivity. They will almost certainly become dissatisfied. And, since they are the most competent they are likely to find it easiest to leave the group (i.e., they have the best CL_{ALT}). This condition tends to lower both group productivity and group cohesion.

Equality

Still another allocation rule that has received some research attention is equality. To give equal outcomes to all members without reference to their inputs is "fair" in the sense that each person can be regarded as an equal member of the group, entitled to $1/N$ share of its resources/rewards. Expressions such as "all for one and one for all," "share and share alike," express this idea of fairness and hint at its value in attaining high cohesion or solidarity of the group. Leventhal (1976) sees equality as the rule of choice for allocating when the top priority is to increase within-group harmony and reduce dissension, with increasing productivity having a lower priority. The equality norm has advantages when the group's task requires close cooperation among members, and one would suppose it to be especially useful for the kind of tasks that Steiner (1972) calls conjunctive (see chapter 5). It is also a valuable strategy when *differences* between inputs of different members are vague and hard to measure. It really begs the "relative input" question, but does so in a not outrageous way. But while allocation on the basis of an equality rule may tend to maximize within-group solidarity, it is not at all designed to increase group member motivation to work harder or perform better.

Equity and equality may be regarded as ends of a continuum. Equity, based on relative value of members' contributions, yields a distribution of payoffs to members that gives them differential outcomes. Equality, based on the fact of membership, yields equal pay-offs to all. No allocation scheme has been proposed as *fair* that gives pay-offs *more* in favor of high input persons than the equity norm would deliver—although there certainly are many such "rich-get-richer" phenomena in real life. Several schemes have been proposed that lie "beyond" the equality norm—that is, that give more to the lower producers than to the higher producers (like a "progressive tax" system). One of them is the idea of pay-offs in relation to need, and it will be discussed below. Another is the idea of *over-rewarding* low producers in the hope that they will work harder. This is the *advantageous inequity* case discussed earlier. As noted, it is much more likely to lead to an upward reassessment of the value of own inputs than to an upward shift in effort and task effectiveness.

There is evidence in several areas that people use some mix of, or compromise between, equity and equality norms. Allocations of pay-offs in coalition formation experiments (see chapter 9) show a blend of equality and equity.

Komorita and Chertkoff's (1973) "bargaining model" of coalitions explicitly uses equity and equality norms as the two competing norms used in the bargaining process. Komorita's (1979) "equal excess" model of coalitions specifically postulates that a coalition will tend toward an allocation in which each member gets back his or her "input"—likely to differ among them—and then all members split the remainder of the pay-off equally. There is considerable empirical support for both of these models. Leventhal (1976) reports a number of studies in which people shifted their allocations from "pure" equity toward—*but not all the way to*—equality, apparently to appease or to motivate potentially dissatisfied low input members. Such compromise, or "equal excess," or other combination of equity and equality rules, reflect the trade-off between motivation to increase task productivity and to decrease within-group dissatisfaction. That experimental coalitions, hypothetical allocators, and real life groups all use such mixes of equity and equality norms is perhaps further evidence for a recurrent theme of Part II of the book, namely, *Groups tend to leaven principles* (e.g., "truth wins," "majority rules," equity, equality) *with a pinch of pragmatism.* As a consequence, there are fewer hung juries and aborted negotiations than would follow from undiluted use of any one of the limiting-case, ideal-state single principles that group researchers have posed for them.

Need

Another potential allocation norm can be stated as a paraphrase of the Marxian motto: "From each according to ability, to each according to need." While exchange theorists have talked little about this potential norm—and, indeed, it is somewhat antithetical to the "maximize individual gain" premise of exchange theory—the need norm does in fact seem to operate quite strongly in some group settings. Families with small children, for example, expect:

1. Differential contributions of members, based on their ability to contribute, with one or two adults making major economic and labor contributions, with some older children perhaps contributing minor low-skill labor such as baby-sitting.
2. Differential allocation of resources, based on individual need, with different family members "needing" different amounts of spending money, of clothing, and of food, as well as different amounts of support and autonomy, based on age, functional role, and perhaps gender.

Indeed, it would be absurd for families to use either equity or equality as the sole allocation rule. There are vast disparities among members in their possible contributions, and equally vast disparities among them in what resources, and how much of them, they can effectively use. We all know from our own experience that identical treatment of different individuals is not always "fair" treatment (i.e., is not always equally "profitable" to all of them). Exchange theory or equity theory might account for such experiences by proposing that there are some additional, perhaps intangible "commodities" being exchanged in families—love, comfort, support, and so on. But it is pretty tenuous to argue that an infant is actually giving an amount of these equivalent in value to the contributions the infant is receiving from family members—at least in the short run. It is also difficult to argue that the infant or very young child calculates equity ratios and acts to balance them. So the "need" norm in family interaction is hard for equity theory to handle, and requires a broadened view of social exchange (as will be discussed later in this chapter).

But as soon as one leaves the family, or very family-like groups (e.g., communes), the "need" norm poses difficulties as a normative standard for allocation. In work settings, for example, if contributions differ widely there will be pressures from those making the largest contributions to get the largest payoffs, perhaps in terms of prerequisites or status if not in direct payment. (The classic line from Orwell's *Animal Farm,* that all animals are equal but some are more equal than others, suggests this same idea.) There may also be pressures from members to get their "needs," hence their pay-offs, defined upward. Komorita (1979) suggests, for the allocation of rewards in a coalition, that those with the highest resources may invoke an equity norm, while those with lowest resources may invoke an equality norm. If a "need" norm is being used, those with highest contributions may similarly invoke an equity norm, or may become dissatisfied with the group. Those whose needs are defined as low—who may be high, average, or low producers—may also become disaffected, may push for either an equity or an equality norm (depending on their relative contributions), or may push for a redefinition of need.

The preceding discussion assumes that individuals are somehow naturally motivated toward maximizing their own individual gain, at least in work relations and economic matters. That, of course, is a basic premise of exchange theory and especially of equity theory, and it is one heavily laden with culturally delimited values. Some non-kin groups (e.g., various religious sects) do run true communes successfully, though not all such attempts succeed or survive. Even some whole cultures or social systems have run on such communal premises, though these tend to be rather small-scale (tribes) and preindustrial. On the other hand, it is not unheard of for equity, equality and high need norms to be invoked by family members, as a rationale for increasing own net pay-off, even in families that operate relatively successfully on communal premises.

Other forms of work groups, and non-kin groups, may develop communal norms. Military units that are actually engaged in combat tend to modify prior normative systems toward the communal norms of ability based differential inputs and need based differential rewards. This does not necessarily imply a shift in the formal status hierarchy in relation to power of command—indeed, the presence of combat conditions may serve to intensify hierarchical command structures. It refers to the normative basis for allocation that will be used within such structures, not the "fairness" or "equality" of the structure itself.

One further feature of the operation of the need, or communal, norm requires clarification. While there is no reason to expect a correlation *across* members between level of contribution (based on ability) and the level of pay-off (based on need), there does tend to be pressure to produce a high correspondence between level of contribution *relative to ability potential* (i.e., level of effort) and the *level of pay-off in relation to needs* (i.e., proportion of needs fulfilled). In groups operating under such communal norms, there is often the implication that contributions below one's ability imply less than top effort, which in turn implies less than full commitment to the group. It would be remarkable if such implications did not lead to some negative sanctioning of the lazy members, if not to direct reduction of their pay-offs. In turn, this suggests a further contrast. The equity norm refers to an equality between the pay-off/input ratios of two people—with the further implication that the ratio should be as high as the circumstances permit for all members. In contrast, the need norm refers to a relation between the two parts of the individual's ratio, with pay-offs reflecting the same proportion of "needs fulfilled" as contributions reflect a proportion of "potential ability realized," and with the further implication that the ratio should be equal to 1.00 for every member of the group. Such a formulation represents a somewhat revised statement of the communal norm: insofar as each member contributes as much as he or she can in relation to own abilities, each should have all of his or her own needs fulfilled. This begins to converge with the *effort* norm discussed earlier.

NONALLOCATION RULES
THAT CONSTRAIN BEHAVIOR
IN GROUPS

Keeping Commitments

Some regard this as a fundamental rule of interaction, a sine qua non for effective behavior by mutually interdependent people. Any patterned sequence of mutually interdependent behavior requires interpersonal trust. A must be confident that B will do the behavior that B has promised and A now expects. Leventhal (1976) views the norm of keeping past commitments as one way in which an allocator can build up a reputation as being trustworthy. One can extend the idea of keeping past commitments one step further, to the idea of *meeting expectations*. That idea underlies the force of role expectations in a group.

Reciprocity

Another general norm that has been proposed as a key factor in interaction is the idea of *reciprocity*. One rendering of that idea is the maxim known as the golden rule: "Do unto others as you would have them do unto you." Other renderings, some less benign, include "an eye for an eye...", "tit for tat", "I'll scratch your back, you scratch mine", and the like. Reciprocity as a *description* of interactive behavior, in relation to increasing intimacy, for example, was discussed in chapter 13; it will be discussed again in the next chapter. What is here considered is reciprocity as a *normative standard* for interpersonal relations (that is, not so much how people in interaction *do* behave, but how they *should* behave, how they are *expected to* behave by their interacting partners).

In considering reciprocity, it is useful to distinguish between *matching behavior* (if A does X, B does X) and *matching outcomes* (if A does X to give B an outcome of value q, then B will do Y to give A an outcome of value amount q). Reciprocity of reward does not necessarily mean similar behaviors, nor even pay-offs identical in form, but rather pay-offs equivalent in value.

While reciprocity has been proposed as a broad and general process pervading social interaction as exchange, the evidence is not so clear (see, e.g.,

Altman, 1973, for a review). Altman suggests that reciprocity of self-disclosure tends to operate for encounters between strangers, but is far less apparent in encounters between intimates. Furthermore, self-disclosure among strangers tends to be composed of extensive discussion of surface or nonintimate topics, rather than disclosure of more intimate matters. The matter of reciprocity of intimacy was discussed in chapter 13, in the context of equilibrium. Increases in the complex of factors bearing on interpersonal intimacy (proximity, eye contact, body orientation, touch) sometimes led to a reciprocal response (thus producing increased intimacy) and sometimes led to a compensatory response (thus reestablishing the previous level of intimacy).

Reciprocity, or a tit for tat strategy, is the most effective one for "shaping" the behavior of a partner in a prisoner's dilemma game toward cooperation (see chapter 9). Note, however, that reciprocity in the PDG involves movement from a competing to a cooperating response, and continued reciprocity would mean continuation of that response. For both self-disclosure and the intimacy pattern (distance, gaze, touch, etc.) continued reciprocity between interactants would lead to maximum possible intimacy—a level of intimacy intolerable for most potential interaction occasions. Unmitigated reciprocity in *exchange behavior* would lead to many unthinkable situations.

Reciprocity considered as a *normative standard* for appropriate treatment of groupmates is another matter. It obviously plays some part in accounting for both positive behavior (paying back favors) and negative behavior (revenge). Foa and Foa (1975) make it the central principle of their theory of resource exchange, which will be discussed later in this chapter.

Mutual Responsiveness

Still another norm proposed as a basis for regulating interaction is the norm of *mutual responsiveness* (e.g., Leventhal, 1976; Pruitt & Kimmel, 1977). This norm implies that each partner, in a close and highly positive interpersonal relation, has an *obligation* to satisfy the other's needs. This is both a variant of the need norm and a variant of the reciprocity norm. That is, mutual responsiveness implies a reciprocity of obligation to respond to the other's needs. It does not imply reciprocal behavior, nor even reciprocal value of pay-offs. At the same time, mutual responsiveness implies attention to the needs of the other, not just to the amount of reward given and received. Mutual responsiveness may, in fact, be an accurate statement of the norms guiding behavior in families and other close relationships.

Perhaps it could be proposed that, while *constrained reciprocity* guides interaction in superficial, or less intimate, relationships (as in tit for tat strategy in PDG, and the reciprocity of superficial self-disclosure among strangers), mutual responsiveness to others' needs guides interaction in more intimate relationships (e.g., family relationships). At the more superficial levels of relationships, pay-offs received by A need to be in some reasonable relation to resources expended by A, at least in comparison to those matters for others involved in the interaction (B, C, etc.), lest A become disaffected from the relationship. This is the equity idea. At the more intimate levels, it is not the sheer quantity of pay-offs, but their kind and quality in relation to resources *needed* by A, that determines A's continuation in and satisfaction with the relationship.

It is perhaps also reasonable to point to an analogy between these two "interaction rules" for superficial and close relationships—*constrained reciprocity* and *mutual responsiveness*—and the two features affecting interpersonal attraction early and later in the relationship, namely, *similarity of values and attitudes* and *complementarity of needs*. If one accepts that parallel relation just suggested, then one can further suppose that equity is a proper or fair normative standard for superficial relationships (work relationships, distribution of pay-offs within a coalition in an experimental setting, and so forth), while need is a fair allocation rule for intimate relationships (family, intimate couple). This suggests that social exchange relationships are characterized by a pattern of *similarity/limited reciprocity/equity* at early or superficial levels of those relationships; and by a pattern of *complementarity/mutual responsiveness/need* at more fully developed, more intimate levels of those relationships. There is a sharp contrast between the two items of each pair: similarity and complementarity as bases of attraction; limited reciprocity and mutual responsiveness as interaction norms; and equity and need as resource allocation rules. Perhaps those features of relationships could be used to assess the degree of closeness of relationships at any given time, and the degree to which they have developed uniformly across the three aspects (attraction, interaction, allocation), rather than pursuing all-or-nothing questions.

TYPES OF RESOURCES IN SOCIAL EXCHANGE

All of the discussion of social exchange is based on an implicit assumption that there are many varieties of rewards and of costs. Thibaut and Kelley specifically discuss various types of rewards and costs, but assume that, at least in principle, they can all be translated into a single value dimension. Foa and colleagues (e.g., 1975, 1976) attempt to specify the major classes of resources that become involved in interpersonal exchange, and to postulate some rules for that exchange. The Foa formulation posits six kinds of resources, arrayed in a circular pattern (technically, a circumplex). The six classes of resources, shown in Figure 15–2, are: Love, Status, Services, Goods, Information, and Money. The two dimensions defining the space of the circumplex are universal versus particular, and abstract versus concrete. Love defines the particularistic end and money the universalistic end of the first dimension. Money is totally transferable from one person to another, but love is very much particular to the lover-loved-object pair. Status and services are two variations that are one step less "particularistic" than love. The first, status, is highly abstract; the second, services, is highly concrete. Information and goods are, similarly, two variations that are one step less "universalistic" than money. The first, information, is highly abstract; the second, goods, is highly concrete.

Foa underpins that theory with a reciprocity assumption: In social interaction, people exchange resources of equal amounts or value, and they tend to respond "in kind." A gift of love will be responded to by a reciprocal gift of approximately the same amount of love. Money given begets money received. But that is not always feasible. So, Foa and Foa hypothesize that people will re-

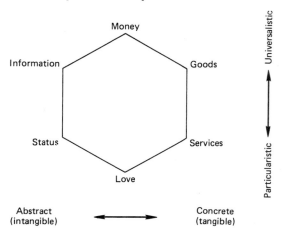

FIGURE 15-2   Foa's Circumplex of Resources in Social Exchange

spond as nearly in kind as they can. Love might be returned in services or in status giving; it certainly would not be "repaid" in the form of money. "Goods" are paid for in money or services, services in love or goods.

While Foa and Foa cite some empirical evidence in support of these premises, only limited research has been done by others on these questions. A study by Brinberg and Castell (1982) found support for two of the premises: (a) the proposition that resources are paid back in equal amounts; and (b) the hypothesis that the closer the two types of resources are to one another (in the circumplex space) the more likely they are to be substituted for each other in exchanges. They also found general support for the locations of the six types of resources in relation to one another.

Perhaps such resource exchange can also be construed in terms of surface versus deep relationships. Perhaps money and goods and information can be regarded as the proper "coin" of superficial relationships—we buy goods for money or barter with other goods; we buy or exchange information. Perhaps services, status and especially love are the "coins" of intimate relationships. And while we may exchange services for services (or love), the services given and services received may differ in content—so as to be responsive to the other's needs—even though they may be similar, somehow, in "value." Moreover, in line with the rule of "contributions according to abilities, pay-offs according to needs," receipt of needed "services" (e.g., child care) may be repaid with "love" or "status" if the recipient (e.g., small child) does not have the ability to deliver "services" needed by the adult caretaker. So perhaps it is possible to add types of resources exchanged to the pattern characteristic of surface versus deep relationships: For superficial or early stages of relationships, similarity based attraction, limited reciprocity in interaction, equity in allocation and exchanges involving universalistic-generic type resources; for later and deeper stages of relationships, complementarity of needs as a basis of attraction, mutual responsiveness in interaction, need based allocation and particularistic type resources in exchange. These patterns are shown in Figure 15-3.

FIGURE 15-3 Parallel Dimensions of Interaction over Stages of Development

TYPE OF INTERACTION	TEMPORAL STAGES OF RELATION	BASIS OF ATTRACTION	INTERACTION NORM	ALLOCATION NORM	TYPE OF RESOURCE EXCHANGED	LEVEL OF INTIMACY
ENCOUNTER	Early	Proximity/ Physical At- traction/ Demographic Similarity	Constrained Reciprocity	Equity	Money	SHALLOW
					Goods Information	
ACQUAINTANCE	Later	Attitude and Value Similarity	Shared Expectations	Equality		
ROMANCE					Service Status	
LONG–RUN FRIENDSHIP	Long-run	Need Compatibility	Mutual Responsiveness	Need		
MARRIAGE					Love	DEEP

CHAPTER SIXTEEN
INTIMACY AND PRIVACY:
THE DYNAMICS
OF INTERACTION

In spite of the long established use of the term *group dynamics,* remarkably little of the research on groups has dealt with dynamic, rather than static, aspects of groups. Studies of interpersonal attraction, and even most studies of the acquaintance process, are done from a static rather than a dynamic point of view. That is, they study patterns of relations among group members at one point in time or, at most, examine differences between static patterns at two or a few points in time. They are done as if there is a specific relation between any two people at any one time (they *are or are not* "friends," for example) and as if there is a step by step progression of that relation, from encounter to acquaintance to friend or "date" to close friend or "romantic partner." Most studies deal with only a fixed and limited period of time. Even those that trace a relation over a long period of time generally deal only with *before* versus *after* differences, rather than with the flow of events and relations *during* that time.

Similarly, the exchange view of social interaction, though somewhat less static in its treatment of relationships, still focuses on relatively static patterns. For example, while Thibaut and Kelley do trace the path of development of interdependence in dyads, yielding sequential patterns of mutually responsive behaviors, such patterning is set within a narrow-band and static matrix that has relatively unchanging actors, alternatives and pay-offs.

There has been a limited body of work on interpersonal relations, most of it fairly recent, that has a more dynamic character. This chapter will present some of that work. The first part will deal with the development of (and retreat from) intimacy in groups. The second part will deal with the ongoing regulation of privacy. The third part will present a view that tries to tie that pair of related opposites, intimacy and privacy, to one another in what is called a dialectic approach. The fourth part describes a quite different approach: a formal computer simulation model of the development of interpersonal relationships. That model, called RELATE, lets us examine the pattern of interpersonal relationships that results from interaction under different sets of conditions reflecting different sets of theoretical assumptions.

SOCIAL PENETRATION THEORY: DEVELOPMENT OF INTERPERSONAL INTIMACY

Altman and Taylor (1973; Altman, 1973) present a treatment of interpersonal relationships that paints a more dynamic picture than most research in the area. They build on work by Jourard and others (e.g., Jourard, 1964) on patterns of self-disclosure in groups. They also build on work by Argyle and others (e.g., Argyle & Dean, 1965, Argyle & Kendon, 1967) on the interrelations among parts of a pattern of factors (gaze, distance, other verbal and non-verbal aspects of behavior) that reflect the level of intimacy of a relationship.

Altman and Taylor (1973) propose that an interpersonal relationship between two people develops as if each of the two people were "penetrating" each other's "social self" to successively deeper (more intimate) levels, and at the same time, on a successively broader basis at any one level. The penetration process is like a wedge; it encompasses broader areas at more surface levels as it penetrates, narrowly, into deeper, more intimate areas. Altman and Taylor (1973) also concern themselves with the depenetration process—the reversal of the social penetration process, in which the parties withdraw to shallower and narrower bases of interaction—and they are virtually the only theorists who do so. But short of the undoing of a social relationship—a depenetration process—social penetration theory assumes that the course of a relationship is directional and cumulative. That is, relationships progress from shallower to deeper, more "open" interaction, and simultaneously from narrower to broader areas of interaction. The rate and shape of that progression, and the level to which it progresses, depend on the rewards and the costs ensuing from the interaction. When net pay-offs are high and positive, relationships move to broader and deeper levels. If they become negative, depenetration begins. The rate, shape and level of relationships also depend on characteristics of the individuals (e.g., their tendency toward openness) and of the situations (e.g., the degree of intimacy they call for) involved in them.

Moreover, the degree and pattern (i.e., depth and breadth) of intimacy of a relationship *involves and is displayed by* the interplay of many levels of behavior, including verbal, paraverbal, and nonverbal interpersonal actions and environmentally oriented behaviors. These all function as a unified system. Many aspects of verbal behavior, such as level of self-disclosure; paraverbal features such as voice tone and intensity, pauses and interruptions; aspects of nonverbal behavior such as smiling, looking, touching, body orientation and posture; and environmentally oriented actions such as interpersonal distance, territorial behavior, use of markers—all are part of an organized *pattern* of behavior that expresses the level, form, and intimacy of the social relationship between the interactants. These and many behavioral expressions of the relationship are both conjunctively linked (i.e., they go together) on the one hand, and compensatory (i.e., they can substitute for one another) on the other, as the relationship progresses, retrogresses, and/or is maintained at some particular level.

The reciprocal and complementary features of this intimacy pattern were discussed in an earlier chapter, in the context of a discussion of different meanings of equilibrium. The main points raised in that discussion apply here as well. Level of interpersonal intimacy is both defined and displayed by a pattern of verbal and nonverbal behavior. A shift in levels of intimacy may be accomplished by change in one or more behaviors of that pattern. A change in intimacy by one partner, A, may be reacted to by a compensatory change by the other partner, B. Alternatively, a change in intimacy by A may be viewed by B as a signal for a shift in the relationship, to which B may respond by an incrementing rather than a compensating change. Any of these kinds of changes can be accomplished in a variety of ways by varying different parts of the behavior pattern. A smile, a look, a touch, a change of topic or a change of tone of voice, all may signal a desire for greater intimacy or indicate the attaining of it.

The social penetration view has some strengths and some limitations. Its main strengths are its more complex treatment of interpersonal relationships and its more dynamic view of their development and dissolution. Its main limitations arise from an apparent underlying assumption that ''more open'' is necessarily better. This feature led Altman and his colleagues to develop an alternative view of interpersonal relations—concentrating on privacy—that is to be discussed next.

PRIVACY REGULATION THEORY: CONTROL OF INTERPERSONAL INTERACTION

Altman (1975) developed a theory of privacy regulation that contrasts quite sharply with his social penetration theory. In it, he tried to bring together several research areas that had become very popular areas of study but that had been treated only as separate areas: use of personal space, territorial behavior, and crowding. Hall's (1966) ideas of different interpersonal zones—intimate, personal, social and public—for different situations have already been discussed (see chapter 13). *Personal space* refers to a sort of bubble of space around people that serves as an extension of their own interpersonal selves. Much of the research on personal space involves people reacting negatively, by stress, withdrawal or defense, when others intrude into their personal space bubbles. (See EXRT 35.) *Territoriality* refers to how people claim, occupy, mark, and attempt to control areas in the physical environment, and how they

EXRT 35:   *SOMMERS'S PERSONAL SPACE INTRUSION PARADIGM*

Main Study Procedures: An experimenter-confederate sits down either next to or at more distant positions from individuals (usually students) who are already seated in various settings such as cafeterias and libraries.

Main Dependent Variables of Interest: Reactions of individuals who are intruded upon (withdrawal; use of personal possessions as barriers; changes in body orientation; time before departure from the setting) compared to controls who were not intruded upon.

Main Variations: Type of setting; distance and orientation of chosen seat; characteristics of intruder and subject (gender, age, race, apparent status, assertiveness, and the like).

References: Altman (1975); Altman & Vinsel (1977); Hall (1966); Sommers (1959).

---

sometimes defend these areas in response to intrusion. *Crowding* refers to how people react in trying to cope with situations in which so many people occupy such a small space that they impede each others' social behavior and task performance. All three of these areas—personal space, territoriality, and crowding—emphasize the importance of people being able to *close themselves off from others,* and the negative consequences of not being able to do so. Research on personal space emphasized the negative responses to intrusions. Territoriality research stressed how territorial behavior enhanced the smooth functioning of social systems by minimizing conflict. Research on crowding emphasized the negative physiological and psychological effects and after-effects of short- and long-term crowding, and how people struggle to try to avoid or reduce its effects. In all of these cases, emphasis is on the dangers of being overly open to others and on the virtues of people being able to close themselves off from others. This is in sharp contrast to social penetration theory, which stresses (actually, overstresses) the importance of people becoming progressively more open to one another. (See EXRT 36.)

Altman's privacy regulation theory tried to handle this contrast by incorporating the opposing ideas, of openness and closedness to others, in the same formulation. The theory postulates that privacy regulation involves a balancing of two opposing processes, interpersonal opening and closing; and that the desirable point of balance of these two differs over individuals, over situations, and over times. The net balance of the two, at any one time, leads to behaviors aimed at either increasing or decreasing interpersonal accessibility. Privacy regulation theory kept the ideas from social penetration theory about a multi-level *system* of behaviors—verbal, paraverbal, nonverbal and environmentally oriented behaviors—that were both conjunctively linked and compensatorily substitutable, and that were mechanisms by which shifts in desired level of accessibility were accomplished. It dropped the assumption from social penetration theory that there is a *directionality* to the development of social relationships. But it also dropped that theory's emphasis on development. It concentrated, instead, on the short-term oscillations—toward intimacy and

EXRT 36:   *THE ALTMAN/HAYTHORN GROUPS-IN-ISOLATION PARADIGM*

Main Study Procedures: Volunteer male navy enlistees are assigned to groups (usually two-person), either on a random basis or in terms of an intended group composition pattern. Each group is given the mission of staying together in a small room(s) for an extended period of time (e.g., eight days), and carrying out a series of experimental tasks (some individually and some in a group) during that time, with essentially no contact with anyone or anything outside the room.

Main Dependent Variables of Interest: Interaction patterns and topics; territorial behavior (development of consistent use of certain furniture and spaces by one member); task performance; accuracy of time estimates; interpersonal attraction/hostility; ability to complete the mission.

Main Variations: Size and composition of groups; types and difficulty of tasks; size and equipment of room(s) and degree of potential privacy for various functions; degree of stimulation from outside the isolation (e.g., recorded music; newscasts; reading material).

References: Altman & Haythorn (1965, 1967a, 1967b); Altman & Taylor (1973).

---

toward privacy, opening and closing—in interpersonal relationships. In doing so, it seemed to imply some form of optimal balance of openness and closedness, toward which all social relationships "strive," and some homeostatic mechanisms underlying their regulation.

Altman and colleagues later proposed yet a third formulation, one that attempts to integrate the other two into a unified theory of the development and management of social relations. That third formulation is described next.

ALTMAN'S DIALECTIC THEORY OF SOCIAL RELATIONSHIPS

Altman and colleagues (Altman, Vinsel, & Brown, 1981) presented a third, dialectic formulation that attempts to mold the strengths of social penetration theory and privacy regulation theory into a single unified *theory of social relationships*. That theory is built on a *dialectic* view of interactive processes, and a brief discussion of that concept is therefore useful here.

The Dialectic Concept

The term dialectics has been used with a variety of meanings, and has even become a catchword in certain areas of political, economic and social science. (See Altman et al., 1981, for a review of such usages.) Altman uses it only in a limited and definite form, to include three basic ideas: (a) the idea of opposition or polarity; (b) the idea that there is a unity or relatedness between opposites; and (c) the idea that that relation between opposites is dynamic, that it shifts over time.

Altman posits two fundamental oppositions or polarities in social relationships: openness-closedness and stability-change. The two poles of each opposition are related, and help define one another. The two polarities are themselves related, as part of a unified system and not just as two parallel, independent processes. It is the pattern of openness (or closedness) to which the idea of stability (or change) refers. Moreover, the relative strengths of these opposites—of openness and closedness, of stability and change—shift over time.

Neither pole of an opposition ever completely dominates. Even very close relations contain some areas in which the parties are "closed" to one another. Even very stable relations contain some elements for potential change. Indeed, each polarity at the extreme is self-limiting, so the system tends back from its limits. But these dialectic oppositions do not necessarily tend toward a fifty-fifty balance, *nor toward any particular ideal state.* In any given case, the "balance point" of a relationship depends on the participants, their past histories, their present needs and opportunities, and the situation in which they are interacting. Furthermore, such a balance point only applies temporarily. It shifts from moment to moment, because all those underlying things (histories, needs, opportunities, situational factors) shift over time.

The Concept of Change

Altman's idea of *change* also merits comment here. Most psychological and social psychological theories (e.g., those of Freud, Erikson, Helson, Piaget) and even many philosophers who have used dialectic ideas in their work (e.g., Hegel), postulate a *directionality* to changes—a teleological or goal seeking force, a directional growth, a fixed homeostasis, a final synthesis. Altman rejects both the idea that social relationships are homeostatic or equilibrium seeking, and the idea that the development of social relationships is directional or "ideal state seeking." He holds that *change in social relationships is cumulative but not necessarily directional.* It is cumulative in the sense that a relationship at any one time "contains" all of its past history—or at least contains the residual effects of that past in the perceptions of the interactants. Such change is not necessarily directional. There is no "ideal state" toward which all social relationships tend.

The schema Altman builds upon these underlying philosophical and theoretical assumptions is summarized (Altman, et al., 1981) as follows:

> We assume that human social interaction can be viewed as functioning in accordance with two dialectical processes: openness-closedness and stability-change. We further assume that the oppositional components . . . operate as a unified and dynamic system, that each pole of the two oppositions is equally important to social functioning, and that the interplay . . . is not directed at . . . some ideal state. (p. 127)

Interpersonal Boundary Regulation

Openness-closedness is not an all-or-none matter. A person can be differentially accessible to different partners, in different content areas, or at different levels of intimacy. A person can also be differentially open with regard to receiving from and expressing to others. The desire for more or less accessibility in one or more of these aspects of openness-closedness is both *expressed and accomplished* by means of a spectrum of behavioral possibilities: verbal self-disclosure or hostility, looking, touching, smiling, closing the door, turning the back, moving closer. All of these and other behaviors can be viewed as parts of a unified *boundary regulation system*. In those terms, the degree of openness-closedness can be viewed as the degree of permeability or impermeability of the interpersonal boundary, in either or both directions.

Every organism (and suborganisms, such as cells and organs) must have some capacity to regulate transactions with its environment if it is to remain viable as an interdependent entity. So it is, Altman argues, for the individual in regard to transactions with the social environment. But that regulation is not accomplished by means of a single fixed barrier, with variable permeability, plus a few orifices or "gates" (as in the "skin" of an organism and the membrane of a cell). Rather, it is carried out by means of a unified system of behavior. Verbal, paraverbal, nonverbal and environmentally oriented actions serve both as the *mechanisms regulating the flow of interpersonal interaction* and the *content or substance of the interpersonal interaction* that is being regulated. Note that, in these terms, use of personal space and territorial behavior are simply subsystems of the interpersonal boundary regulation system—relatively "peripheral" subsystems. Similarly, the smile-look-touch-orient segment of nonverbal behavior, plus distance, discussed by Argyle and Dean (1965) as an equilibrium seeking system for maintaining a proper level of intimacy (see chapter 13), is also a subsystem of the overall interpersonal boundary regulation system. But while these components may function in a compensatory manner with respect to each other in any given setting, the overall system is *not* equilibrium seeking, and is not "striving toward" any specific pattern or balance or ideal state.

In this same context, "crowding" is a term identifying extreme conditions under which the interpersonal boundary regulatory system (for convenience, the IBRS) has broken down or is on the verge of it. The threatened system breakdown is in the direction of the individual being unable to limit interpersonal interactions. The individual is "flooded," so to speak, and viability as an independent organism is threatened. It is also worth considering the case of system breakdown or near-breakdown at the other extreme of accessibility—extreme and continued interpersonal isolation. While there has been some research on effects of social isolation (see Altman & Haythorn, 1965, 1967a, 1967b), that work has seldom been discussed in relation to crowding, or even in relation to the dynamics of "normal" interaction. Social isolation, like crowding, refers to an extreme condition in which the individual's IBRS has broken down, or is on the verge of it. In this case, the problem is one of too little flow of interaction across the system boundary. If crowding is a flood, isolation is a drought. As with crowding, the individual will experience discomfort, sometimes extreme stress, and will struggle in various ways to cope with and alter that system condition. For crowding, those coping strategies include a variety of actions to impose "barriers" that will prevent or reduce unwanted interaction—closed body positions; perhaps aggressive defense of near-body space and territory; perhaps hostile verbal and paraverbal behaviors; withdrawal when that is possible. For isolation, unless the individual can reestablish interpersonal contact, the coping strategies are more geared to generating *substitutes for actual social contact*—by remembering, anticipating, fantasizing and, in extreme cases, hallucinating.

Stability and Change

Altman specifically rejects one assumption that underlies virtually all current theories of social psychology, namely, that change occurs in the service of achieving balance, consistency or equilibrium. Such theories postulate that imbalance, inconsistency, dissonance, or disequilibrium are aversive and stressful. Such a view implicitly treats change either as (a) externally imposed, equilibrium disturbing, and therefore unwanted and to be gotten rid of; or as (b) internally generated, in reaction to such external perturbations, and in pursuit of reestablishing the prior equilibrium (or, if necessary, a new equilibrium). These views thus treat change as *epiphenomenal, undesirable and transitory*. In contrast, Altman treats change as a *fundamental* and *persistent* feature of social interaction that is *neither desirable nor undesirable* (or, is both). He assumes that people seek *both* stability and change, and that the two are equally important in social interaction and are diametrically opposed aspects of it. Stability and change (of many aspects of a relationship, but specifically of its openness-closedness) can vary on several dimensions. Altman posits four: (1) *frequency,* or number of "cycles" of open-closed per unit time; (2) *amplitude,* or degree or magnitude of openness-closedness for a given cycle; (3) *regularity,* or the degree to which successive cycles have the same periodicity (i.e., the *stability of changes*); and (4) *relative duration* of openness versus closedness within a given cycle.

Stability and change can also be regarded from short-run and long-run stances. Some relationships may exhibit short-run cyclical fluctuations in openness-closedness that are embedded within stable long-run cycles. (The opposite possibility is also of interest, though not mentioned by Altman in the chapter cited. That opposite is the case of relationships with short-run stable patterns that are embedded within systems of relationships that are themselves changing. For example, certain features of a husband-wife relationship may remain very stable over time, even though they, their children, and others are involved in a network of relationships that is both changing and aging.)

Like openness and closedness, stability-change can apply differentially to different aspects of a relationship: different content areas, different levels of intimacy, different behavioral levels (verbal, nonverbal, etc.). Stability serves the function of increasing predictability in an interpersonal relationship. Change serves the function of infusing variety into that relationship. *Both* are desirable at different times, under different circumstances, and for different specific relationships. A maximum of either, hence an absence of the other, is intolerable, unadaptive.

Adaptation and Ideal States

Altman assumes that adaptive (that is, effective) social functioning involves a *momentary congruence of psychological processes with the demands of the situation*. As that situation changes (or the interactants change), so does what is required for adaptive congruence. Furthermore, even for any one situation, congruence can be attained in many different ways. Multiple patterns of openness-closedness, and stability-change, are equipotential ways of adapting to any given situation. No one pattern should be regarded as "optimal" or "desirable" even for one momentary adaptive congruence. Furthermore, not only is change inevitable, it is desirable—though so is stability. A social bond that is completely stable (or nearly so, since complete stability is not possible) is not likely to permit adaptation to new circumstances, and new circumstances are inevitable as a consequence of both external and internal forces. A totally unchanging relationship, therefore, is not likely to survive. On the other hand, continuous change and instability, hence unpredictability, are also intolerable in a relationship. Some minimum patterning of norms, expectations and behaviors is necessary for viability.

Altman, thus, reverses the usual roles of change and adaptation. For most psychological theories, change is accidental, transient and undesirable, while adaptation is a "resting state"—basic, desirable and pervasive. For Altman, it is *adaptation* that is epiphenomenal, and transient. *Change* is fundamental and pervasive. So is stability. And both stability and change (and openness and closedness) are *both desirable and undesirable,* under different circumstances. Adaptation is accidental and momentary, perhaps "desirable" in an abstract sense, but only incidentally and temporarily to be attained.

Implications

Altman applied these concepts to lay out some hypotheses in several areas: (a) the development of interpersonal relationships; (b) the impact of "crises" in a relationship; (c) the intimacy levels of exchanges; (d) interaction styles; and (e) matching and timing of interaction within the interpersonal unit. In all of these areas, the dialectic view not only takes into account the features of relationships dealt with in social penetration and privacy regulation theory, but integrates and extends them by positing more complex, more dynamic, and more variable patterns of relations. This formulation also opens up some quite new territory. For example, Altman and colleagues (1981) comment that the reason why the search for stable individual difference factors associated with self-disclosure has been unfruitful may have been because a search for persistent traits or behavior patterns of the individual is an inappropriate approach. From the dialectic viewpoint, a far better approach would be to search for persistent patterns of openness-closedness over time. As another example, the much more complex, dynamic formulation resulting from the dialectic view makes it possible to treat the *temporal and behavioral fit* (or lack of fit) *between the two interaction partners,* over time, as properties of the interacting dyad rather than just as behavior of the individuals. At this level too, a dialectic enters. The authors postulate that while there is a need for at least a minimal degree of *congruence between partners* in temporal and substantive features of the interaction, it is also the case that mistiming and noncongruence of substantive aspects can serve some positive functions by providing stimulation and unpredictability that lead to further exchange, exploration, and development of the relationship.

The same features of the Altman dialectic approach that are its chief strengths are also the wellsprings of its chief weaknesses, as is fitting of course for a dialectic view! It is by far the most complex, dynamic and fluid treatment of interpersonal relations that has been attempted to date within the social-psychological literature. It thereby seems to come closer than other formulations do to fitting what we know about interpersonal relationships from our own day to day experience, as well as fitting what we know from past formal research on groups. It places emphasis on intact, relatively molar social units, and integral "chunks" of interpersonal behavior, rather than taking an overly analytic approach that studies narrowly defined molecular segments of individual behavior. It also tries to break away from some of the pervasive assumptions about human behavior—such as homeostasis and goal directed development—that have long dominated social science research, and that have helped to make past theories at the same time both more tractable and less consonant with our own experience. All of these are powerful and valuable features that give this view great potential as a guide for new theoretical conceptions regarding group interaction process.

But these very same features, of complexity, flexibility, dynamic and molar emphasis, and departure from past assumptions, pose serious problems for Altman's dialectic approach. Thus far, the substantive detail is only partially fleshed out. To put substantive meat on such a complex and dynamic conceptual skeleton is an extremely demanding task. Moreover, while there has been considerable research bearing on social penetration, personal space, territoriality, and the like, which provides some empirical basis for forming hypotheses within this theory, little empirical research has yet been done to *test* the formulations of this theory. Moreover, the very complexity and fluidity of Altman's theory make it extremely difficult to devise strong empirical tests of its hypotheses. And its radical shift in assumption base—from the more familiar and tractable ideas of equilibrium and goal directedness, to some as yet unclear alternatives—may involve a trade-off of apparent realism for tractability that few researchers will be willing to buy. So, while Altman's dialectic, IBRS theory has much potential value, its actual contribution to our understanding of group interaction remains to be determined on the basis of its future development.

LEVINGER'S INCREMENTAL EXCHANGE MODEL

Levinger and colleagues (Huessman & Levinger, 1976; Levinger, 1980) have developed and applied a formulation of interpersonal interaction that is both similar to and quite different from Altman's theory. The two approaches are similar in that they both insist on the treatment of interaction as a relatively dynamic and complex process, they both are concerned with *development* of relationships, and they both aim at treatment of a molar and dyadic social unit rather than a more molecular and monadic one. They differ in that, while Altman's formulation insists on almost complete fluidity, allows almost all possible patterns to occur, and imposes a minimum of structure, Levinger's approach is a formal computer model (called RELATE) whose use requires de-

tailed quantitative specification along a number of parameters. Both build on
Thibaut and Kelley's exchange theory, and both go beyond it—but in different
ways.

The RELATE model begins with the exchange theory idea of a pay-off
matrix, but does not hold it constant. Instead, the relationship entails choices
within a *systematically linked series of matrices,* Levinger also posits a depth
dimension (as did social penetration theory), but changes the assumptions
about the relation between depth and amount of reward. Altman and Taylor
(1973) postulated that higher rewards accelerated the development to deeper
levels of relationship. Huessman and Levinger (1976) assume that deeper levels
of involvement bring higher potential rewards—but also higher potential costs,
hence more variable potential pay-offs.

At any given point, actors are faced with a given matrix of alternatives
and pay-offs. The actors' joint choices yield a separate pay-off for each, as in
Thibaut and Kelley's theory; but also move the pair to a different "state". Each
state has a *different matrix,* that may involve same or different choice alternatives and pay-offs. As relationships continue, they increase in involvement
and in depth, and the size of potential rewards and costs both increase. Hence,
the variability of pay-offs increases, and the array of behavior alternatives increases. *Anticipated future behaviors* of the partner, and their consequences,
are taken into account, but people differ in how far ahead they look. Furthermore, people *learn* from past experience about the partner's probable
responses, but learn at different rates. At the same time, anticipated future
rewards are *discounted,* probably because the future is uncertain. People differ
in the discount rates they use, although the discounting is always monotonic
with time; that is, far-future rewards are discounted more than near-future ones.

An actor chooses, at any given time, in a way that will maximize *expected
pay-offs* for a *weighted sum of own and partner's pay-offs, for some specified
time into the future.* As the relationship develops, the weight given to the *partner's* pay-offs increases, from a near zero level at the outset to a substantial
level for deep, highly involved relationships. The model permits the setting of
several parameters independently, for any given "trial": the functional form of
increase of the weight given to the other's pay-offs; the number of steps into the
future ("depth of search") for which expected pay-offs and other's expected
behavior are taken into account; the learning rate from partner's past performance; and the discount rate applied to anticipated pay-offs that lie at different
distances into the future. In that way, the model can be used to explore the quite
complex consequences of different combinations of parameter values for these
several dimensions of the model.

Huessman and Levinger (1976) apply the RELATE model to explore
several specific topics, some of which are touched upon elsewhere in this book:
altruism, similarity and attraction, reciprocity in self-disclosure, and romantic
relationships. The RELATE model is not a tool for empirical research; and it is
not a substitute for empirical research. It is a form of theoretical development,
complementary to empirical research. At the same time, the RELATE model is
not a specific theory, but rather a medium within which a variety of specific
theories of dyadic interaction can be stated, and the consequences of their sets
of assumptions systematically explored. The RELATE model can be used as a

device for checking the feasibility and potential consequences of a specific set of theoretical premises *before* conducting extensive empirical research. It can also clarify concepts, both by forcing a clear statement of premises and by showing distinct patterns of consequences. For example, under certain assumptions RELATE shows that altruism is tied to discount rate and to depth of search (how far ahead one looks). In analysis of similarity and attraction, RELATE shows that it is *not symmetry of pay-offs* for A and B, but rather *within-cell pay-off correspondence* between A and B, that predicts continued deepening of a relationship.

Huessman and Levinger (1976) point out that while RELATE is a very versatile tool for exploring alternative theoretical formulations, it does not escape the central fault of all reward/cost based formulations: a failure to specify just what is a reward (and cost) and how to determine its magnitude. Nevertheless, the RELATE model, and the incremental exchange theory underlying it, offer a very great advance over more limited, static formulations. That model and Altman's dialectic formulation have complementary strengths and limitations. While they are diametrically different in *style,* the two of them together seem to offer much potential for future advance in theoretical exploration of interpersonal interaction.

CHAPTER SEVENTEEN
THE INFLUENCE PROCESS: EFFECTS OF INTERACTION ON GROUP MEMBERS

The logic of the framework used here to analyze interaction (see chapter 1) is that group interaction involves the development of communication patterns, task performance patterns, and interpersonal relations patterns, and that these have effects on each other and on the group's participants. One major set of consequences of group interaction is the set of effects that interaction has on those participants, the members of the acting group. Group interaction can influence members' attitudes, perceptions, judgments, their feelings about themselves and others, and their learning and task performance. These matters are the topic of this chapter.

While individuals affect one another in a myriad of ways, many of those ways of influence can, but do not have to, take place within the context of an acting group. Some seem to take place whenever individuals are in one another's presence. The chapter begins with consideration of such "mere presence" effects, and proceeds to consideration of effects of individuals on others that seem to take place only when those individuals stand in some kind of continuing relation to one another—that is, when they are part of a group.

SOCIAL INFLUENCE EFFECTS ON LEARNING AND PERFORMANCE

Social Facilitation and Inhibition by Audiences and Coactors

Very early work on groups (e.g., Allport, 1920; Triplett, 1898) centered on the apparently robust finding that individuals performed certain tasks better when in the presence of other people than when performing alone. For example, Triplett (1898) found that bicycle racers achieved better times when in competition with an opponent than when performing alone against the clock. Even when additional motivational factors such as rivalry were taken into account, the effect still seemed present. Allport (1920) gave this phenomenon the name "social facilitation," because at that time many believed that it came about because the sights and sounds of others served an arousing or motivating function that led to increased effort, hence to increased performance. But the effect seemed to hold when the others were in the role of audience, even an unseen audience, as well as when they were coactors.

However, Allport and other researchers soon began to find that, with certain kinds of tasks, the presence of others had a debilitating rather than a facilitating effect on performance. Efforts were made to account for these differences in terms of type of task—simple versus difficult, or motor versus intellectual, for facilitation as against debilitation respectively. But none of these task distinctions accounted for the total set of data very well. As a consequence of the ambiguity of the empirical evidence on the problem—and of a total lack of theoretical clarity in discussions of it—the social facilitation topic dropped from the field for over forty years.

Then, in the middle of the 1960s, there were at least two more or less simultaneous treatments of the social facilitation phenomenon, arriving at quite compatible reformulations (Zajonc, 1965; Paivio, 1965). Zajonc's formulations, in particular, cleared up much of the inconsistency in the past empirical evidence and did so in theoretically tractable form. He applied the concepts of classical learning theory. He made the assumption that the presence of other people, either as audience or as coactors, functions as a stimulus to increase drive level. In learning theory terms, to learn a new response to a specific stimulus means that that response has become more probable as a response to that stimulus. When a response is well learned, it is the most probable—it is highest in the habit hierarchy. Increasing the drive level has the effect of increasing the probability that the already most probable (that is, the best learned) response will occur, and to decrease the probability of other responses. The presence of other people, Zajonc argues, serves to increase drive level, hence, to make the most probable response more likely, and to make it occur with greater intensity. But at the same time, it makes any other response less likely to occur. So, the presence of other people ought to enhance the performance of already well learned responses, but hinder—indeed, render improbable—the learning or acquisition of new responses. That distinction appears to be supported by the evidence from the early social facilitation studies, as well as by evidence from more recent work. (See Geen & Gagne, 1977, for an excellent recent review of this area.) (See EXRT 37.)

Zajonc's (1965) reformulation stimulated a multitude of new studies of the social facilitation phenomenon. Some of that work questioned Zajonc's assumption that "mere presence" of other persons is sufficient to produce the effects, arguing, instead, that the persons must be in a position to observe and at least potentially evaluate the performance for the effect to occur (e.g., Cottrell, Wack, Sekerak & Rittle, 1968). While those questions are still matters of controversy, the weight of the evidence apparently favors the idea that mere presence may produce some effect, although presence in a form that permits observation and potential evaluation, especially negative evaluation, enhances the effect (e.g., Geen & Gagne, 1977). There is also a line of research, reflected in

EXRT 37:   *THE SOCIAL FACILITATION PARADIGM*

Main Study Procedures: Subjects are asked to perform some task, either alone or in the presence of one or more others. The others can be either coactors (doing the same tasks) or audience (watching the focal subject).

Main Dependent Variables of Interest: Indices of task performance effectiveness (speed, intensity, errors, quality); indices of subject arousal or stress (e.g., palmar sweat, pulse rate).

Main Variations: Proximity or immediacy of audience (visible, hidden); audience size, and activities (e.g., evaluating, razzing, coacting, rivalling, being merely passively present); types of task, and prior experience of subject on that task (e.g., effective performance may require acquisition of new responses or performance of highly practiced ones).

References: Allport (1920); Cottrell, Wack, Sekerak, & Rittle (1968); Easterbrook (1959); Geen & Gagne (1977); Paivio (1965); Triplett (1898); Zajonc (1965).

---

the work of Easterbrook (1959), arguing that the presence of others (as well as many other "stress" conditions) has its effects not by increasing drive but by narrowing the bandwidth of cues to which the individual attends. When such stress conditions increase from low to medium, the effect is to reduce attention to irrelevant cues but focus on task important cues, thus enhancing performance. As that effect continues, to high levels of stress, the continued narrowing eventually leads to a situation where task-critical cues are ignored, and this leads to decreased performance effectiveness. The point of decrease comes at a lower level of stress for tasks for which a more complex batch of cues is crucial—that is, for more difficult or more complex tasks.

It is difficult to devise a crucial test that would clearly distinguish between these two explanations, the "increased arousal/drive" versus the "restricted attention to cues." In any case, for purposes of this book the important point can be summarized as follows. Mere presence, and/or active, evaluating behavior by other people, affects the individual. This occurs either by increasing his or her level of drive or arousal or by altering his or her attention to task/environmental cues—or, very likely, both. This in turn affects the individual's performance of tasks and learning of new tasks. If the presence of other people in highly artificial experimental situations (the case for most of the research in this area) has such important effects, it seems quite likely that the physical presence of groupmates, or even the "psychological" presence of members of one's standing group(s), would also have important—but not necessarily identical—effects. Such effects are incorporated into many current models in the form of terms like "social norms" or "role expectations" or "conformity pressures."

Models: Learning by Observation

Another line of study that strongly supports the general proposition that people are influenced by other people—sometimes in and sometimes outside of group contexts—is the area called modelling or social learning (see Bandura

1962; Bandura & Walters, 1963). This work has an ancestry that goes back as far as the French sociologist, Tarde (1903), who proposed that much human behavior could be accounted for in terms of "imitation." The concept of imitation, as it was used in very early social psychological work, was taken to be an explanation when in fact it was merely a relabeling of what had been observed, namely, sometimes people do what they see others do. But to relabel an observation does not really help "explain" it or understand how and why it comes to be. So the idea of imitation, as either the main or one of the many "instincts" that trigger and guide human behavior, faded into obscurity until the second quarter of this century. Then, some classical learning theorists (Miller & Dollard, 1941) began to try to extend learning theory to a broader array of behaviors than had been done in the earlier animal studies. They broke down the old idea of imitation into several categories—for example, mere copying, involuntary responses (e.g., yawning when someone else yawns), and so forth. Some of the categories involved learning processes, to be accounted for along lines of classical learning theory; others were nonlearning phenomena to be accounted for by involuntary (perhaps instinctual) mechanisms.

At about the same time, there was a parallel line of research, more social psychological in its formulation, on what was termed "behavioral contagion" (Polansky, Lippett, & Redl, 1950). That work was done mainly with children, most of it in play situations. It focused on the characteristics of those children whose behavior was imitated and on social properties of the situation (e.g., social status differences) that appeared to facilitate or hinder such "behavioral contagion." This work did not really consider imitation as some kind of universal human trait or instinct; rather, it looked for individual differences among persons, both as active "imitators" and as models to be imitated.

In the 1950s, Bandura and his coworkers (e.g., Bandura, 1962; Bandura & Walters, 1963) resurrected the fundamental idea of imitation in a way that combined the two streams of work, one by the neoclassical learning theorists and the other by the social psychologists studying behavioral contagion. Bandura (1962) considered modelling to be a matter of social learning—learning from the behavior of social objects in the environment. In a series of ingenious studies, Bandura had young children watch films or live performances of other children or adults performing relatively unlikely but clearly aggressive sequences of behavior (such as punching an inflated clown doll). He then observed how often, and under what conditions, those children produced some sequence of behavior akin to what had been modelled.

Bandura made two important distinctions. First, he highlighted the distinction between acquisition of a response (that is, learning it, whether or not it is exhibited), and performance of a response. Second, he argued that children clearly learn new responses *without practice and without reinforcement* (which classical learning theory held to be necessary conditions for increasing the probability of a response, that is, for learning). But acquisition was enhanced when there was reinforcement, either to the person or to the model; and *performance* of the response (as opposed to its acquisition or learning) *required reinforcement*. In other words, the child could learn from watching someone else perform, and could perform the response him or herself, but was unlikely to unless given some reason (motivation/reinforcement) to do so. It was as if the child

EXRT 38:   *BANDURA'S SOCIAL LEARNING (MODELLING) PARADIGM*

Main Study Procedures: Children watch (live, film or video) an adult execute some relatively unfamiliar behavior sequences of aggressive behavior (e.g., hitting an inflated doll).

Main Dependent Variables of Interest: Whether, and how well, children later reproduce the model's behavior sequences; whether acquisition occurred (as evidenced by performance when asked to do what the model did) even if such performance does not occur spontaneously.

Main Variations: Modelling conditions (e.g., reinforcement received by the model, source of such reinforcement); status of the model; complexity and novelty of modelled sequences.

References: Bandura (1962); Bandura & Walters (1963).

---

learned, vicariously, from observing the model's behavior and the consequences of the behavior for the model. (See EXRT 38.)

Modelling is, in a sense, the "flip side" of the audience effects discussed under social facilitation. Here, instead of the individual's behavior being influenced by presence (and evaluative behavior) of an audience, members of the audience are influenced by (i.e., acquire and perhaps perform) behaviors exhibited by the individual, construed now as a "model." This attests to the two-directional nature of social influence. Much work in social psychology, and even in the group research area, explores only one direction of influence. For example, much leadership research is posed as if the leader influenced members, but the reverse was not so. But, in fact, it is reasonable to argue that all social influence situations, however imbalanced in power they may appear to be on the surface, should be regarded as two-way influence situations. Parents train children, but children just as much (though not necessarily just as self-consciously) train parents. Leaders and followers are mutually interdependent and exercise mutual influence. Teachers and students, therapists and clients, masters and slaves, all are in situations of mutual interaction and mutual influence.

Inactive Bystanders Helping in an Emergency

Still another line of social psychological research that highlights the effects that presence of other people can have on individuals (although again in a nongroup and one-way influence context) is the work initiated by Latané and Darley's (1968) now-classic study of bystanders' failure to act in emergency situations. In a series of ingenious experimental arrangements, they showed that an individual is much less likely to help someone in trouble/danger/difficulty if there are a number of other people present than if that individual is the only one present. The phenomenon is relatively robust, at least for laboratory situations. (See EXRT 39.)

Levy and colleagues (Levy, Lundgren, Ansel, Fell, Fink & McGrath, 1972) have shown the effect in demand situations far short of emergency. There

EXRT 39:   *THE LATANÉ-DARLEY BYSTANDER PARADIGM*

> *Main Study Procedures:* The subject is performing a paper and pencil task in an experimental setting. An experimental confederate (posing either as a subject or as an experimental assistant), and usually in an adjacent room, appears to be having an emergency of some kind—suffering illness or extreme pain or having an accident. Some subjects are exposed to this while working in a room alone; others are exposed while working in a room with other coactors.
>
> *Main Dependent Variables of Interest:* Whether and how quickly the subject will respond to the emergency or offer help to the victim, given that none of the other bystanders respond to it.
>
> *Main Variations:* Nature of the emergency or need for help (e.g., apparent heart attack, in a lab setting or on a subway; request to make an emergency phone call; request to enter the experimental room; dropping personal items or packages on the floor or street); number of (inactive) bystanders; gender composition of set of bystanders and gender of victim; prior relationships among set of bystanders (e.g., friends, opponents, strangers).
>
> *References:* Latané & Darley (1968, 1970); Levy, Lundren, Ansel, Fell, Fink & McGrath (1972); Piliavin, Rodin & Piliavin (1969).

are some questions about its generalizability to field situations, for example, to helping an apparent drunk, or an apparent victim of illness, on a city subway at night (Piliavin, Rodin, & Piliavin, 1969). Latané and colleagues have tried to establish a functional relation between number of inactive bystanders and the probability of response, but the "alone" versus "others present" difference is by far the most striking effect.

We can regard the bystander effect as an inhibition of behavior by the presence of others—a modelling of the *inaction* of the others. While researchers have tried to account for it in terms of "diffusion of responsibility" and similar conceptualizations, there is really no adequate theoretical explanation at this time. It is a further indication of the considerable impact that mere presence and relatively limited behavior (or even inaction) of other human beings can have on cognitive (e.g., attention to cues), emotional (e.g., arousal) and behavioral (e.g., task performance, helping behavior) aspects of individual response.

SOCIAL INFLUENCE EFFECTS ON ATTITUDES, PERCEPTIONS, JUDGMENTS, AND DECISIONS

Attitude Change

Some of the earliest interest in groups was spurred by the conviction that groups had powerful effects on their members. The early work of Kurt Lewin (e.g., Lewin, 1948, 1953), often taken to be the start of the "group dynamics" movement, was designed to change the attitudes of individuals by working through groups of which they were members. In one case, for example, he studied the attitudes of housewives toward using less popular cuts of meat—kidney, liver, etc.—during the wartime meat shortage. He found that a group discussion, followed by a group decision, was a powerful force leading to individual behavior change (the actual use of such cuts of meat, as reported on a follow-up). Even though later studies raised doubts that a group decision, or even a group discussion, was a necessary condition for such attitude changes (see Bennett, 1955; also see discussion later in this section), Lewin's early studies had powerful influence in the field. (See EXRT 40.)

From these Lewinian ideas and studies sprang two movements. The first was a group dynamics movement that became one major force in the development of what we would now regard as the subfield of small group research. The focus of that movement was an attempt to apply the methods of science to the study of group processes, structures and consequences. That is the topic of this book. The second was a group dynamics movement that was ancestor to a host of applied systems for accomplishing personal change through group methods. That set includes such recent and current "movements" as training or T groups (originally started by some of Lewin's colleagues), sensitivity groups, encounter groups, and many other similar activities. The central purpose of those "group methods" is to use the power of groups to produce particular changes in the group's members—not so much attitudes toward things like eating less popular cuts of meat as attitudes toward oneself and one's significant others. These are not the topic of this book. (Excellent reviews of these activities can be found in Back, 1972; Hartman, 1979; Lieberman, 1976).

In those early Lewin studies, groups of housewives were gathered, either to hear an expert lecture on, or to participate in a group discussion of, the topics of concern (that is, buying and serving their families less popular cuts of meat to ease the wartime meat shortage). The discussion was followed by an effort to get a public commitment to use the unpopular meats. Lewin's interpretation of results viewed the group methods as superior to the lecture, both in getting a

EXRT 40:   *THE LEWIN GROUP DISCUSSION / ATTITUDE CHANGE PARADIGM*

Main Study Procedure: Subjects of appropriate types (e.g., housewives) are brought to group meetings at which they are exposed to either a lecture or an investigator-led group discussion of the advantages of doing the target behavior (e.g., using cheaper but available cuts of meat, during wartime meat shortages).

Main Dependent Variables of Interest: Post-session expressions of intention to do the target behaviors; subsequent reports of actual target behaviors.

Main Variations: Whether or not individuals made a commitment, did so publicly, and / or witnessed others' public commitments to do the target behaviors; characteristics of group members, and the salience of their relationships with others in the group (e.g., indicating that all members of a particular group were of one religious or ethnic group, for an attitude topic for which that membership might be relevant).

References: Bennett (1955); Lewin (1953).

commitment at that time (attitude change) and in subsequent actual buying (behavior). In later studies, however, (e.g., Bennett, 1955) it was pointed out that at least four things were involved: group discussion; perceiving that others said they were going to do the recommended action; making a personal decision to do so; and making such a commitment publicly. Not all proved equally effective. And not all are really "group effects." For example, it is possible to reproduce the perception of social consensus outside of group settings (as will be discussed later in this chapter); and it is possible to get a personal decision made without the commitment being made in public. So, in these areas, it is not clear that the effects are enhanced by some aspects of group settings. Note, also, that the "groups" in question are by no means established, continuing groups (standing groups in the vocabulary of this book) but rather are acting groups or quasi-groups with relatively fleeting lives.

Perceptions and Judgments

Another early study that had much impact was by Sherif (1936). He took a relatively well established phenomenon from the psychology of perception—the autokinetic phenomenon—and used it as a tool for studying the influence of groups on the judgments of their individual members. If you put someone in a totally dark room, arrange matters so that he or she has relatively few orientation cues and then present light from a fixed point source, that light will appear to move (at least to most people). Sherif asked his subjects—sometimes working alone, sometimes working within groups—*how far* the light moved. He found the following:

1. Each individual rather quickly established a range within which most of his or her own judgments would fall. That range, or its middle, can be called a norm.

2. When individuals worked together in groups, all members shifted their individual judgments so that they fell within a common range; that is, they established a *group norm.*

3. When individuals worked alone after having worked in a group, the range and midpoint of their group's norm continued to influence their judgments; that is, the group norm persisted outside the group itself.

Note that this use of *norm* differs from uses elsewhere in this book. It is descriptive (what people do do, on the average) rather than normative (what people should do). (See EXRT 41.)

These findings are a clear-cut and relatively robust case of social influence, though hardly group influence in the more limited way I am using the term "groups" in this book. It is not an influence on attitudes, but on judgments of what ought to have been objective matters of fact.

The autokinetic phenomenon, though, is designed to be a highly ambiguous situation. Perhaps it is only in such conditions of high ambiguity that people influence one another's judgment of such objective matters. Asch (1951) attempted to test such a proposition by setting up relatively strong, clear-cut stimulus conditions along with rather strong social influence conditions. He had subjects judge, aloud and in turn, which of three lines was longest, under conditions where the stimulus differences were clearly discernible by all of the

EXRT 41:   *SHERIF'S GROUP NORM PARADIGM*

Main Study Procedures: Subjects are placed in a room in which position and orientation cues are minimized (e.g., darkness, seated on a stool high enough so that feet don't touch floor). They are exposed to a stationary point source of light which, under such low orientation conditions, appears to most people to move. (This is known as the autokinetic phenomenon.) Subjects are asked to judge how far the light moved, on each of a series of trials. Some subjects do this alone, some do it in relatively small groups in which judgments are reported aloud.

Main Dependent Variables of Interest: The extent to which the judgments of a given individual working alone tend to cluster around some average value (that individual's "norm"); the extent to which the judgments of all the individuals working in a group tend to cluster around the same average value (that group's "norm"); the extent to which such a group norm persists when those individuals subsequently work alone.

Main Variations: Number of trials; size of group; sequences of solitary and group judgments; transmission of a norm over group "generations."

Reference: Sherif (1936).

---

respondents. In certain trials, though, he had prearranged with all but one of the respondents (who were, in fact, his confederates) to give an objectively wrong answer. The questions asked by the study were whether, how often, and under what conditions the lone naive subject (always responding next to last) would yield to the social pressure of the others' judgments. Asch (1951) was apparently shocked to find that a very large proportion of subjects yielded, on a very large proportion of key trials; that only a few individuals remained "independent" on all trials; and that they—rather than the yielders, who had violated objective veridicality—were the ones who felt uncomfortable in the situation. Many studies of such conformity to social pressure followed, including investigations of effects of different numbers of others (apparently, up to about three, the number of others increases the effect, but with no further increases for still larger numbers); unanimous majorities versus majorities with some dissenters (the really powerful effects occur with unanimous majorities, and even one ally is sufficient to reduce the proportion of "yielding" substantially); effects of allies who "defect" on later trials (the "resistance" to pressure bestowed by having an ally fades away entirely when that ally "defects"); and the like. (See EXRT 42.)

These early studies by Lewin, Sherif and Asch, and studies by many others following their leads, opened up several areas of social psychology that became important in the 1950s, 60s and 70s, including conformity pressures; dissonance; reactance; obedience; attitude change; risky shifts and polarization effects. From the point of view of this chapter, their importance lay in firmly establishing the social influence effects that people have on one another's attitudes, judgments and perceptions.

EXRT 42:   *THE ASCH CONFORMITY PARADIGM*

Main Study Procedures: A group of ostensive subjects are brought to an experimental room, seated in a row, and asked to make judgments of the relative lengths of lines. All but one of those persons are actually confederates of the experimenter; that one naive subject is seated so that he or she will always respond next to last. On all trials, stimulus differences are large enough so that they pose no problems of visual acuity. On some trials, including the first several, confederates give correct answers (and, presumably, the naive subject does too). But on certain predetermined trials, *all* of the confederates give the same objectively wrong answer.

Main Dependent Variables of Interest: Whether, and how often (proportion of key trials) the naive subject "yields" to the (implicit) pressure of the unanimous though objectively incorrect majority and gives an objectively wrong answer; postsession perceptions and feelings of subjects.

Main Variations: Judgment tasks permitting the subject to give a "compromise" wrong answer; size of majority; variations in the majority (unanimous, versus one confederate who allies with naive subject, versus such an ally who later "defects"); instrumental/procedural variations (e.g., use of light and switch panel, with no actual other persons present, to give feedback to the subject about others' ostensive answers).

Reference: Asch (1951).

Polarization Effects of Group Discussion: Normative and Informational Effects

The substantial literature on the phenomenon known as the "risky shift" has already been reviewed in large part in chapter 7 dealing with group performance of tasks for which there is not a single correct answer. It was noted there that, although often considered along with other group task performance material, the risky shift phenomenon is not actually a group task performance phenomenon. While some of that work deals with shifts from pre-group to group decisions, most of it deals with shifts between individual responses pre-group and individual responses after the group decision. Furthermore, recent work suggests that the polarization effects produced in such studies may not necessarily require a group discussion. Rather, these polarization effects may be produced by either of two kinds of inputs: information about positions of others on the subject, and persuasive arguments for one or another side of the subject. Both of these usually accompany group discussion, but either or both of them could be conveyed in ways other than by means of a group discussion. It is suggested here that polarization effects of group discussions on choice shift items (and on gambling risks and other decisions) may be produced by persuasive arguments or by social comparison information (the two dominant theories currently viable). It is also suggested that either of those effects could be accomplished either through group discussion or by direct input of information: (a) material on persuasive arguments for one side or the other; and (b) material on the prediscussion beliefs of the group members themselves, or some other set of normative information. These are standard attitude change operations, used frequently in studies not dealing with polarization or risk. They in no sense require a group discussion for their impact.

This matter brings to mind the questions raised after the initial success of the early Lewinian attitude change experiments. Was it really group discussion, or group decision, that led to the change effects? Or, instead, was it the making of a personal commitment, and/or the perception of consensus on the part of the others, that produced the effects? It became clear, in later studies of attitude change in general, that group discussion was one format that could facilitate and perhaps even enhance some of these attitude change factors, but that it was in no way essential to them. Perhaps it is the same with the group risky shift effects: group discussion is one way to implement effects of persuasion on informational grounds, and to communicate social comparison information, normative information, on questions dealing with risky decisions. But group discussion may be by no means an essential condition for producing those special social influence effects now called polarization. As with many other behavioral phenomena presented in this book, a "group" view is one, but only one, perspective from which the matter can be approached. Certain information will be heightened, and other information lost, if we approach such questions only from one such approach. So, while it is clear that much social influence takes place among individuals, and that a great deal of it takes place within group contexts, it is not at all the case that such influences *require* a group context. As with many other aspects, groups may serve, largely, to *intensify, or enhance,* effects of various kinds of social forces.

Other Social Influence Effects

The discussion so far has concerned several relatively clear-cut and relatively well studied ways in which individuals are subject to social influences: the arousing and/or distracting effect of presence and/or evaluative activity of others; the social learning effects of observation of a behavior model; the inhibiting effects of presence and inactivity of others during an emergency; and attitude change and judgment influences from social and informational inputs. There are a number of other ways that individuals are affected by others, in group and nongroup contexts. Some of those other forms are complex, and for some the evidence is not at all clear-cut, so the discussion will be limited.

Sometimes, for example, having a lot of people in a relatively fixed space leads to perceptions of *crowding.* This, in turn, may lead to a series of negative consequences that can include competition for available space and other resources; interference with instrumental or goal directed behavior; and overstimulation or cognitive and emotional "overload." Sometimes, of course, the same number of people in the same space would not be perceived as crowding, in a pejorative sense, and would not yield such negative consequences. For example, having a large number of people per square foot in the stadium seats at a football game or at a cocktail party not only might not lead to feelings of crowding but actually might add to positive feelings because of the stimulus increments they entail. The same density in a classroom or a work setting might yield very strong negative feelings of crowding, with the consequences noted above.

Other people represent sources of *emotional comfort and support,* as well as sources of *annoyance and interference with goals.* There is a set of studies, for example, in which people expecting an unpleasant experience (e.g., pain from an injection, or from an electric shock) preferred to wait in the presence of other people rather than alone. (See Schachter, 1959.) The other people were strangers but were presumed to be in the same predicament. The effect apparently does not hold if the others are not also "sweating out" an unpleasant experience, or if the anticipated experience is embarrassing rather than painful.

Even though the experimental evidence about preferring to wait with others when anticipating unpleasant events isn't altogether clear, and may not be general over a wide range of conditions, it is clear from evidence of other kinds that other people serve very important emotional functions for the individual. In studies of small groups of individuals in isolation, for example, (e.g., Altman & Haythorn, 1965, 1967a, 1967b) it is clear that being in intense and continuous interaction with a very small set of other people, and only with them, has powerful effects on the individual's feelings, behavior, and interpersonal relationships. When small groups are in such situations, either in laboratory experiments in which the isolation is prearranged for research purposes, or in real life situations—such is the case for the crews of nuclear submarines, wintering-over parties in the Arctic, and other expeditions—the few other people available to them become extremely important sources of both *positive and negative reinforcements.* On the positive side are such things as *information* or anticipations about the situation, *feedback* about own behavior, and just plain *social interaction.* On the negative side are such things as *annoyance at habits, competition or territorial behavior or attempts to dominate,* and *interruption of privacy* (or withdrawal when interaction is desired). These matters were discussed in chapter 16. The point to be made here is that the presence and behavior of other people (and, in a sense, the absence and the inactivity of other people) help to define the meaning of situations for the individual and can have a powerful impact on his or her behavior, attitudes and feelings in those situations. Thus, there is much reason from nongroup situations to suppose that the presence of other group members, and their interactions, will have major consequences for the individual who is a member of that group. The discussion to follow deals with such group influences on the individual member.

THE COMMUNICATION/COHESION/CONFORMITY COMPLEX: THE FESTINGER PROGRAM ON SOCIAL INFLUENCE IN GROUPS

In the late 1940s, working out of the Group Dynamics Research Center that had been established by Lewin (first at the Massachusetts Institute of Technology, later at the University of Michigan), Leon Festinger and a group of colleagues launched what was perhaps the first systematic program of research on social influence processes in groups. It incorporated conduct of some field studies, formulation of some theoretical propositions, and design and conduct of a series of laboratory experiments intended to test, revise and extend those propositions. Although there were earlier field, lab and theoretical efforts, and others were taking place at more or less the same time, this systematic and programmatic attack on a delimited set of phenomena perhaps marks the real beginning of what might be called experimental research on small groups. It included both the formulation of coherent theory to deal with the phenomena and the devising of means for testing the propositions of that theory under relatively controlled and precise laboratory conditions.

Much of the work of that program is reported in two monographs: Festinger, Schachter, and Back (1950), and Festinger, Back, Schachter, Kelley, and Thibaut (1952). The first reports a set of field investigations of communication, friendship and attitude patterns in two housing developments. The second presents a theoretical statement and reports a series of laboratory experiments to test portions of that theory. The gist of the program's findings will be discussed here, although much more of its flavor and details can be had by reading those monographs, or other sources reporting that work in detail. (See Back, 1951; Festinger, 1950; Festinger & Thibaut, 1951; Kelley, 1951; Schachter, 1951; Thibaut, 1950). (See EXRTs 43, 44, 45.)

In the field studies, Festinger and his colleagues explored how the locations of apartments within buildings, or of houses within "courts" of a housing development, affected the probability that the residents of those houses would become acquainted with one another. They found that functional distance (actual physical distance, modified by such factors as location in relation to common pathways, stairways, mailboxes and the like) played a very large part in determining probability of encounter by members of any two families; and that probability of encounter was, of course, a key factor in (though not totally determinant of) probability of those two families establishing an acquaintance and then a friendship. They also found that friendship patterns followed func-

EXRT 43:   *FESTINGER AND COLLEAGUES' COHESIVENESS MANIPULATION*

Main Study Procedures: Subjects who have completed a questionnaire at an earlier time are formed into small task groups. Members of some groups are told that they will be in a group whose members have been matched (on the basis of that earlier material) so that it is very likely that they will be quite congenial. Members of other groups are told that, while some of the groups were composed for high congeniality, their particular group was made up of members who would not necessarily be congenial with one another.

Main Dependent Variables of Interest: Resulting "cohesiveness," or positive attraction of members for one another and for the group; level of task productivity; level of pressure toward conformity/agreement; rate, pattern and content of within-group communications.

Main Variations: Instructions that base the attraction on the group's prestige, or the desirability of the group's assigned task, rather than on congeniality.

References: Back (1951); Festinger, Back, Schachter, Kelley & Thibaut (1952); Schachter, Ellerton, McBride, & Gregory (1951); Thibaut (1950).

EXRT 44:   *SCHACHTER'S DEVIATING CONFEDERATE PARADIGM*

Main Study Procedures: A number of clubs (eight- to ten-member), were composed, using male college students. All clubs were asked to discuss and reach a joint decision on a discussion task. Three members of each club were actually confederates. Subjects were asked their opinions on the task before the discussion started. One confederate took the group's modal position. The other two took the most extreme deviating position they could at the outset. During the discussion, one of the deviators gradually shifted position until in agreement with the group, but the other one did not change from the maximum deviation position.

Main Dependent Variables of Interest: Amount and type of communication to each of the confederates and shifts over time in that pattern; interpersonal attraction choices regarding the three confederates before and after the discussion.

Main Variations: Size and composition of groups; topic or task; requirement for a unanimous decision; group cohesiveness; status of the deviating members within the group.

Reference: Schachter (1951).

EXRT 45:   *BACK'S INFORMATION-DISCREPANCY TECHNIQUE*

Main Study Procedures: Two subjects are given copies of a picture, ostensibly identical but actually different in a number of details. They are asked to make some judgments/decisions about the picture, individually. Then, they are put into two-person groups and asked to reach group agreement on those same questions. They cannot directly determine that their stimulus materials are not identical.

Main Dependent Variables of Interest: Amount and content of communication and its distribution over the two members; amount of "conformity" of each to the other's positions; whether a group reaches or fails to reach a set of joint decisions.

Main Variations: Different levels of group cohesiveness; different stimulus materials (e.g., verbal versus pictorial content); differential statuses of members (e.g., power, prestige, age, gender differences).

Reference: Back (1951).

---

tional distance lines, and that friendship patterns were closely aligned with patterns of shared attitudes about issues pertinent to the housing situation.

From these findings, they developed the following general theoretical stance: For a set of people sharing common space and resources, communication, interpersonal attraction, and interpersonal influence are three processes that go together, or constitute a *system*. By *system* we mean that the three processes (parts of the system) vary together, and exercise mutual influence on one another; not that any one of them causes the other, but that each of them has effects on and is affected by both of the others. Thus, if one could observe some major shift in one process (perhaps from some force outside the system), one ought to be able to observe concomitant shifts in one or both of the other processes. If there is a major shift in communication patterns, there ought to be a commensurate shift in interpersonal attraction and/or interpersonal influence patterns. If there is a major shift in interpersonal attraction, there ought to be a commensurate shift in communication and/or influence.

Proximity increases chances of interpersonal encounter, hence of communication. Communication leads to attraction, hence to subsequent communication. When a set of people communicate, and are attracted, they generate forces toward agreement on at least those issues related to their common situation. Such forces toward agreement constitute social pressures on the individual to modify his or her attitudes and opinions when they are not in accord with those of the group. Such pressures should be the greater the more the group and its members are attractive to the individual; they should also be the greater the more communication there is from others in the group to the individual. Conversely, interpersonal attraction should be greater the more there is communication from, and agreement with, others in the group. Finally, communication, too, will tend to be more for those others with whom there is attraction and agreement (except for certain special circumstances, when communication increases, at least for brief periods of time, in attempts to reduce disagreements). Thus, the three are interdependent; they form a system, such that changes in any one of them presage changes in one or both of the others. This line of argument implies that the system has some balanced state, or equilibrium—much as many biological systems and subsystems are thought to have—and that forces producing imbalances will be reacted to by internal system forces, thereby reestablishing balance. Indeed, one of the fundamental ideas of Lewin's early group theory, from which this work grew, was the idea that groups are systems in states of what he called "dynamic equilibrium"—that is, a balanced but dynamically changing state that continually maintains a patterned (but not constant) relation to a probably-changing external environment, and an internal pattern balanced in those terms. The Festinger theory, and many others that followed it, was indeed a theory based on the assumption of forces toward equilibrium in social systems, large and small.

But how to test such a theory? In natural settings, such as the housing development, all three of the processes—communication, attraction and influence—(and many others) vary together. It is not possible to tell, in such situations, whether any one causally influences any other, or indeed whether some other, unnamed process is in fact the "cause" of changes in all of them. It is standard practice in science to try to reproduce such problems in the laboratory and conduct an experiment by deliberately, experimentally, varying one process to note what changes, if any, occur in other processes. That procedure posed two major questions for Festinger and his group. First, their theory did not posit a simple directional model of causation. It was a system theory, proposing that each process affected and was affected by each of the others. So, it would be necessary, at least, to run a series of experiments, experimentally manipulating each of the basic processes in turn, to study the effects caused by (or, at least, following after) its manipulation. Second, there was no readily apparent means by which some of the processes in question could be "manipulated." So, they quite literally had to invent a "technology" for experimentation with groups. They needed means both for measuring and for manipulating such group factors as communication (pattern and frequency), friendship or attraction, and influence or conformity.

Festinger and colleagues posited the concept of *cohesiveness,* defined as the sum total of all the forces attracting members to a group (Cartwright, 1968). They noted at least three common bases of such attraction or cohesion: liking for the other group members; attraction to the task that the group did (and which often could not be engaged in without being a part of such a group); and attraction of the status that was bestowed on members by being members of the group (for example, belonging to a prestigious club). While they regarded these as more or less substitutable one for another, they relied mostly on the first—interpersonal attraction—as the basis for manipulating group cohesion.

The key feature in social influence was conformity to group positions or norms. Festinger's theory argues that groups tend to generate forces toward uniformity of opinion among members, at least on matters of consequence to the group. This has several advantages to the group. It allows people to agree on "what is what." That is, in many cases groups and members of groups rely on a social consensus to define "reality." This is especially so for questions for which there either is no physical reality or it is difficult or impossible for the individual to determine physical reality on his or her own. But it also applies under some circumstances in cases where the physical reality is all too clear, as in the Asch studies of conformity regarding judgments of lines that were clearly different in length. In a range of circumstances, then, individuals rely on others—particularly others with whom they interact regularly, and to whom they are attracted, that is, other members of cohesive groups—to help define social reality, "what is so." Moreover, uniformity of attitudes among group members helps make everybody's behavior more predictable; and both groups and individuals gain an advantage by being able to predict behavior, at least regarding matters of central consequence to the group.

Given such functional value of agreement, when there is variation of attitudes among group members (on matters of importance) there will be pressures toward uniformity. If most members agree, the pressures will rest most heavily on dissenters. Those pressures will be enacted via communication, perhaps increased communication from others to the dissenter(s), designed to produce conformity to the group view. Thus, direction (who to whom), content (messages concerning conformity) and frequency of communication within the group are pertinent to the question of pressures toward uniformity of opinion in groups. And, since it is expected that high cohesive groups will have much more influence on members than groups less attractive to their members, and that failure to achieve conformity will lead to reduction in attraction of the member, the attraction aspect also affects and is affected by the conformity pressures in groups.

This series of theoretical propositions received strong support in most cases in the program of experiments run by the Festinger group. Groups manipulated so as to have high cohesiveness (e.g., by instructing members that they had been matched in such a way that they almost certainly would get along with each other very well) had greater influence on members' attitudes. Group members who deviated from group norms (often confederates) were initially the target of much more than average communication, presumably in the interest of persuasion. But when that member proved intractable (again, by experimental design), the communication to that member eventually dropped virtually to zero, and post-session responses indicated that the member had been rejected by the others. When groups had members of different status levels (established by assigning high and low status roles), communication tended to flow from low to high rather than the other way. When group members disagreed on matters central to their joint task (arranged by giving them different information at the start) those that had been designed to have high cohesiveness (as described above) compromised more and were better able to resolve their disagreements than groups with low cohesiveness.

Many further interesting implications of this theory were tested with various degrees of support within that program of studies. One example is the relation of productivity to group attraction. While there was some indication that groups who were very unhappy often did not do well on the job, it was clear that high productivity was not just a simple matter of high morale or having a happy group. Festinger and his colleagues' theory implies that cohesive groups—whose members valued membership for any of a variety of reasons—ought to have more power to influence their members toward group norms than would less cohesive groups (that is, groups less valued by their members). But that should be so whether the group's norm is toward higher or lower productivity. This proposition was tested in an experiment in which group cohesiveness was manipulated and so was the direction of influence of communications to the member from other group members. (The experimenter permitted communication only by notes, with the notes having been prearranged to urge either higher or lower productivity.) The results were clear in one direction: groups can influence members toward higher productivity and cohesive groups can do so more so, in such experimental circumstances. But, for the populations studied (college students, working with strangers, in a contrived situation), there is apparently a built-in "hard work" bias, so that the negative manipulation was not clearly effective, even in the cohesive groups. It should be noted, though, that such negative effects of group norms are often observed in real life work situations, and indeed appear to be endemic in such situations, especially for established groups of workers under industrial production line conditions. (See, for example, the early "Hawthorne" studies: Mayo, 1933; Roethlisberger & Dickson, 1939.) So one must view these laboratory study results with some caution. (Some of the methodological issues about the status of findings from experimental groups versus findings from natural groups—both of which have major limitations—were discussed in chapters 3 and 4.)

In summary, this systematic and programmatic attack on group processes had several important consequences for the topic of this book. For one thing, it established group research as a field amenable to experimental study, and to formulation and test of theory. Second, it helped stimulate research on many areas of groups, and indeed had a major role in launching what became a veritable flood of group research studies. Third, it established the three processes in question—communication, cohesion, and conformity—as the focal processes in group dynamics, related to one another as interdependent elements of a system.

Three subsequent theoretical developments take these factors into account. First, Heider (1958), working more or less independently but from a Lewinian background, talked about conditions under which an individual (P) will perceive another (O) and an object (X) as interdependent (as a unit) and positively or negatively. Heider's work laid the groundwork for much of the subsequent development of the study of interpersonal perception, and for the later-to-bloom areas of impression formation and attribution. Second, Festinger developed a theory of dissonance (Festinger, 1957) that received widespread attention throughout social psychology. Many of its features seem to have origins in the work just described here. For example: dissonance is an equilibrium principle; perception of a discrepancy in cognitions leads to internal pressures to reduce that discrepancy; and attitudes, attractions and communications will be used by the individual in pursuit of such dissonance reductions. (See EXRTs 46, 47.) Third, Newcomb (1953) took ideas quite similar to Heider's and extended them to interpersonal communications (as distinct from intraindividual processes, which was the case for both Heider's theory and Festinger's dissonance theory). Newcomb posited forces toward balance in interpersonal systems (of attitudes toward one another and toward issues and objects of mutual relevance), as well as in intrapersonal systems (of attitudes toward, and perceptions of others' attitudes toward, one another and toward issues and objects). He also posited communication, persuasion, attitude change, and changes in interpersonal attraction, as complementary methods for reestablishing such balanced states. All of these developments build on the central ideas embodied in the Festinger group research program (although some of them, including Festinger's own later work on dissonance, are done outside a group context). Their effects are reflected in many aspects of social psychology today. All point, too, to the broad-band forms and degrees of influence that people can have on one another, both inside and outside of group contexts.

EXRT 46:   *SNYDER'S BEHAVIORAL CONFIRMATION (SELF-FULFILLING PROPHECY) PARADIGM*

Main Study Procedures: Pairs of subjects talk to each other by telephone. One of them (A) has been given some information about the other (B) before the conversation (e.g., a male (A) is told that the person to be talked with, B, is an attractive female, or he is told that she is not attractive). B does not know that A has been given any information about her.

Main Dependent Variables of Interest: Observation of differences in B's behavior during the phone conversation as a function of differential information A is given about B.

Main Variations: Characteristics of members of the dyads; characteristics of the information about the target person.

Reference: Snyder (1974).

EXRT 47:   *FESTINGER'S FORCED COMPLIANCE (DISSONANCE) PARADIGM*

Main Study Procedures: Subjects are induced to perform some behaviors that are not in accord with their prior attitudes (e.g., they are induced to tell ostensive next subjects that the experimental task is interesting when in fact it is boring). They are induced to do so by an extrinsic reward (e.g., money) that is either insufficient, or very much more than sufficient, to justify compliance.

Main Dependent Variables of Interest: The extent to which subjects change their expressed attitudes, to make them less dissonant with their behavior, as a function of whether the extrinsic rewards under-justified or over-justified the counter-attitudinal behavior.

Main Variations: Types of counterattitudinal behaviors; types and levels of rewards.

References: Aronson & Mills (1959); Festinger (1957).

SOCIAL-IMPACT THEORY: A RECENT INTEGRATION

Latané and his colleagues have recently developed *social-impact theory,* which is an attempt to integrate evidence over a wide range of kinds of social influence in groups (Latané, 1981; Latané & Nida, 1980; Latané & Wolf, 1981). Social-impact theory postulates that the degree of social impact (pressure to change) on any given target person in a given situation is a multiplicative function of the *strength, immediacy,* and *number* of other persons who are potential sources of influence in the situation. *Strength* refers to the person's status or power. *Immediacy* refers to the person's proximity in time and space (or, in terms of earlier chapters of this book, to how broad band the communication channels between them are). It also proposes that there is a marginally decreasing impact of number of influence sources, with each additional source producing less impact than the previous source. The theory also incorporates propositions about the impact on group members of influence pressures from outside the group. Essentially such impact is *divided among* the group members as targets, hence a diminishing function of size of the focal group.

Latané and colleagues use this schema to interpret a wide range of social influence findings, including conformity to a majority, bystander inaction in emergencies, influence effects of a persistent minority, and some aspects of effects of group size on group task productivity. It is a broad theory—really, a formal model rather than a substantive theory. It will accommodate a wide range of substantive hypotheses that have been proposed to account for various specific social influence findings. (See Latané, 1981, and Latané & Wolf, 1981, for a review of some of those applications). It is a flexible model, because it allows the particulars of each situation to serve as "weights" in its formulations. In this way, the level and shape of the impact curve is calculated from the data rather than predicted by the theory in advance. Although generality and flexibility are valuable features for a model to have, at the extreme they also make that model difficult if not impossible to refute. Social-impact theory may be so broad and flexible that it will fit all possible evidence—and, if a theory cannot be tested and refuted it cannot be supported either. On the other hand, social-impact theory offers great promise as a schema for conceptual integration of the voluminous, and until now quite divergent, research evidence on social influence of groups on their members.

CHAPTER EIGHTEEN
INTERACTION AND GROUP STRUCTURE: INTERPERSONAL RELATIONS AND ROLE PATTERNS IN THE STANDING GROUP

In addition to the influence processes discussed in chapter 17, there is a second major set of consequences of group interaction: the pattern of interrelations that develops (or changes) among group members—that is, the structure of the group as a standing group. This is manifested, first of all, in the development of differentiated patterns of behavior among group members—differentiated roles. Such behavior patterning becomes stabilized and leads to the development of *expectations* for how others, and oneself, will and should behave. These *role expectations* serve as guides to and normative standards for group member behavior. They contain prescriptions for communication, task behavior and influence relations among members. Such *role systems,* considered as *structural consequences of interaction process,* are the topic of this chapter. The chapter also contains a discussion of one area of study that constitutes an important portion of a group's role system, and is a topic that has received much attention in group research, namely, *the leader role and leadership behavior.* The chapter ends with a section on what is perhaps the most ubiquitous of all types of natural groups, and certainly the prototypical group, but a type of group that has received only limited research attention: *the family.* The discussion of research on families makes clear the interdependence of patterns of process and structure in determining how groups and their members behave.

In a previous chapter, I suggested that norms of several kinds develop in the service of decreasing the costs, hence increasing the pay-offs, of interaction. Some of these norms have to do with sequential patterns of interaction (e.g., alternation to balance rewards); some have to do with allocating resources among members (e.g., equity, equality); some have to do with more general principles of interactive response (e.g., reciprocity, mutual responsiveness). One very important set of norms that develops in groups deals with functional differentiation of behavior among the members. In continuing groups, whose members deal with one another in terms of a relatively broad band of activities, a "division of labor" tends to develop. That is, the group develops a patterned distribution of "who does what when." Furthermore, groups tend to develop expectations about such patterns—that is, they tend to develop rules or norms that certain members *will* and *should* do certain kinds of things and not others. These functional norms are often called *role expectations*.

DIFFERENTIATION OF ROLES IN GROUPS

One very striking feature of much of the data gathered by means of Bales's IPA was that the group member who had the highest amount of behavior in the "task" area was seldom the member who had the most social-emotional behavior. In fact, the most active member, A, was almost always the most active in *task* categories; while the second most active member, B, was usually the most active in social-emotional categories. Furthermore, in many groups, A and B talked more to each other than to any other member; and *effective* groups, especially, were likely to have this pattern of alliance between the two most active members.

Bales and his colleagues tended to interpret these findings as evidence that groups use role specialization as one way to deal with the equilibrium problem. The task activity of the task leader (i.e., the member who is most active, on the task and overall) generates social-emotional strains. Often, such strains can be handled more effectively by someone other than the task leader who is generating them. Hence, a second role, that of a social-emotional specialist or leader, becomes differentiated.

Further evidence for the strain reducing basis for this role differentiation comes from postsession ratings. The most active was usually judged the leader and the most influential on the task, but *not* the best liked. The second most active, the social-emotional leader, was usually judged best liked. It was not just activity that made one influential, but *task* activity; and it was not just high activity, or low activity, that was associated with popularity, but high social-emotional activity.

Proponents of this view speculated that such dual-leadership roles—or perhaps multi-leader roles—might be the state of things for most "natural" groups. They drew an analogy between task and social-emotional leaders in ad hoc laboratory problem-solving groups and "father" and "mother" roles in the family. (With considerable ethnocentric bias, even for the 1950s, they seemed never to consider that "mothering" and "fathering" might not be all that differentiated and specialized in all families in all cultures; and with acceptance of gender stereotypes that was typical of the 1950s, they quite unquestioningly assumed a "natural" gender-role match: task-oriented-instrumental-male role and social-emotional-expressive-female role.)

To some extent one can regard this particular pattern of role specialization—a task leader and a social-emotional co-leader—as an artifact of the IPA system, plus the baserates of those categories in the laboratory groups on which IPA baseline data were developed. One could not find a role specializing in questioning, or in negative social-emotional acts, much less a person specializing in asking for suggestions, because the baserates of those categories are quite low. Other researchers, using other data systems, searched for various specialized roles in continuing groups: the "joker" (which might also be high in tension release acts), the "scapegoat," the "deviate" or the "antagonist." All of these, too, depend on the sets of observation categories (or rating scales for post-meeting judgments by members or observers) that are used to search for those distinctive roles.

Note that all of this discussion deals with roles as differentiated patterns of interactive *behavior* in groups. It does not carry any implications that group members develop differentiated *expectations* for one another's behavior. Norms have to do with such expectations. The term, expectation, has two meanings that need to be distinguished. One is a *descriptive* meaning: A expects B to give a hearty greeting, because that is what B always does. The other is a *prescriptive* meaning: A expects B, a close friend, to support A's candidacy, because friends *should* support one another. Norms, and role expectations, involve both of these meanings; and at times the second may grow out of the first. But the two meanings are distinct and matters should not be confused by ignoring that distinction.

Thibaut and Kelley's exchange theory proposes that when a set of people continues to interact over time (a) they will develop patterned ways of behaving in relation to one another; (b) they will come to expect the others to behave in certain ways under certain circumstances in the descriptive sense of expectations; and (c) they will also come to expect others, in a prescriptive sense, to behave in certain ways in certain situations. It is the latter—the *prescriptive* expectations—that give norms their powerful role in social exchange. Members *call upon a norm as a means for influencing the others without exercising informal personal control.* So it is only when the patterned differentiated behavior of group members becomes expected of them—in a prescriptive sense as well as a descriptive sense—that one can speak of norms for differentiated role behavior or, more succinctly, *role expectations.*

Researchers and theorists who used results of Bales's IPA to identify differentiated roles in groups tended to search for totally general patterns of role behavior, thus, for "the" set of roles characteristic of *all* groups. This approach has quite limited potential as a means for analyzing groups, because the behaviors that *all* groups exhibit must be described at very abstract levels (e.g., instrumental versus expressive). On the other hand, the exchange theory idea of patterned behaviors, partly based on normative expectations, allows for every group (actually every dyad in every group) to develop its own unique pattern of interaction for every type of situation. With such diversity and specificity, it is not surprising that exchange theory does not usually deal with descriptions of groups in terms of patterned roles, role expectations, and role behaviors. But there is a middle ground between the two: neither a totally general set of roles, characteristic of all groups, nor a totally specific set of patterned behaviors, backed by norms idiosyncratic to the specific interactants and situations. That middle ground, called *role systems,* is described next.

GROUPS AS ROLE SYSTEMS

The role-system approach, while applicable in principle to any group, is actually geared for description and analysis of relatively formal groups, and is most often used on work groups. Moreover, several quite different bodies of research and theory use the key term *role.* One is a dramaturgical view of groups exemplified in the work of Goffman (1959) and Moreno (1934). A second has to do with a particular set of techniques for group therapy, called role playing (see e.g., Sarbin & Allen, 1968). A third use of the term *role* is in a set of theoretical ideas derived from two early sociologists, Mead (1934) and Cooley (1902), who talk about development of self, self-esteem, and the like, as expressions of the individual's learning to take the role of (i.e., the perspective of) the generalized other. A fourth use of the term *role* is to denote an important social attribute or set of attributes, or an important basis of the person's social status, as in "the role of women" or "the role of the elderly" (e.g., Merton, 1957). A fifth use, and the meaning intended here, is as a description of the expectations and behaviors of the incumbents of an interrelated set of positions, or role system (e.g., Katz & Kahn, 1976). Biddle and Thomas (1966) provide a comprehensive and excellent description of these many uses of role terms.

Basic Role System Concepts

There are several basic assumptions involved in considering groups as role systems. First, the ideas are most easily applied to formally organized groups, but can also be applied to less formal and more natural groups. Second, continuing groups, especially those *designed* for specific functions within larger ongoing organizations (such as work groups), but also many less formally structured groups, can be conceived of as a differentiated set of positions (or offices). Those positions are differentiated "bundles" of rights, responsibilities and duties, in relation to the group's tasks and in relation to the other group members. Such a "bundle" of rights, responsibilities and duties is a *role.* A role is not a characteristic of a particular person, but rather is a characteristic of the behavior of the *incumbent of a particular position.* Who occupies a given position may change from time to time. For example, a work group may get a new boss. When that takes place, the person who enacts that role will also change. Moreover, any one person may—indeed, almost always does—occupy more than one position. Hence any one person has more than one role. Third, the person who is occupying a given position is expected (by others and by self) to carry out the rights, responsibilities and duties, that is, the role, that goes with that position. He or she is expected to do certain tasks, in certain ways and at certain times, and to do so in relation to the behavior of the occupants of other positions in the set (that is, to coordinate and synchronize behavior). The individual role incumbent is evaluated—by others in the role set, often by others outside the role set, and by self—in terms of how well his or her role performance matches those role expectations.

Katz and Kahn (1976) talk about a role episode for a given role (here, referred to as the focal role) as a small unit of role behavior. They regard a role episode as having four stages or segments or links: (a) communication of role expectations, from role senders to the occupant of the focal role, about the what and how of behavior in that role; (b) receipt of those role messages, and interpretation of them, by the person in the focal role; (c) role behavior by the person in the focal role, in response to those role messages as they get filtered through the focal person's perception and interpretation of them; and (d) feedback, from the role senders, about how well role behavior fits those role expectations.

Role expectations are communicated to the role holder from a variety of sources. A role sender can be anyone who has a legitimate basis for caring about how the person in the focal role performs. That includes incumbents of all of the roles with which the focal role is directly or indirectly connected. That usually includes the incumbents of the rest of the positions in the role system within which that focal role is embedded. It often also includes incumbents of some roles that are not in the immediate role set but that are in a related role set within a larger role system in which the focal role is embedded. In work groups, for example, one's role behavior is of consequence to one's work group peers, to the group's supervisor, to that boss's boss, and to people in work groups whose tasks depend on one's own group's outputs. In families, the adult woman's role behavior is of concern to her children, to her husband, perhaps to her parents and in-laws, and, for some matters, to her employer and to her children's teachers. The incumbents of all of these relevant roles "send" role expectations about how the incumbent of the focal role should behave. And they all observe subsequent behavior, evaluate it, and, to some degree, transmit that evaluation back to the focal role incumbent.

But role prescriptions come from two other sources as well. For some fairly general roles, there are some very general culture wide expectations. Bosses should not cheat workers out of their pay. Male bosses should not sexually harass female employees. Mothers should love and nourish their children. Parents should not beat small children. Teachers should not use incorrect grammar. These are transmitted to the role incumbent early, often, and through a variety of means—books, metaphors, newspapers, humor, songs—as well as by direct tuition by members of the role sets involved.

It is here that the role system description overlaps with the use of the term, role, to refer to behavior associated with very broad social status characteristics, as noted earlier in this chapter. The "role of the woman" is too broad for the usage of this book. But the "role of a mother" is not. The latter refers to the very general but powerful set of role expectations, held broadly within the culture or some subculture of it, for behavior by adult women in relation to their natural-born or adopted children. In this general sense, virtually everyone in a culture—past and present—is a legitimate role sender for such general role expectations.

Finally, we hold role expectations for ourselves, in regard to behavior in at least many of our roles. We form these expectations in part because, as members of the culture, we share the culture wide role expectations for those roles. We also form them in part from our own past experience in the related roles of those role sets. Men learn how to be fathers in part from their own experiences as sons. People learn to be bosses in part from their own experience interacting with bosses. We also learn role expectations for our own role behavior in part from the direct experience of behaving in that role. It is at this point that the role system description overlaps with the Mead-Cooley ideas of learning about self by "taking the role of the generalized other." We learn how we should behave, how well we did behave, and indeed who we are, in part by interpreting the behavior of others toward us, that is, by receiving and interpreting the role expectations and evaluative feedback they send to us.

So the incumbent of the focal role receives sent role messages—role expectations—from three kinds of sources: from people in interdependent roles; from people reflecting culture-wide role prescriptions; and from self. The clarity of these messages, and the consensus among them, are crucial features affecting the individual's role perceptions and role behavior, and their consequences.

Sources of Role Problems in Groups

Role expectations, transmitted by role senders, are messages about how the role incumbent *should* behave. These prescriptions are like other norms—they constitute a kind of impersonalized influence, or pressure, to conform to those prescriptions. They are received not only as *information* about what is expected, in a descriptive sense, but also as *normative pressures* about what is *proper* for the incumbent of the focal role to do, about what is expected in a prescriptive sense. They, therefore, can be regarded as role pressures, i.e., pressures for role behavior to conform to those sent role expectations.

In the second link of the role episode, the focal role incumbent must receive these messages, clarify and/or interpret them if they contain any ambiguity, integrate them somehow if they contain any conflicting implications, and decide how to behave in order to fulfill them (or whether or not to try to fulfill them).

In a very large proportion of occasions, all of the sent role messages will be clear in their implications for the focal role; the messages from different sources will all be congruent; whether or not to comply with them will not be in question because one of the agreeing "sources" is self; and it is clear what behavior needs to be done to comply. In such cases, received role will jibe with all sent roles, role behavior will fulfill role expectations, and evaluations of role behavior will be positive. In such situations, role expectations will not be problematic and will not be experienced as pressure to conform—after all, you are doing what you expect of yourself, too. Role behavior will not be seen, by self or others, as compliance or conformity—you will be "doing what comes naturally." And role evaluations will be implicit, low key. In fact, such no-problem role episodes will occur virtually unnoticed by all parties to the interaction. If matters always went that smoothly, one would hardly use or need role system concepts to describe them.

But on a substantial percentage of occasions, one or more features of the role episode may go otherwise than perfectly smoothly, and thereby may give rise to perturbations, or disturbances, of this smooth and unproblematic flow. First, some of the role messages may be unclear, giving rise to role ambiguity. Second, some of the role messages may imply different and even mutually conflicting actions, not all of which can be done at the same time. This can be called role conflict, and there are several important forms of it (to be discussed below). Third, even if what is to be done is clear and does not contain internally conflicting prescriptions, those prescriptions may be beyond the capabilities in qualitative terms—the role incumbent just can't do it. Or, there may simply be too many role requirements to be done in the time period involved, even though each of them could be done. Both of these are problems of role load, the first being qualitative and the second quantitative overload. Thus, role expectations, received as role pressures, can give rise to problems of role *ambiguity,* role *conflict* and role *overload*.

These three forms of role problems are distinct but related concepts. Role conflict has several different aspects; so do role ambiguity and role load. Figure 18-1 shows a classification of several variations of these kinds of role perturbations. The form of the diagram is intended to stress the dual nature of most of them. Some forms of role perturbation are mostly matters of conflict, but partly matters of load; others are mostly matters of conflict but partly ambiguity; and so forth.

Figure 18-1 shows nine types of role problems, three each under ambiguity, conflict, and load. The three forms of role based *conflict* are:

C1   Disparity among role messages of different senders.
C2   Disparity between sent role expectations and personal values/principles.
C3   Disparity between level of role performance demanded and level of ability.

The three forms of role based *ambiguity* are:

A1   Disparity among messages of one role sender.
A2   New or changing role.
A3   Lack of clarity on how to translate expectations into behaviors.

The three forms of role based *load* are:

L1   Unspecified priorities among multiple role demands.
L2   Too many role demands.
L3   Competition between different roles.

Of the three types of role conflict, Figure 18-1 suggests, C1 is related to ambiguity, C3 is related to load, and C2 is "pure" conflict. Of the three types of ambiguity, A1 is related to conflict, A3 is related to load, and A2 is "pure" ambiguity. Of the three types of role load problems, L1 is related to ambiguity, L3 is related to conflict and L2 is "pure" load. These nine represent *classes of role problems,* which are things that can go wrong in the transmission, reception, and reaction to role expectations within role episodes.

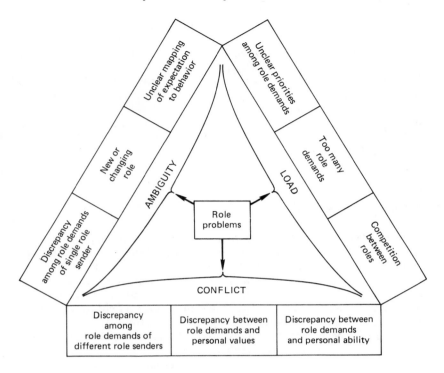

FIGURE 18-1   A Typology of Role Problems

Kahn and colleagues (Katz & Kahn, 1976; Kahn, Wolfe, Quinn, Snoek & Rosenthal, 1964) treat role ambiguity, load and conflict as three types of stress in role systems. They found very high base rates for problems based on *load*. These seemed to involve all three aspects of load: amount, priorities, and inter-role competition. They also found high stress to be characteristic for persons in certain types of "marginal" roles: (a) supervisors who probably had lots of between-sender conflict (C1); (b) persons who spanned the boundaries of two role systems, such as those in liaison roles, who also probably had lots of between-sender conflict (C1); (c) persons occupying emerging or changing roles, who probably had lots of role ambiguity in regard to those roles (A2). They found little evidence of conflicts between role demands and personal values (C2), and relatively little between role demands and performance abilities (C3). Perhaps the latter findings occur because, in natural and continuing groups, before people become incumbents of work roles there tends to be a two-way matching of jobs to people, in regard to both values and abilities. Kahn and colleagues did not report base rates of ambiguities among messages from a single sender or lack of clarity of the demand-to-behavior mappings, but other studies of work settings have reported stress based on those forms of role problems.

In terms of the frame of reference of this book and of its treatment of group interaction, we can regard such role systems as *structured patterns of relations among the interacting members.* Such a role system contains role expectations, or normative standards, or rules, (statements about "who-to-whom,-when, how,-about what,-to what effect) for interaction among the incumbents of those roles. It is a pattern that both reflects and prescribes the communication pattern, the task performance pattern, and the interpersonal relations pattern among those role incumbents. In other words, such role systems can be regarded as *structured patterns of relations among group members.* They are the *standing group* structures that result from prior interaction, and that in turn shape future interaction of members of the acting group who are their role incumbents.

THE LEADER ROLE AND LEADERSHIP BEHAVIOR

The idea of the role of leader has already been introduced in talking about differentiation of roles in groups. Indeed, leadership behavior has been a topic of central importance, historically, in the study of groups. It has been an extremely attractive topic to group researchers; at times it has seemed to receive a very large portion of the total resources available for group research. It has often been accorded a central conceptual place in the group field. (Here, in contrast, it is given only a minor role as a part of the larger topic of role structure.) But it has not really been as fruitful a research topic as one would expect, given the attention and resources it has received.

Early efforts in the leadership area were concerned with identifying the attributes of people who became leaders (versus non-leaders), or successful leaders (versus unsuccessful ones). This proved a phantom chase. People acquire formal positions of leadership for many reasons (e.g., inheritance, seniority) besides their own talents. Moreover, some groups succeed, others fail, for reasons far beyond the abilities and performances of their leaders. The best military commander in the world, if in charge of a badly equipped, ill trained and disloyal army, is likely to be unsuccessful against well equipped, well trained troops in the hands of even an average leader. (For good reviews of past leadership research, see Fiedler, 1967; Gibb, 1954; Stodgill, 1974.) (See EXRTs 48, 49.)

Efforts later shifted to the study of the leader of successful groups, using concepts that tried to take into account the impact of group members and of the situation. Perhaps the most complete expression of this point of view is Fiedler's Contingency Theory of Leadership (Fiedler, 1967) which, though still controversial, is nevertheless the dominant theoretical view of leadership at the present time.

Fiedler argues that effective leadership depends on the group members and the situation in two senses. Leader effectiveness is contingent on the group and the situation in the sense that task abilities and behavior of members, and attributes of the situation, affect the group's task success—hence the leader's success. Furthermore, leader effectiveness is also contingent on group and situation in the sense that different types or styles of leader behavior will be more and less effective depending on which combination of group and situational factors exists.

EXRT 48:   *THE CARTER-BASS EMERGENT LEADER PARADIGM*

Main Study Procedures: Subjects are assigned to (relatively small) groups and asked to discuss a problem or issue and to provide a group decision on it. (Tasks are usually of the decision/discussion type, though sometimes of various other types.)

Main Dependent Variables of Interest: Whether or not some group member emerges as a "leader," as reflected in observations of amount of talking time, and/or in post-session ratings by members; characteristics of members who do exercise influence; comparison of behavior of emergent vs appointed leaders.

Main Variations: Size of group; characteristics of members (e.g., prior activity levels, gender, prestige); type of task; social and physical aspects of the situation (e.g., seating positions, social status differences).

References: Bass & Klubeck (1952); Bass, Pryer, Gaier, & Flint (1958); Carter, Haythorn, & Howell (1950); Carter, Haythorn, Shriver, & Lanzetta (1950); Pepinsky, Hemphill, & Shevitz (1958).

EXRT 49:   *THE LEWIN-LIPPETT-WHITE LEADER STYLE PARADIGM*

Main Study Procedures: Boys who volunteered for activity clubs are assigned to groups with one of several adult leaders. Each adult leader adopts one of three leader styles to use in meeting with a particular group of boys (and the three leader styles are balanced among the adult leaders for different groups): (a) an autocratic style, in which the leader is highly directive, decides what activities the group will engage in, insists on orderly meetings, and the like; (b) a democratic style, in which the leader helps the boys make decisions collectively; and (c) a laissez-faire style in which the adult leader neither directs the group nor helps the boys direct themselves.

Main Dependent Variables of Interest: Group productivity (number and quality of products, such as paper masks); amount of on-task activity and time; scapegoating; indicators of interpersonal harmony.

Main Variations: Temporary absence of leader; switching leader styles; presence of a disrupting outsider.

Reference: Lewin, Lippett, & White (1939).

Fiedler represents the group and situation in terms of three main variables:

1.   How positive is the relationship between leader and members?
2.   How structured is the group's task?
3.   How powerful is the leader's formal position in the group?

All three of these affect how favorable the situation is for the exercise of leadership. A leader in a strong formal position can use rewards and punishments to try to improve group performance. If the group's task is structured, the leader can allocate subtasks, monitor performance, and so on. A leader who is liked by group members can influence them more than one who is not. The more a situation has these three attributes, the more favorable it is for the exercise of influence by the leader on the group's task performance.

Fiedler's main leader variable is a bipolar measure of leadership style. One pole reflects a strong instrumental task orientation, and the other represents an interpersonal orientation. Fiedler holds that leaders who are high in task orientation are more effective *in very favorable and in very unfavorable situations;* whereas leaders high in interpersonal orientation are more effective in *situations of intermediate favorableness.* In the highly favorable situation, task orientation by the leader works better for group task performance than does an interpersonal orientation (though the latter might work better for interpersonal relationships). As the situation gets less favorable for the leader, an orientation that deals effectively with interpersonal matters begins to be needed *even for group task performance.* As the situation becomes still more difficult, a strong task orientation by the leader is again needed to drive the group to any performance at all, perhaps creating unfavorable interpersonal effects at the same time. (This is reminiscent of the task/social-emotional equilibrium process in Bales's interaction analysis; see chapter 12.)

Some of the discussion in chapter 13, dealing with effects of restricted communication channels and modalities, speculated about a continuum of communication ranging from "pure task" messages (in the highly restricted communication systems) to messages rich in interpersonal information as well as in task information (in the less constrained, face to face, full channel communication systems). I speculated there, also, that certain features important for group performance—size, task difficulty, complexity, shifts in group membership, tasks involving conflicts, and the like—might function *as if* they imposed constraints on the group's communication system or increased the demand for richer information. I want to speculate further, here, that the features of the situation dealt with by Fiedler may function to increase or decrease the need for interpersonally rich information, while the task instrumental leadership style may function to constrain, or narrow, the bandwidth of leader-group interaction. If such a set of relations could be described, elaborated, and verified empirically, so as to tie the contingency theory of leadership to the more general area of communication effectiveness, it would be a major advance in integration of research on groups.

STRUCTURE AND INTERACTION
IN NATURAL GROUPS:
RESEARCH ON FAMILIES

It was noted at the beginning of this chapter that findings using Bales's IPA show a differentiation of leader roles in ad hoc laboratory problem-solving groups, into instrumental or task oriented, versus expressive or interpersonal oriented leaders or specialists. It was also noted there that some group theorists generalized these findings to imply these two "roles" as general ones for groups, and specifically to generalize them to families (e.g., Parsons & Bales, 1955; Parsons, Bales, & Shils, 1953). These theorists further presumed that, in the family, not only is there a differentiation of instrumental and expressive roles, but that that differentiation is sex linked (or, more accurately, gender linked). Waxler and Mishler (1970), in an excellent review, point out some serious discrepancies between this assumption and the empirical evidence from research on families.

Three types of studies are useful in addressing this question. One type of study deals with "natural" families, sometimes by retrospective reports and sometimes by observation during experimenter-arranged interaction sessions in the lab or in the home. A second type of study deals with what Waxler and Mishler (1970) call "artificial families." The main structural factors in families are age and sex. An "artificial family" might be composed of one adult male, one adult female, and one adolescent male, who are *not* kin to one another. Such an artificial family might be compared to a "natural" family composed of mother, father and teen-age son. In this way, it is possible to separate out some of the effects on behavior of age based and sex based status from effects of factors associated with the particular family members and their histories. (See EXRT 50.) A third type of study useful in considering effects of role structure in families are studies of ad hoc laboratory groups. In these, members are not kin; they usually are homogeneous in age and gender. So they represent a kind of baseline control, against which findings pertaining to artificial families and natural families can be compared. (See chapter 4 for more elaboration of this rationale.)

A review of many studies of all three types leads Waxler and Mishler (1970) to conclude that the differentiation of instrumental and expressive specialists is really most descriptive for ad hoc groups; that it holds to a substan-

EXRT 50:   *THE ARTIFICIAL FAMILY PARADIGM*

Main Study Procedures: Groups are composed of members who are not kin but who are selected so that the composition of the group matches some particular family pattern (for example, a family with a male and female parent and a male teen-age child), with which it is to be compared. These "artificial families" are then asked to perform a set of tasks together. The tasks may require them to make a series of joint decisions of the kinds families make, or to negotiate a series of disagreements on issues. Artificial families can be compared to natural families doing similar laboratory tasks or simulations; natural families on "natural" tasks in their homes; ad hoc laboratory groups with homogeneous age and gender compositions.

Main Dependent Variables of Interest: Individual and group task performance; individual participation, influence and types of behavior (e.g., task versus social-emotional); member satisfaction with decisions.

Main Variations: Group composition and size; types of tasks; past experience on similar tasks, and in groups of similar composition.

References: Leik (1963); O'Rourke (1963); Waxler & Mishler (1970).

tial degree, and is sex linked in "artificial families"; but that it is much less descriptive of "natural" families. Specifically, the adult females in natural families are very active in both instrumental and expressive areas, although such adult females "fall into" the expressive specialization (expected of them by the cultural stereotype) when they are placed in "artificial families." Another way to view the latter point is to say that, at the start of a new group, members apply role expectations brought with them from the general culture—in this case, the gender differentiated roles. As that group continues over time (which families do but artificial families do not), or, alternatively, as that group becomes a more real and important part of the person's life (which families do and artificial families do not), the role expectations of the other members of that role set, and of self, become more powerful in shaping interpersonal patterns in that group. That latter point, in turn, can be restated as a principle: *Any given group becomes more unique, more idiosyncratic, in its patterns of norms and roles, the longer it continues and the broader the band of activities it subsumes.*

Findings in real families are even more complex than the preceding discussion indicates. In some studies (e.g., Leik, 1963), both parents are high in task activity, while the mother (and daughters!) are social-emotional specialists. In other studies (e.g., Strauss, 1967), it is the father who displays a dual role, directive and supportive, in both parent-child and spouse-spouse interaction. It is likely that just which pattern is displayed by which parent depends on how the culture stereotypes the specific topic or area of activity (i.e., as a "male" or "female" area of activity). It may also depend in part on the sex of the child with whom interaction is taking place, and the particular culture and subculture of the family. Bronfenbrenner (1961) suggests that in lower-class families parents discipline the child of the same sex, and indulge the child of the opposite sex. O'Rourke (1963) found fathers more expressive with daughters than mothers were. O'Rourke also found an important difference for interaction patterns when the *same* (natural) families were studied in the home and in a laboratory. In the lab, families shift toward a pattern such as Parsons and Bales predict: father instrumental, mother expressive. At home, fathers drop in instrumentality, mothers increase, and the opposite holds for expressiveness. So, again, the differentiated and gender specialized role patterns seem associated with greater artificiality, less "naturalness."

Another interesting difference between families and ad hoc groups is in studies of "coalitions" in decision-making. Ad hoc groups most often exhibit a consistent coalition of two who mutually reject and isolate the third (Mills, 1953). In families, such a two-against-one pattern is also common but the isolate is given much greater support by the dominant pair. In families—and perhaps in any group that has temporal continuity and anticipates continuation as a group—even a low status member who has little power in decisions still receives emotional support and interpersonal rewards that sustain him or her as a member of the group. In terms of Thibaut and Kelley's exchange theory, the low status member must have net pay-offs at or above the comparison level of available alternatives. For family members, to drop family membership—by divorce for adult members, by running away for child members, or perhaps by extreme withdrawal for members of any age—carries extremely high costs. Hence, even relatively low pay-offs may exceed the (CL_{ALT}).

There have been some studies of patterns of family interaction in the sense of behavioral consistency or predictability over time (i.e., the *descriptive* side of norms or role expectations). Families with schizophrenic children showed more short-run predictability of interaction (successive speakers acknowledging prior speaker), but less long-run patterning, than families with normal children. Short-run predictability might be considered a kind of rigidity. Long-run patterning reflects continuity of relations. "Normal" families can keep a predictable process going for an extended time, but in the short run they are more flexible, less rigid, in their interactions. One might expect more artificial groups to be more like the "abnormal" families: to display more short-run predictability or rigidity of patterning and less long-run patterning. One might also expect that such groups would learn to be more flexible, as well as to have more unique role differentiation patterns, as they become more "real" and continue over time.

As with many aspects of group interaction discussed in earlier parts of this book, these findings regarding natural families and various simulations or ad hoc groups to which they have been compared, suggest that certain differences may reflect the operation of fairly general processes. First, a task versus expressive role specialization is found, repeatedly, in ad hoc laboratory groups. It has been presumed by theorists to apply to groups in general, and to be gender linked in families. However, such specialization is not found in distinct form in natural families in natural settings. Instead, both adult members of families may engage in lots of both instrumental and expressive behavior, with amounts and relative amounts of each displayed by male and female parent (and adolescent children) depending on the culture, the subculture, the situation and the particular history of that group. When various degrees of artificiality are introduced by studying natural families in the lab, by studying "artificial families" composed of nonkin in family-like gender and age combinations, and by studying ad hoc laboratory groups, the role specialization into task and social-emotional leaders increases, and it is gender linked when members of both sexes are in the group. Men tend to take instrumental roles and women tend to take expressive roles when they are interacting with strangers (as in the artificial families) or when they are interacting in unnatural circumstances (as when natural families are studied in the lab). But when "at home" in their natural groups under natural conditions, men act less instrumentally, more expressively, and women act more instrumentally, less expressively. It is as if both men and women take on what they know to be the culturally shared stereotypes about male and female behavior when they are "out in public" and interacting with strangers; but that they shed these stereotypes when they are "off stage" at home.

However, the artificiality under which this question has been studied confounds two features: the *temporal continuity* of the group, hence the degree of acquaintance of the interactants with one another; and the degree of restriction of form and scope of activities involved in the interaction, hence the degree of artificiality of the interaction settings and tasks. We do not know what would happen if experimentally created "artificial families" (or ad hoc groups) continued to interact, in family-like fashion, over a long period of time. There have been a few studies of strangers isolated together for long time periods (e.g., Altman & Haythorn, 1965, 1967a, 1967b). But these were same-sex groups, often groups of two or three; the studies were not designed to focus on role specialization; and many other factors, including severe isolation and confinement, were very central to the settings of these studies. We do know from informal observation that sets of people interact differently when they have known each other well for a long time than when they are strangers or casual acquaintances. So it is reasonable to suppose that temporal continuity and/or degree of acquaintance is one important feature of these findings.

On the other hand, we know that gender stereotyped role specialization increases when natural families are studied in the lab; and that when families are observed doing artificial tasks a pattern of role specialization develops that depends on the "gender-linked" nature of the tasks. It is reasonable, therefore, to suppose that the broad-band scope of the activities in families, compared to the restricted scope of activities in the groups or quasi-groups of various research settings, is also a major feature of those findings. So it is reasonable to conclude that *the gender-linked role specialization, prevalent in laboratory studies of groups, tends to disappear or diminish as the scope of the group's activities and/or the continuity of the group over time increases.* As a group continues over time, and as its activities encompass a bigger and bigger slice of its members' time and attention, the group develops patterns of norms and role expectations, hence patterns of behavior, that are more and more reflective of its own members' idiosyncratic attributes and history of interpersonal relations, and less and less "typical" of some type of group or type of task or type of cultural pattern. The focal group becomes less and less "a family" (or "a dating couple" or "a basketball team"). It becomes more and more "this family," Stewart and Jane Little, and all the little Littles, of 502 Maplewood Drive, Haven, Illinois.

Let me digress briefly, from consideration of role specialization in groups, to note that these caveats and complexities have a certain similarity to the kinds of statements one might make about falling bodies under "natural" versus "artificial" conditions if one had only a pre-Newtonian science of physics. If we arrange to study falling objects under highly artificial conditions—near-vacuums—they fall in a very predictable path and with a very predictable time course. But natural objects falling under natural conditions, where there is variation in atmospheric pressure, wind and friction, and where objects vary in shape and size, do not fall in such predictable paths or time courses. Indeed, some of them don't "fall" at all, but "float." Because we do have some knowledge of the physical laws involved, we do not brush off the artificial results of studies in a near-vacuum as meaningless, and accept the complexity of the natural situation as "true," unanalyzable, and not amenable to scientific study. Instead, we recognize that the actual behavior of falling bodies under natural conditions incorporates those basic relations isolated in the artificial situations, but also incorporates other relations as well (e.g., effects of air resistance). When we see a glider sail or an eagle fly we do not for a minute think that gravity isn't operating just because it is not the only thing operating.

The principles identified under artificial conditions are a crucial part of, but not a comprehensive description of, the forces operating under natural conditions.

So it is, perhaps, with families and other natural groups, in natural settings compared to various artificial groups or settings. The role specialization found in ad hoc groups and artificial settings may be one of various counteracting tendencies operating in natural groups. It is probably the case that all groups divide up what they have to do among members. If a group has only one thing to do, and only has to do it once, it is a reasonable thing for members to divide it up and each do certain parts. If the group does that same thing repeatedly, it is not unreasonable for the same people to do the same parts on successive trials; to do so is undoubtedly efficient; performance improves with practice and so does coordination. But over time, it would undoubtedly become boring; task interest requires some degree of variety and challenge. So even if a group does only one thing but does it repeatedly over a long time, members may vary what each of them does (as Thibaut and Kelley suggest, for dyadic interaction). If a group does many different tasks, it will probably divide up each task; but there is little reason to expect a group to divide up and allocate parts among members in the same way for all tasks. For example, in broad-band groups, even of relative strangers, men may take the instrumental lead in tasks that the culture regards as "male" (e.g., repairing a broken lawn mower), with women taking supportive roles, while women may take the instrumental lead on culturally defined "female" tasks (e.g., repairing a torn drape), with men taking supportive roles. In long-term natural groups, though, the instrumental lead on task X may be taken by A because *A likes to do X,* while task Y may be "led" by B, because *B is skilled at doing Y,* quite independent of the gender or age or "generation" of A or B, and of the cultural stereotypes for tasks X and Y. As a concrete example, consider a family faced with two household chores: painting a chair and putting photos in an album. Either task might be done by the parent of either gender, by an adolescent or even pre-adolescent child of either gender, or by a grandparent of either gender or either side of the family. That activity might be given social-emotional support by any, all, or none of the others. Moreover, there is no reason at all to suppose that the same person—or even a person of the same generation or gender—would do them both, or would act supportively toward whoever did them both. Who does what in a given family depends on activity preferences, skills, available time, past experience, and rewards and costs involved in the activities. It may well be easy to predict which member of a particular family will do a given task, if you have enough information about *that* family. But there is no reason why their role allocations ought to correspond, by gender or generation, to the role allocations of other specific families, or even to their own role pattern at a later time (when, for example, Johnnie is older and thus will handle the photos with more care; when Grandmother can't see well enough to paint). That statement is analogous to saying that, if you have enough information about the *specific* objects and situations, you can predict the path and time course of actual falling bodies under natural conditions—which indeed is the case—even though those bodies do not follow the "law" by falling in a perfect parabola at thirty-two feet per second.

So it is with the study of groups. Chapter 3, on methods, discussed how the researcher is always faced with trade-offs among generalizability, realism, and precision. That constraint applies to research on family patterns. If you want to predict with precision you must either restrict naturalness (by using artificial situations), or restrict generalizability (by trying to predict only for this group at this time), or, more likely, both. If you want to state general laws—about *all* groups, or even all families—you must either give up precision (by making only general and abstract statements, such as $B = f (P,E)$ or "behavior equals some function of person and environment"), or else restrict naturalness (by concentrating, for example, only on two-person groups playing a prisoner's dilemma game), or both. If you want to retain maximum realism, then you must either reduce precision by forgoing powerful but obtrusive methods (such as continuous observation of behavior) or reduce generalizability by restricting study to a narrow range of groups or activities (e.g., studying families who have come to some clinic for help; or studying only the on-court behavior of basketball teams), or both. It is not possible to maximize precision, generalizability, and naturalness all at the same time. This is not a limitation of research on families, or even of research on groups. Rather it is a limitation on empirical research of any kind. The physical sciences have overcome those limitations of empirical studies by systematic accumulation of findings from overlapping studies guided by strong and fully developed theory. The same kind of progress by the same tactics is possible, in principle, for the social and behavioral sciences in general, and for group research in particular. But we are still a very long way from that state, in regard to theory, method and empirical results, in the knowledge we have gained from the study of groups. Much empirical and theoretical progress is yet needed before we can give firm answers to most of the crucial questions that have been raised about the nature and consequences of human groups.

REFERENCES

ADAMS, J. S.   Inequity in social exchange. In L. Berkowitz (Ed.), *Advances in experimental social psychology* (Vol. 2). New York: Academic Press, 1965.

ALLPORT, F. H.   The influence of the group upon association and thought. *Journal of Experimental Psychology,* 1920, *3,* 159–182.

ALLPORT, F. H.   *Social psychology.* Boston, MA: Houghton-Mifflin, 1924.

ALLPORT, G. W.   The historical background of modern social psychology. In G. Lindzey (Ed.), *Handbook of social psychology.* Cambridge, MA: Addison-Wesley, 1954.

ALTMAN, I.   Reciprocity of interpersonal relationships. *Journal for the Theory of Social Psychology,* 1973, *3,* 249–261.

ALTMAN, I.   *The environment and social behavior: Privacy, personal space, territoriality and crowding.* Monterey, CA: Brooks-Cole, 1975.

ALTMAN, I., & HAYTHORN, W. W.   Interpersonal exchange in isolation. *Sociometry,* 1965, *28,* 411.

ALTMAN, I., & HAYTHORN, W. W.   The ecology of isolated groups. *Behavioral Science,* 1967, *12*(3), 169–182. (a)

ALTMAN, I., & HAYTHORN, W. W.   The effects of social isolation and group composition on performance. *Human Relations,* 1967, *20*(4), 313. (b)

ALTMAN, I., & TAYLOR, D. A.   *Social penetration: The development of interpersonal relationships.* New York: Holt, Rinehart & Winston, 1973.

ALTMAN, I., & VINSEL, A. M.   Personal space: An analysis of E. T. Hall's proxemics framework. In I. Altman & J. F. Wohlwill (Eds.), *Human behavior and environment: Advances in theory and research* (Vol. 2). New York: Plenum Publishing Corporation, 1977.

ALTMAN, I., VINSEL, A. M., & BROWN, B. B.   Dialectic conceptions in social psychology: An application to social penetration and privacy regulation. In L. Berkowitz (Ed.), *Advances in experimental social psychology* (Vol. 14). New York: Academic Press, 1981.

APFELBAUM, E.   On conflicts and bargaining. In L. Berkowitz (Ed.), *Advances in experimental social psychology* (Vol. 7). New York: Academic Press, 1974.

ARGYLE, M.   *The scientific study of social behavior.* New York: Philosophical Library, 1957.

ARGYLE, M., & COOK, M.   *Gaze and mutual gaze.* London: C.U.P., 1976.

ARGYLE, M., & DEAN, J.   Eye contact, distance and affiliation. *Sociometry,* 1965, *28,* 289-304.

ARGYLE, M., & KENDON, A.   The experimental analysis of social performance. In L. Berkowitz (Ed.), *Advances in experimental social psychology* (Vol. 3). New York: Academic Press, 1967.

ARGYRIS, C., & SCHON, D.   *Theory in practice.* San Francisco: Jossey-Bass, 1974.

ARONSON, E., & MILLS, J.   Effects of severity of initiation on liking for a group. *Journal of Abnormal and Social Psychology,* 1959, *59,* 177-181.

ASCH, S.   Effects of group pressure upon the modification and distortion of judgment. In H. Guetzkow (Ed.), *Groups, leadership and men.* Pittsburgh: Carnegie Press, 1951.

AXELROD, R.   *Conflict of interest.* Chicago: Markham, 1970.

BACK, K. W.   Influence through social communication. *Journal of Abnormal and Social Psychology,* 1951, *46,* 9-23.

BACK, K. W.   *Beyond words: The story of sensitivity training and the encounter movement.* New York: Russell Sage Foundation, 1972.

BALES, R. F.   A set of categories for the analysis of small group interaction. *American Sociological Review,* 1950, *15,* 257-263. (a)

BALES, R. F.   *Interaction process analysis: A method for the study of small groups.* Cambridge, MA: Addison-Wesley, 1950. (b)

BALES, R. F.   The equilibrium problem in small groups. In T. Parsons, R. F. Bales & E. A. Shils (Eds.), *Working papers in the theory of action.* Glencoe, IL: Free Press, 1953.

BALES, R. F., & COHEN, S. P.   *SYMLOG: A system for the mutilevel observation of groups.* New York: Free Press, 1979.

BALES, R. F., & SLATER, P. E.   Role differentiation. In T. Parsons, R. F. Bales and others (Eds.), *The family, socialization, and interaction process.* Glencoe, IL: Free Press, 1955.

BALES, R. F., & STRODTBECK, F. L.   Phases in group problem solving. *Journal of Abnormal and Social Psychology,* 1951, *46,* 485-495.

BANDURA, A.   Social learning through imitation. In M. R. Jones (Ed.), *Nebraska symposium on motivation, 1962.* Lincoln, NB: University of Nebraska Press, 1962.

BANDURA, A., & WALTERS, R.   *Social learning and personality development.* New York: Holt, Rinehart & Winston, 1963.

BARKER, R. G.   Explorations in ecological psychology. *American Psychologist,* 1965, *20,* 1-14.

BARKER, R. G., & WRIGHT, H. F.   *Midwest and its children: The psychological ecology of an American town.* New York: Harper & Row, 1955.

BASS, B. M.   *Leadership, psychology and organizational behavior.* New York: Harper & Row, 1960.

BASS, B. M., & KLUBECK, S.   Effects of seating arrangements on leaderless group discussion. *Journal of Abnormal and Social Psychology,* 1952, *47,* 724-727.

BASS, B. M., PRYER, M. W., GAIER, E. L., & FLINT, A. W.   Interacting effects of control, motivation, group practice, and problem difficulty on attempted leadership. *Journal of Abnormal and Social Psychology,* 1958, *56,* 352-358.

BAVELAS, A.   A mathematical model for group structure. *Applied Anthropology,* 1948, *7,* 16–30.

BENNETT, E. B.   Discussion, decision, commitment and consensus in "group decision." *Human Relations,* 1955, *8,* 251–273.

BENNIS, W. G., & SHEPHERD, H. H.   A theory of group development. *Human Relations,* 1956, *9,* 415–437.

BERKOWITZ, L.   Personality and group position. *Sociometry,* 1956, *19,* 210–222.

BERMENT, G., NEMETH, C., & VIDMAR, N. (Eds.).   *Psychology and the law: Research frontiers.* Lexington, MA: Lexington Books, 1976.

BERSHEID, E., & WALSTER, E.   *Interpersonal attraction* (2nd ed.). Reading, MA: Addison-Wesley, 1975.

BIDDLE, B. J., & THOMAS, E. J. (Eds.).   *Role theory: Concepts and research.* New York: Wiley, 1966.

BION, W. R.   *Experiences in groups: And other papers.* New York: Basic Books, 1961.

BLAU, P. M.   *Exchange of power in social life.* New York: Wiley, 1968.

BLAU, P. M., FALBE, C. M., MCKINLEY, W., & TRACY, P. K.   Technology and organization in manufacturing. *Administrative Science Quarterly,* 1976, *21,* 20–40.

BORGATTA, E. F.   A systematic study of interaction process scores, peer and self-assessments, personality and other variables. *Genetic Psychology Monographs,* 1962, *65,* 219–291.

BORGATTA, E. F.   A new systematic interaction observation system: Behavior scores system (BSs). *Journal of Psychological Studies,* 1963, *14,* 24–44.

BORGATTA, E. F., & BALES, R. F.   Interaction of individuals in reconstituted groups. *Sociometry,* 1953, *16,* 302–320.

BORGATTA, E. F., COUCH, A. S., & BALES, R. F.   Some findings relevant to the great man theory of leadership. *American Sociological Review,* 1954, *19,* 755–759.

BRAY, R., & KERR, N.   *The psychology of the courtroom.* New York: Academic Press, 1981.

BREAUGH, J. A., & KLIMONSKI, R. J.   The choice of a group spokesman in bargaining: Member or outsider? *Organizational Behavior and Human Performance,* 1977, *19,* 325–336.

BREHMER, B.   Social judgment theory and the analysis of interpersonal conflict. *Psychological Bulletin,* 1976, *83,* 985–1003.

BREWER, M. B.   In-group bias in the minimal intergroup situation: A cognitive motivational analysis. *Psychological Bulletin,* 1979, *86,* 307–324.

BRINBERG, D., & CASTELL, P.   A resource exchange theory approach to interpersonal interactions: A test of Foa's theory. *Journal of Personality and Social Psychology,* 1982, *43*(2), 260–269.

BRONFENBRENNER, U.   Toward a theoretical model for the analysis of parent-child relationships in a social context. In J. C. Glidewell (Ed.), *Parental attitudes and child behavior.* Springfield, IL: Thomas, 1961.

BRUNSWICK, E.   Representative design and probabilistic theory in a functional psychology. *Psychological Review,* 1955, *62,* 193–217.

BYRNE, D.   *The attraction paradigm.* New York: Academic Press, 1971.

BYRNE, D., & CLORE, G.   Effectance arousal and attraction. *Journal of Personality and Social Psychology Monographs,* 1967, *6,* 4, Whole No. 638.

CAMPBELL, D. T., & STANLEY, J. L.   *Experimental and quasi-experimental designs for research.* Chicago, IL: Rand-McNally, 1966.

CAMPBELL, J., & DUNNETTE, M. D.   Effectiveness of T-group experiences in managerial training and development. *Psychological Bulletin,* 1968, *70,* 73–104.

CAPLOW, T.   A theory of coalitions in the triad. *American Sociological Review,* 1956, *21,* 489–493.

CARTER, L. F., HAYTHORN, W. W., & HOWELL, M.   A further investigation of the criteria of leadership. *Journal of Abnormal and Social Psychology,* 1950, *45,* 350–358.

CARTER, L. F., HAYTHORN, W. W., SHRIVER, B., & LANZETTA, J.   The behavior of leaders and other group members. *Journal of Abnormal and Social Psychology,* 1950, *46,* 589–595.

CARTWRIGHT, D.   The nature of group cohesiveness. In D. Cartwright & A. Zander (Eds.), *Group dynamics: Research and theory* (3rd ed.). New York: Harper & Row, 1968.

CARTWRIGHT, D.   Determinants of scientific progress: The case of research on the risky shift. *American Psychologist,* 1973, *28*(3), 222–231.

CARTWRIGHT, D., & ZANDER, A. (Eds.),   *Group dynamics: Research and theory* (1st. ed.). Evanston, IL: Row, Peterson, 1953.

CARTWRIGHT, D., & ZANDER, A. (Eds.),   *Group dynamics: Research and theory* (2nd. ed.). Evanston, IL: Row, Peterson, 1960.

CARTWRIGHT, D., & ZANDER, A. (Eds.),   *Group dynamics: Research and theory* (3rd. ed.). New York: Harper & Row, 1968.

CHAPPLE, E. D.   The measurement of interpersonal behavior. *Transactions of the New York Academy of Science,* 1942, *4,* 222–233.

CLORE, G.   Interpersonal attraction: An overview. In J. Thibaut, J. Spence & R. Carson (Eds.), *Contemporary topics in social psychology,* Morristown, NJ: General Learning Press, 1976.

COCH, L., & FRENCH, J. R., JR.   Overcoming resistance to change. *Human Relations,* 1948, *1,* 512–532.

COLLINS, B. E., & GUETZKOW, H.   *A social psychology of group processes for decision-making.* New York: Wiley, 1964.

COMPTE, A.   *The positive philosophy* (Vol. I). London: Trubner & Co. 1853, (Original French edition, 1830).

COOK, M., & LALLIJEE, M.   Verbal substitutes for visual signals in interaction. *Semiotica,* 1972, *3,* 212–221.

COOK, T. D., & CAMPBELL, D. T.   *Quasi-experimental design: Design and analysis issues for field settings.* Chicago: Rand, McNally, 1979.

COOLEY, C. H.   *Human nature and the social order.* New York: Chas. Scribner's Sons, 1902.

COTTRELL, N. B., WACK, D. I., SEKERAK, G. I., & RITTLE, R. H.   Social facilitation of dominant responses by the presence of an audience and the mere presence of others. *Journal of Personality and Social Psychology,* 1968, *9,* 245–250.

COUCH, A. S., & CARTER, L. F.   *A factorial study of the rated behavior of group members.* Paper read at Eastern Psychological Association meeting, March, 1952.

DABBS, J. M., JR.   *Indexing the cognitive load of a conversation.* Unpublished paper, Georgia State University, Atlanta, Georgia, 1980.

DALKEY, N. C.   *Experiments in group prediction.* Santa Monica, CA: Rand Corp., 1968.

DALKEY, N. C.,   The Delphi Method: An experimental study of group opinion. *Management Science,* June, 1969.

DAVIS, J. H.   *Group Performance.* Reading, MA: Addison-Wesley, 1969.

DAVIS, J. H.   Group decision and social interaction: A theory of social decision schemes. *Psychological Review,* 1973, *80,* 97–125.

DAVIS, J. H.   Group decision and procedural justice. In M. Fishbein (Ed.), *Progress in social psychology* (Vol. 1). Hillsdale, NJ: Erlbaum, 1980.

DAVIS, J. H., BRAY, R. M., & HOLT, R. W.   The empirical study of social decision processes in juries: A critical review. In J. Tapp & F. Levine (Eds.), *Law, justice and the individual in society: Psychological and legal issues.* New York: Holt, Rinehart & Winston, 1977.

DAVIS, J. H., KERR, N. L., ATKIN, R. S., HOLT, R., & MEEK, D.   The decision process of 6- and 12-person juries assigned unanimous and 2/3 majority rules. *Journal of Personality and Social Psychology, 1975, 32,* 1–14.

DAVIS, J. H., LAUGHLIN, P. R., & KOMORITA, S. S.   The social psychology of small groups: Cooperative and mixed-motive interaction. *Annual Review of Psychology, 1976, 27,* 501–541.

DAVIS, J. H., & RESTLE, F.   The analysis of problems and prediction of group problem solving. *Journal of Abnormal and Social Psychology, 1963, 66,* 103–116.

DAWES, R. M.   Social dilemmas. *Annual Review of Psychology, 1980, 31,* 169–183.

DELBECQ, A. L., VAN DE VEN, A. H., & GUSTAFSON, D. H.   *Group techniques for program planning.* Glencoe, IL: Scott, Foresman, 1975.

DEUTSCH, M.   A theory of cooperation and competition. *Human Relations,* 1949, *2,* 129–152. (a)

DEUTSCH, M.   An experimental study of the effects of cooperation and competition upon group process. *Human Relations,* 1949, *2,* 199–231. (b)

DEUTSCH, M., & KRAUSS, R. M.   Studies of interpersonal bargaining. *Journal of Conflict Resolution,* 1962, *6*(1), 52–76.

DION, K. L., BARON, R. S., & MILLER, N.   Why do groups make riskier decisions than individuals? In L. Berkowitz (Ed.), *Advances in Experimental Social Psychology* (Vol. 5). New York: Academic Press, 1970.

DITTES, J. E., & KELLEY, H. H.   Effects of different conditions of acceptance on conformity to group norms. *Journal of Abnormal and Social Psychology,* 1956, *53,* 100–107.

DUNNETTE, M. D., CAMPBELL, J., & JAASTAD, K.   The effect of group participation on brain storming effectiveness for two industrial samples. *Journal of Applied Psychology, 1963, 46,* 30–37.

DUNPHY, D. C.   *Social change in self-analytic groups.* Unpublished doctoral dissertation, Harvard University, 1964.

EASTERBROOK, J. A.   The effect of emotion on cue utilization and the organization of behavior. *Psychological Review, 1959, 66,* 183–201.

EILS, L. C., III., & JOHN, R. S.   A criterion validation of multiattribute utility analysis and of group communication strategy. *Organizational Behavior and Human Performance, 1980, 25,* 268–288.

EINHORN, H. J., HOGARTH, R. M., & KLEMPFER, E.   Quality of group judgment. *Psychological Bulletin, 1977, 84,* 158–172.

FESTINGER, L.   Informal social communication. *Psychological Review, 1950, 57,* 271–292.

FESTINGER, L.   *A theory of cognitive dissonance.* New York: Harper & Row, 1957.

FESTINGER, L., BACK, W., SCHACHTER, S., KELLEY, H. H., & THIBAUT, J. W.   *Theory and experiment in social communication.* Ann Arbor, MI: Edwards Brothers, 1952.

FESTINGER, L., & HUTTE, H. H.   An experimental investigation of the effect of unstable interpersonal relations in a group. *Journal of Abnormal and Social Psychology,* 1954, *49,* 513–522.

FESTINGER, L., SCHACHTER, S., & BACK, K. W.   *Social pressures in informal groups: A study of human factors in housing.* New York: Harper Bros., 1950.

FESTINGER, L., & THIBAUT, J. W.   Interpersonal communications in small groups. *Journal of Abnormal and Social Psychology,* 1951, *46,* 92–99.

FIEDLER, F. E.   Assumed similarity measures as predictors of team effectiveness. *Journal of Abnormal and Social Psychology,* 1954, *49,* 381–388.

FIEDLER, F. E.   *A theory of leadership effectiveness.* New York: McGraw-Hill, 1967.

FOA, E. B., & FOA, U.   Resource theory of social exchange. In J. W. Thibaut, J. Spence & R. Carson (Eds.), *Contemporary topics in social psychology.* Morristown, NJ: Academic Press, 1976.

FOA U., & FOA, E. B.   *Resource theory of social exchange.* Morristown, NJ: General Learning Press, 1975.

GAMSON, W. A.   A theory of coalition formation. *American Sociological Review,* 1961, *26,* 373–382.

GAMSON, W. A.   Experimental studies of coalition formation. In L. Berkowitz (Ed.), *Advances in experimental social psychology* (Vol. 1). New York: Academic Press, 1964.

GEEN, R. G., & GANGE, J. J.   Drive theory of social facilitation: Twelve years of theory and research. *Psychological Bulletin,* 1977, *84,*(6), 1267–1288.

GIBB, C. A.   Leadership. In G. Lindsey (Ed.), *Handbook of social psychology* (Vol. 2). Cambridge, MA: Addison-Wesley, 1954.

GLANZER, M., & GLASER, R.   Techniques for the study of group structure and behavior: I. Analysis of structure. *Psychological Bulletin,* 1959, *56,* 317–322.

GLANZER, M., & GLASER, R.,   Techniques for the study of group structure and behavior: II. Empirical studies of the effects of structure in small groups. *Psychological Bulletin,* 1961, *58,* 1–27.

GOFFMAN, E.   *The presentation of self in everyday life.* New York: Doubleday, 1959.

GOODACRE, D. M., III.   Group characteristics of good and poor performance combat units. *Sociometry,* 1953, *16,* 168–178.

GORDAN, K. A.   A study of aesthetic judgments. *Journal of Experimental Psychology,* 1923, *6,* 36–43.

GOTTMAN, J. M.   Detecting cyclicality in social interaction. *Psychological Bulletin,* 1979, *86,* 336–348. (a)

GOTTMAN, J. M.   *Marital interaction: Experimental investigations.* New York: Academic Press, 1979. (b)

GOTTMAN, J. M., NOTARIUS, L., MARKMAN, H., BANKS, S., YOPPI, R., & RUBIN, M. E.   Behavior exchange theory and marital decision making. *Journal of Personality and Social Psychology,* 1976, *34*(1), 14–23.

GREER, F. L., GALANTER, E., & NORDLIE, P. G.   Interpersonal knowledge and individual and group effectiveness. *Journal of Abnormal and Social Psychology,* 1954, *49,* 411–414.

GURNEE, H.   A comparison of collective and individual judgments of facts. *Journal of Experimental Psychology,* 1937, *21,* 106–112.

GUSTAFSON, D. H., SHUKLA, R. M., DELBECQ, A. L., & WALSTER, G. W.   A comparative study of differences in subjective estimation made by individuals' interacting groups, Delphi groups and nominal groups. *Organizational Behavior and Human Performance,* 1973, *9,* 280–291.

HACKMAN, J. R.   Effects of task characteristics on group products. *Journal of Experimental Social Psychology,* 1968, *4,* 162–187.

HACKMAN, J. R.   Group influences on individuals. In M. D. Dunnette (Ed.), *Handbook of Industrial and Organizational Psychology,* Chicago, IL: Rand-McNally, 1976.

HACKMAN, J. R.   The design of self-managing work groups. In B. T. King, S. S. Streufort & F. E. Fiedler (Eds.), *Managerial control and organizational democracy.* Washington, D.C.: Winston & Sons, 1977.

HACKMAN, J. R., BROUSSEAU, K. R., & WIESS, J. A. The interaction of task design and group performance strategies in determining group effectiveness. *Organizational Behavior and Human Performance,* 1976, *16,* 350–365.

HACKMAN, J. R., JONES, L. E., & MCGRATH, J. E. A set of dimensions for describing the general properties of group-generated written passages. *Psychological Bulletin,* 1967, *67,* 379–390.

HACKMAN, J. R., & MORRIS, C. G. Group tasks, group interaction process, and group performance effectiveness: A review and proposed integration. In L. Berkowitz (Ed.), *Advances in experimental social psychology* (Vol. 8). New York: Academic Press, 1975.

HACKMAN, J. R., & MORRIS, C. G. Group process and group effectiveness: A reappraisal. In L. Berkowitz (Ed.), *Group Processes.* New York: Academic Press, 1978.

HACKMAN, J. R., & OLDHAM, G. R. The Job Diagnostics Survey: An instrument for the diagnosis of jobs and the evaluation of job redesign projects. *Journal of Applied Psychology,* 1975, *60,* 159–170.

HACKMAN, J. R., & OLDHAM, G. R. *Work redesign.* Reading, MA: Addison-Wesley, 1980.

HALL, E. T. *The hidden dimension.* Garden City, NY: Doubleday, 1966.

HALL, J. Decisions, decisions, decisions. *Psychology Today,* November 1971, pp. 51–54.

HALL, J., & WATSON, W. H. The effects of a normative intervention on group decision-making performance. *Human Relations,* 1971, *23*(**4**), 299–317.

HAMMOND, K. R., STEWART, T. R., BREHMER, B., & STEINMANN, D. O. Social judgment theory. In M. F. Kaplan & S. Schwartz (Eds.), *Human judgment and decision processes.* New York: Academic Press, 1975.

HAMMOND, K. R., TODD, F. J., WILKINS, M., & MITCHELL, T. O. Cognitive conflict between persons: Application of the "lens model" paradigm. *Journal of Experimental Social Psychology,* 1966, *2,* 343–360.

HARDIN, G. R. The tragedy of the commons. *Science,* 1968, *162,* 1243–1248.

HARE, A. P. Theories of group development and categories for interaction analysis. *Small Group Behavior,* 1973, *4*(3), 259–304.

HARE, A. P. *Handbook of small group research* (1st ed.). New York: The Free Press of Glencoe, 1962.

HARE, A. P. *Handbook of small group research* (2nd ed.). New York: The Free Press of Glencoe, 1976.

HARE, A. P., BORGATTA, E. F., & BALES, R. F. *Small groups: Studies in social interaction* (1st ed.). New York: Knopf, 1955.

HARE, A. P., BORGATTA, E. F., & BALES, R. F. *Small groups: Studies in social interaction* (2nd ed.). New York: Knopf, 1965.

HARTMAN, J. J. Small group methods of personal change. *Annual Review of Psychology,* 1979, *30,* 453–476.

HAVRON, M. D., FAY, R. J., & GOODACRE, D. M., III. *Research on the effectiveness of small military units.* Adjutant General Department PRS Report 885, Washington, DC, 1951.

HAVRON, M. D., & MCGRATH, J. E. The contribution of the leader to the effectiveness of small military groups. In L. Petrullo & B. M. Bass (Eds.), *Leadership and interpersonal behavior.* New York: Holt, Rinehart & Winston, 1961.

HEARN, G. Leadership and the spatial factor in small groups. *Journal of Abnormal and Social Psychology,* 1957, *54,* 269–274.

HEIDER, F. *The psychology of interpersonal relations.* New York: Wiley, 1958.

HEMPHILL, J. K. Situational factors in leadership. *Ohio State University Educational Research Monographs, 32,* 1949.

HEROLD, D. M.   Improving the performance effectiveness of groups through a task-contingent selection of intervention strategies. *The Academy of Management Review,* 1978, *3*(2), 315–325.

HILL, C., RUBIN, Z., & PEPLAU, L.   Breakups before marriage: The end of 103 affairs. *Journal of Social Issues,* 1976, *32,* 147–168.

HOMANS, G. C.   Social behavior as exchange. *American Journal of Sociology,* 1958, *63,* 597–606.

HORVATH, W. J.   A mathematical model of participation in small group discussion. *Behavioral Science,* 1965, *10*(2), 164–166.

HUESSMAN, L. R., & LEVINGER, G.   Incremental exchange theory: A formal model for progression in dyadic social interaction. In L. Berkowitz & E. Walster (Eds.), *Advances in experimental social psychology. Equity theory: Toward a general theory of social interaction.* (Vol. 9). New York: Academic Press, 1976.

HUSTON, T. L., & LEVINGER, G.   Interpersonal attraction and relationships. *Annual Review of Psychology,* 1978, *29,* 115–156.

JENNESS, A.   Social influence in the change of opinion. *Journal of Abnormal and Social Psychology,* 1932, *27,* 279–296.

JOURARD, S. M.   *The transparent self: Self-disclosure and well-being.* New York: Van Nostrand, 1964.

KAHN, R. L., WOLFE, D. M., QUINN, R. P., SNOEK, J. D., & ROSENTHAL, R. A. *Organizational stress: Studies in role conflict and ambiguity.* New York: Wiley, 1964.

KATZ, D., & KAHN, R. L.   *The social psychology of organizations* (2nd. ed.). New York: Wiley, 1976.

KELLER, R. T.   Dimensions of management system and performance in continuous-process organizations. *Human Relations,* 1978, *31*(1), 59–75.

KELLEY, H. H.   Communication in experimentally created hierarchies. *Human Relations,* 1951, *4,* 39–56.

KELLEY, H. H., & THIBAUT, J. W.   Experimental studies of group problem-solving process. In L. Lindzey (Ed.), *Handbook of social psychology.* Reading, MA: Addison-Wesley, 1954.

KELLEY, H. H., & THIBAUT, J. W.   *Interpersonal relations: A theory of interdependence.* New York: Wiley, 1978.

KENT, R. N., & MCGRATH, J. E.   Task and group characteristics as factors influencing group performance. *Journal of Experimental Social Psychology,* 1969, *5*(4), 429–440.

KERCKHOFF, A. C., & DAVIS, K. E.   Value consensus and need complementarity in mate selection. *American Sociological Review,* 1962, *27,* 295–303.

KLIMONSKI, R. J., & BREAUGH, J. A.   When performance doesn't count: A constituency looks at its spokesman. *Organizational Behavior and Human Performance,* 1977, *20,* 301–311.

KNIGHT, H. C.   *A comparison of the reliability of group and individual judgments.* Unpublished masters thesis, Columbia University, 1921.

KOMORITA, S. S.   Concession making and conflict resolution. *Journal of Conflict Resolution,* 1973, *17*(4), 745–762.

KOMORITA, S. S.   A weighted probability model of coalition formation. *Psychological Review,* 1974, *81*(3), 242–256.

KOMORITA, S. S.   A model of the N-person dilemma type game. *Journal of Experimental Social Psychology,* 1976, *12,* 357–373.

KOMORITA, S. S.   An equal excess model of coalition formation. *Behavioral Science,* 1979, *24,* 369–381.

KOMORITA, S. S., & CHERTKOFF, J. M.   A bargaining theory of coalition formation. *Psychological Review,* 1973, *80*(3), 149–162.

LAMM, H., & MYERS, D. G. Group induced polarization of attitudes and behavior. In L. Berkowitz (Ed.), *Advances in experimental social psychology* (Vol. 11). New York: Academic Press, 1978.

LANDSBERGER, H. A. Interaction process analysis of the mediation of labor-management disputes. *Journal of Abnormal and Social Psychology,* 1955, *51,* 552–558.

LAPLANTE, D. *Communication, friendliness, trust and the prisoner's dilemma.* Unpublished Masters thesis, University of Windsor, Windsor, Canada, 1971.

LATANÉ, B. Psychology of social impact. *American Psychologist,* 1981, *36,* 343–356.

LATANÉ, B., & DARLEY, J. M. Group inhibition of bystander intervention in emergencies. *Journal of Personality and Social Psychology,* 1968, *10*(3), 215–221.

LATANÉ, B., & DARLEY, J. M. *The unresponsive bystander: Why doesn't he help?* New York: Appleton-Century-Crofts, 1970.

LATANÉ, B., & NIDA, S. Social impact theory and group influence: A social engineering perspective. In P. B. Paulus (Ed.) *Psychology of group influence.* Hillsdale, N.J.: Erlbaum, 1980.

LATANÉ, B., & WOLF, S. The social impact of majorities and minorities. *Psychological Review,* 1981, *88*(3), 438–453.

LAUGHLIN, P. R. Social combination processes of cooperative, problem-solving groups as verbal intellective tasks. In M. Fishbein (Ed.), *Progress in social psychology* (Vol. 1). Hillsdale, NJ: Erlbaum, 1980.

LAUGHLIN, P. R., & ADAMOPOULOS, J. Social decision schemes on intellective tasks. In H. Brandstatter, J. H. Davis & C. Stocker-Kreichgauer (Eds.), *Group decision making.* London: Academic Press, 1982.

LAUGHLIN, P. R., & JACCARD, J. J. Social facilitation and observational learning of individuals and cooperative pairs. *Journal of Personality and Social Psychology,* 1975, *32,* 873–879.

LAUGHLIN, P. R., & JOHNSON, H. H. Groups and individual performance on a complementary task as a function of initial ability level. *Journal of Experimental Social Psychology,* 1966, *2,* 407–414.

LAUGHLIN, P. R., KERR, N. L., DAVIS, J. H., HALFF, H. M., & MARCINIAK, K. A. Group size, member ability, and social decision schemes on an intellective task. *Journal of Personality and Social Psychology,* 1975, *31,* 522–535.

LAUGHLIN, P. R., KERR, N. L., MUNCH, M. M., & HAGGERTY, C. A. Social decision schemes of the same four-person groups on two different intellective tasks. *Journal of Personality and Social Psychology,* 1976, *33,* 80–88.

LAUGHLIN, P. R., MCGLYNN, R. P., ANDERSON, J. A., & JACOBSON, E. S. Concept attainment by individuals versus cooperative pairs as a function of memory, sex, and concept rule. *Journal of Personality and Social Psychology,* 1968, *8,* 410–417.

LAUGHLIN, P. R., & SWEENEY, J. D. Individual-to-group and group-to-individual transfer in problem solving. *Journal of Experimental Psychology: Human Learning and Memory,* 1977, *3,* 246–254.

LEARY, T. *Interpersonal diagnosis of personality.* New York: Ronald, 1957.

LEAVITT, H. J. Some effects of certain communication patterns on group performance. *Journal of Abnormal and Social Psychology,* 1951, *46,* 38–50.

LEBON, G. *Psychologie des foules.* Paris: F. Olean, 1895. (*The Crowd.* London: T. Fisher Unwin, 1896.)

LEIK, R. K. Instrumentality and emotionality in family interaction. *Sociometry,* 1963, *26,* 131–145.

LEISERSON, M. *Coalitions in politics.* Unpublished doctoral dissertation, Yale University, 1966.

LEISERSON, M.   Factions and coalitions in one-party Japan: An interpretation based on the theory of games. *American Political Science Review,* 1968, *62,* 770–787.

LEVENTHAL, G. S.   The distribution of rewards and resources in groups and organizations. In L. Berkowitz & E. Walster (Eds.), *Advances in experimental social psychology* (Vol. 9). *Equity theory: Toward a general theory of social interaction.* New York: Academic Press, 1976.

LEVINGER, G.   Toward the analysis of close relationships. *Journal of Experimental Social Psychology,* 1980, *16,* 510–544.

LEVINGER, G., SENN, D. J., & JORGENSON, B. W.   Progress toward permanence in courtship: A test of the Kerckhoff-Davis hypothesis. *Sociometry,* 1970, *33*(4), 427–443.

LEVY, P., LUNDGREN, D., ANSEL, M., FELL, D., FINK, B., & MCGRATH, J. E.   Bystander effect in a demand-without-threat situation. *Journal of Personality and Social Psychology,* 1972, *24*(2), 166–171.

LEWIN, K.   *Resolving social conflict: Selected papers on group dynamics.* New York: Harper, 1948.

LEWIN, K.   *Field theory and social science.* New York: Harper, 1951.

LEWIN, K.   Studies in group decision. In D. Cartwright & A. Zander (Eds.), *Group dynamics: Research and theory* (1st ed.). Evanston IL: Row, Peterson, 1953.

LEWIN, K., LIPPETT, R., & WHITE, R.   Patterns of aggressive behavior in experimentally created "social climates." *Journal of Social Psychology,* 1939, *10,* 271–299.

LEWIS, S. A., & FRY, W. R.   Effects of visual access and orientation on the discovery of integrative bargaining alternatives. *Organizational Behavior and Human Performance,* 1977, *20,* 75–92.

LIEBERMAN, M. A.   Change induction in small groups. *Annual Review of Psychology,* 1976, *27,* 217–250.

LORGE, I., FOX, D., DAVITZ, J., & BRENNER, M.   A survey of studies contrasting the quality of group performance and individual performance, 1920–1957. *Psychological Bulletin,* 1958, *55,* 337–372.

LORGE, I., & SOLOMON, H.   Two models of group behavior in the solution of Eureka-type problems. *Psychometrika,* 1955, *20,* 139–148.

LOWE, R., & MCGRATH, J. E.   *Stress, arousal, and performance: Some findings calling for a new theory.* Project report, AF 1161–67, AFOSR, 1971.

MANN, R. D., GIBBARD, G. S., & HARTMAN, J. J.   *Interpersonal styles and group development.* New York: Wiley, 1967.

MARQUART, D. I.,   Group problem-solving. *Journal of Social Psychology,* 1955, *41,* 103–113.

MAYO, E.   *The human problems of an industrial civilization.* New York: McMillan, 1933.

MCCLINTOCK, C. G., MESSICK, D. M., KUHLMAN, D. M., & CAMPOS, F. T.   Motivational bases of choice in three-choice decomposed games. *Journal of Experimental Social Psychology,* 1973, *9*(6), 572–590.

MCDOUGALL, W.   *An introduction to social psychology.* London: Methuen & Co. Ltd., 1908.

MCGRATH, J. E.   A social psychological approach to the study of negotiations. In R. V. Bowers (Ed.), *Studies in behavior in organizations.* Athens, GA: University of Georgia Press, 1966.

MCGRATH, J. E.   A multifacet approach to classification of individual, group and organizational concepts. In B. Indek & K. Berrian (Eds.), *People, groups and organizations: An effective integration.* New York: Teachers College Press, 1968.

MCGRATH, J. E.   Stress and behavior in organizations. In M. D. Dunnette (Ed.),

Handbook of industrial and organizational psychology. Chicago, IL: Rand-McNally, 1976.

MCGRATH, J. E.   Small group research. *American Behavioral Scientist,* 1978, *21*(5), 651–674.

MCGRATH, J. E., & ALTMAN, I.   *Small group research: A synthesis and critique of the field.* New York: Holt, Rinehart & Winston, 1966.

MCGRATH, J. E., & JULIAN, J. W.   Interaction process and task outcome in experimentally created negotiation groups. *Journal of Psychological Studies,* 1963, *14*(3), 117–138.

MCGRATH, J. E., & KRAVITZ, D. A.   Group research. *Annual Review of Psychology,* 1982, *33,* 195–230.

MEAD, G. H.   *Mind, self and society* (Posthumous. C. M. Morris, Ed.). Chicago, IL: University of Chicago Press, 1934.

MEDLEY, D. M., & MITZEL, H. E.   A technique for measuring classroom behavior. *Journal of Educational Psychology,* 1958, *49,* 86–92.

MEHRABIAN, A.   Verbal and nonverbal interactions of strangers in a waiting situation. *Journal of Experimental Research in Personality,* 1971, *5*(2), 127–138.

MERTON, R. K.   *Social theory and social structure* (rev. ed.). New York: Free Press, 1957.

MILGRAM, S.   Some conditions of obedience and disobedience to authority. *Human Relations,* 1965, *18*(1), 57–75.

MILLER, N.   A questionnaire in search of a theory. In L. Berkowitz, (Ed.), *Group Processes.* New York: Academic Press, 1978.

MILLER, N. E. & DOLLARD, J.   *Social learning and imitation.* New Haven: Yale University Press, 1941.

MILLS, T. M.   Power relations in three-person groups. *American Sociological Review,* 1953, *18,* 351–357.

MILLS, T. M.   *Group transformation.* Englewood Cliffs, NJ: Prentice-Hall, 1964.

MONAHAN, J., & LOFTUS, E. F.   The psychology of law. *Annual Review of Psychology,* 1982, *33,* 441–475.

MORENO, J. L.   *Who shall survive?* Beacon, NY: Beacon House, 1934.

MORGAN, W. R., & SAWYER, J.   Bargaining, expectations, and the preference for equality over equity. *Journal of Personality and Social Psychology,* 1967, *6,* 139–149.

MORLEY, I. E., & STEPHENSON, G. M.   Interpersonal and interparty exchange: A laboratory simulation of an industrial negotiation at the plant level. *British Journal of Psychology,* 1969, *60,* 543–545.

MORLEY, I. E., & STEPHENSON, G. M.   Formality in experimental negotiations: A validation study. *British Journal of Psychology,* 1970, *61,* 383–384.

MORLEY, I. E., & STEPHENSON, G. M.   *The social psychology of bargaining.* London: Allen & Unwin, 1977.

MORRIS, C. G.   Task effects on group interaction. *Journal of Personality and Social Psychology,* 1966, *4*(5), 545–554.

MURNIGHAN, K.   Models of coalition behavior: Game-theoretic, social psychological, and political perspectives. *Psychological Bulletin,* 1978, *85,* 1130–1153.

MYERS, D. G., & LAMM, H.   The group polarization phenomenon. *Psychological Bulletin,* 1976, *83*(4), 602–627.

NEMETH, C.   Jury trials: Psychology and law. In L. Berkowitz (Ed.), *Advances in experimental social psychology* (Vol. 14). New York: Academic Press, 1981.

NEWCOMB, T. M.   *Personality and social change.* New York: Drysden, 1943.

NEWCOMB, T. M.   An approach to the study of communicative acts. *Psychological Bulletin,* 1953, *4,* 183–214.

NEWCOMB, T. M.   *The acquaintance process.* New York: Holt, Rinehart & Winston, 1961.

NOWAKOWSKA, M.   A model of participation in group discussion. *Behavioral Science,* 1978, *23,* 209–212.

O'ROURKE, J.   Field and laboratory: The decision making behavior of family groups in two experimental conditions. *Sociometry,* 1963, *26,* 422–435.

OSBORN, A. F.   *Applied imagination* (rev. ed.). New York: Scribner's, 1957.

OSGOOD, C. E.   *An alternative to war or surrender,* Urbana, IL: University of Illinois Press, 1962.

PAIVIO, A.   Personality and audience influence. In B. Maher (Ed.), *Progress in experimental personality research* (Vol. 2). New York: Academic Press, 1965.

PARSONS, T. C.   An outline of the social system. In T. Parsons et al. (Eds.), *Theories of society.* New York: The Free Press, 1961.

PARSONS, T. C., & BALES, R. F.   *The family, socialization and interaction process.* Glencoe, IL: The Free Press, 1955.

PARSONS, T. C., BALES, R. F., & SHILS, E. A.   *Working papers on the theory of action.* Glencoe, IL: The Free Press, 1953.

PARSONS, T. C., & SHILS, E. A. (Eds.),   *Toward a general theory of action.* Cambridge: Harvard University Press, 1951.

PATTERSON, M. L.   An arousal model of interpersonal intimacy. *Psychological Bulletin,* 1976, *83*(3), 235–245.

PENROD, S., & HASTIE, R.   Models of jury decisionmaking: A critical review. *Psychological Bulletin,* 1979, *86,* 462–492.

PEPINSKY, P. N., HEMPHILL, J. K., & SHEVITZ, R. N.   Attempts to lead, group productivity and morale under conditions of acceptance and rejection. *Journal of Abnormal and Social Psychology,* 1958, *57,* 47–54.

PEPLAU, L. A.   Impact of fear of success and sex-role attitudes on women's competitive achievement. *Journal of Personality and Social Psychology,* 1976, *34*(4), 561–568.

PILIAVIN, I. M., RODIN, J., & PILIAVIN, J. A.   Good Samaritanism: An underground phenomenon? *Journal of Personality and Social Psychology,* 1969, *13*(4), 289–299.

PILISUK, M., & SKOLNICK, D.   Inducing trust: A test of the Osgood proposal. *Journal of Personality and Social Psychology,* 1968, *8,* 121–133.

PLATT, G.   Social traps. *American Psychologist,* 1973, *28,* 641–651.

POLANSKY, N., LIPPETT, R., & REDL, F.   An investigation of behavioral contagion in groups. *Human Relations,* 1950, *3,* 319–348.

PRUITT, D. G., & KIMMEL, M. J.   Twenty years of experimental gaming: Critique, synthesis, and suggestions for the future. *Annual Review of Psychology,* 1977, *28,* 363–392.

PSATHAS, G.   Phase movement and equilibrium tendencies in interaction process in psychotherapy groups. *Sociometry,* 1960, *23*(2), 177–194.

RAPOPORT, A.   Optimal policies for the prisoner's dilemma game. *Psychological Review,* 1967, *74*(2), 136–148.

RAPOPORT, A., & ORWANT, C.   Experimental games: A review. *Behavioral Science,* 1962, *7*(1), 1–37.

RESTLE, F., & DAVIS, J. H.   Success and speed of problem solving by individuals and groups. *Psychological Review,* 1962, *69,* 520–536.

RIECKEN, H. W., & HOMANS, G. C.   Psychological aspects of social structure. In G. Lindzey (Ed.), *Handbook of social psychology.* Cambridge, MA: Addison-Wesley, 1954.

RIKER, W. H.   *The theory of political coalitions.* New Haven, CT: Yale University Press, 1962.

ROETHLISBERGER, F. J., & DICKSON, W. J. *Management and the worker.* Cambridge, MA: Harvard University Press, 1939.

ROHRBAUGH, J. Improving the quality of group judgment: Social judgment analysis and the Delphi technique. *Organizational Behavior and Human Performance,* 1979, *24,* 73–92.

ROSEBOROUGH, M. E. Experimental studies of small groups. *Psychological Bulletin,* 1953, *50,* 275–303.

ROSEN, S., & TESSER, A. On reluctance to communicate undesirable information. The MUM effect. *Sociometry,* 1970, *33,* 253–263.

ROSENTHAL, H. Size of coalition and electoral outcomes in the Fourth French Republic. In S. Groennings, E. S. Kelley & M. Leiserson (Eds.), *The study of coalition behavior.* New York: Holt, Rinehart & Winston, 1970.

ROSS, E. A. *Social Psychology.* New York: McMillan, 1908.

RUBIN, J. Z. Experimental research on third-party intervention in conflict: Toward some generalizations. *Psychological Bulletin,* 1980, *87,* 370–391.

RUBIN, J. Z., & BROWN, B. R. *The social psychology of bargaining and negotiations.* New York: Academic Press, 1975.

RUNKEL, P. J., & MCGRATH, J. E. *Research on human behavior: A systematic guide to method.* New York: Holt, Rinehart & Winston, 1972.

RUTTER, D. R., & ROBINSON, B. An experimental analysis of teaching by telephone: Theoretical and practical implications for social psychology. In G. M. Stephenson & J. H. Davis (Eds.), *Progress in applied social psychology.* New York and London: Wiley, 1981.

RUTTER, D. R., & STEPHENSON, G. M., AYLING, K., & WHITE, P. A. The timing of looks in dyadic conversation. *British Journal of Social and Clinical Psychology,* 1978, *17,* 17–21.

RUTTER, D. R., STEPHENSON, G. M., LAZZARINI, A. J., AYLING, K., & WHITE, P. A. Eye-contact: A chance product of individual looking? *British Journal of Social and Clinical Psychology,* 1977, *16,* 191–192.

SARBIN, T. R., & ALLEN, V. L. Role theory. In G. Lindsey & E. Aronson (Eds.), *The handbook of social psychology* (2nd ed.). Reading, MA: Addison-Wesley, 1968.

SCHACHTER, S. Deviation, rejection and communication. *Journal of Abnormal and Social Psychology,* 1951, *46,* 190–207.

SCHACHTER, S. *The psychology of affiliation.* Stanford, CA: Stanford University Press, 1959.

SCHACHTER, S. The interaction of cognitive and physiological determinants of emotional state. In L. Berkowitz (Ed.), *Advances in experimental social psychology* (Vol. 1). New York: Academic Press, 1964.

SCHACHTER, S., ELLERTON, N., MCBRIDE, D., & GREGORY, D. An experimental study of cohesiveness and productivity. *Human Relations,* 1951, *4,* 229–238.

SCHUTZ, W. C. *FIRO: A three-dimensional theory of interpersonal behavior.* New York: Holt, Rinehart & Winston, 1958.

SHAW, MARJORIE E. Comparison of individuals and small groups in the rational solution of complex problems. *American Journal of Psychology,* 1932, *44,* 491–504.

SHAW, MARVIN E. Some effects of individually prominent behavior upon group effectiveness and member satisfaction. *Journal of Abnormal and Social Psychology,* 1959, *59,* 382–386.

SHAW, M. E. Communication networks. In L. Berkowitz (Ed.), *Advances in experimental social psychology* (Vol. 1). New York: Academic Press, 1964.

SHAW, M. E.   Scaling group tasks: A method for dimensional analysis. *JSAS Catalog of Selected Documents in Psychology*, 1973, *3*, 8.

SHAW, M. E.   *Group dynamics: The psychology of small groups* (2nd ed.). New York: McGraw-Hill, 1976.

SHAW, M. E.   Communication networks 14 years later. In L. Berkowitz (Ed.), *Group processes.* New York: Academic Press, 1978.

SHERIF, M.   *The psychology of social norms.* New York: Harper, 1936.

SHERIF, M., HARVEY, O. J., WHITE, B. J., HOOD, W. R., & SHERIF, C. W.   *Intergroup conflict and cooperation.* Norman, OK: Institute of Group Relations, 1961.

SHIFFENBAUER, A., & SCHIAVO, R. S.   Physical distance as attraction: An intensification effect. *Journal of Experimental and Social Psychology*, 1976, *12*, 274-282.

SHIFLETT, S.   Toward a general model of small group productivity. *Psychological Bulletin*, 1979, *86*(1), 67-79.

SHUBIK, M.   *Game theory and related approaches to social behavior.* New York: Wiley, 1964.

SIEGAL, S., & FOURAKER, L. E.   *Bargaining and group decision making: Experiments in bilateral monopoly.* New York: McGraw-Hill, 1960.

SIMMEL, G.   *The sociology of Georg Simmel* (K. H. Wolff, Ed. and trans.). Glencoe, IL: The Free Press, 1950.

SIMON, H. A.   *The new science of management decisions.* New York: Harper, 1960.

SLATER, P. E.   *Microcosm: Structural, psychological and religious evaluation in groups.* New York: Wiley, 1966.

SMITH, P. B.   Controlled studies of the outcome of sensitivity training. *Psychological Bulletin*, 1975, *82*, 597-622.

SMOKE, W. H., & ZAJONC, R. B.   On the reliability of group judgments and decisions. In J. H. Criswell, H. Solomon & P. P. Suppes (Eds.), *Mathematical models in small group processes.* Stanford, CA: Stanford University Press, 1962.

SNYDER, M.   Self-monitoring of expressive behavior. *Journal of Personality and Social Psychology*, 1974, *30*(4), 526-537.

SOCIAL GROUPS,   *Encyclopedia Britannica* (3rd ed.). 1974.

SOMMERS, R.   Studies in personal space. *Sociometry*, 1959, *22*, 247-260.

STEIN, M. K.   *Stimulating creativity* (Vol. 2). New York: Academic Press, 1975.

STEINER, I. D.   Models for inferring relationships between group size and potential group productivity. *Behavioral Science*, 1966, *11*, 273-283.

STEINER, I. D.   *Group process and productivity.* New York: Academic Press, 1972.

STEINER, I. D.   Whatever happened to the group in social psychology? *Journal of Experimental Social Psychology*, 1974, *10*(1), 94-108.

STEINER, I. D., & RAJARATNAM, N.   A model for the comparison of individual and group preference scores. *Behavioral Science*, 1961, *6*(2), 142-147.

STEINZOR, B.   The spatial factor in face to face discussion groups. *Journal of Abnormal and Social Psychology*, 1950, *45*, 552.

STEPHAN, F. F.   The relative rate of communication between members of small groups. *American Sociological Review*, 1952, *17*, 482-486.

STEPHAN, F. F., & MISHLER, E. G.   The distribution of participation in small groups: An exponential approximation. *American Sociological Review*, 1952, *17*, 598-608.

STOCK, D., & THELEN, H. A.   *Emotional dynamics and group culture: Experimental studies of individual and group behavior.* New York: New York University Press, 1958.

STODGILL, R. M.   *Handbook of leadership.* New York: The Free Press, 1974.

STONER, J. A. F.   *A comparison of individual and group decisions involving risk.* Unpublished masters thesis, Massachusetts Institute of Technology, 1961. (Cited in Wallack, M. A., Kogan, W., & Bem, D. J. Group Influence in individual risk taking. *Journal of Abnormal and Social Psychology,* 1962, *65,* 75–86.)

STRAUSS, M.   The influence of sex of child and social class on instrumental and expressive family roles in a laboratory setting. *Sociological and Social Research,* 1967, *52,* 7–21.

STROOP, J. R.   Is the judgment of the group better than that of the average member of the group? *Journal of Experimental Psychology,* 1932, *15,* 550–562.

SWINGLE, P. G. (Ed.).   *The structure of conflict.* New York: Academic Press, 1970.

TALLAND, G. A.   Task and interaction process: Some characteristics of therapeutic group discussion. *Journal of Abnormal and Social Psychology,* 1955, *50,* 105–109.

TAPP, J. L.   Psychology and the Law: An overture. *Annual Review of Psychology,* 1976, *27,* 359–404.

TAPP, J. L.   Psychology and policy perspectives on the law: Reflections on a decade. *Journal of Social Issues,* 1980, *36*(2), 165–192.

TARDE, G.   *The laws of imitation* (trans.). New York: Henry Holt, 1903.

TAYLOR, D. W., BERRY, P. C., & BLOCK, C. H.   Does group participation when using brainstorming facilitate or inhibit creative thinking? *Administrative Sciences Quarterly,* 1958, *3,* 23–47.

TAYLOR, D. W., & FAUST, W. L.   Twenty questions: Efficiency in problem solving as a function of size of group. *Journal of Experimental Psychology,* 1952, *44,* 360–368.

TAYLOR, F. W.   *The principles of scientific management.* New York: Harper, 1911.

THELEN, H. A.   Emotionality of work in groups. In L. D. White (Ed.), *The state of the social sciences.* Chicago, IL: University of Chicago Press, 1956.

THELEN, H. A., STOCK, D., & OTHERS.   *Methods for studying work and emotionality in group operation.* Chicago, IL: University of Chicago, Hyman Dynamics Laboratory, 1954.

THIBAUT, J. W.   An experimental study of the cohesiveness of underpriviledged groups. *Human Relations,* 1950, *3,* 251–278.

THIBAUT, J. W., & KELLEY, H. H.   *The social psychology of groups.* New York: Wiley, 1959.

THOMAS, E. A. C., & MALONE, T. M.   On the dynamics of two-person interaction. *Psychological Review,* 1979, *86*(4), 331–360.

THOMAS, E. J., & FINK, C. F.   Models of group problem solving. *Journal of Abnormal and Social Psychology,* 1961, *63,* 53–63.

THOMAS, E. J., & FINK, C. F.   Effects of group size. *Psychological Bulletin,* 1963, *60,* 371–385.

THORNDIKE, R. L.   On what type of task will a group do well? *Journal of Abnormal and Social Psychology,* 1938, *33,* 409–413.

TORRANCE, A. P.   The behavior of small groups under the stress of conditions of "survival." *American Sociological Review,* 1954, *19,* 751–755.

TRIPLETT, N.   The dynamogenic factors in pace-making and competition. *American Journal of Psychology,* 1898, *9,* 507–533.

TRIST, E. L. & BAMFORTH, K. W.   Some social psychological consequences of the longwall method of goal-getting. *Human Relations,* 1951, *4,* 3–38.

TSAI, Y.   Hierarchical structure of participation in natural groups. *Behavioral Science,* 1977, *22,* 38–40.

TUCKMAN, B. W.   Developmental sequence in small groups. *Psychological Bulletin,* 1965, *63*(6), 384–399.

VAN DE VEN, A. H.   *Group decision-making effectiveness.* Kent State University, Kent, Ohio, Center for Business & Economic Research Press, 1974.

VAN DE VEN, A. H., & DELBECQ, A. L.   Nominal vs interacting group processes for committee decision-making effectiveness. *Academy of Management Journal,* 1971, *14*(**2**), 203–212.

VIDMAR, N., & MCGRATH, J. E.   Forces affecting success in negotiation groups. *Behavioral Science,* 1970, *15*(**2**), 154–163.

VINACKE, W. E., & ARKOFF, A.   Experimental study of coalitions in the triad. *American Sociological Review,* 1957, *22*, 406–415.

WALLACK, M., KOGAN, N., & BEM, D.   Group influence on individual risk taking. *Journal of Abnormal and Social Psychology,* 1962, *65*, 75–86.

WALSTER, E., WALSTER, G., & BERSHEID, E.   *Equity: Theory and research.* Boston: Allyn & Bacon, 1978.

WALTON, R. E., & MCKERSIE, R. B.   *A behavioral theory of labor negotiations: An analysis of a social interaction system.* New York: McGraw Hill, 1965.

WAXLER, N. E., & MISHLER, E. G.   Experimental studies of families. In L. Berkowitz (Ed.), *Advances in experimental social psychology* (Vol. 5). New York: Academic Press, 1970.

WEBB, E. J., CAMPBELL, D. T., SCHWARTZ, R. D., & SECHREST, L.   *Unobtrusive measures: Non-reactive research in the social sciences.* Chicago, IL: Rand-McNally, 1966.

WHYTE, W. F.   *Street corner society: The social structure of an Italian slum.* Chicago, IL: University of Chicago Press, 1943.

WHYTE, W. H., JR.   *The organization man.* Garden City, NY: Doubleday & Co., 1957.

WICHMAN, H.   Effects of isolation and communication on cooperation in a two-person game. *Journal of Personality and Social Psychology,* 1970, *16*, 114–120.

WICKER, A. W., & KIRMEYER, S. L.   From church to laboratory to national park. In S. Wapner, B. Cohen & B. Kaplan, (Eds.), *Experiencing the environment.* New York: Plenum Publishing Corporation, 1976.

WILLIAMS, E.   Experimental comparisons of face-to-face and mediated communication: A review. *Psychological Bulletin,* 1977, *84*, 963–976.

WINCH, R. F.   The theory of complementary needs in mate selection: Final report on the test of the general hypothesis. *American Sociological Review,* 1965, *20*, 552–554.

WOODWARD, J.   *Industrial organization: Theory and practice.* London: Oxford University Press, 1965.

ZAJONC, R. B.   Social facilitation. *Science,* 1965, *149*, 269–274.

ZANDER, A. F.   The psychology of small group processes. *Annual Review of Psychology,* 1979, *30*, 417–451.

AUTHOR INDEX

SUBJECT INDEX